sixth edition

ROCK MUSIC STYLES

a history

sixth edition

ROCK MUSIC STYLES

a history

Katherine Charlton

Mt. San Antonio College
Walnut, California

Connect
Learn
Succeed™

ROCK MUSIC STYLES, SIXTH EDITION

ISBN 978-0-07-802507-5
MHID 0-07-802507-9

Vice President & Editor-in-Chief: *Michael Ryan*
Vice President EDP/Central Publishing Services: *Kimberly Meriwether David*
Publisher: *Bill Glass*
Senior Sponsoring Editor: *Chris Freitag*
Executive Marketing Manager: *Pamela S. Cooper*
Editorial Coordinator: *Marley Magaziner*
Senior Project Manager: *Jane Mohr*
Design Coordinator: *Margarite Reynolds*
Cover Designer: *Mary-Presley Adams*
Lead Photo Research Coordinator: *Nora Agbayani*
USE Cover Image Credit: *Ingram Publishing/SuperStock*
Production Supervisor: *Susan K. Culbertson*
Media Project Manager: *Sridevi Palini*
Compositor: *Glyph International*
Typeface: *10.5/12.5 Garamond*
Printer: *Worldcolor*

Library of Congress Cataloging-in-Publication Data
Charlton, Katherine.
   Rock music styles : a history / Katherine Charlton. — 6th ed.
      p. cm.
   Includes index.
   ISBN-13: 978-0-07-802507-5 (alk. paper)
   ISBN-10: 0-07-802507-9 (alk. paper)
   1. Rock music—History and criticism.   I. Title.
   ML3534.C45 2010
   781.6609—dc22
                                             2009052942

To the memory of my late first husband,
Andrew Charlton, who loved the blues.

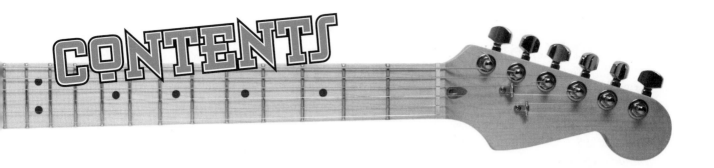

CONTENTS

1980s

Rock Music Styles: A History is intended to be used as a text for a college-level course on the history of rock music. My primary concern has been to help students develop an understanding of both the musical and cultural roots of rock music and the ability to hear a direct relationship between those roots and the music currently popular. To that end, I identify the various styles of music that influenced the development of rock and discuss the elements of those styles along with the rock music to which they relate. Careful listening is necessary for one to hear and identify those basic elements of music and then understand how they help define characteristics of the individual styles. The kind of listening I am asking students to do is not about deciding whether the music is pleasing or not, but rather to analyze exactly what one is hearing.

The listening guides to individual recordings in this book are intended to aid students in such analytical listening. Each guide begins with the tempo of the recording. To identify that basic beat in the recording all one has to do, in many cases, is look at the second hand or number on a clock while listening to it. We know that there are sixty seconds in a minute, so if the tempo is 120, the beats are the pulses in the music that are heard at the rate of two per second. Even if the tempo is 72, one can listen for pulses that are just a bit faster than the seconds to pick out the basic beat. Listening to the music is the most important part of this process, but many nonmusicians will need to force themselves to avoid the "tone bath" type of listening they might be used to and listen much more carefully.

After the tempo, the listening guides discuss the form of the recordings. Form in music is the overall structure of the music as defined by repetition and contrast. A song like "Hound Dog," for example, has lyrics in an AAB form. In other words, we hear one line of lyrics, A (the first letter of the alphabet is used for the first section of music), and then we hear that line repeated. Those two A lines are followed by new lyrics, so we identify those new lyrics by a new letter, B. When we get into the music analysis we will be outlining when melodies repeat or are contrasted with new melodies. With either lyrics or melody, when we listen for form we listen for a musical element to repeat or for a new and contrasting element to be played or sung.

"Features" in the listening guides vary with the recordings and are my way of describing other musical elements or characteristics that are special in a particular recording and that help to define the general style of the music. This presentation does not allow for the type of detail that a musician who notates and analyzes music note by note or chord by chord uses, but that type of analysis is not the subject of this book. As I said earlier, what I have tried to do here is teach the interested student about the musical characteristics of many different types of music and help that student learn to listen critically so that he or she can make stylistic connections on his or her own.

Lyrics are very important in most rock music, and for that reason, each listening guide includes a simple explanation of the song's lyrics. In some light pop songs that explanation may say as much as do the lyrics themselves, but in most cases lyrics contain complexities that are open to many different interpretations that would go beyond the scope of this book. I hope that my representations of lyrics will be used as a point of departure for further thought and discussion about the meaning(s) conveyed in each song.

Most rock listeners are well aware of the controversial aspects of some rock music, particularly its lyrics. In these cases, I have mentioned some of the issues but avoided imposing personal judgments in the text. My goal is to be as objective as possible and provide the reader with an understanding of what the music means to the performer and his or her fans. Discussions about any possible negative impact the music or lyrics may have on some listeners can, and I expect will, take place in individual classrooms without any biased opinions from the textbook.

The ideal version of this book would come with a set of CDs that would include all of the recordings discussed in the listening guides in the text. My editors at McGraw-Hill and I have tried many times to make that possible, but the cost is very high for the recordings that are available and in many cases permission to reproduce a given recording is impossible to obtain at any cost. Now, however, many Internet sites make recordings available at very low prices, so I have added more listening guides to this edition and urge readers to seek out these Internet resources.

New to This Edition

Based on reviewer comments, a substantial effort has been made to improve the quality of the photographs and update the content of *Rock Music Styles: A History* for the sixth edition. Most notably, more listening guides are featured than were available in previous editions. Some guides new to this edition replace outdated listening guides used in previous editions; others provide additional tools for students as they learn to analyze individual songs. Better coverage of essential examples can be found in new guides in chapters on the following topics: Teen-Styled Rock Music ("Venus" by Frankie Avalon and "Be My Baby" by the Ronettes), Folk Rock ("Blowin' in the Wind" by Peter, Paul, and Mary, "Sounds of Silence" by Simon and Garfunkel, and "Help Me" by Joni Mitchell), Rap ("Rapper's Delight" by the Sugar Hill Gang, "The Message" by Grandmaster Flash, "It's Like That" by Run-DMC, and "Straight Outta Compton" by N.W.A.), and Rock Styles of the 2000s ("The Middle" by Jimmy Eat World, "Karma Police" by Radiohead, and "Freak on a Leash" by Korn).

Billboard chart information about the recordings has been included in the listening guides so that the information is easier to find. Previously this information was in the text and perhaps not as obvious as it should have

been. The chart listings now include the Country, Rhythm and Blues, and British charts, in addition to the Pop charts. It is instructive to notice how one artist's recording of a specific song ranked on the *Billboard* chart when compared with others: for example, Elvis Presley's recording of "Hound Dog" was number one on the Rhythm and Blues chart almost as long as Willie Mae Thornton's recording of the same song. That fact highlights Elvis's appeal to African Americans as well as his tremendous success measured by the Pop charts.

In this edition, some material was rearranged to clarify important connections between musical styles and the decades in which they were important. Chapter 1, "Roots of Rock," now includes early blues examples by Robert Johnson and Bessie Smith because those delta and classic blues styles are, indeed, roots of the blues and blues-rock styles of the fifties and later. The decade introduction to the 1950s was moved to precede Chapter 2 because the urban, Chicago, and rhythm and blues styles discussed in that chapter are all styles from the fifties, as are the gospel, doo-wop, and country styles discussed in Chapter 3. Although Curtis Mayfield was an important musical figure in the 1960s, information about this soul and funk artist is now included in Chapter 17, "Funk and Disco," to stress the importance of Mayfield's developments in funk and the socially conscious statements he made in his songs for the soundtrack of the film *Super fly*.

Summaries have been updated throughout the book to reflect the changes made in the chapters. New end-of-chapter Discussion Questions were added to this edition and can be used by instructors to engage students' critical thinking skills in the classroom.

New copies of *Rock Music Styles,* Sixth Edition, include a discount card allowing students to receive a Rhapsody Unlimited online music subscription at a special four-month introductory rate of only $10/month (normally $12.99/month). Rhapsody lets you connect to over 9 million full-length songs, including many of the songs featured in listening guides in *Rock Music Styles*.

Acknowledgments

This book is dedicated to my first husband, Andrew Charlton, for many reasons, not the least of which is that it was only with his support and encouragement that I wrote the first three editions. Having lost him to cancer in 1997, I spent several years as a grieving zombie. I finally met and married another wonderful man, Jeffrey Calkins, and it is only with his patience and support that I have been able to dedicate myself to writing later editions. Jeff is an attorney with a master's degree in political science, and his advice has been a tremendous help in writing the political and social background sections for the book. I hope his conservatism has successfully neutralized my liberalism to allow for the kind of political balance I think the book needs. I am grateful to my record collector and eternal rock-fan friend in Cleveland, Pat Phillips, who has introduced me to much wonderful music that I might otherwise have missed. The A.I.F.S. staff members at the University of London were a great help to me in organizing "rock tours" for my students during the semester (or "term" to the British) I taught there, and, while I cannot name everyone who helped me, I appreciate the support I received.

Rock historians whose advice was a great help to me include

Jason Chevalier, Mt. San Antonio College
Jeff Jones, Mt. San Antonio College
Peter Winkler, SUNY—Stony Brook
Paul Feehan, University of Miami—Coral Gables
John R. Harding, University of North Carolina—Charlotte
Ron Pen, University of Kentucky
Darhyl S. Ramsey, University of North Texas
Jim Albert, Eastern Washington University
Albert LeBlanc, Michigan State University
David H. Stuart, Iowa State University
Richard Weissman, University of Colorado—Denver
Robert Bozina, Santa Clara University

Carl Woideck, University of Oregon
Mark Forry, University of California at Santa Cruz
Stephen Young, University of Tennessee
Don Carroll, Mt. San Antonio College
John Webb, University of Wisconsin at Whitewater
Gerard Aloisio, Minnesota State University
Kirk Higgins, Yavapai Community College
Janet Kopp, Cambridge Community College
Dennis Anderson, California State University, Fullerton
Stan Breckenridge, California State University, Fullerton

Others whose support was invaluable include Francie and Richard French, Ed Huddleston, Karen Speerstra, and Lorraine Zielinski. Thanks also to Chris Freitag, Marley Magaziner, Preston Thomas, Sonia Brown, Jocelyn Spielberger, Jason Huls, and Emily Hatteberg at McGraw-Hill Higher Education. Thank you to Gary O'Brien, Alan Boyd, Probyn Gregory, and Denise McCabe. And a special thanks to the following individuals who provided reviews for this edition:

Cindy Ison, Indiana University Kokomo
Morten Kristiansen, Xavier University
Robert Lehmann, Bunker Hill Community College
John Limeberry, Jefferson Community and Technical College
Gary Pritchard, Cerritos College
Donald Brad Sherman, Western Washington University
Joseph Taylor, James Madison University
Randy Wright, Chandler-Gilbert Community College

Of course, I must remember that it is my students who have asked questions requiring me to look at rock music from many different perspectives who are really the only reason this book exists. I thank them all and hope for many more exchanges of ideas with students in the future.

Katherine Charlton Calkins

chapter

1

Roots of Rock Music

"The way to write American music is simple. All you have to do is be an American and then write any kind of music you wish."

—VIRGIL THOMSON, COMPOSER

Was there life before rock and roll? Died-in-the-wool rock fans might think not, or at least think that whatever life there was was not worth living, but that, of course, was not the case for those who lived before the emergence of rock and roll. People have always entertained themselves and one another with songs, dances, and other types of music. Music that is simple and catchy enough to immediately appeal to large numbers of people is generally dubbed "popular," and a large body of popular music existed before rock and roll and alongside rock music through to the present time.

Much popular music today is rather complex and would be beyond the ability of an average person to perform. Before the existence of such twentieth-century inventions as radio, television, and good-quality record, tape, or CD players, the only way most people could hear music was to perform it themselves, hire performers to play for them, or go to a public performance. Because of this, popular music of past times was often either relatively simple or composed to be part of large-scale public extravaganzas. Through the years popular music has become very big business and is usually produced primarily to generate financial gain for the writer, publisher, and performer.

The earliest popular songs in America were brought to the colonies by British and other European settlers. The business of producing, publishing, and selling music in America was aided by the passage of the first American National Copyright Act in 1790. A **copyright** protects the composer's credit and allows him or her and the publisher to receive payment for the sale of published songs and maintain control of their distribution. With many people willing to pay for printed music, the popular music industry in the United States grew rapidly during the nineteenth century. It exploded in the twentieth century with the availability of phonograph recordings in the first decade of the century, radio beginning in the twenties, and television in the forties. Rock music developed into a large-scale industry of its own in the fifties, but that happened only after and because of the popular music that preceded it.

Of the many types of music popular in various different parts of the United States during the late nineteenth century, ragtime, Tin Pan Alley, the blues, and jazz all directly influenced the development of rock music. By the 1890s, all four styles were well established and independent of one another and yet all also influenced one another. The one distinguishing factor that separates the blues and jazz from the other two is that the blues and jazz were improvised music. Unfortunately, the late nineteenth-century versions of improvised music are unknown to us today because they were not recorded and **improvisation** is not written down. Improvisation happens when a musician decides what to play while he or she is playing it. It wasn't until the first jazz recording was made in 1917, and the blues somewhat later, that we can really tell what they sounded like. Ragtime and Tin Pan Alley music was composed and published as sheet music, and performances were, for the most part, played and/or sung directly from that notation. Once recordings came into common use, that changed for many people and popular music became more of a thing to listen to than to perform.

Ragtime

Ragtime was primarily, although not exclusively, an African American style. It might well have been first performed on the banjo in the mid-nineteenth century, but piano rags became more common. It was named for the "ragged" or **syncopated rhythms** played by the pianist's right hand, or the main melody played by the banjo or the band. The ragged lines were generally accompanied by a steady alternation between a single note and a **chord** (three or more notes played together) in the bass or lower band parts. The music had existed for some time before any of it was published. **Scott Joplin** (1868–1917) is the best-known ragtime composer. The sheet music to Joplin's "Maple Leaf Rag" (1899) had sold more than a million copies while he was still alive to receive royalties from the sales.

Although ragtime is related to some of the same interesting rhythms that were part of early jazz, it is not really a jazz style. The primary characteristic that keeps it from being jazz is that it is completely notated and is performed just as it is written. Improvisation, or spontaneous playing of unwritten music, is an essential part of jazz. Ragtime was, however, an important influence on the development of the jazz piano style known as "stride" in which the pianist's left hand moved back and forth rapidly from a single low note to a chord played much higher. Such jazz pianists as James P. Johnson and Eubie Blake had played ragtime before becoming known for their stride piano styles. The spread of ragtime and other popular music was aided by the invention of new sound devices such as the player piano, the phonograph, and jukebox-time players. Ragtime's direct influence on rock music had to do with its energy and fun, syncopated rhythms, and its influence on the development of stride piano, which became an element of many rhythm and blues piano styles used in rock music.

Tin Pan Alley

The term **Tin Pan Alley** referred to the thin, tinny tone quality of cheap upright pianos used in music publishers' offices on New York's West Twenty-Eighth Street between Fifth Avenue and Broadway during the late nineteenth and early twentieth centuries. The increasing popularity of **vaudeville shows** and the tremendous amount of new music they required helped the New York publishers gain much control of the popular music publishing industry because of the concentration of vaudeville houses and numbers of shows that began there before traveling to other parts of the country. Songwriters would travel to Tin Pan Alley to play their songs for publishers in hopes of getting them performed on vaudeville stages and also printed, distributed, and sold to amateur musicians who saw the shows. Some of the publishers also contracted professional songwriters whose job it was to write material similar to the songs that were already selling well. Generally, the songs were sentimental ballads or songs that portrayed the "gay nineties" as full of fun and as an escape from life's realities. Many songs were based on popular dance rhythms. The most common feature of the songs was that they were simple and easy to remember. "Take Me Out to the Ball Game" is one such song that is still known to many baseball fans.

The clever, catchy, and easy-to-remember types of pop melodies in much Tin Pan Alley music created an important model for many of the more pop-oriented rock songs, ballads, and dance music. The biggest difference between Tin Pan Alley music and the rock music derived from it was that rock music was usually sold as records whereas Tin Pan Alley music was sold as sheet music for the consumers to play themselves.

The Beginnings of Jazz in New Orleans

New Orleans has always been a very musical city. By the late nineteenth century, the main emphasis of musical interest in New Orleans had shifted from opera and classical music to popular band music and then gradually to jazz. As early as 1840, band music had become an important part of New Orleans's musical traditions. The Sunday parades where bands vied with each other for audience acclaim became common. The more popular groups found themselves in demand to play for funeral processions, park concerts, picnics, and other social events as well as for dancing in many of the halls, taverns, and clubs that abounded in the city. The music that they played would range from marches to popular dances of the day. Bands in New Orleans were usually small and made up of African American musicians or those of mixed (Creole) blood, although there were a few all-white bands in the city as well.

The African American and Creole musicians who played in the bands in New Orleans, for the most part, had some formal training on their instruments and could read music. They were playing a large variety of types of music, and the musicians began to add improvisations to the written lines. The African American musicians, in particular, added energy to their performances with syncopated African rhythms and other influences of the blues and black gospel music with which they were familiar. Gradually this transformed music began to be referred to as "hot" music.

Early hot bands generally included one trumpet (or cornet), one clarinet, and one trombone as the principal solo instruments (called the **front line**) and a **rhythm section** composed of banjo, guitar, or piano, or some combination of them; string bass or tuba; and drums. (*Rhythm section* is a general term for the instruments in any band that keep the beat and play the chords.) The clarinet often played a florid part above and around the cornet, and the trombone played countermelodies and bass-line passages below the cornet. Where the music of large bands was written out, a hot band would use collective improvisation when they played. This meant that the cornetist played the melody, but rather than performing it "straight," or as written, he embellished it in various ways by clipping certain notes short, adding other tones around the given notes of the tune, adding syncopations and blue tones (notes slightly lowered in pitch), introducing a "growl"

Joe ("King") Oliver and His Orchestra. Left to right, Baby Dodds, Honore Dutrey, Oliver, Louis Armstrong, Bill Johnson, Johnny Dodds, and Lil Armstrong

into his tone, and generally playing in a swinging manner. Other members of the front line improvised melodic lines all related to the succession of harmonies played by a chordal instrument such as the guitar or banjo or implied by the notes played in the bass. Extended improvisations by a solo instrument, unaccompanied by the rest of the front line, were not a part of the style of this early type of jazz although very short (usually not more than two measures or bars) **solo breaks** for an individual instrumentalist to be featured alone were common. The earliest (1917) hot or jazz band to record was made up of white musicians who called themselves the Original Dixieland Jazz Band.

Jazz did not remain confined to New Orleans or even the South for long. African American touring groups traveled to various parts of the country as early as 1908 to perform in vaudeville and minstrel shows. The popularity of social dancing was one element that contributed to the spread of jazz. The energetic and "raggy" rhythms of jazz were perfect for dances such as the charleston, which became popular during the twenties. Jazz remained a dancers' music through the swing era of the late thirties and early forties. Both Chicago and New York were

important centers for the development of the next important jazz style, swing.

> " If it hadn't been for him, there wouldn't have been none of us. I want to thank Mr. Louis Armstrong for my livelihood. "
>
> –Dizzy Gillespie

Swing Dance Bands

Beginning around 1934 and lasting through the end of World War II eleven years later, a couple's idea of a perfect night out would be one spent dancing to the music of a big band. **Swing** bands played jazz-related music, and individual musicians were allowed to improvise solos in a jazz style; but the bands themselves were bigger than earlier jazz bands, and improvisation time was limited. Most of the time the bands played music from written **arrangements** that were carefully planned for playing swing dance rhythms rather than the types of complex music of other jazz styles. Where earlier New Orleans jazz bands used one trumpet (or cornet), one clarinet, and one trombone as the principal solo instruments, swing bands were much larger, comprised of numbers of trumpets, trombones, and saxophones in addition to the rhythm instruments. A typical rhythm section in the New Orleans bands was composed of banjo or guitar, string bass or tuba, and drums. The smoother style of swing dance music used string bass, piano, and drums.

Swing music not only increased the number of band instruments used but also brought about new ways of playing them. The old bass lines played on tuba were usually single notes pumping back and forth between the first and third beats of a bar of four beats. Swing bassists created a much smoother effect by "walking" from note to note by playing a new note on every beat and occasionally between the beats to decorate the rhythmic flow. This bass style became known as **walking bass** and was later used in rhythm and blues and rock and roll.

Swing bands often backed male singers who sang in a style known as **crooning.** Crooning was different from earlier popular singing styles in that it was developed as a way of using a new invention, the microphone. Sound engineers were better able to control and amplify a soft and gentle voice than a loud, resonant one. In the crooning style men softened their natural voices into a smooth, gentle tone, sliding from one note to another to create the effect of warm sentimentality. Popular crooners of the swing era included Bing Crosby (1903–1977) and Perry Como (1912–2001). These crooners all had an influence on the pop rock singers of the fifties and early sixties known as *teen idols.*

The Blues

The very earliest roots of the blues lie not only in Africa but also in music from parts of Arabia, the Middle East, and even Spain during the Moorish occupation (eighth through the fifteenth centuries). Because that early music originated centuries before the advent of recorded sound and had not been notated, one can only listen to modern-day music from those parts of the world to hear similarities and assume intercultural exchanges among those peoples and Africans in the past. Musical devices, such as Arabic scale structures and melodic sequences, melodic and rhythmic patterns in Turkish ceremonial music, and the sense of rhythmic freedom used by Spanish singers, all share similarities with some types of African music and, ultimately, the blues.

To find the nearest direct predecessor of the blues, the ancestral music of African Americans must be examined. A potential problem in undertaking such a study is that

Africa is a very large continent and the people who were brought to the New World as slaves came from many widely separated areas. Understanding this, we believe that the easiest single place to find preblues African musical traditions is Freetown, Sierra Leone. Freetown was given its name when it was established as a colony of Africans who were to be shipped to the New World as slaves but were freed by an antislavery authority. It is interesting to note that although the people of Freetown represented nearly the same mixture of Africans as those who came to the New World, the blues as we know it did not develop in Freetown. The music there continued to be performed according to African traditions and ceremonies that were of and by the dominant culture of that part of the world. However, some of those musical practices clearly point the way to the blues.

Accompanied songs sung by **griots** (prouounced gree-ōs) from Sierra Leone share characteristics with early American blues songs. In Sierra Leone, as in many parts of Africa, griots have functioned for centuries as oral poets who tell the history of the people and their leaders. Before their society had a system of writing, griots maintained a social standing that was high and respectable, and the oral tradition continued on even after many Africans were able to write down their own history and poetry. Musical characteristics of griot songs include an expressive but somewhat rough vocal tone production, duple rhythm patterns, a vocal line that avoids following the rhythmic flow of the accompaniment, and an accompaniment without harmonic changes. Of those characteristics, the vocal tone and the duple rhythms are found in early American blues styles, but American blues singers tended to follow their accompaniment patterns more often than was common in the African tradition.

Although African griot songs heard today and the American blues have enough similarities to assume that they developed out of a similar source, American blues is not merely a transplanted version of the griot song. Part of the reason the blues had to be different from the griot song was that the blues functioned as a personal expression of an individual who suffered from a lack of human respectability, where the griot song was central to the dominant social structure in Africa. African Americans also had been exposed to music from white European traditions, particularly the hymns sung in churches, and that music influenced their use of a three-chord harmonic progression and short verses that were equal to one another in length. From all of this one can see that the blues developed out of ancient musical traditions from many parts of the world, traditions that were synthesized by African Americans in the southern United States.

Some of the musical traditions that influenced the development of the blues come from the experience of slavery. During very hard group work, such as chopping wood to clear a field or digging dirt for planting a crop, slaves would often fall into the old African tradition of singing in a **call-and-response** style. Call-and-response means that a leader sings out a phrase, then the group sings a copy version, or "response," to that phrase. Call-and-response was done in Africa when a group was dancing or otherwise celebrating, but it also worked for New World slaves as a way of keeping the work motion going. This type of singing during slave work is called **work songs.** When we study the blues, we will hear much use of call-and-response, particularly when we hear instruments respond to singers at the end of each vocal phrase.

Another type of singing done by working slaves is called the **field holler.** The field holler is different from the work song in that it was done by an individual worker who often sang laments about the tasks required of him or her. Field hollers had a less regular rhythm than work songs; they were also usually slower and included much improvisation. We will hear such individual improvisation in solos by blues and jazz singers and instrumentalists.

Both work songs and field hollers sometimes referred to a "captain" as the person who oversaw their work. Sometimes these references fell into what we call **signifying,** or having double meanings in a text. To the slaves the song might really be about their discontent, but to the ears of the overseer it seemed respectful. We will also see this kind of double meaning in a text when we study spirituals as a root of black gospel music. The spoken word with multiple meanings attached to it has long been important in African traditions, way back to the tribal importance of the griot singers. That vocal tradition will also be an element of the later style of rap.

Because of their origins in rural areas of the United States, particularly the South, the earliest-known blues styles were called **country blues.** The composers and performers of country blues were, for the most part, people to whom the blues was an integral part of life. They usually accompanied themselves on battered guitars (if they were accompanied at all), and the texts they sang were often rough yet highly expressive.

The blues developed its form and style some time in the late nineteenth or early twentieth century, but the earliest recordings were not made until the twenties. Exactly how the blues sounded at the beginning of the century can only be inferred from these later recordings. Even putting the performers in front of a microphone to record them must have affected the musical results to some degree.

Although much variation existed in the country blues styles that developed in various parts of the South, the style that had the most direct influence on the development of rock music came from the Mississippi Delta and was called **delta blues.** The lyrics were very expressive

about the lives the singers really led. It was highly emotional and rough when compared to country blues styles from such places as the Carolinas, but its expressiveness and rhythmic vitality caused its popularity to spread. Delta blues musicians such as Robert Johnson, Charley Patton, and Son House accompanied their singing with guitars, strumming chords that they interspersed with melodic fills.

Delta blues guitarists would often break off the neck of a bottle, file down the rough edges, put it on the third or fourth finger of the hand controlling the fingerboard of the instrument (usually the left hand), and slide it from note to note on the upper strings of the guitar, leaving the other three fingers of that hand to play simple chords or bass lines. Breaking bottles soon became unnecessary as tubes (called **bottlenecks**) of glass or steel were made commercially available. Other guitarists, Leadbelly (Huddie Ledbetter, 1885–1949) for one, achieved a similar effect by sliding a knife along the guitar strings. Blues players like Big Joe Williams, who recorded for Vocalion as early as 1929, and Muddy Waters, who began to record for Aristocrat Records in 1945 (renamed Chess Records in 1948), were later musicians who retained the essence of the delta blues bottleneck guitar style, while also updating it by using amplification and adding other instrumentalists.

Part of the general character of the blues was created by bending the pitches of notes to what were called **blue notes.** The exact origin of blue notes may never be known for certain, but they came either from **pentatonic** (five-tone) **scales** used in much world music or perhaps even from Islamic influences on African music. In the blues as it was played by early blues artists, the commonly lowered blue notes were the third and seventh degrees of a major scale. In the key of C, for example, one of the blue notes was somewhere between E and E♭ and the other was between B and B♭. To perform these notes with the voice and on some musical instruments, an E or a B could be bent down in pitch to produce the blue note. On many instruments, the piano for one, a note could not be bent to produce a blue tone, so the player simply lowered the tone a full half step. The following example shows the C scale with the blue notes a piano would play in parentheses:

Other scales, such as the pentatonic minor scale, were also often used in the blues, but even in these scales the lowered third and seventh degrees remain the common blue notes. In more advanced jazz styles such as **bebop,** the lowered fifth scale degree also became a blue note, but it was not often used as such in early blues.

Although pianists were limited to either lowering the pitch of a blue note a full half step or hitting two adjacent notes simultaneously to suggest the one in between, the pitch level of blue notes was much less exact on instruments that could bend notes. One reason for the popularity of playing the guitar with a bottleneck was that the bottleneck could be used to slide through the blue notes that fell between the frets (metal bars across the fingerboard behind which the strings were stopped). Another technique for playing blue notes on a guitar without a bottleneck was to play the fret just below a blue note and then push or pull the string, causing it to tighten and then loosen gradually, raising and lowering the pitch within the area of the blue note. This technique was called **string bending.**

The blues developed into a fairly consistent formal structure, influenced by European song forms, that was made up of repeated and contrasting lines of specific length. The form used in most blues could be outlined by the letters AAB. In that outline, the first letter A referred to the first line of melody (four measures) and the first phrase of words. The second A represented a repetition of the same words and a melody that was exactly or nearly the same as the first. The letter B stood for a contrasting line of text (often rhyming with line A) and a contrasting melody that functioned as a response to the words and melody of the A sections. In other words, blues lyrics usually had two lines of text, the first of which was repeated. Songs can still be the blues when this lyric structure is not followed, but it is common in traditional blues.

The rhythm of the blues form was organized into four-beat patterns, each of which was called a bar (or measure), and each section of the melody was made up of four bars. As the three phrases had four bars each, the complete structure for each AAB blues verse, chorus, or stanza (these terms are used interchangeably) had a total of twelve bars. For that reason, it was often referred to as the **twelve-bar blues.** Following is an example of a stanza of blues showing how the poetic (lyric) form was structured:

I love my man when he treats me fine (The first A section)

I love my man when he treats me fine (The second A section)

I just wish he wouldn't drink so much wine (The B section)

A practice not always followed in blues-based rock music, but typical of traditional blues styles, involved the use of the West African practice of call-and-response, in which a leader would call out to a group, and the group responded to the call. The blues singer usually played the part of the caller by singing from the first beat of each section of melody through the first beat of the third bar, and the remainder of the four-bar section was filled by an instrumental response. The response could be played by one or more players on a variety of instruments, by the singer on the guitar or piano, or by the singer repeating one or more of the words at the end of each line of text. The following diagram shows the placement of the text, the instrumental or vocal fill (response to the singer's call), and the chord progression as it became standardized in the twelve-bar blues. In the key of C the tonic chord is C, the subdominant chord is F, and the dominant chord is G. All three are often seventh chords. (Early blues musicians often kept playing the G^7 chord through the first two bars of the B section instead of playing the F chord in the second bar.) Each repetition of the chord name represents a beat on which the chord would be played, and the vertical lines divide those beats into four-beat bars.

Twelve-Bar Blues Form

A Lyric Sung text_____Instrumental fill
C C C C | C C C C | C C C C | C C C C |

A Lyric Sung text_____Instrumental fill
F F F F | F F F F | C C C C | C C C C |

B Lyric Sung text_____Instrumental fill
$G^7G^7G^7G^7$ | F F F F | C C C C | C C C C |

As was also true of most jazz styles, the beats were usually subdivided unevenly, creating a smooth flow of long-short-long-short in which each long note was twice the length of each short note, as shown by the following notation:

Even beat subdivision   *Uneven beat subdivision*

The uneven rhythm pattern was called a shuffle beat when the bass was played on the beat and the chord was played on the last part of the beat. When performed slowly, the uneven **beat subdivisions** created a relaxed feeling that was well suited to and became a characteristic of the blues. Even beat subdivisions are common in folk and country music.

One of the most influential country blues singer/guitarists who recorded during the thirties was **Robert Johnson** (1911–1938). Not much is known about his life, other than that he was poor, grew up on a plantation in Mississippi, and was reputedly either husband or lover to just about any woman who would have him. The lyrics of most of Johnson's songs expressed his insatiable desire for wine, women, and song. He recorded only twenty-nine songs, although when one includes alternate takes of some of those songs his recordings total forty-one. His recordings were done in makeshift studios in hotel rooms or office buildings, and the distribution of those recordings in his own time was extremely limited because large record companies simply were not interested in his kind of music. The recordings were reissued in later years, and consequently many blues-loving rock musicians have been influenced by them.

Johnson did not perform in formal situations for large groups, so relatively few people heard him in person. Those who did spread stories about the expressiveness of his music, and from those stories arose the Faustian myth that he had sold his soul in order to play so well. That myth was dramatized in the 1986 movie *Crossroads*.

Johnson's songs did follow the traditional AAB lyrical scheme and the chords of the basic blues progression as it was described earlier (with only two chords in the B section), but he was not confined by the rhythmic strictness observed by later blues musicians. He added extra beats to bars and extra bars to phrases seemingly at random, and sometimes even sang in a rhythmic pattern that differed

from what he was playing on his guitar. The simultaneous use of more than one rhythm (**polyrhythm**) was known in some African musical traditions, and he may have been familiar with music based in such practices. The essentials of Johnson's musical style can best be discussed with reference to one of his recordings. A listening guide for his "Cross Road Blues" is below.

Two years after the recording of "Cross Road Blues" was made, Johnson's wild and free lifestyle was responsible for his death. Only twenty-seven years old, he was poisoned either by a woman with whom he had been involved or by the husband of such a woman. Johnson's songs have been recorded by many rock groups, including the Rolling Stones, who recorded "Love in Vain" and "Stop Breaking Down"; Cream, who recorded "Cross Road Blues" (although they called it "Crossroads"); and Fleetwood Mac, who recorded "Hellhound on My Trail."

Listening Guide

"Cross Road Blues"
as recorded by Robert Johnson (1936)

Tempo: The speed of the basic beat is approximately 88 beats per minute, but Johnson speeds up and slows down at will.

Form: Johnson plays slightly less than a four-bar introduction on the guitar using a bottleneck. (The introduction has been cut short, perhaps because the recording machine was turned on just after he had begun playing.)

After the introduction, the twelve-bar blues form is followed throughout. As was common in delta blues, the B section has two bars of a dominant chord (the G^7 in the outline of the blues form) followed by two bars of the tonic chord (the C chord in the outline).

Features: Johnson sings four stanzas of blues lyrics, providing his own responses on the guitar without any backup by other musicians.

The influence of polyrhythms can be heard in two ways:

1. Johnson's beat is usually subdivided into uneven parts, as is typical of the blues, but he occasionally breaks the pattern and uses sections of even beat subdivisions.

2. His singing often departs from the beat played by the guitar, following a different rhythm pattern, producing a polyrhythmic effect.

Lyrics: The main image is a lonely black man in the American South of the 1930s who cannot "flag a ride" out of his environment, yet must leave the crossroads before dark (an allusion to curfews that were imposed on blacks in the South at the time). But the imagery suggests a deeper loneliness that transcends the singer's place and time: He falls to his knees seeking a way out of his existential predicament, yet no one stops to help him out, which parallels his failure to connect with a "lovin' sweet woman."

Although most of the country blues singers who attracted the attention of record companies were men, women also sang and played the blues, and some had fairly successful careers. One such musician was Lizzie "Kid" Douglas, who recorded under the name Memphis Minnie (1897–1973). Her recordings can be found on several labels including Columbia, Victor, Vocalion, OKeh, Decca, and JOB.

Female singers in the classic blues style did not accompany themselves as did Memphis Minnie. Most were from the South and had grown up hearing country blues, but they developed powerful and gutsy vocal styles needed to be heard over the sound level of their accompanying jazz bands. Their style was called **classic blues.** Two classic blues singers who served as inspiration for such later rock singers as Etta James, La Vern Baker, and Janis Joplin were Ma Rainey and Bessie Smith. Ma Rainey (born Gertrude Malissa Pridgett, 1886–1939) was sometimes called the Mother of the Blues because of her nickname, Ma (from Malissa), and also for her influence on singers who followed her. Rainey recorded with such jazz greats as Coleman Hawkins and Louis Armstrong, but much of her performing was done on tour with tent shows, in which she had to belt out over the sound of a band without the aid of amplification. Her style included gutsy moans, dramatic pauses, expressive bending of blue notes, and sliding from one melody note to the next. Rainey retired from touring in 1935 and succumbed to a heart attack four years later.

Bessie Smith on stage in 1928

Bessie Smith (1894–1937) toured and performed with Ma Rainey—who was about ten years her senior—and was very much influenced by Rainey's singing style. Smith took Rainey's ideas about the bending of blue notes

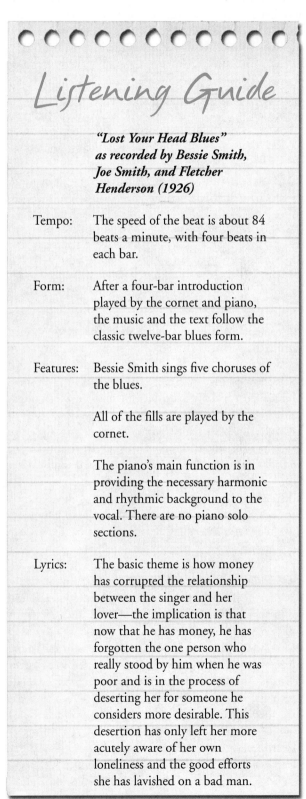

Listening Guide

"Lost Your Head Blues"
as recorded by Bessie Smith,
Joe Smith, and Fletcher
Henderson (1926)

Tempo: The speed of the beat is about 84 beats a minute, with four beats in each bar.

Form: After a four-bar introduction played by the cornet and piano, the music and the text follow the classic twelve-bar blues form.

Features: Bessie Smith sings five choruses of the blues.

All of the fills are played by the cornet.

The piano's main function is in providing the necessary harmonic and rhythmic background to the vocal. There are no piano solo sections.

Lyrics: The basic theme is how money has corrupted the relationship between the singer and her lover—the implication is that now that he has money, he has forgotten the one person who really stood by him when he was poor and is in the process of deserting her for someone he considers more desirable. This desertion has only left her more acutely aware of her own loneliness and the good efforts she has lavished on a bad man.

and the use of dramatic expression in her delivery beyond what Rainey herself had done, and she eventually earned the title the Empress of the Blues. Smith was featured in the 1929 film *St. Louis Blues* and throughout her career sang with such jazz pianists as Clarence Williams and Fletcher Henderson, swing bands led by Jack Teagarden and Benny Goodman, and, like Ma Rainey, with instrumental soloists Coleman Hawkins and Louis Armstrong. She was on a theater tour with a group called Broadway Rastus Review when she was in a car accident and died from her injuries. A listening guide to Bessie Smith's classic recording of "Lost Your Head Blues" is on page 9.

Other classic blues singers included Alberta Hunter, Mamie Smith, and Ida Cox. Billie Holiday is sometimes referred to as a blues singer, but she recorded few songs that were technically the blues. She is better known as one of the greatest of the female jazz singers who recorded during the thirties through the fifties. One of the best examples of her blues recordings was her own composition "Fine and Mellow" (1939).

The Beginnings of Rock and Roll

Instrumental, vocal, and dance styles that were popular during the forties had a certain amount of influence on the development of rock music. It is important, however, to understand that rock music also had its roots in styles of music that had not yet gained the nationwide popularity of the Tin Pan Alley songs or the swing bands. For example, delta blues and rhythm and blues, which served as the basis of much early rock music, were mostly played and sold in African American neighborhoods and neither heard nor understood by the general American public. Similarly, some country music styles that influenced early rock music had their own particular regions of popularity and, therefore, rather limited numbers of fans. Racism and the forced segregation of African Americans was one of the reasons for this division of musical tastes.

In addition to the types of popular music previously discussed, which aided the development of rock music, several technological innovations in the late forties and early fifties were also very important for rock. Magnetic tape recorders not only provided a dramatic improvement in the sound quality of musical recordings but also were handy in the recording studio. Fifties pop and rock musicians made much use of their ability to create echo effects and use **overdubbing** to enhance music already recorded. Some famous examples include Elvis Presley's recording of "Heartbreak Hotel" (1956), which used echo, and Eddie Cochran's "Summertime Blues" (1958), which was made by overdubbing his own playing several times to create an effect that he could never achieve live without the help of other musicians. Recordings became so important in rock music that many performers would **lip sync** to the recordings of their songs on television rather than try to perform them live.

Three technological developments in 1948 were especially important. Transistor radios, 33⅓ rpm long-playing (LP) records, and 45 rpm single records became commercially available. Transistor radios were lighter and easier to move around than the old vacuum tube radios, and by the early sixties they were made small enough to carry around all day long. It was not until 1954 that the new 33⅓ and 45 single records replaced older types, so many early rock recordings were originally released on the old 78s. The new 45 singles were particularly popular because they allowed for the inexpensive purchase of an individual song with another on the reverse (or "B") side. They were also used in jukeboxes, which were becoming common in soda fountains, restaurants, bars, and other public gathering places. Jukeboxes played songs from their list of available 45 records when coins were dropped in them. Because they could be heard by everyone in the place, not just the person who chose and paid for the song, they helped many people hear popular songs even without the radio.

Racial barriers slowly eroded when white teenagers began to listen and dance to the rhythm and blues of such jump bands as Louis Jordan and his Tympany Five in the late forties.

Also in the late forties, a big change occurred in what music could be heard on radio stations. Previously, only four national stations were available, all of which played music and programs geared to a largely white middle-class audience. Now small, independent stations sprang up all over the country playing music geared to local tastes. These new independent stations used disc jockeys as entertainers and were not afraid to play rock recordings. They also played black rhythm and blues, another important type of music in which rock music was rooted. It was primarily through the radio that white teenagers became acquainted with rhythm and blues because rhythm and blues records were generally only available in black neighborhoods.

Radio and television were both very important in popularizing rock music from its very beginnings. As hard as it is to imagine, it was not until 1951 that televisions were inexpensive enough to be purchased by average middle-class family consumers. Even so, TVs soon became important vehicles for rock performers, and they allowed for dance shows such as *American Bandstand* to be viewed nationwide. At first, many white radio-station and record-company owners resisted making music by African American performers widely available. Certainly, airtime on radio during the thirties and forties was crowded with programs by white entertainers. The increased availability of televisions and the subsequent movement of many former white radio programs from radio to television left room for broader radio programming. By 1951, the smooth rhythmic sounds of African American vocal groups like the Platters and the Moonglows were reaching white teens through radio programs hosted by maverick disc jockeys who refused to perpetuate racial exclusion, the most famous of whom was Cleveland's **Alan Freed.** The increased availability of radios, especially car radios during the early fifties and portable transistor radios several years later, was important in bringing both rhythm and blues and rock music to the teen audience. Bands and audiences were still segregated for the most part, but early rock music did help bridge some of the gap.

In 1954, the Supreme Court decided that equality could not exist when people remained separated by race. After deciding the case known as *Brown v. Board of Education,* the court demanded that public schools be integrated. It still took years before integration became more common, but attitudes gradually changed from the extreme racist attitudes of the past. The popularity of rock music that developed directly from both African American and white styles of music can be given a part of the credit for helping to relax racist attitudes. Of course, rock music did not replace other types of popular music when it finally came into being, and many other types of popular music still maintain a large following. For the purposes of this book, however, it is rock and roll and its development that will be discussed further.

New York was an important center for several styles of popular music originating in Tin Pan Alley. Swing dance bands and the crooners who sang with these bands helped keep American optimism and spirit alive through World War II. The blues was performed by African Americans living in the rural areas of the southern United States around the beginning of the twentieth century. In its earliest form, country blues music was used to express the longings of people whose lives were generally very difficult. West African influences on the development of the blues included the use of polyrhythms and blue notes and the practice of call-and-response between a leader and a group. European musical traditions such as a regular four-beat pattern in each bar, a repeating and contrasting AAB lyrical scheme, and a twelve-bar chord progression also became elements of the blues.

During the early years of the development of recording technology, blues musicians began moving to larger cities and working with organized jazz bands or at least instruments from them in smaller groups. Rock music developed out of a number of different styles of music that existed in the forties and became a style of its own in the early fifties. More than any of the prerock styles we discussed, rock music depended on recording technology that came into common use in the late forties. In many ways, the popularity of rock music among both black and white musicians and fans aided the movement toward racial integration and mutual respect of people of any ethnic background.

Summary

America's earliest popular music was brought to the New World by British and other European settlers. Eventually, American-born composers began to compose and publish their own music, providing popular songs that expressed more purely American interests and lifestyles. By the 1890s ragtime music was heard up and down the Mississippi River and had become popular in many big cities.

discussion questions

To what degree did early rock music depend on sociological changes as distinct from technological developments? What were some of those sociological changes and how did they help create and popularize rock music? How might the blues be different if slavery had never existed and African Americans had been welcomed immigrants in the United States?

The NINETEEN FIFTIES

"Radioactive poisoning of the atmosphere and hence annihilation of any life on earth has been brought within the range of technical possibilities. . . . In the end, there beckons more and more clearly general annihilation."

–Albert Einstein (1950)

"We will bury you!"

–Soviet Premier Nikita Khrushchev (1956)

"Rock and roll is a means of pulling down the white man to the level of the Negro. It is part of a plot to undermine the morals of the youth of our nation."

–ASA Carter, North Alabama White Citizens' Council (1956)

The Decade of the Fifties

With memories of World War II still fresh in the minds of most Americans, a new threat was dawning on the horizon in 1950: the communist states of the Soviet Union and the People's Republic of China. In the years immediately following World War II, the Soviet Union occupied much of Eastern Europe; at the other end of the continent, the People's Republic of China had aided the North Korean government against Western allies in the Korean War. The Soviet Union had more planes, tanks, and troops than did the United States and had even already tested its own atomic bomb. Americans were scared. Some who could afford to do so dug into their backyards and installed heavily shielded bomb shelters to save their families from the destruction of the "bomb." Drop drills were practiced in schools to teach kids to drop to the floor, get under their desks, and cover their heads and necks to protect them from window glass that would shatter if a bomb were dropped in the vicinity of the school.

Along with fear of a war with the Soviet Union was fear of the influence that Russian communism might have in the United States. Julius and Ethel Rosenberg were executed (1953) for selling secrets to the Russians. Senator Joseph McCarthy was one of many who was obsessed by the thought that we could be overtaken by oppressive communism. He started his investigations in the early fifties by accusing members of the State Department of having communist ties. His televised questioning of members of the U.S. Army in 1953 gained national attention, but it was ended by the Senate for his obviously having overstated the case. Even so, McCarthy had drawn widespread attention to the communist threat. At the same time, the House Un-American Activities Committee investigated the entertainment industry in search of communists. Its "blacklist," or list of people it determined might be communists, was successful in curtailing or destroying the careers of many people in Hollywood. It also had unknown effects on the work being produced by people who managed to stay in the industry because controversial subjects in television, movies, or other modes of entertainment might lead to the writer's questioning, blacklisting, and subsequent job loss or jail stay. The average American citizen saw this tremendous amount of investigating at home and also saw that the Soviet Union was overtaking more and more countries around its borders, a move that was reminiscent of what Hitler had done. All of those news items added together to create a fear in many Americans that lasted through the cold war (1950–1990). U.S. involvement in the Korean War was in many ways a reaction to perceived communist expansion into the Korean peninsula.

Despite this pressure to avoid communism and the bomb, the fifties was a decade of relative prosperity for most white middle-class Americans. With the exception of a recession in 1958, unemployment and inflation remained low. During this time fertility rates increased and most of the members of what became known as the baby boom generation were born. Women were also working outside the home in greater numbers than they had before, even during the war. Where families had suffered wartime rationing of food and other supplies, they finally had a fairly decent chance to buy their own homes and live comfortably. Some of these new parents had had to work to contribute to the family income during their own teenage years and responded by giving their kids more freedom and money to enjoy. When preteen or teenaged young people had their own money to spend on the things that appealed to them, their tastes began to dictate what was popular.

In part, the emerging youth culture had a dark, albeit exciting, side in the popular image of the rebellious antihero. Movies such as *The Wild One* (1954), in which a young Marlon Brando played the leader of a tough motorcycle gang, helped to popularize that image of rebellion for its own sake. That movie was followed by others, including *Blackboard Jungle* (1955) about juvenile delinquency in an all-male high school, and James Dean's *Rebel without a Cause* (1955). Some rockabilly singers such as Gene Vincent and Eddie Cochran wore the black leather jackets associated with that image and sang songs about young people needing to break free of adult authority figures, but the rock artists did not create that image. The movies did.

Rebellion was not limited to teenagers in the fifties. Writers and poets of the Beat movement questioned the values of American society and found it to be hypocritical and oppressive compared to the popular belief that America was a place that gave freedom to all. Statements made by the Beats became central to the thinking of many young people during the sixties and later. Their influence aided the development of several styles of rock music of later decades, including folk-rock, psychedelic, glitter, punk, and industrial.

Televisions got less and less expensive, and by the end of the decade most middle-class households had one. Ironically, the image popularized by television contradicted that of the rebellious teenager portrayed in the cinemas. Despite the seriousness of the statements made by the Beat writers, the beatnik (follower of the Beat writers) Maynard G. Krebs on *Dobie Gillis* was a comic character. The parents in *Ozzie and Harriet, Father Knows Best,* and *Leave It to Beaver* had no problems of their own and were always available to see to their children's every need. Lucille Ball did sometimes buck the image of the obedient housewife with her many efforts to gain control of her life in *I Love Lucy,* but she was only able to sell that effectively because she was such a brilliant comedian. The idea of a wife really having equality with her husband was not popular. Overall, the fifties can be seen as a time when many people of the large white middle class were enjoying the fruits of a lifestyle that was clean and comfortable and were anxious to avoid the bomb, communism, and almost anything foreign.

For African Americans it was a time of serious recognition of their unequal status and for their gradual and finally unified decision to change it. For the most part, segregation had given them lower-quality lifestyles than whites had. Even such issues as the right to vote were in dispute. African Americans had previously been given that right by the Fifteenth Amendment to the Constitution, but it was not practiced fairly in parts of the South. In such places, African Americans were given tests that were impossible for anyone to pass, and their failure kept them from being allowed to vote. Sometimes they were charged fees called poll taxes, so they could not afford to vote. Whites did not have either restriction on their voting rights. The images of African Americans on television were also extremely unequal. The actors on all of the popular shows were white, with African Americans and other minorities only cast in the roles of servants in such comedies as *Make Room for Daddy* and the *Jack Benny Show.*

In the *Brown v. Board of Education* (1954) decision, the Supreme Court forced schools that had previously been segregated by race to integrate. The new law took some years to become common practice and be accepted by the majority of the U.S. population. More than two thousand school districts had still not integrated by 1960.

It was in Montgomery, Alabama, in 1955 that the weary Rosa Parks refused to give up her seat on a bus to a white man and was arrested and tried for it. Dr. Martin Luther King led a 381-day bus boycott following the incident. The legal battles that ensued took time, but the Supreme Court did finally outlaw the segregation of seats on vehicles for public transportation. The civil rights movement had gotten well under way.

Most entertainment venues had always been racially segregated. In cases such as New York's famous Cotton Club, where Duke Ellington and other jazz greats of the thirties often performed to white audiences, African Americans were not allowed to mix with the white patrons. By the fifties, some clubs would have "black" nights for African American patrons and "white" nights for whites. At times the groups could be at the same club at the same time, but there was a rope across the floor segregating the crowd. As rhythm and blues and blues-based rock music began to be popular with more and more white teenagers, that segregation was unacceptable to them. The separate nights gradually became one and the ropes came down. As Chuck Berry said at the time, "Well, look what's happening, salt and pepper all mixed together." Rock music was, in many ways, a music of integration.

Chronology Chart

Historical Events	Happenings in Rock Music
1945 U.S. drops first atomic bomb. End of WWII, beginning of postwar prosperity. Beginning of baby boom. Truman becomes president.	Louis Jordan's "jumpin' jive" style becomes popular with white teens. The Delmore Brothers record "Hillbilly Boogie."
1947 Truman orders all federal government buildings to be racially integrated. The Marshall Plan aids Europe.	Country musicians begin to cover African American blues recordings. Atlantic Record Co. formed.
1948 Apartheid policy becomes official in South Africa. U.S.S.R. blockade of Allied sectors of Berlin. Goldmark invents microgroove system, making LP albums possible.	Pete Seeger and Lee Hays form the Weavers. 33⅓ and 45 rpm records first marketed.
1949 U.S. troops withdraw from Korea. Berlin blockade is lifted. NATO established.	*Race music* begins to be called *rhythm and blues.*
1950 Truman authorizes production of H-bomb. U.S. military advisers agree to aid South Vietnam against communist North. Senator Joseph McCarthy's search for communists begins.	Chess Brothers change label name from Aristocrat to Chess. Cool jazz develops from bebop jazz. "On Top of Old Smoky" and "Good Night Irene" hit for the Weavers.
1951 U.S. involvement in Korean War. First transcontinental TV and first color TV marketed in U.S.	Car radios become common. Bill Haley and the Saddlemen record "Rocket 88." Popularity of rhythm and blues among white teens increases. Alan Freed's debut on Cleveland radio.
1952 Immigration and Naturalization Act passes. U.S. explodes first hydrogen bomb.	Bill Haley's Saddlemen become the Comets. Riot at Alan Freed's Moondog Coronation Ball in Cleveland. *Bandstand* on television.

1953	Rosenberg executions. Eisenhower becomes president. Korean War ends. U.S.S.R. tests hydrogen bomb.	Weavers break up after HUAC investigation. Hank Williams dies.

1954   McCarthy hearings end with Senate condemnation of McCarthy. Racial integration in public schools begins. Some whites resist efforts toward integration of races. U.S. sends military units to South Vietnam as French troops leave.

Bill Haley's first release of "Rock Around the Clock." Alan Freed on WINS in New York. 45s replace 78s at RCA and Mercury. "Sh-Boom" by the Chords enters the pop charts. Marlon Brando portrays a rebellious teen in *The Wild One.* Elvis Presley records for the Sun Record Co. Fender releases the Stratocaster. First stereo recorded on tape.

1955   Atomically generated power is used. Bus boycott is organized by African Americans in Montgomery, Alabama. Labor unions merge to form AFL-CIO.

Blackboard Jungle and *Rebel without a Cause* are released. Chess label signs Chuck Berry. The Platters have a pop chart hit. First radio broadcasts in stereo. James Dean dies.

1956   Martin Luther King becomes recognized leader of civil rights movement. Supreme Court overturns Alabama Intrastate Bus Segregation Law. First transatlantic telephone cable put into operation.

Ska begins to develop in Jamaica. Elvis Presley's first RCA recording sessions and movie *Love Me Tender.* Elvis Presley makes first TV appearance on the Tommy Dorsey Show. Carl Perkins is injured in an auto accident. Buddy Holly and the Crickets sign first record contract. Dick Clark becomes host of *American Bandstand.* Many bans on rock concerts sought due to brawls and riots at previous concerts.

1957   U.S.S.R. launches first satellites (Sputniks I and II). Eisenhower Doctrine seeks to keep communism out of the Middle East. International Atomic Energy Agency is founded. Federal troops sent to Arkansas to protect African American students at formerly all-white high school.

American Bandstand broadcast on national TV. Little Richard quits performing to enter the ministry. Jerry Lee Lewis marries thirteen-year-old cousin. Boston bans the Everly Brothers' "Wake Up Little Susie." Paul McCartney joins John Lennon's Quarry Men in Liverpool. Burrough's novel *Naked Lunch* is published. Last 78s are released.

1958   Congressional committee investigates unethical practices in broadcasting industry (payola scandal). U.S. launches Explorer I satellite. First recordings made in stereo.

Army drafts Elvis Presley. Violence causes cancellations of Alan Freed shows. NBC bans rock music. St. Louis DJs break rock records on radio. Aldon Music and Brill Building centers for New York pop songwriting. First Newport Folk Festival. Transistor radios are marketed. Big Bill Broonzy dies.

1959   Alaska and Hawaii join U.S. as states. First ballistic missile submarine and first atomic-powered merchant ship are launched. Castro takes power in Cuba. Soviet premier Khrushchev visits U.S.

Buddy Holly records first rock record using a string section. Alan Freed is fired because of payola scandal. Motown Record Co. starts in Detroit. Buddy Holly, Ritchie Valens, and the Big Bopper die.

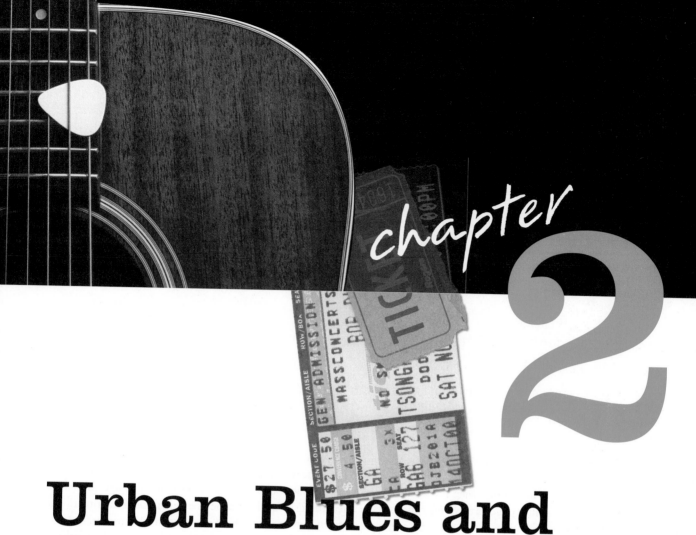

Urban Blues and Rhythm and Blues

"Muddy Waters is the godfather of the blues."
—CHUCK BERRY

The term *blues* has long been used to describe feelings of sadness and hopelessness. The music called the blues developed out of a very unhappy situation indeed—that of people taken forcibly from their homes and brought to a new world to live in slavery. Even long after they were released from servitude, African Americans were not accepted by the white society that had granted them their freedom. Despite that difficult fact, the blues was not always a sad music. It was often music used by African Americans to help them cope with the problems and frustrations they encountered in the harshness of their daily lives. The lyrics of many blues songs included an element of hope and the anticipation of better times. Some told stories, often including sexual references, sometimes euphemistically, sometimes blatantly; but in general they were an emotional outpouring by a people who had been relegated to existing on the fringes of a society that considered them social and genetic inferiors. One, perhaps the first, type of rock music was played by rhythm and blues musicians who added more energy and a stronger **backbeat** (accents on the second and fourth of each four-beat bar) to their music than was typical of most earlier rhythm and blues. Bo Diddley was one such musician who was really a rhythm and blues guitarist and singer but whose music is also an early type of rock music.

Urban Blues

The U.S. involvement in World War I (1914–1918) required many men of military age to leave their industrial jobs in large northern cities and go to Europe to fight in the war. Around that same time, many African Americans in the Mississippi Delta were losing jobs because of the boll weevils' attacks on cotton crops. The result of these two events was that many southern African Americans ended up moving to such northern cities as Kansas City, Chicago, and New York in order to find jobs. Once settled in the North, the first of these workers found that they suffered less from the kinds of racial discrimination they had in the South; and that word spread, causing others to move north. Racism still existed in the North to the point that neighborhoods were segregated so separate African American communities developed in each city. Among those workers who were newly grouped together and living a much more urban, or city-oriented, lifestyle than they had in the rural South were many musicians whose training was in country blues. When these musicians banded together into small groups instead of just singing and accompanying themselves on guitars, a new style of blues developed: **urban blues.**

Most urban blues was played by groups of instruments that included a rhythm section (bass, drums, guitar or piano) and solo instruments such as the saxophone or other wind instruments. The instrumental group, which at times was a full jazz band, accompanied the singer, played responses to the singer's lines, and also played instrumental choruses. A piano was loud enough to be used as a solo instrument, but an unamplified guitar did not project well enough (although some acoustic guitar solos were played on recordings). For that reason, the guitar was used primarily to strum rhythms until the invention of the electric guitar. Guitarist Floyd Smith and trombonist/guitarist Eddie Durham were pioneer electric guitarists who recorded solos in the thirties. Another jazz guitarist, Charlie Christian, further developed the innovations of Smith and Durham by playing melodic lines patterned after the solos of jazz horn players.

Urban blues guitarist Aaron Thibeaux Walker, nicknamed **T-Bone Walker** (1910–1975), was among the first musicians to use the electric guitar as a solo blues instrument. Born in Texas, Walker grew up playing country blues guitar in the style of Blind Lemon Jefferson, who was also from Texas. Jefferson played with the same casual approach to rhythm that delta singers like Robert Johnson had used, but his style differed in that the lines he played as fills between his vocal phrases were much longer and more complex than those of most delta guitarists. After years of playing both the blues and rhythm and blues, Walker grew away from his early rural roots and developed a flashy solo style in which he played highly embellished versions of the melody. He was a terrific showman who did things like play the guitar behind his back, and he became a strong influence on both blues guitarist B. B. King and rock guitarist Chuck Berry.

B. B. King (born in 1925) came from Mississippi, the homeland of the delta blues. His very lyrical and expressive

B. B. King in concert.

Listening Guide

"Three O'Clock Blues"
as recorded by B. B. King (1951)

Tempo: The speed of the beat is slow (about 76 beats per minute), with four beats in each bar.

Form: Both the music and the text follow the classic twelve-bar blues form.

The recording starts with a four-bar guitar introduction, followed by four full choruses of the twelve-bar form, the third of which is instrumental with the guitar improvising on the harmonic progression.

Features: King sings and then plays guitar lines that function as a response to his vocal lines. (He plays the instrumental fills on the last seven beats of each section of the twelve-bar form.) The guitar lines imitate and expand on the vocal melody to which they respond and often use string bends to reach blue notes.

A chordal accompaniment is supplied by saxophones playing sustained (long-held) notes. The drums are very soft (under-recorded?), with little or no accenting of the backbeat (beats 2 and 4 of a four-beat pattern). A bit of urban sophistication in the arrangement is the occasional use of half-step slides into some of the main chords of the progression. Most of the time King slides down to the proper chord, but he reverses that and slides up to the tonic chord at the final cadence (ending).

Lyrics: Finding, in the wee hours of the morning, that his lover has left him, the singer is suicidal, though going to the local pool hall may offer some solace.

Billboard rhythm and blues charts: number one for five weeks

solo style was an important influence on many rock guitarists, including Eric Clapton, Jimmy Page, Jimi Hendrix, and Mike Bloomfield. King's initials, "B. B.," were derived from his nickname, "Blues Boy"; his real name was Riley B. King. An analysis of King's recording of "Three O'Clock Blues" (1951) showing the important elements of his playing is on page 19. "Three O'Clock Blues" was a number one hit on the *Billboard* rhythm and blues charts for five weeks.

"I can hear myself singing when I play. That may sound weird, but I can hear the words that I'm saying and a lot of times they don't mean as much to me as the way I say it."

–B. B. King

It is helpful to compare the rhythmic informality of Robert Johnson to the formal regularity of the beat pattern and song structure of "Three O'Clock Blues" to hear the urbanization of the later style. Also, King's urban blues guitar style includes playing lines that are of equal importance to the lines he sings. Certainly no single recording could show all of B. B. King's abilities as either a guitarist or a singer. He has performed as featured soloist with jazz bands and groups of all sizes, as well as with large orchestral string sections playing arrangements of blues songs. He also performed with U2 in their 1988 movie *Rattle and Hum.* King's interest in playing melodic lines rather than chordal accompaniments was evident in that performance. Just before King went on stage with U2, he requested that "the Edge" take care of the chords. King's career continued on in the nineties with several new albums and even a performance on *Simpsons Sing the Blues* (1990). On the album *Blues Summit* (1993), King played a series of duets with John Lee Hooker, Lowell Fulson, and Robert Cray.

"I still don't think there is a better blues guitarist in the world than B. B. King."

–Eric Clapton

Although the urban blues was more complex than country blues, this style was not necessarily better. Rock musicians have taken advantage of both styles, drawing elements from the music of both the relatively untrained but tremendously expressive style of country blues artists and the musical sophistication of urban blues artists.

Blues-based rock styles may differ greatly from each other, but this is proof that through the years the blues has remained a very adaptable and flexible music.

"Maybe our forefathers couldn't keep their language together when they were taken away from Africa, but then the blues was a language we invented to let people know we had something to say. And we've been saying it pretty strong ever since."

–B. B. King

Chicago Blues

Chicago was one of the large industrial cities that attracted many African American workers during World War I. Soon after the end of that war, African American neighborhoods in Chicago's West Side and South Side were populated by as many as 200,000 people. That population more than doubled during World War II, again because of job availability in the city. As had happened in other northern cities, Chicago musicians urbanized their styles by joining into groups and by replacing the older acoustic guitars with electric ones. The blues style that developed in Chicago combined swing jazz and boogie-woogie piano influences with the passion of the delta blues. This style came to be called **Chicago blues.**

Chess Recording Studios in Chicago must be given much credit for its recordings of the blues during the forties and fifties. The company was owned and run by two brothers, **Phil and Leonard Chess,** who had immigrated to the United States from Poland. Almost all of the blues artists discussed earlier were with the Chess label at one time or another; and while their styles were generally rural, country blues when they first came to Chicago, Chess gave them backup musicians and amplification that resulted in a more urban style.

As you listen to music by the delta singers, you will notice that while many of their songs fit the twelve-bar form of the traditional blues described earlier, others avoided both the AAB lyrical structure and the prescribed chord progressions. Some songs had no more than a single chord throughout but kept a general blues style by using other elements such as blue notes and uneven beat subdivisions. In other words, not every "blues-sounding" song played by a blues musician necessarily fit the formal structure of the twelve-bar blues. To aid the inexperienced listener's understanding of the basic differences between

the sound of the twelve-bar structure (and some common variants) and the sound of the blues-style chant over a single chord, this section concludes with some comments about the structure and other characteristics of a few representative songs by Chicago blues musicians, along with some information about their careers.

Willie Dixon (1915–1992) worked as a writer, producer, contractor, bass player, and occasional singer at the Chess Recording Studios in Chicago, but he became better known as a blues songwriter than as a singer. He wrote many hits for others, including "You Shook Me" and "I Can't Quit You Baby," which have been recorded by many blues and blues-rock musicians. "You Shook Me" and another of his songs, "(I'm Your) Hoochie Coochie Man," represented a variant on the twelve-bar blues structure because both had an extra-long (eight-bar) first A section on each vocal chorus, followed by A and B sections of the usual four bars each, extending each full blues chorus to sixteen bars. "Little Red Rooster" and "I Can't Quit You Baby" followed the twelve-bar blues form. As a performer, Dixon played bass on many Chess recordings.

Although the origin of **Muddy Waters**'s (1915–1983) stage name is not known for certain, popular legend has it that he was so called because he liked to "muddy" for fish (reach into water and catch fish with his hands) in a pond near his father's home in Rolling Fork, Mississippi. As a songwriter, Muddy Waters used his real name, McKinley Morganfield. His style, which often included the whining sound of a bottleneck guitar, was rustic and was actually close to country blues in his early blues hits like "Rollin' Stone" (1948). That song was not a twelve-bar blues but instead had only one chord played throughout, with the

lyrics structured in eight-bar periods. Waters's bending of blue notes and relaxed flow of uneven beat subdivisions created a blues feel without the standard structure.

Although Muddy Waters began playing and singing in the rural delta blues style, his change to the electric guitar and the addition of a band that included Little Walter on blues harp, Jimmy Rogers on guitar, and Waters's half-brother, Otis Spann, on piano shifted his sound from country blues to urban blues. It was for this latter style that he became best known. Waters never actually played rock and roll, but he often performed in rock concerts, including the Band's final concert in 1976 (subsequently made into the movie *The Last Waltz*) and a tour with Eric Clapton in 1979. Over the years, Waters won many Grammy awards in the categories of "Best Ethnic" and "Best Traditional" recordings. He died in 1983 having spent over forty years performing and recording the blues.

A listening guide to Muddy Waters's recording of Willie Dixon's song "(I'm Your) Hoochie Coochie Man" is on page 22. "(I'm Your) Hoochie Coochie Man" reached number three on the rhythm and blues charts but did not make the pop charts.

"There was quite a few people around singing the blues, but most of them was singing all sad blues. Muddy was giving his blues a little pep."

–"(I'm Your) Hoochie Coochie Man" songwriter Willie Dixon

Listening Guide

"(I'm Your) Hoochie Coochie Man" as recorded by Muddy Waters (1954)

Tempo:	The tempo is about 76 beats per minute with four beats in each bar.
Form:	The form is based on a twelve-bar blues with the first A section being eight bars long resulting in a sixteen-bar chorus.
	The introduction is two bars long.
	The introduction is followed by three sixteen-bar choruses.
Features:	Each A section has a two-beat instrumental stop time segment.
	The drums maintain an uneven beat subdivision with little or no backbeat.
	The piano usually plays triple-beat subdivisions, but at times lapses into a duple subdivision, creating a polyrhythm with the drums.

The recording has no instrumental choruses.

Lyrics:	The theme is the singer's *supernatural* sexual prowess. *Hoochie coochie* is a term for sexual desire (to dance the hoochie coochie is to perform an erotic dance). The supernatural nature of the singer's "studliness" is shown in every verse, from the references to a gypsy fortune teller who prophesies that the singer will make women "jump and shout," to black cats, good luck charms ("I got a mojo too"), and a birth on the seventh hour of the seventh day of the seventh month. Indeed, the supernatural force of multiples of seven goes back at least as far as the Old Testament's Book of Joshua, where seven priests blowing seven trumpets for seven days cause the walls of Jericho to "come a tumbling down" the way that the singer brags that his own association with the number seven will undermine the defenses of any woman he has chosen to sexually conquer.

Billboard rhythm and blues charts: number three

Elmore James (1918–1963) claimed to have met and played with Robert Johnson, who, James said, suggested that he try using a metal pipe to slide along the strings in much the same way that others were using a bottleneck. Like Muddy Waters, James eventually moved from Mississippi to Chicago to perform and record. Instead of just accompanying his singing with his own guitar as he had in the past, James took advantage of the availability of jazz musicians in Chicago and was among the first of the delta blues musicians to work regularly with groups including saxophone, piano, and drums. Through his work with those groups, he gained a reputation as one of the early modernizers of the delta blues. While his groups gave his music a modern sound, his own guitar playing was an example of bottleneck country blues. Elmore James's recording of Robert Johnson's twelve-bar blues song "I Believe I'll Dust My Broom" exemplified that synthesis of urban and delta blues.

James's slide guitar style was copied by many rock guitarists, including British blues players Eric Clapton, Brian Jones (an original member of the Rolling Stones), and Jeremy Spencer (of the original Fleetwood Mac) and Americans Jimi Hendrix and Duane Allman. His lifestyle must have included Robert Johnson's fondness for women, because when James died of a heart attack in 1963 at age forty-five, six women claimed to have been married to him.

Blues harpist (the **blues harp** is a harmonica) and singer **Sonny Boy Williamson** No. 2 (Rice Miller, 1899–1965) was called "No. 2" because he actually stole the stage name of another blues singer, John Lee Williamson (Sonny Boy No. 1), in order to associate himself with Williamson's reputation before he gained one of his own. He toured

Chart Listings

Information about the relative popularity of songs in this book has been gathered from books published by *Billboard,* a weekly magazine on popular music. First published in 1894, the earliest issues of *Billboard* magazine were comprised of articles of interest to people in the business of popular music, but it did not begin having chart lists until 1940. Information needed to compile the charts was gathered from radio station playlists and from record sales. Since neighborhoods where records were sold and radio stations aired were segregated and a variety of styles of music were being evaluated, *Billboard* listed songs on three different charts: popular, currently called pop; hillbilly, later called country and western and currently country; and sepia (a dark reddish brown color), later called race and currently rhythm and blues. Given that the rhythm and blues charts generally reflect the tastes of African Americans; the country charts those of white Americans, particularly in the South and West; and the pop charts those of the very largest, multiracial, but primarily white population, it can be interesting to compare how a particular song or artist rated on the various different charts. The primary goal of this text is not to take the place of the *Billboard* books in reporting the listings for every song that is discussed; but the ones of particular interest to the subject of general popularity of rhythm and blues and early rock music will be included here.

Britain in 1963 and recorded live albums with the Yardbirds and the Animals. Because Williamson was willing to sit down and perform with the British groups at the very beginning of the blues revival, he had a great deal of influence in the development of their blues-styled playing. Dead of tuberculosis by 1965, he did not live to see how popular his rock musician disciples would make the blues among young people.

Chester Arthur Burnett originally called himself Big Foot Chester, but the wolflike growls and howls that were part of his act earned him the name **Howlin' Wolf** (1910–1976). He played both the guitar and the harp and claimed to have played with Robert Johnson, who influenced his guitar style, and with the original Sonny Boy Williamson, from whom he learned to play the harp. Burnett's aggressive, sometimes raunchy sound was not suited for the pop charts, but such recordings as "Little Red Rooster" (written by Willie Dixon) were often played by blues revivalists, including the Rolling Stones and the Grateful Dead. "Little Red Rooster" was a traditional twelve-bar blues, but many other recordings by Howlin' Wolf were not. "Smokestack Lightnin'," for example, was chanted over a single chord. His songs were also recorded by the British groups Cream, the Yardbirds, and Led Zeppelin, and in America by the Doors and the Electric Flag.

In 1972, Burnett (Howlin' Wolf took writer's credit under his real name) recorded the album *The London Sessions,* which included some of the rock musicians who had begun their careers playing his music—Eric Clapton, Steve Winwood, Bill Wyman, and Charlie Watts. After a long and successful career, Burnett died of kidney disease in 1976.

John Lee Hooker (1917–2001) was based in Detroit rather than Chicago and recorded on a variety of labels, including Modern and Riverside Records, but he toured with some of the Chicago bluesmen and also had an influence on rock musicians who recorded his songs. His dramatic delta-based guitar style and deep, rich voice gave him a career that lasted almost six decades. His twelve-bar blues song "Boom Boom" became a rock hit when recorded by a British group, the Animals, in 1965. Both recordings used a **break,** in which the instruments stopped playing during the vocal line and then responded by playing on the second, third, fourth, and first beats that followed. The break created an effective type of call-and-response that was used in other blues and blues-rock recordings as well. Other songs originally written and recorded by Hooker were also recorded by the Spencer Davis Group and by the later American blues revivalists Canned Heat and George Thorogood. Hooker was featured in the 1980 film *The Blues Brothers,* and he toured and recorded albums well into the eighties. On his album *The Healer* (1988) he was joined by Santana, Bonnie Raitt, Robert Cray, Canned Heat, Los Lobos, George Thorogood, and Charlie Musselwhite. Hooker has recorded several new albums, and collections of his old recordings were released during the nineties. He stopped touring in 1995, but vowed to continue to sing and record for the rest of his life. He died in 2001, six years later.

The Chess Record Company was sold to GRT Corporation after Leonard Chess died in 1969. The company continued to do minimal recording, but it no longer promoted musicians' careers. The catalog of recordings was preserved, however, and eventually purchased by MCA, later known as the All Platinum/Sugarhill Company. The new owners have continued to reissue the great Chicago blues recordings of the past.

Many early rock songs were based on the blues form and style, making the blues one of the most important roots of rock music. The blues is not rock by itself, however. Other important styles of music that melded with the blues to create rock music are discussed in the next chapter.

Rhythm and Blues

The blues might not have had as great an impact on the development of rock music of the fifties and sixties had it not been for the tremendous popularity of a related style, **rhythm and blues.** Called *race music* until the end of the forties, rhythm and blues was a type of rhythmic dance music in which every second and fourth beat of each four-beat bar was accented. Because it was more common in other styles of music to accent the first and third beats of each bar, that stress on the "off" beats was called a backbeat. The backbeat was used in the blues, but it became more obvious and important in rhythm and blues.

Whereas the blues developed as music reflective of the problems of African American life, rhythm and blues was a dance music that expressed the enjoyment of life. It originated in the African American ghettos of large cities and was played by organized, rehearsed groups that included a variety of instruments. These groups put on energetic stage shows in which saxophone players often swiveled their hips, lowered themselves to the floor (or into the audience), and rolled around on their backs while playing. Singers shouted out their lyrics while maintaining a high level of physical activity. This excitement and energy, as well as the rhythm and backbeat of rhythm and blues, formed the very basis of much fifties rock and roll. The sexual suggestiveness of the lyrics of many rhythm and blues songs also helped to contribute to some of the backlash against rock music that was based on it.

During the late thirties and through the forties, **Louis Jordan** (1908–1975) played alto saxophone and clarinet in various large jazz bands and finally formed his own band, Louis Jordan and His Tympany Five. His group often played big theaters like the Apollo in New York and the Regal in Chicago, and through these performances he gained a following as much for his sense of humor as for his musical ability. Jordan called his rhythmic style of playing the blues "shuffle boogie" or "jumpin' jive," and his group was often described as a "jump band." His music was so danceably rhythmic, his stage personality so

engaging, and his songs so full of humor that his records were as popular with whites as they were with African Americans. Having heard and liked Jordan's jump band, white rock musicians such as Bill Haley imitated its shuffle beat in the early fifties. Newer tributes to Jordan's popular appeal include the rerecording of some of his songs on Joe Jackson's album *Jumpin' Jive* (1981) as well as the musical revue *Five Guys Named Moe* that opened in London in 1990 and then moved on to Broadway in New York. Jordan was also a big influence on the "jump blues" rock style of Little Richard.

Bo Diddley, born Ellas Bates (1928–2008), strummed his guitar in a constantly throbbing, rhythmic style that sounded almost as if he were playing drums. His name was legally changed to Ellas McDaniel by the adoptive parents who raised him, and he used that name as a songwriter. He studied the violin for a time before he decided to change to the guitar, an instrument that was more acceptable to the other kids in his rough Chicago neighborhood. Many stories have been told about the source of his stage name, but he claimed that his friends gave it to him back when he was a boxer because of his originality in coming up with new fighting tricks. It was quite possible that his friends chose Bo Diddley after the diddley-bow, a single-stringed instrument of African origin that was played by African Americans in the South.

Bo Diddley's strongly rhythmic style was rock-oriented, although it was considered rhythm and blues during the fifties. In fact, his only top forty hit on the *Billboard* pop charts was "Say Man," which reached number twenty in 1959. His first record was "Bo Diddley" backed by "I'm a Man," and it was a number one hit on the rhythm and blues charts. Bo Diddley was very influential on American rock musicians during the fifties and was copied by British blues-revival rock groups of the sixties in their covers of his songs as well as in their own material. The Yardbirds did his "I'm a Man"; the Rolling Stones, his "Mona"; and the Animals, his "Bo Diddley." None of these three songs were in the blues form; in fact, both "Mona" and "Bo Diddley" were based on a single chord throughout. In both of these songs, Diddley used a bottleneck to slide up and down between the fifth and seventh frets on his guitar, giving the effect of more chord changes during breaks in the melody. "I'm a Man" used a modified form of an instrumental break that was also common in the blues. The harp and piano break (stop playing) during the vocals, but the drums continue throughout the song, repeating the characteristic rhythm known as the "Bo Diddley beat," which is notated in the listening guide on page 26. Of course Bo Diddley was not the first musician to ever play this beat

Guitarist Bo Diddley poses for a portrait with his Gretsch electric guitar and Jerome Green on his right playing maracas circa 1958 in New York City

pattern, but it has taken his name because of the characteristic energy with which he strummed it and the fact that he popularized it.

> **"I'm a rhythm fanatic. I played the guitar as if I were playing drums."**
>
> –Bo Diddley

The Bo Diddley beat has been used in many rock songs, including Buddy Holly's "Not Fade Away," Johnny Otis's "Willie and the Hand Jive," the Who's "Magic Bus," Bruce Springsteen's "She's the One," U2's "Desire," and the Pretenders' "Cuban Slide." In addition to covering Diddley's recordings, the Animals also recorded a tribute to him they called "The Story of Bo Diddley," in which they gave Diddley much of the credit for starting rock and roll. Bo Diddley himself was still performing, writing, and recording in the nineties, and the influence of his rhythmic, blues-based style was apparent in the music of younger blues musicians including George Thorogood.

One of the most important rhythm and blues pianists to influence rock and roll was New Orleans's **Professor Longhair** (Henry Roeland Byrd, 1918–1980), whose rollicking boogie-woogie bass lines became essential elements in the rock styles of Fats Domino, Huey "Piano" Smith, Dr. John (Malcolm "Mac" Rebennack), and Allen Toussaint, to name only a few. **Boogie-woogie,** a spirited and rhythmic piano style developed by African Americans in the South during the twenties and copied by many white performers, eventually became basic to most rock piano styles from both blues and country roots. In boogie-woogie, the pianist's left hand played a fast, repeated note pattern with two notes played in the time of each single beat. Its effect was that of doubling the basic beat, creating a fast, motoristic, rhythmic drive. Some common boogie-woogie piano patterns are notated as follows:

These examples are notated in even note values, but they were also often played in a shuffle beat pattern. Over these left-hand bass patterns, the right hand often played short bits of melody (called **riffs** when repeated several times). Boogie-woogie most often employed the classic twelve-bar blues harmonic form. However, Professor Longhair also used pop song forms for some of his songs; his rhythm and blues hit from 1949, "Bald Head," is an example of this. In addition to his own successes and his

Listening Guide

"Bo Diddley"
as recorded by Bo Diddley (1955)

Tempo: The tempo is approximately 104 beats per minute, with four beats in each bar.

Form: The recording begins with four bars of instrumental introduction that establish the beat pattern that will repeat throughout the rest of the song.

The form is based on a series or chain of two-bar phrases, at least in the sections that have vocals. In those sections the first bar of the phrase is sung and the second repeats the instrumental pattern established in the introduction. The sections that begin with the vocal melody used just after the introduction vary in length; the first is seventeen bars, the second is twenty-four bars, and the third is nineteen bars. There seems to be no set pattern to the number of bars the instrumental rhythm pattern is repeated.

Features: Even beat subdivisions are maintained by the maracas.

There is no stress on the backbeat other than the fact that the second and fourth beats are played as part of the basic Bo Diddley beat that is followed throughout the recording.

The Bo Diddley beat is notated as follows:

Along with this basic beat there are other beat patterns that, at times, create an almost polyrhythmic effect. Most of the variants make changes in the second beat of the four-beat pattern, maintaining the stress on beat one, the second half of beat three, and on beat four.

After the sections with vocals, the repetitions of instrumental bars are colored by rhythmic strums on the guitar stopped by a bottleneck on the seventh, the fifth, and then the seventh frets.

Lyrics: The mythical Bo Diddley goes to great expense and effort to seduce his "pretty baby," from buying her a diamond ring to trying black magic, but the ultimate result is that she won't go for it.

Billboard rhythm and blues charts: number one for two weeks

influences on others, Longhair's music continues to be remembered in his hometown when his "Mardi Gras in New Orleans" is played every year as the famous Mardi Gras carnival's theme song.

Summary

In urban blues the guitar moved beyond its earlier role as an accompaniment instrument to that of a solo instrument playing along with piano, drums, and other instruments. Chicago blues was a particular type of urban blues that was heavily influenced by swing jazz and boogie-woogie piano styles. Urban blues, from Chicago and other large cities, lead directly to the development of rock guitar styles of the fifties.

Rhythm and blues made use of blue notes and other musical characteristics of the blues but did not usually follow the twelve-bar blues form. It was intended as light-hearted entertainment rather than as a reflection of the difficulties of day-to-day living. Often used as dance music, rhythm and blues shared a type of formalism with urban blues because it was usually performed by groups of musicians playing written or memorized arrangements, and yet the performances were wild and full of sexual innuendo. Both the blatant sexuality and the backbeat of rhythm and blues became basic characteristics of rock music.

discussion questions

Listen, again, to "Three O'Clock Blues" by B. B. King and then to "Bo Diddley" by Bo Diddley. As you listen, compare the tempos, the feel of the rhythms, and the lyrics of the two recordings. What basic differences between the blues and rhythm and blues can you name based on this comparison? Can you tell why the term *rhythm* is there in rhythm and blues?

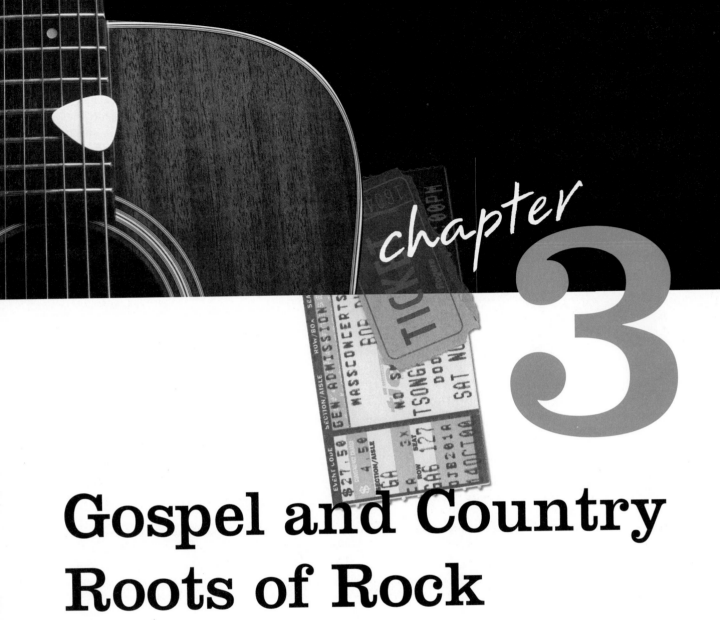

Gospel and Country Roots of Rock

"Blues are the songs of despair, but gospel songs are the songs of hope."
—MAHALIA JACKSON

Rock music developed from the combination of a number of different styles of music that existed before it. The blues is a primary root of rock, but then the blues is the blues. It didn't become rock until it was combined with other music to create something new. One can say that much fifties rock is a combination of blues and country music, but then country musicians had been playing songs based on a twelve-bar blues form for years without sounding like they were playing rock. If they played their instruments and sang in a distinctively country style, their "blues" songs sounded like country music. A new type of rock music was created when musicians who grew up playing and singing the blues, rhythm and blues, and gospel, such as Fats Domino, Chuck Berry, and Little Richard, added country-styled characteristics to their music. Rock music was also created when country-trained musicians such as Bill Haley, Elvis Presley, Buddy Holly, and many others not only played songs in a blues form but added blues characteristics such as blue notes and uneven beat subdivisions to their playing and singing. In order to be able to pick out the characteristics of each of the styles of music that came together to create rock and roll, those prerock types of music need to be discussed. That is the purpose of this chapter.

Spirituals

Christians were directed to sing "spiritual songs" in the New Testament of the Bible (Ephesians 5:19 and Colossians 3:16). Accordingly, the term **spiritual** was given to religious folk songs from both the white and the African American traditions from the middle-eighteenth century through the nineteenth century. Over time terms such as *psalm* or *hymn* became more commonly used for songs by white composers, and *spiritual* became associated with songs by African American composers. As was true of folk music in general, the original spirituals were not written down but were passed by memory from singer to singer. Exactly what the early spirituals sounded like can only be guessed from the descriptions written in slave owners' diaries or included in the earliest printed editions of the lyrics. According to *Slave Songs of the United States,* written by William Francis Allen, Charles Pickard Ware, and Lucy McKim Garrison in 1867, spirituals were not sung in the prearranged, multivoiced structures that whites called *part singing,* but African American singers did not always sing the same melody at the same time either. Lead singers improvised, sliding from one note to another and singing "turns" around the melody notes. Other sources indicate that a similar style was used in African American work songs and field hollers. The use of leaders improvising while other singers stay in the background with the plain melody became common in black gospel singing styles of the twentieth century.

Texts of spirituals varied from slow, melancholy sorrow songs such as "Nobody Knows the Trouble I've Seen" to fast and highly energetic jubilees such as "Didn't My Lord Deliver Daniel?" Both types of spirituals often contained coded messages that the singers did not want whites to understand. The messages were cleverly designed to sound on the surface as if they were being sung to celebrate the belief that Christianity would bring them to heaven, when they were really communicating the way to escape from slavery in the South to freedom in the North.

"Wade in the Water," for example, was about baptism on the surface, but it also communicated the suggestion that escaping slaves should travel in streams so that their "owners'" dogs could not track their scent. Granted, the reference to the owner is "A band of angels coming after me," but subtlety was essential. Other lyrics like "We'll stand the storm" helped to encourage patience and endurance until the dream of freedom came true.

The Fisk Jubilee Singers from Fisk University in Nashville, Tennessee, helped to popularize spirituals during the late nineteenth century through their performances in various parts of the United States and Europe. Modern choral groups from Fisk University and many other universities, colleges, community groups, and churches continue to perform and record spirituals in as close to the early tradition as possible, although most modern groups sing from modern arrangements and rely less on improvisation than did the earliest spiritual singers.

Gospel Music

Black gospel music developed from the same musical roots as spirituals and the blues. These roots included certain scale structures and the call-and-response tradition from parts of West Africa. European musical traditions contributed formal structure, harmonies, regular beat patterns, and use of such musical instruments as the guitar and piano. The blues and gospel music developed into different, but related, styles because the blues was the personal expression of an individual singer, whereas gospel was used to voice the shared religious beliefs of a group of worshippers.

The development of black gospel music came about as it did because of the manner in which African Americans were introduced to Christianity. African American slaves attended church with their white owners (or under the watchful eye of someone who represented the owners) because it was thought dangerous to allow large groups of slaves to meet together without the presence and dominance of whites. White churches had separate sections for African American congregations, but both groups sang the same hymns and came to share the same beliefs in the "good news" of the Gospels. Because churches were organized for white congregations, hymns were performed with white European traditions—a steady beat with even beat subdivisions and accents on the first and third beat of each four-beat pattern. Known as "white gospel," the music followed many of the same traditions as hillbilly music.

After the Civil War and the abolishment of slavery, African Americans built their own churches. White gospel music continued to be sung in the white churches, but African Americans developed their own style of religious music. Spirited by the new taste of freedom, they sang music that displayed the characteristics and energy of pre–Civil War camp meeting and jubilee spirituals, like "Swing Low, Sweet Chariot" and "In That Great Gettin' Up Morning." The African call-and-response tradition, as it was practiced in a church service, involved the preacher calling out a phrase from the Bible, to which the congregation would respond with statements about their belief in its truth or with the next biblical verse. Call-and-response was also employed during the singing of hymns, when the preacher or lead singer would sing verses and a group of singers would respond with the refrain of the hymn. By the thirties, the term *gospel* began to be applied to sophisticated religious music by such composers as Thomas A. Dorsey and Lucie Campbell.

Probably first intended as an expression of enthusiasm for the religious subjects of the music, a number of highly stylized vocal devices or patterns were improvised by gospel singers, and those improvisations became characteristic of the vocals in soul styles that followed gospel. One such device, sometimes called a *turn* (or **melisma** in its more elaborate form), was a type of embellishment that involved sliding around notes both above and below the melody note, thereby dramatically delaying that note, and then finally resolving to it. Another stylized vocal practice was breaking a single syllable of a word into several parts by punctuations or aspirations of breath. The effect was to build the intensity of the word.

As another result of the congregations' emotional involvement with religion, highly energetic and syncopated rhythms entered the performance of music in church services, along with dancing in the aisles, hand clapping, and shouting. It was not uncommon in some southern churches for preachers to become caught up in the fervor of these activities and faint during the service, something that became part of the stage act of many soul singers.

The **Soul Stirrers,** from Texas, recorded for the Library of Congress archives as early as 1936. They influenced many other gospel groups with their **falsetto** (higher than standard tenor range and generally somewhat breathy in tone quality) lead singing, use of polyrhythms, and textual improvisations. A rock singer and writer popular in the late fifties and early sixties, **Sam Cooke** (originally Cook), and the Memphis soul singer Johnny Taylor both did their first professional singing with the Soul Stirrers. The recording discussed in the listening guide on page 31 was made by the Soul Stirrers when eighteen-year-old Sam Cooke was their lead singer.

The Queen of Gospel was **Mahalia Jackson** (1911–1972). Born in New Orleans, she grew up enjoying recordings by the classic blues singers Ma Rainey, Bessie Smith, and others, but she did so in secret. Her very religious family and friends would not have approved of her appreciation of the blues because of the secular lifestyle that was described in most blues lyrics. She moved to Chicago when she was sixteen years old and was soon singing gospel music professionally. During the late thirties and through the forties, she toured with the famous gospel composer Thomas A. Dorsey. Her recording of "Move on Up a Little Higher" (1947) made her famous. After that she toured Europe, had radio and television shows of her own, and was a featured soloist at President John F. Kennedy's inauguration in 1961.

Female gospel groups became popular during the forties. Among the best known were the Clara Ward Singers, who gained such a following through their recordings and tours during the fifties that they left the church and concert hall circuit in 1961 to perform in Las Vegas. Although numerous gospel groups performed in secular settings, many popular gospel and, later, soul performers

Listening Guide

"How Far Am I from Canaan?"
as recorded by the Soul Stirrers with
Sam Cooke (1952)

Tempo: The tempo is approximately 96 beats per minute, with four beats per bar for the first half of the recording, but then doubles to approximately 192 beats per minute for the second half. A doubling of the tempo is called **double time.**

Form: The slow beginning section of the recording is made up of four eight-bar phrases, each of which ends with words that lead into the phrase that follows. The fast section has four sixteen-bar phrases, the last of which functions as a **coda** in that it includes short, repeated sections from earlier parts of the song that help bring the song to a musically satisfying conclusion.

Features: Sam Cooke sings the lead melody throughout the recording, often adding melismas to embellish the melody.

The Soul Stirrers sometimes sustain chords to accompany Cooke's lead vocals and at other times separate somewhat and sing portions of lyrics from the lead line. Even with their occasional breaks into separate lines, the Soul Stirrers never cover Cooke's lead or improvise melismas to the extent that Cooke does on his lines.

Only a drummer accompanies the singers. The drummer maintains a steady beat with thumps on the bass drum and accents the backbeats with a high hat cymbal.

Uneven beat subdivisions are used throughout the recording.

Lyrics: Canaan was another name for the Promised Land, which the singer identifies with heaven. The singer yearns to hear the angels singing, to have his troubles over, to meet his mother and join his Savior. The tension is in the haunting question—"how far" is the singer from obtaining this beatific state, which suggests recognition of the fact that there is yet more striving ahead in this world before he can enter the next one.

were uneasy about taking gospel music out of the church and using it in nonreligious performances.

Although small groups of four or five singers remained popular, a full-choir style of gospel music based on a tradition began by Thomas A. Dorsey in the early thirties was popularized by pianist/arranger Edwin Hawkins in Oakland, California, during the sixties. Hawkins replaced the small vocal group with a large choir and accompanied it with a rock beat played by keyboards, bass, and drums. His group, the **Edwin Hawkins Singers,** recorded gospel songs that became hits on the pop charts. In their recording of "Oh Happy Day," soloist Dorothy Morrison used the stylized vocal devices that had long been traditions in gospel singing, and because the large choir could not use those devices in their responses to her singing, her improvisations clearly stood out above their singing. Particularly on the words "oh" and "day," Morrison adds various melismas not sung by the choir in their repetitions of the same words. The recording also includes a high female voice improvising above the choir, a characteristic often copied in disco recordings. "Oh Happy Day" was number four on the pop charts and number two on the rhythm and blues ones. A listening guide to this recording follows on page 32.

The Edwin Hawkins Singers

Listening Guide

"Oh Happy Day"
as recorded by the Edwin Hawkins
Singers (1969)

Tempo: The tempo is approximately 112 beats per minute, with four beats per bar.

Form: The performance begins with a ten-bar introduction played by pianos and percussion.

The musical form is based on eight-bar phrases that are often extended by repetition of individual bars.

The first vocal section is fourteen bars long, with repetition of several lines of text and melody.

The entire fourteen-bar section repeats immediately after the first time it is performed and repeats again several times later in the recording, with additional extensions toward the end.

Features: The beat subdivisions are even.

The rhythm section maintains the steady beat while the vocalists gradually speed up, often ending phrases one-half beat early. This pushing of the tempo produces an effect of enthusiasm and fervor.

Dorothy Morrison sings the lead, and a large chorus sings responses. Her vocals use the stylized devices mentioned earlier; the chorus repeats her basic melody, but without her turns and inflections.

A contrasting section with new lyrics follows the repeat of the first section. The chorus is louder in this section, and a woman (possibly Morrison) sings above the chorus in a free and energetic style.

(continued)

<table>
<tr>
<td>The new section is eight bars long, not having the repetitious extensions of the first vocal section.</td>
<td>Lyrics:</td>
<td>This is a simple spiritual, in which the singers exclaim their joy at the experience of religious conversion (the image of washing is a clear allusion to the Christian rite of baptism), with the caveat (in the words "fight and pray") that trouble and temptation still loom ahead in this world.</td>
</tr>
<tr>
<td>The eight-bar section is repeated later in the recording, accompanied by hand clapping on the backbeat during one of the last repeats.</td>
<td></td>
<td></td>
</tr>
</table>

Billboard pop charts: number four; *Billboard* rhythm and blues charts: number two for two weeks; British hit singles: number two

Hawkins's large-choir gospel style was copied by other groups as well, but the smaller groups in which each singer, or several of the singers, could have an opportunity to solo and improvise remained more common. Hawkins continued to play gospel music in the nineties, but the Edwin Hawkins Singers broke up after a series of personnel changes.

Doo-Wop

Secular music sung by gospel-oriented African American vocal groups was popular as early as the twenties. The term *doo-wop* came to be used to identify the vocal group sound, as the groups usually had a lead singer who was accompanied (or responded to) by other singers singing nonsense syllables or repeating a few words from the lead singer's line. The general label doo-wop referred to the nonsense syllables—"ahs" or "dum, dum, de-dums"—that the backup singers used. Two early African American pop vocal groups whose influences could be heard in the later doo-wop style were the Mills Brothers, who sang four-part harmony in a smooth, sophisticated style, and the Ink Spots, whose high-tenor lead singer often dropped out after a chorus to allow the bass singer to speak the lyrics, accompanied by the rest of the group humming chords.

In 1945, the Ravens took the mellow vocal style of the Mills Brothers and added the Ink Spots' lead bass idea to bring to their New York audiences a musical combination of pop, gospel, and rhythm and blues. Even when the bass singer was not singing lead lines, he maintained a moving bass part that imitated the lines a string bass might play instead of merely singing the same rhythm pattern as the rest of the group, a technique the Mills Brothers pioneered. The Ravens worked with a pianist who played a constant triplet pattern behind the group's vocals; the basic rhythm was used in much doo-wop to follow. As doo-wop was essentially a vocal style, instruments were relegated to secondary roles as accompaniment. The Ravens began to record and tour nationally and were eventually copied by many other vocal groups, some of which also used bird names, such as the Crows, the Penguins, the Cardinals, and the Flamingos.

A group from Baltimore, Maryland, took the name the Orioles from their state bird. The **Orioles** did not imitate the Ravens, because their sound depended more on the light lead tenor vocal style that the Ink Spots had used. The Orioles' recording of "Crying in the Chapel" (1953) was one of the first recordings by African American artists to be successful on the pop charts. Additionally, it was a **cover** (rerecording) of a country song by a white singer, Darrell Glenn (his father, Artie Glenn wrote the song). (Actually, the Orioles' recording was the third cover released; others by June Valli and Rex Allen were made after Glenn's but before the Orioles'.) Glenn's recording reached number six on the pop charts and number four on the country ones. The Orioles' recording reached number eleven on the pop charts and was number one for five weeks on the rhythm and blues charts.

The styles were so different from each other that a comparison of the two by Glenn and the Orioles demonstrates the basic contrast between white and black gospel styles. White gospel music followed the steady beat and instrumental practices common in country music, while black gospel used a shuffle rhythm and backbeat, vocal improvisation, and a backup chorus. The recordings are discussed in the listening guide on page 34.

"Crying in the Chapel" was covered again by Elvis Presley in 1960, and his version was much closer to the style of the Orioles than to Glenn's. The Orioles broke up in 1954, but their Ink Spots–influenced sound was copied by many other groups.

Despite the Glenn/Orioles example, it was much more common for white groups to cover African American material than the reverse. As with blues and rhythm and blues songs, many of the white covers had changes in

Listening Guide

"Crying in the Chapel"
by the Orioles (August 1953)

The tempo is about 69 beats per minute, with four beats per bar.

The song is made up of one chorus of the AABA song form that uses Darrell Glenn's lyrics, but not in the same order as on the earlier recording.

Each A section is eight bars long; the B section is the same length as in Glenn's recording.

Sonny Til sings the lead, with the other Orioles singing "ahs" and a few words taken from the lyrics in response to his lead lines.

Til varies the melody with many turns and other black gospel stylizations.

Uneven beat subdivisions are maintained throughout the recording.

Instruments include trumpet, alto saxophone, Hammond organ, bass, and drums.

The drums keep a strong backbeat.

The song uses the (literally) puritan image of a "plain and simple chapel" to juxtapose the singer's spiritual joy in the experience of repentance (he gains "peace of mind") with the spiritual void and emptiness the song associates in the general world. The key to that spiritual joy is humility (note the references to "humble people" and being on one's knees).

Billboard rhythm and blues charts: number one for five weeks

by the **Crew-Cuts,** a white group from Canada. The Crew-Cuts did not make any substantive changes in the song's lyrics, but they did make other changes to take out African American musical characteristics and "whiten" their sound.

Other changes that were made included backing by a full swing-style dance band instead of the small rhythm section plus saxophone that played on the Chords' recording. As often happened when white groups covered material by African American ones, the covers outsold the originals. The Chords' recording reached number two on the rhythm and blues charts and number five on the pop charts, whereas the Crew-Cuts' version was number one on the pop charts. A listening guide to the two recordings appears on page 35.

The chord progression of $I–vi^7–ii^7–V^7$ ($C–Am^7–Dm^7–G^7$, in the key of C) used in "Sh-Boom" was the harmonic basis of many songs in the doo-wop style. Some songs varied it slightly, but the regular use of this same basic chord progression at about the same rhythmic rate was the reason so many of the doo-wop songs sounded similar. It is commonly referred to as the **doo-wop progression.**

Another musical characteristic found in a large percentage of doo-wop is the constant pounding of repeated chords at the rate of three chords per beat with the bass line and the melody following that triplet pattern through their use of uneven beat subdivisions. An example of a simple form of a typical doo-wop accompaniment follows:

lyrics, instrumentation, and production style that were supposed to make them more salable to the white audience than the African American originals. One of the most famous examples of this was the song "Sh-Boom," which was written and first recorded in 1954 by the **Chords,** an African American vocal group, and covered

One doo-wop group whose music generally did not follow the stock doo-wop progression was the Platters. Their manager/arranger, Buck Ram, had studied jazz arranging and was able to incorporate more advanced harmonic ideas into their arrangements. The Platters also differed from many other doo-wop groups because they had

Listening Guide

"Sh-Boom"
as recorded by the Chords (1954)

"Sh-Boom"
as recorded by the Crew-Cuts (1954)

Tempo: The tempo is about 134 beats per minute, with four beats in each bar.

The tempo is about 134 beats per minute, with four beats in each bar.

Form: Most of the song is structured in eight-bar periods, each of which consists of two four-bar phrases. The only exceptions are the four-bar introduction and one four-bar extension sung in nonsense syllables after the first full eight-bar period of lyrics.

Most of the song is structured in the same eight-bar periods as in the Chords' version, except that the ninth period is shortened to only seven bars. The four-bar extension after the first verse of the Chords' version is not present in the Crew-Cuts' recording.

The chords and melody of all periods except that sung by a solo bass singer are similar enough to be called A sections of a song form. The bass sings the contrasting B section, or **bridge,** of the song form.

The same A and B periods are used, except that the bridge is repeated to fit a standard AABA format followed by another AABA theme.

Features: The vocal group is accompanied by a rhythm section consisting of a guitar, string bass, drums, and saxophone for instrumental solos.

The vocal group is accompanied by a full swing-style dance band including several saxophones, brass instruments, a rhythm section, and a kettledrum.

Beat subdivisions are uneven.

Beat subdivisions are uneven.

The recording begins with an introduction in which the vocal group sings **a cappella** (without instrumental accompaniment) for two bars and then is joined by the instruments for two more bars.

The recording begins with instruments accompanying a solo singer for a four-bar introduction.

Most of the lyrics are sung by the vocal group, except for the bridge, which is sung by a solo bass singer (showing the Ink Spots' influence).

The introduction and first four eight-bar periods are sung by solo singers (not always the same one). The last seven periods are sung by the full group. None of the soloists is a bass.

The sixth and seventh full eight-bar periods are instrumental, with a tenor saxophone improvising in a jazz style.

There is no instrumental section except for occasional fills between lines of text. During the fifth and sixth periods, the vocal group sings nonsense syllables and the band fills in behind them. After dramatic pauses at the end of each of those periods, the band returns with a strong

(continued)

Lyrics:	The doo-wop air of simple love and sexual desire ("if you do what I want you to Baby . . .") is emphasized in the repitition of nonsense syllables, reference to "paradise," and (shades of "Row, Row, Row Your Boat") the possibility that life could be a dream.	beat and glissando on a kettledrum. (Its pitch is raised as it rings.) The lyrics are the same as those sung by the Chords, except that the nonsense syllables have been changed, with repetitions of "sh-boom" and "la la las."

Billboard pop charts: number nine; *Billboard* rhythm and blues charts: number two for two weeks

Billboard pop charts: number one for seven weeks; British hit singles: number twelve

a woman in their backup vocal group and used a strong rhythm section (with Ram on piano).

The **Drifters** were given their name because the members were known to drift from group to group; in fact, not a single member stayed with the group throughout its career. The Drifters added a Latin beat to some of their songs, an example of which could be heard in their recording of "Honey Love" (1954). The lead bass that the Ink Spots and the Ravens had introduced was copied by the Drifters in their recording of "White Christmas" (1954). The original Drifters broke up in 1958, but their manager retained the copyright on the group's name and renamed a group that had called themselves the Five Crowns (with Ben E. King singing lead) the Drifters. The old Drifters had recorded songs that made the rhythm and blues charts, but the new group broke through to the top of the pop charts at number two with "There Goes My Baby." That record was not the first to use orchestral strings—Buddy Holly had done that with his last hit "It Doesn't Matter Any More"—but it was the first rhythm and blues record to use such a full, thick background, which became a trend toward the early sixties. The song was written and the recording produced by Atlantic Record Company's Leiber and Stoller, who had earlier written "Hound Dog" for Willie Mae Thornton. A listening guide to the recording that put the orchestral background into early sixties rock appears on page 37.

Other doo-wop groups who had hits during the fifties included the Moonglows, the Coasters, the Five Satins, the Rays, the Clovers, Little Caesar and the Romans, and the Capris (in addition to the various "bird" groups mentioned earlier). Doo-wop groups named after cars became popular with the advent of the Cadillacs, the Impalas, the Fleetwoods, the Imperials, and the Edsels. The vocal styles of the Mills Brothers, the Ink Spots, the Ravens, and the Orioles were the main influences on all

of the doo-wop groups. The general style was a fairly consistent, smoothly romantic, moderately slow, danceable sound in which the lead singers often used gospel singing devices including repeated breath punctuations on words needing emphasis and stylized embellishments at phrase endings.

The smooth, pop-oriented doo-wop style gave way to gutsier African American vocal styles from the late fifties through the early seventies. That music came to be called

The Drifters

Listening Guide

"There Goes My Baby"
as recorded by the Drifters (1959)

Tempo: The tempo is approximately 126 beats per minute, with four beats in each bar.

Form: The song is comprised of eight, eight-bar periods without clear contrasting sections of new melodies or new chord progressions.

A variant version of the doo-wop progression is followed in each period, with each of the four chords lasting for two bars and IV replacing the ii^7 ($I–I–vi^7–vi^7–IV–IV–V^7–V^7$).

The recording ends with the beginning of a new period, but then fades out.

Features: Even though a single melody and chord progression repeats throughout the recording, it does not sound repetitious because the vocals and background instruments vary from one period to another as follows:

1. Bass solo voice with backup vocal group, and no instruments until the strings swirl in during the final bar.

2. Ben E. King sings lead with instrumental accompaniment, but no backup vocals.

3. King continues to sing lead and the backup vocal group sings soft responses.

4. The backup vocal group takes the lead and King sings responses.

5. King again sings lead without backup vocals and the lower strings supply a dramatic accompaniment.

6. King continues with the strings and the backup vocalists return sustaining chords.

7. King sings lead and the swirling violins return to accompany him.

8. The full vocal group returns to back King on this final period.

The orchestral string group provides most of the instrumental accompaniment with kettledrums accenting beats.

No backbeat is accented.

Beat subdivisions are uneven throughout the recording.

Lyrics: The singer's lover, or "baby," has gone away brokenhearted and not said exactly why she left or whether or not she loves him. The singer wishes he could tell her of his love for her.

Billboard pop charts: number two; *Billboard* rhythm and blues charts: number one

---

soul. The term *soul* was first used for African American music in reference to gospel groups' ability to "stir people's souls." By the early sixties, however, it came to refer to secular music by and, for the most part, for African Americans, during a time of struggle for recognition in a white society. In general terms, soul music was not imitative of white styles, and it developed as an expression of African American pride.

Gospel and doo-wop were alive, well, and extremely popular in the nineties and early two-thousands with such singers and groups as Amy Grant, Take 6, All 4 One, Boyz II Men, and many others.

Cover Records

A cover record is a recording of a song made after the original recording. In the fifties, the practice of white groups covering black blues or rhythm and blues records was common, although race was not always a factor. Just about everyone who thought they could make a record that would sell covered whatever song they wanted, and sometimes more than one version of the same song would make the charts at the same or close to the same time. As long as the writer's credit on the cover record was given to the original writer, the writer could not prevent the cover from being made or have any control over changes that might be made in the music or lyrics. The writer did, and still does, however, receive the royalty income generated by the performances of the cover, so many writers benefited from the fact that they wrote songs that became hits when performed by others.

Songwriters have the right to control the first recording of their songs. They can also have some controls over the use of their work if their publication contracts state that they maintain the right to approve of the use of their song in a movie or commercial. As will be seen in many examples of rock music, covers often change lyrics, completely change vocal or production styles, and even change the basic beat or meter of the song. Yet at other times, covers obviously imitate the production style of the original recording. Either way, the performers of the covers have the right to record or perform the song any way they choose.

Of course, attempts have been made to sue parties who made covers that the copyright owners did not like. In the early nineties, the Acuff-Rose Publishing Company sued 2 Live Crew over their parody cover of Roy Orbison's "Oh, Pretty Woman," which 2 Live Crew called "Bald-Headed Woman." Acuff-Rose claimed that the cover denigrated the value of Orbison's song. After several court cases and appeals, the Supreme Court decided in favor of 2 Live Crew because they had a right to parody the preexisting work. People who regularly parody the work of others often request permission first. They do this as a courtesy, as well as a protection against a potential lawsuit.

Songwriting credit can be sold, won as part of the settlement of a lawsuit, or given to someone by the writer. Songwriting credit and royalties may be shared with a publisher or record company depending on the terms of the contracts signed by the writer. A major change was made in the United States Copyright Law in 1978. Before that year, copyright remained in effect for twenty-eight years from the publication date and was renewable for another twenty-eight years. After January 1, 1978, copyright is in effect for the writer's life plus fifty years. The additional fifty years allowed the writer's heirs to collect royalty income generated by the song for that period of time. After the copyright has expired, the song is in the public domain, which means that anyone can use the song without any concern about paying a writer's royalty.

Note: This information applies to recordings. The writer's or publisher's written permission is needed to use someone else's melody in a written work one might like to publish.

Country Music

Country music is a commercial form of folk music that developed into a variety of styles of its own sometime during the nineteenth century. The earliest forms of country music were first called *hillbilly,* a name used for backwoods southerners of British descent who played them.

From the seventeenth through the nineteenth centuries, large numbers of settlers from the British Isles made their way to the mountainous regions of what is now the southern and southwestern United States, bringing with them many centuries of rich musical traditions that they maintained as cultural links with the Old World. Their dance music included simple rhythmic dances such as the jig, the reel, the polka, the waltz, and various types of round dances. Their vocal music included hymns and folk ballads as well as other types of songs. Much of their dance music was played by a fiddle, a folk term for the violin dating back to a medieval European bowed-string instrument, the *fidula* or *fidel.* The British settlers sang their songs either unaccompanied or backed with instruments such as the guitar, the plucked and strummed dulcimers, the piano, and later the harmonica. African Americans in the South developed the banjo out of an African instrument, the *banza,* and it was adopted by the white players of British-derived folk music around the time of the Civil War. By the end of the thirties, instruments such as the string bass, the steel guitar, and the autoharp had also come into common use in southern folk music.

> " Country music is three chords and the truth. "
>
> –Harlan Howard

With the growing importance of radio and the developments in recording technology in the twenties, the folk music of the South was brought to the attention of the rest of the country. It was not long before radio stations were springing up across the country, bringing live music broadcasts into homes and gathering places. One of the most popular types of radio programs, the barn dance show, featured live performances of rural dance music for which people collected in barns or other large buildings to dance. *The WSM Barn Dance* (WSM were the radio station's call letters) was first broadcast in 1925, and its name was changed to the *Grand Ole Opry* as a playful commentary on the classical operatic program that preceded it.

Hillbilly music developed into several different musical styles. During the thirties and forties, a style called **western swing** became popular in Texas. Its origins lay in the music played by fiddle-and-guitar barn dance bands, which gradually adopted characteristics of African American blues and jazz. From the blues, western swing bands took some of their songs or instrumental works, borrowing the twelve-bar blues form and using blue notes in melodies. From jazz they took syncopated rhythms, instruments commonly used in jazz such as the saxophone, and improvisational practices in which individual musicians took turns playing solos. From both the blues and jazz, western swing bands borrowed the typical uneven beat subdivisions and the stress on the backbeat. Western swing was one of the few hillbilly styles that used drums, which were usually avoided in most country styles partly because of their association with African American music. In Texas, the king of western swing was fiddler Bob Wills (1905–1975), who led the Texas Playboys. Another fiddler, Spade Cooley (Donnell Clyde Cooley, 1910–1969), popularized the style in California. Both western swing and another blues-influenced country style called hillbilly boogie became important in the development of rock and roll through the music of Bill Haley.

A **honky-tonk** was a bar or saloon, often found outside the limits of "dry" towns (towns that prohibited alcoholic beverages). The honky-tonk atmosphere was one of boisterous, noisy camaraderie, and for that reason it was not the place for unamplified music like that played by bluegrass groups, or, for that matter, any groups with the slightest bit of subtlety in their style. The music in honky-tonks had to be loud (therefore amplified) and had to have a steady, danceable beat. Honky-tonk pianists played with a strong beat and rollicking boogie-woogie bass patterns. Honky-tonk song themes often stressed depression over a lost job or an untrue lover. Ernest Tubb (born in 1914 and also known as the Texas Troubadour), George Jones (born in 1931), and Hank Williams Sr. (1923–1953) were all popular honky-tonk singers and writers. John Fogerty revived Hank Williams's honky-tonk style with his Blue Ridge Rangers' hit "Jambalaya (On the Bayou)" in 1973.

The use of amplified guitar, bass, and drums in honky-tonks influenced the development of the rockabilly styles of Elvis Presley, Eddie Cochran, and Gene Vincent during the mid-fifties, and Jerry Lee Lewis took his rockabilly piano style from the music of honky-tonk pianists.

Country music of the fifties existed in many styles, but descriptions are, of course, only of value in addition to (and not in place of) listening to examples of each style. What follows is an attempt to guide the listener's ear to those general elements of country music that influenced the rock and roll played by country musicians.

1. The beat is steady, and all musicians play exactly on that beat. Other styles of music have a steadiness to the beat, but musicians often play slightly "behind" it, thereby relaxing within that beat. Pure country style is based on a crisp, exact beat.

2. The beats are patterned with either four, two, or three beats per bar (four is standard in rock).

3. Four-beat patterns have even subdivisions. Even subdivisions have a "boom-chunk" feel, or to refer to music notation, an even eighth-note flow.

4. The harmonies are usually **triadic** (triads are simple three-note chords with no added sevenths).

5. Most of the music follows a repeating pattern of **eight-bar periods,** each composed of two **four-bar phrases.** The blues form is also often used.

6. The bass often plays the root of the chord on beat one and the fifth of the chord on beat three in a four-beat pattern, creating a regular alternation between those notes called **two-beat bass.**

7. Song lyrics often tell stories or are intended to express the singer's feelings about some person, event, or political issue, and they are meant to be heard over the accompaniment.

8. Vocals often have a nasal tone quality and are sung with either a deadpan style of delivery or with an intensity that gives the impression that the singer is on the verge of tears.

9. Hillbilly vocal duos often sing the melody below a high, slower-moving part. Vocal trios add another low part, and quartets another below that.

10. Except for the bass, which usually slaps down exactly on the beat, voices and instruments often slide from note to note. The steel guitar is played with a bar and pedals that can bend entire chords, not just single notes.

Jimmy Rodgers (1897–1933) is often called the Father of Country Music. Rodgers had a very distinctive vocal style described as "blue yodeling" (a type of singing that rapidly changes back and forth between high and low notes). The term *blue* refers to the fact that Rodgers sang many songs that followed the twelve-bar blues form, creating a combination of black and white musical styles as early as the 1920s. He also broke away from the previous country and folk tradition of singing mostly old traditional songs and performed and recorded newly written songs. By doing that, he established a new tradition that led directly to the highly acclaimed song writing of Hank Williams, Johnny Cash, and many other country artists to follow.

The late, great **Hank Williams Sr.** (1923–1953) certainly deserves some attention. "I'll Never Get Out of This World Alive" was a number-one hit on the country charts in 1952. A listening guide to that recording is on page 41. It was his last single to be released. Williams was only twenty-eight years old when he recorded the song, but problems in his personal life and a dependency on painkillers and alcohol brought on his untimely death by heart attack only one year later.

An important country star whose career developed around the same time that rock music was becoming popular was **Johnny Cash** (1932–2003). In fact, Elvis Presley was already recording at Sun Records when Cash auditioned there and released his first single "Cry, Cry, Cry" (1955). That single and Cash's next release, "Folsom Prison Blues" (1956), were hits on the country charts, but he actually *crossed over* (succeeded in becoming popular with an entire new audience) into success on the pop charts the same year with "I Walk the Line." "I Walk the Line" was number one for six weeks on the country charts and reached number seventeen on the pop charts. A listening guide to that recording is on page 42.

Cash's career continued to be very successful with his biggest pop chart hit being the very clever "Boy Named Sue" (1969), which was number two for three weeks. In the song the singer is angry with his father for naming

Hank Williams

American country singer and musician Johnny Cash wearing a tuxedo, performing with a guitar on stage during a television appearance.

Listening Guide

"I'll Never Get Out of This World Alive"
as recorded by Hank Williams (1952)

Tempo: The tempo is approximately 118 beats per minute, with four beats per bar.

Form: Two fiddles play a two-bar introduction with three eighth-note **pickups.**

The musical form is that of a standard pop song (AABA) in which each A and B period is eight bars long. The first full AABA section has vocals on each period, but the first two A sections in the next are instrumental followed by a B and another A with vocals. The recording ends with a two-bar extension.

Features: The beats are very steady, but a western swing feel is created by uneven beat subdivisions.

A string bass is played in a two-beat bass pattern alternating chordal notes on beats one and three of each four-beat bar.

Acoustic rhythm guitar accents the backbeats.

The steel guitar and a pair of fiddles alternate four-bar sections during the two instrumental A sections. They often slide from one note to another.

Drums provide a very subtle support to the beat played by the other instruments.

The harmonies are simple and triadic with few additions of sevenths.

Williams's voice has a nasal tone quality and he occasionally ends words with hiccuplike slides away from the pitch, giving the impression that he is about to cry.

Lyrics: The song is archetypical of the lost-your-woman, lost-your-dog, lost-your-pickup-truck country western bad luck lament. The singer virtually glories in his continuing bad luck (a theme established in the first stanza: "I had lots of luck but it's all been bad") as he plays with all sorts of permutations of how things can go wrong (basically can't win for losin').

Billboard country charts: number one

him Sue, but then finds out that his father gave him a girl's name to help make him tough enough to deal with the world. One must hear Cash's recording to appreciate the dramatic ending when he comes to understand his father's thinking and then tells what name he intends to give his own son some day. The song was so popular that it was played on rock stations. Given the many other important musical events of the psychedelic sixties, including the Woodstock Festival, it took a great country song and performance to be that popular with the rock audience of the era. Johnny Cash was always an individual. At a time when country performers tended to deck themselves out in colorful, sparkling outfits, Cash preferred to wear black, and he became known as the "Man in Black."

Cash sang on Bob Dylan's *Nashville Skyline* album (1969). He later connected with a number of important rock musicians through his contract with Rick Rubin, known for his work with such rap artists as the Beastie Boys, Run-DMC, and the metal band Slayer. As Rubin said about his interest in Cash, "From the beginning of rock and roll, there's always been this dark figure who never really fit. He's still the quintessential outsider. In the hip-hop world, you see all these bad-boy artists who are

Listening Guide

**"I Walk the Line"
as recorded by Johnny Cash (1956)**

Tempo: The tempo is approximately 216 beats per minute, with four beats in each bar.

Form: The overall form is strophic, which means that each verse is sung to the same melody.

After a nineteen-bar instrumental introduction, the first verse begins with a three-beat pickup.

All five verses are sixteen bars long.

Between verses the instruments play eight-bar instrumental sections that do not include any new melody lines, but "vamp" (or repeat a rhythmic pattern) to fill before the next verse begins.

The recording ends with a fade out in the seventh and eighth bars of the final instrumental section.

Features: Even beat subdivisions are followed throughout.

The "two-beat bass" sound (notes alternating between beats one and three of each four-beat bar) typical of traditional country music is played by both the bass and the bass strings of a guitar.

Cash has a piece of wax paper wound through his guitar strings to give his guitar a slightly muffled sound.

Drums are so subdued that they are barely audible.

Lyrics: This is one of country music's great paeans to fidelity and monogamy—"walking the line" being a metaphor for the lover being true, keeping a "close watch" on his heart and keeping his eyes "wide open" against temptation. The theme of fidelity is heightened by the reference to separation with its possibilities for relationships with others.

Billboard pop charts: number seventeen; *Billboard* country charts: number one for six weeks

juggling being on MTV and running from the law. John was the originator of that."

Tom Petty and the Heartbreakers played on Cash's *Unchained* album (1996). Cash even covered a Nine Inch Nails' song, "Hurt" (2003), in the year he died. The musical expression of pain is not unusual for Trent Reznor or Cash and as Cash said of the song, "There's more heart, soul and pain in that song than any I've heard in a long time. I love it." Cash had overcome severe drug problems and had a very long, successful career, but he was in ill health through most of the 1990s to the end of his life. He died of complications from diabetes.

Country music continues to appeal to very large audiences, and it has diversified into many later styles. Alternative country music by bands such as Uncle Tupelo and Wilco are discussed in Chapter 21.

Summary

Like the blues, black gospel music originated with influences from both African and European musical traditions. But unlike the blues, which tended to be a vehicle for personal expression, gospel was religious and was often sung by groups of people who used their music to share the beliefs that unified them. Early gospel songs were called spirituals, and they were usually sung by groups of believers in a highly energetic style that displayed the fervor of their religious commitment. As part of that display, gospel singers stylized their vocals with ornaments that were not part of the basic melodies but were improvised by soloists and changed with each performance. Generally, choirs did not embellish the melodies they sang, resulting in an interesting variation between the style of the soloist and that of the responding group.

Professional gospel groups formed to record and tour as early as the twenties. Groups such as the Mills Brothers and the Ink Spots formed secular versions of professional gospel groups. By the forties, other groups who imitated them developed a style called doo-wop. Many doo-wop groups were popular during the fifties, and some added pop-style instrumental backgrounds and remained on the charts into the sixties. Gospel and doo-wop were revived by new singers and groups in the nineties.

Country music is a commercial form of folk music. Called hillbilly music until the early fifties, country styles included songs that told stories and dances accompanied by such instruments as the fiddle, the guitar, the dulcimer, the piano, the harmonica, and the mandolin. Eventually drums and saxophones from jazz and blues influenced some country styles, but many country performers at the time resisted association with music that was commonly played by African American musicians.

Musical elements typical of most country music styles included a steady beat that was subdivided into two equal sections, simple triadic chords, four-bar phrases that formed repeating eight-bar periods, two-beat bass, the practice of sliding from one note to the next, and group vocals in which the second from the highest part carried the melody. Partly because the songs often told stories that developed as the song progressed, the vocals were never obscured by the instruments that accompanied them. The blues form was sometimes used in traditional country music, but usually the uneven beat subdivisions and blue notes commonly used by African American performers were not.

Various styles of country music have influenced rock music in a variety of ways at different times during the course of rock's development. Western swing and hillbilly boogie were the basis for early rock music played by Bill Haley. Another country style to use drums and amplified instruments, honky-tonk, was combined with the blues to create rockabilly. Bluegrass group vocals and the use of instruments common in bluegrass such as the banjo became important in the country-rock music popular during the late sixties.

discussion questions

Both blues and country lyrics can express downheartedness. What are some differences in the kinds of expression between the two styles, and what are some reasons for the differences?

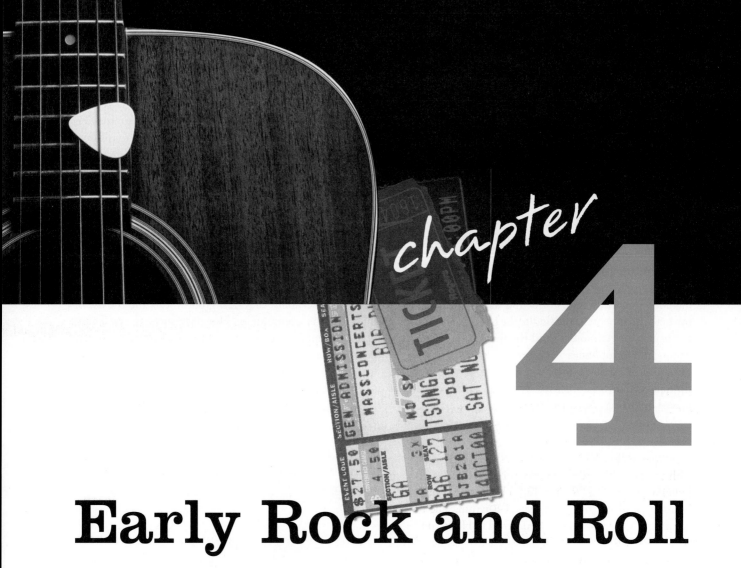

Early Rock and Roll

"The blues had a baby and they called it rock and roll."

—MUDDY WATERS

It might be difficult for today's fans of fifties rock music to imagine, but rock was considered to be a new sound when it was created. Actually, many rock historians consider blues and rhythm and blues recordings of the forties to be rock music. In many ways they were. When disc jockey Alan Freed first used the term rock and roll, he was using it to identify rhythm and blues. Certainly early or protorock music was blues- or rhythm and blues–based in practically all cases. Finding the point at which rock really begins is impossible, or at least greatly disputed, but we can listen to recordings by particular artists of the fifties and hear a variety of styles that are definitely rock, if not the very earliest rock. The musical characteristics that make them rock will be discussed in some detail and connected to the roots of rock music that were presented in the previous chapters.

Musicians with Backgrounds in Country Music

Bill Haley

Bill Haley (1925–1981) was a country singer and guitarist from Michigan who played in western swing bands. A disc jockey during the late forties, he formed the Four Aces of Western Swing to play on his radio program. When the group broke up, he formed another group, the Saddlemen, with which he recorded country songs. In 1951, Haley's group did a cover of "Rocket 88," a blues record by Jackie Brenston with Ike Turner's Kings of Rhythm. The record did not sell well, but when he performed it, Haley could see how much white teens enjoyed the beat and vitality of the blues. He decided to drop his country image the next year, changing his group's name to the Comets (after Halley's comet), and record blues and rhythm and blues. Bill Haley and the Comets signed with Decca Records in 1954 and covered two blues songs, "(We're Gonna) Rock Around the Clock" (recorded by Sunny Dae in 1952) and Joe Turner's "Shake, Rattle and Roll."

Joe Turner (1911–1985) had been singing jazz since the late twenties and had become an accomplished singer of slow, jazz-styled blues as well as the faster jump blues. As a jump blues singer, he was often described as a "blues shouter" because of his rousing performances in which he made his voice match the honking sounds of the saxophones. As was common in jazz and blues, Turner's songs were often full of sexual references that white singers who wanted their music played on the radio in the fifties had to remove. A comparison of Joe Turner's and Bill Haley's versions of "Shake, Rattle and Roll" can be found on page 46.

Bill Haley and the Comets

Listening Guide

	"Shake, Rattle and Roll" as recorded by Joe Turner (1954)	*"Shake, Rattle and Roll"* as recorded by Bill Haley and the Comets (1954)
Tempo:	The tempo is about 140 beats per minute, with four beats per bar.	The tempo is about 176 beats per minute, with four beats per bar.
Form:	Both the music and the text follow the classic twelve-bar blues form. The recording has nine choruses of the blues.	Both the music and the text follow the classic twelve-bar blues form. The recording has seven choruses of the blues.
Features:	The rhythm section includes boogie-woogie-style piano, string bass playing on all four beats, and hand clapping and a snare drum accenting the backbeats. The fills are played by saxophones playing repeated notes in some choruses and a riff pattern in others. The fifth chorus is instrumental, with a baritone saxophone playing a jazz-style improvised solo. The recording ends with a saxophone line taken directly from the ending to Duke Ellington's recording of "Take the 'A' Train."	The rhythm section includes piano and drums playing together in a shuffle beat pattern and the bass player snapping the strings of his instrument against the fingerboard (the **slapping bass** often used in country music). The backbeat is less obvious than in Turner's recording. The fills are played by saxophone and guitar playing a riff pattern (different from the one used by Turner). The fourth chorus is instrumental, with the saxophone and guitar playing the melody together in unison, with no improvisation. The recording ends with a two-bar **tag** (short ending tacked on after the last chorus).
Lyrics:	The lyrics include several sexual references: in the first verse, the singer and the woman to whom he sings are in bed together; in verse two he voices his appreciation at seeing the sun shine through her dress; in verse six he is looking at her and appreciating the fact that she is a woman.	The lyrics basically follow those of the original, but the references to a bed are removed and the lines about the singer's appreciation of the woman's sexuality have been changed to lines about her being cold (verse two) and her having stopped loving him and treated him wrong (verses five and six).

Billboard rhythm and blues charts: number one for three weeks

Billboard pop charts: number seven; British hit singles: number four

> ❝My love was rock and the blues. I put swing to the blues. I made the blues jump! I wasn't tryin' to change the style. I was just trying to give it life.❞
>
> –Joe Turner

This comparison points out several of the differences between the blues and the early rock music based on the blues. Haley's version is faster than Turner's, it has fewer characteristics of jazz style, and the lyrics are toned down to be more acceptable to a broader audience that might have been offended by the sexual references in the original. Haley probably did not change the beginning of the verse about the "one-eyed cat" because he thought it was subtle enough to get by the listeners who were easily offended and yet would please those who listened for sexual references. Turner's recording did not make the pop charts, but it was number one for three weeks on the rhythm and blues charts. Haley's recording reached number seven on the pop charts.

Bill Haley's recording "(We're Gonna) Rock Around the Clock" (1955) was number one for eight weeks on the pop charts and also reached number three on the rhythm and blues charts. It also followed the twelve-bar blues form, used uneven beat subdivisions (except in the guitar solo), and had saxophones playing in riff patterns unlike the improvisations used by jazz musicians. The lyrics to the song used the word *rock* for dancing and partying, but young listeners certainly made the connection with the way blues singers used the word as slang for sexual intercourse. The recording was not as successful in 1954 as it was after being rereleased as the main-title music for the movie *Blackboard Jungle* (1955). Bill Haley was thirty years old, but because teen rebellion was the theme of the movie, he and his group were seen as reflective of that attitude.

Bill Haley and the Comets toured Britain in 1957, making them the first international rock stars. As popular as their combination of western swing and rhythm and blues was during the fifties, it did not prove to be as lasting and influential a rock style as the combination of honky-tonk, country music, and rhythm and blues called rockabilly.

Elvis Presley

Sam Phillips (1923–2003), an Alabama farm boy, worked as a disc jockey while still in his teens. In 1944, he moved to Memphis and, at the age of twenty-one, started the Memphis Recording Service. Because he liked the blues, most of the artists he recorded were African American blues musicians from the South. He purchased recording equipment and built a studio, where he recorded Jackie Brenston's "Rocket 88" (1951, covered by Bill Haley in the same year) and performances by Howlin' Wolf, Rufus Thomas, and Junior Parker. Phillips's business was too small for him to be able to distribute large quantities of records all over the country, so many of his early recordings were sold to larger companies such as Chess Records in Chicago. By the end of 1951, Phillips formed the Sun Record Company in order to be able to release his recordings himself.

> ❝If I could find a white man who had the Negro sound, and the Negro feel, I could make a million dollars.❞
>
> –Sam Phillips

Phillips was aware of the growing interest white Americans had in the blues and rhythm and blues, but he was also aware of the fact that white Americans tended more often to buy recordings made by white artists. White teenagers wanted to hear references to sex in song lyrics, but record company executives and radio programmers were willing to do anything to keep them out. Sam Phillips knew that what he needed to sell hit records was a white performer who could capture the style and beat of the African American singers and, at the same time, adapt the song lyrics to white tastes. He found that singer in 1954 when the young **Elvis Presley** (1935–1977) came into his studio to record the songs "My Happiness" and "That's When Your Heartaches Begin" to give to his mother for her birthday.

Elvis Presley's recordings at Sun Records introduced **rockabilly** (rock + hillbilly) to American teenagers. The standard accompaniment used for Presley's recordings at Sun was simply an electric lead guitar, an acoustic rhythm guitar, string bass, and subdued drums. Presley's lead guitarist, Scotty Moore, played with the steady, even beat common in country music on some songs, but he varied his style to include uneven picking patterns in others. A country sound was also suggested by Moore's sliding notes up the strings, giving the effect of the steel guitar, while Presley kept the rhythm on an acoustic guitar. Sun's bassist, Bill Black, slapped the strings against the fingerboard of his stand-up bass as he played, creating a sound that became typical of rockabilly. The bass usually played on beats one and three (two-beat bass), or on all four beats of a four-beat bar, while the drums played a rhythm-and-blues style shuffle rhythm and accented the backbeats of each bar. In addition to the way the instruments were played, Phillips used reverberation sound effects that

Elvis Presley in 1955 with bassist Bill Black.

achieved some success locally, Presley was sent by Phillips to audition for the *Grand Ole Opry,* but he was not accepted. His style was too "black" for the *Opry* and too "white" for the rhythm and blues audiences. Despite these racial interpretations of Presley's style, his voice really had no direct precedents in either African American or white traditions. He had a wide, syrupy vibrato that suggested sensual warmth, and yet he could suddenly shift into a falsetto that suggested bottled-up tension and even a barely contained sort of wildness. It was this emotional intensity that made his voice perfect for the young white fans of the rhythm and blues beat. He was clean, good-looking in the rebel image of James Dean, and, although he often sang "cleaned up" lyrics to blues songs that were originally full of sexual suggestions, he put sex into his performances with suggestive poses and hip gyrations.

During 1955, Presley performed on radio programs, mainly in the South, and had his first chance at a television appearance on a local program. At that time, he was considered primarily a country singer, and his success had been limited to the Tennessee area. He traveled to New York but was turned down when he auditioned for Arthur Godfrey's program *Talent Scouts.* When Colonel Tom Parker took over as Presley's manager, he decided that Presley deserved to be with a company that was larger than Sun Records. After the release of "Mystery Train" (by Junior Parker, also of Sun Records) drew sufficient attention to show Presley's potential, the RCA company bought his contract for a mere $35,000. Did Sam Phillips make a mistake? He might not have because Elvis needed more publicity than he could afford.

Under Parker's conscientious and aggressive management, Presley prospered at RCA. With the better publicity that he was given and a more polished sound on his recordings, he became a star within a year. For purist fans of the rockabilly sound, however, Presley's Sun recordings were superior to his RCA recordings.

Presley was not a songwriter, and at RCA many of his songs were written by pop writers and recorded with a clean, studio production that included doo-wop-style group vocals and Fats Domino–style piano accompaniment. Rockabilly instrumentation and style were sometimes used, on "Blue Suede Shoes," for example, but the white pop or pop-style doo-wop sound was more common. Presley's fans were not really concerned about the technical details of the recordings; it was his irresistible performance style that earned him the "King of Rock and Roll" reputation. In 1956, he captured the heart of many a teenage girl (and the resulting wrath of her parents) when he thrust his hips around while singing his hits "Heartbreak Hotel," "I Want You, I Need You, I Love You," "Don't Be Cruel," and "Hound Dog" on the Milton Berle, Steve Allen, and Ed Sullivan television shows

exaggerated the music's throbbing pulse. Presley's Sun recordings, such as "Good Rockin' Tonight" and "Milkcow Blues Boogie," followed the traditional twelve-bar blues form, but the tempos of the songs were almost always faster than those used in blues or rhythm and blues. The faster tempo produced an energetic intensity that was an important characteristic of rockabilly.

> **"From the beginning I could see he had a different outlook on things, just the way he dressed, the way he wore his hair. He was a rebel; really without making an issue of it."**
>
> –Guitarist Scotty Moore, about Elvis Presley

Some of Presley's early recordings were taken from country sources and some from blues sources. One of his first singles had the Arthur "Big Boy" Crudup blues song "That's All Right" on side one and a rockabilly version of the country song "Blue Moon of Kentucky" (by bluegrass writer and performer Bill Monroe) on side two. Having

and the Dorsey Brothers' stage show. The Sullivan show only showed Elvis from the waist up to avoid the sexiness of his moves.

> "It isn't enough to say that Elvis is kind to his parents. That still isn't a free ticket to behave like a sex maniac in public before millions of impressionable kids."
>
> –*New York Journal-American* writer Eddie Condon (1956)

Presley's style of that period included some use of the blues, but his recordings were molded to fit his image and to please his teenaged audience. One example of a blues song that became a hit for Presley was "Hound Dog," written by the songwriting team Leiber and Stoller for Willie Mae "Big Mama" Thornton, who first recorded it. A "hound dog" was African American slang for a man who cheated on his woman, but when Elvis sang the song, the title took on a very different meaning. In his version, he berated a woman by saying she was of no more use than a hound dog that was no good at catching rabbits—a complete shift from Thornton's recording but suitable for Elvis's early tough-guy image. The comparison of the two recordings outlines other changes made in Presley's recording, including an increase in the speed of the beat and the replacement of blues instruments and blues-oriented instrumental improvisations with country-oriented ones. The listening guide is on page 50.

Thornton's recording had been a big hit on the rhythm and blues charts in 1953. It was number one for seven weeks. It never made the pop charts, however. Presley's recording, backed by the equally popular "Don't Be Cruel," was not only number one for eleven weeks on the pop charts, but it was also number one on the rhythm and blues charts for six weeks.

Presley became a movie star with the release of *Love Me Tender* in 1956, and each of his movies was followed by a string of hit songs. He had the world in his hands, but despite his semi-tough-guy image, he never forgot his home or his parents. With the large check he received when he left Sun Records, he bought them both Cadillacs. In 1957, he bought Graceland, the estate he lived in and that enshrined him after his death. Because his mother never learned to drive, her pink Cadillac was parked at Graceland and remained there.

In 1957, Presley made two movies, *Loving You* and *Jailhouse Rock,* which featured the hit songs "Teddy Bear" and "Jailhouse Rock." The next year was not a good one for the new star. While he was shooting *King Creole,* his draft notice arrived. Only a short time after he left for basic training, his mother died before he was able to make it home to see her, an experience he called the worst loss of his life. Thanks to Colonel Parker, Presley's career survived his two-year absence. Parker took great care to keep Presley on the minds of his fans by judiciously releasing prerecorded songs such as "Hard Headed Woman" (from the movie *King Creole* in 1958) and "A Big Hunk o' Love" (1959) while Presley was in the service.

After his return to civilian life, Presley was more of a movie star than a concert performer. The soundtrack

Willie Mae "Big Mama" Thornton with band leader Johnny Otis and a record executive (ca. 1950)

Listening Guide

	"Hound Dog" as recorded by Willie Mae "Big Mama" Thornton (1952)	"Hound Dog" as recorded by Elvis Presley (1956)
Tempo:	The tempo is about 140 beats per minute, with four beats per bar.	The tempo begins at about 176 beats per minute, but speeds up to about 184 during the first chorus. There are four beats per bar.
Form:	Both the music and the text follow the classic twelve-bar blues format. The recording has eight choruses of the blues form. The fourth, fifth, and sixth are instrumental, with a guitar improvising solo lines and Thornton giving occasional vocal responses.	Both the music and the text follow the classic twelve-bar blues format. The recording has eight choruses of the blues form. The fourth and sixth are instrumental, with a guitar playing lead lines and a vocal group singing sustained-note chords in the background.
Features:	Thornton sings using a rough, classic-blues-style tone quality. The rhythm section includes country-blues-style guitar rhythms, a bass playing a regular beat, and hand clapping with a drum stuck on the side (shell) for a very strong backbeat. The fills are played by the guitar in a country-blues style, with the player bending the strings to produce blue notes.	Presley sings in a polished urban blues style and tone quality. The rhythm section includes country-style guitar, a bass playing a riff pattern styled after the saxophone riffs in Bill Haley's version of "Shake, Rattle and Roll," and drums heavily accenting the backbeat. The fills are played by a country-style guitar and by backup singers sustaining chords.
Lyrics:	The lyrics are sung by a woman to a man who has cheated on her, and she responds by vowing to stop seeing him.	The lyrics are sung by a man to a woman whom he sees as being of no more value to him than a hound dog that cannot catch rabbits.

Billboard rhythm and blues charts: number one for seven weeks

Billboard pop charts: number one for eleven weeks; *Billboard* rhythm and blues charts: number one for six weeks; British hit singles: number two

albums from his movies sold well, and beginning in 1968, he made a few concert tours and television films, as well as a number of Las Vegas appearances. He continued to release hit singles through the last year of his life, but his old, rough, rockabilly style was long gone. To lovers of country music, Presley had sold out to a pop style, but by the early sixties rockabilly had already lost its commercial appeal for most of the American audience. Presley's ability to change his style to fit current popular trends was part of the reason he was able to sustain his career through three decades. His image from the fifties was copied by, or was a great influence on, so many later performers that he had become a living legend, unable to go anywhere on earth without being recognized. He died in 1977, in many ways a victim of his legendary status.

> **"Without Elvis, none of us could have made it."**
>
> –Buddy Holly

Presley's voice was so versatile and he sang in so many styles that it would require a large portion of this book to include enough listening guides to cover his career. In an effort to at least recognize the length of his tremendous string of hits, the listening guide discusses his last top ten hit, "Burning Love."

During the five years that followed the release of "Burning Love," Presley continued to record and tour, but his personal life was falling apart. His wife, Priscilla, divorced him, and he spent most of his private time as a recluse on his Graceland estate. By the time he died, he had spent over twenty years trying to avoid the anxious demands of his omnipresent fans. He paid large department stores to stay open in the middle of the night so he could shop with some sense of privacy. Similarly, he would rent whole movie theaters or other attractions to allow himself to enjoy them without the hounding fans. Exactly when he turned to the escape of drugs is not known, or at least not made public, but his dependence on a variety of barbiturates, tranquilizers, and amphetamines certainly contributed to his death at age forty-two.

Carl Perkins

Carl Perkins (1932–1998) grew up on a farm in Tennessee. He had been playing the guitar and singing at country dances when he first heard Presley's recordings on a local radio program. He had always liked the blues and rhythm and blues, and he decided to pattern his style after Presley's. Perkins traveled to Memphis and auditioned and was signed by Sun Records in 1955. Though he did not have Elvis Presley's good looks, his sound was good, and, unlike Presley, he also wrote songs and played lead guitar. His career was launched with a recording of his own composition, "Blue Suede Shoes," in 1956. Part of the reason Sam Phillips released Presley from his contract with Sun was that he felt he had another, possibly bigger star in Perkins. A listening guide to "Blue Suede Shoes" is on page 52. That bright-looking future was dimmed, however, by an automobile accident that injured Carl and claimed the lives of his brother Jay and his manager David Stewart. The group had been on their way to *The Perry Como Show,* where Perkins was to receive a gold record for his recording of "Blue Suede Shoes." That appearance might have led to

Listening Guide

"Burning Love"
as recorded by Elvis Presley (1972)

Tempo: The tempo is approximately 144 beats per minute, with four beats per bar.

Form: The form is based on eight-bar periods, each of which is made up of two four-bar phrases. After a four-bar introduction, the periods follow the pattern AABAABBAAB and end with repetitions of the final phrase and a fade-out. The B sections all begin with the words "Your kisses" except for the third B, in which the B melody is played instrumentally.

Features: The instruments enter one at a time in the introduction in the following order: rhythm guitar, piano, bass, and drums.

Both even and uneven beat subdivisions are kept by the instruments, with the bass and guitar usually maintaining even subdivisions and the piano keeping unevenly subdivided beats. Presley's vocals are generally unevenly subdivided. A strong backbeat is kept in the drums.

The backup vocal group breaks into a black gospel style with two high male soloists during the ending repetitions of the final phrase.

Lyrics: The singer is so aflame with sexual desire that he is burning up.

Billboard pop charts: number two; British hit singles: number seven

Listening Guide

"Blue Suede Shoes"
as recorded by Carl Perkins (1956)

Tempo: The tempo is approximately 168 beats per minute, with four beats per bar.

Form: The form is based on the blues form with pickups and some extensions. The first phrase begins with a one-beat pickup and then two four-beat bars with extensions played by the drums. After that, four-beat bars continue throughout the song. The recording has seven blues choruses, the third and fifth of which are instrumental. The second and fourth each have an additional four bars at the beginning, making them sixteen-bar choruses.

Features: The first, second, fourth, and sixth choruses begin with stop time sections

in which the vocal part is alone with the instruments joining in on the pickup beat four and then the downbeat of each bar. The instruments accompany the vocals throughout the final chorus.

The instrumentation is hollow-body electric lead guitar, acoustic rhythm guitar, stand-up bass played with the strings slapping against the fingerboard, and drums. The drums keep a steady beat with the stick hitting the rim of the drum and a slight accent on the backbeat.

Lyrics: The singer values his blue suede shoes and his ability to dance in them over anything else in his life.

Billboard pop charts: number two for four weeks; *Billboard* rhythm and blues charts: number two for four weeks; *Billboard* country charts: number one for three weeks; British hit singles: number ten

---

many more successes, but Perkins was badly injured and it took him a long time to recover.

> **"That's what rockabilly music, or rock and roll was to begin with . . . a country man's song with a black man's rhythm. I just put a little speed into some of the slow blues licks."**
>
> –Carl Perkins

By the time he was ready to perform again, rockabilly was already being overshadowed by other styles. He did, however, continue as a country recording artist with much success. The Beatles paid him tribute by recording covers of several of his songs. During the sixties and seventies, Perkins performed with Johnny Cash and Bob Dylan, and in 1983, Paul McCartney featured him on his post-Wings album *Tug of War*. A rockabilly revival band

of the early eighties, the Stray Cats, took much of their style from Perkins. Having overcome throat cancer in 1995, Perkins continued to write and record until his stroke-related death three years later. His fans can still enjoy being surrounded by memorabilia from his career at his restaurant, Suede, in Jackson, Tennessee.

Jerry Lee Lewis

Another rockabilly artist whose career in rock was short but influential was pianist/singer **Jerry Lee Lewis** (born in 1935). He grew up in Louisiana listening to both country and blues singers and playing the piano for anyone who would listen to him. A cousin of preacher Jimmy Swaggart, he was also very much influenced by gospel music. After hearing Elvis Presley's recordings on the Sun label, he went to Memphis and signed a contract with Sun Records. Like Bill Haley and Elvis Presley before him, Lewis covered blues songs by African American musicians; his "Whole Lotta Shakin' Goin' On" (1957) had been recorded by Big Maybelle in 1955. The song was full of sexual references, and, unlike Haley and Presley, Lewis chose not to sanitize the lyrics, although he did add to them.

> ❝This man doesn't play rock and roll, he is rock and roll.❞
>
> –Bruce Springsteen, about Jerry Lee Lewis

Jerry Lee Lewis played his honky-tonk piano rock with a tremendous amount of energy. He threw his right hand all over the keyboard with **glissandos** (sliding runs) while his left hand smashed at the keys to maintain a rhythmically pumping bass line. He pushed the bench away and danced while he played, letting his backup band sustain the beat while he banged the piano keys with his feet and even jumped on top of the piano while singing. He deserved his nickname, "The Killer," for his treatment of both the piano and his audience.

> ❝From $10,000 to $250 a night is a hell of a disappointment.❞
>
> –Jerry Lee Lewis

Lewis knew he was a great performer, but he never dreamed that his fans would care about his private life. His career was ruined by an unofficial boycott of his records and performances when it became known that he had married his thirteen-year-old third cousin without having divorced his second wife. Though he remained at Sun Records to record country music and continued to do live performances, Lewis could no longer draw the large crowds he once attracted. In later years, he was remembered by British rock musicians Rory Gallagher, Alvin Lee, and Peter Frampton, who had him join them for an album called *The Session* (1973). During the late seventies and extending into the nineties, Lewis played his old hits on various programs that paid tribute to his importance as an early rock performer, and he continues to tour. In 1995 he released a new album, *Young Blood.*

Eddie Cochran

Although the rockabilly sound was first synthesized in Elvis Presley's recordings of blues songs at Sun Records, the fusion of blues and country music was a natural happening for the time, and it was soon copied by recording artists outside of Sam Phillips's studios. Rockabilly artist **Eddie Cochran** (1938–1960) had only a short career but made a lasting influence on many of the rock stars who followed him. Originally from Oklahoma, he lived in Minnesota and California before settling in Nashville, where he co-wrote songs with his friend Jerry Capehart. He adopted the tough-guy image popularized by James Dean and Marlon Brando, and he was even given an acting role in *Untamed Youth* (1957).

Cochran's biggest recording success was "Summertime Blues" in 1958, which hit number eight on the pop charts. A listening guide can be found below. Both that and his

Listening Guide

"Summertime Blues,"
as recorded by Eddie Cochran (1958)

Tempo: The tempo is approximately 152 beats per minute, with four beats in each bar.

Form: The overall form is ABABAB, with eight bars in each section and an instrumental beginning and ending.

Features: Cochran has overdubbed lead vocals, acoustic rhythm guitar, string bass, hand clapping, and drums.

The repeating rhythmic pattern is a typical rockabilly bar with four even beats and a double accent on both halves of the second beat.

Instrumental breaks are used effectively to draw attention to sections of the vocal lines.

Lyrics: The singer is in agony because, when he should be having fun, everyone is forcing him to work.

Billboard pop charts: number eight; *Billboard* rhythm and blues charts: number eleven; British hit singles: number eighteen

next hit, "C'mon Everybody" (1959), were the result of Cochran's experiments with overdubbing, in which he played and sang all the parts himself. Overdubbing was a new recording technique invented by Les Paul in the early fifties, and although it had been used before, Cochran was among the first rockabilly musicians to use it extensively. Overdubbing techniques soon became a common recording practice.

Cochran saw that the popularity of the rockabilly style was dying with the rise of teen idol pop stars in the late fifties. With his last hit, "Three Steps to Heaven," it appeared that he was going to change his style to include more of this new pop sound. The song was not rockabilly at all; rather, it featured a lightly strummed guitar keeping the rhythm, a doo-wop-style vocal group, and very little bass, drums, or backbeat. He never really got the chance to establish himself in his new style, however. He was killed in an automobile accident on his way to a London airport after a tour of England in 1960.

Gene Vincent

Another rockabilly singer, **Gene Vincent** (Eugene Vincent Craddock, 1935–1971), was with Eddie Cochran on his last tour but survived the accident that killed Cochran. Vincent grew up in Virginia, where he had sung a type of religious country music called white gospel. After serving in the navy during the Korean War, he became interested in the rockabilly style of Elvis Presley and formed a group called the Blue Caps. They sent an audition tape to Capitol Record Company in Hollywood,

which gave them a contract. Vincent's voice was similar enough to Presley's that Capitol saw him as good competition for Presley. In producing his records, they used an echo effect to imitate the rockabilly recordings Sam Phillips made at Sun. "Be-Bop-A-Lula" (1956) was Gene Vincent and the Blue Caps's first recording, and it turned out to be the biggest hit of his career. Vincent's image was a bit rougher than Presley's, although both were styled very much in the James Dean tough-guy tradition. Because of a leg injury he had suffered while in the navy, Vincent could not perform the sexy hip movements that Presley did. Instead, he conveyed a feeling of sexual desperation through his breathy vocals. "Lotta Lovin'" was a hit for him in 1957, but by that time it was clear that rockabilly was beginning to lose popularity in the United States. Instead of trying to change to a pop style, Vincent moved to England, where he continued to perform as a rockabilly artist. In poor health, he returned to America in 1971, and died within a month.

Buddy Holly

Charles Hardin Holley's last name was printed without the "e" early in his career, and he decided to let it stay that way. As **Buddy Holly** (1938–1959), he was another important innovator in rock music who first turned to rock after seeing a 1955 performance by Elvis Presley. Holly was from Lubbock, Texas, and learned to play the fiddle, guitar, banjo, and piano when he was a child. He formed various country and protorock groups and, in 1956, received a contract to record for Decca Records in

Buddy Holly and the Crickets (1957) on Ed Sullivan

Nashville under the name Three Tunes. Holly's Decca recordings were country songs and did not sell well, so he and his drummer, Jerry Allison, decided to go back to Texas, where they performed as a duo. Holly and Allison formed the Crickets and went to New Mexico to record their first hit, "That'll Be the Day" (1957), produced by Norman Petty.

Although he credited Elvis Presley with introducing him to rock and roll, Buddy Holly was certainly no Elvis imitator. He wrote much of his own music, and his witty, personal, and emotional style appealed to male as well as female fans. His vocal style was light, characterized by his trademark hiccup on certain turns of phrase.

Unlike that of leather-jacketed rockabilly stars such as Cochran or Vincent, Holly's image was not one of teen rebellion. He wore suits, ties, and horn-rimmed glasses that gave him the look of a clean-cut, respectable, and even a bit naive young man (an image Elvis Costello would later portray as neurotic).

The Crickets used the standard rockabilly instrumentation of two guitars (one for lead, and one for rhythm), bass, and drums, except that their guitars were electric (Holly's had a solid body), and Jerry Allison played a different and more important role than other rockabilly drummers had. Allison sometimes used subtle and interesting Latin rhythms, unusual for the rock music of the time. Apart from the fact that their bass player played a stand-up bass, not an electric bass guitar, the Crickets' instrumentation was the same as that used by many later rock groups, including the Beatles and the Rolling Stones, both of which covered Holly's songs.

Buddy Holly was one of the first rock guitarists to play a solid-body electric guitar. Bill Haley had played the hollow-body electric guitar commonly used in western swing bands, and the rockabilly singers had often played steel-strung acoustic guitars. The solid body of Holly's instrument gave it a more aggressive tone quality than guitars with an acoustic sound box. Within a short space of time, the solid-body guitar became the standard guitar for rock music.

The listening guide for Buddy Holly's hit recording of "Peggy Sue" (1957) points out characteristics of both the blues and country music that have been molded together to create Holly's rock style. The Crickets' rhythm guitarist, Niki Sullivan, has said that he did not play on the recording of "Peggy Sue," so it is possible that Holly overdubbed the rhythm guitar part after the original recording session.

For two years, Buddy Holly and the Crickets recorded many other hit songs. Late in 1958, however, Holly decided to make some changes in his career. He left the Crickets and their manager, Norman Petty, got married, moved to New York, and started to work on developing his writing skills, changing his style to fit the new pop

Listening Guide

"Peggy Sue"
as recorded by Buddy Holly (1957)

Tempo: The tempo is about 148 beats per minute, with four beats in each bar.

Form: The form is a modified twelve-bar blues. Few blue notes are used.

The four-bar instrumental introduction is followed by seven twelve-bar choruses and a four-bar final extension.

Features: The instrumentation is electric solid-body guitar, acoustic rhythm guitar, string bass, and drums.

On the verses that Holly sings, he strums the solid-body guitar with a pick, but the volume is quite low. The volume is higher on the instrumental fifth chorus, with Holly playing a solo in a strummed pattern with melodic fills, influenced by Chuck Berry's solo style. The strumming of the rhythm guitar is covered up by the amplification of Holly's guitar during his solo.

Throughout the recording the drums keep an energetic four-to-the-beat (sixteenth note) pattern on tom-toms with little or no backbeat.

Holly's characteristic vocal hiccup is most obvious on the fourth, sixth, and seventh choruses.

Lyrics: The song is about the singer's unrequited love for a girl named Peggy Sue.

Billboard pop charts: number three; *Billboard* rhythm and blues charts: number two; British hit singles: number six

trend. His last hit, "It Doesn't Matter Anymore" (1959), was written for him by the songwriting teen idol Paul Anka, whom he met in New York, and was produced with a pop-style orchestral string section instead of the Crickets' instrumentation.

Because Holly's finances were tied up in legal battles with Norman Petty and he needed money, he decided to go on the concert tour that turned out to be his last. On the tour, Holly was backed by a band that included one member of the Crickets, guitarist Tom Allsup, and bass player Waylon Jennings, who would later become a country music star. Other headline performers on the tour were the Big Bopper (J. P. Richardson), Ritchie Valens (Richard Valenzuela), and Dion (Dion DiMucci). The Bopper, Valens, and Holly all died in a plane crash on February 3, 1959, a date that has never been forgotten by many rock fans.

The Everly Brothers

One of the few country-influenced rock groups to maintain popularity in the United States from the late fifties into the early sixties was the **Everly Brothers**. (Don Everly was born in 1937, and Phil Everly was born in 1939.) Phil and Don Everly's parents, Ike and Margaret Everly, were country musicians. They had a radio program on which Phil and

Don performed as early as 1946, when they were only seven and nine years old. The closely harmonized tenor voices of the brothers were accompanied by their own rhythm guitars, electric lead guitarist Chet Atkins, pianist Floyd Cramer, bass, and drums. Their sound was different from the pure rockabilly sound recorded at Sun Records because it was smooth and full and lacked the slapping bass and some of the intensity of Sun rockabilly. The Everly Brothers' voices slid gradually up to high notes, capturing the sound of someone almost on the verge of tears. They signed with Cadence Records in 1957 and recorded many of their best-known songs, including "Bye Bye Love" (1957) and "All I Have to Do Is Dream" (1958). In 1960, they changed to the Warner Brothers label and recorded "Cathy's Clown," which turned out to be their biggest hit. They continued to record through the sixties, but sales did not match those of their earlier records. A breakup was inevitable after a fight on stage in 1973, and it took ten years before they gave a reunion concert. The Everly Brothers' distinctive vocal style influenced many singers who followed them.

> "I didn't think that he [Elvis Presley] was as good as the Everly Brothers the first time

Early Electric Guitar

Buddy Holly's Stratocaster guitar was one of several early solid-body guitars to be used in rock music. Solid-body guitars had a tone quality that was quite different from the types of acoustic guitars or electric acoustic guitars they replaced. Whether it is amplified or not, the body of an acoustic guitar is hollow with a soundhole to let the strings' vibrations bounce around inside of the body. This causes the body top (called a *soundboard*) to resonate, and then that resonated sound comes back out of the soundhole. Early jazz guitarists like Charlie Christian and T-Bone Walker played acoustic (hollow-bodied) guitars with two sound holes (called *f holes* because they were shaped like two small letter f's facing one another) and electric pickups attached to the soundboard. The Gibson model ES-150 is an example of such a guitar. Urban blues guitarists wanted more of a punch to their tone than the full hollow-bodied instruments allowed, so they opted for thinner, semisolid-bodied guitars such as B. B. King's Gibson ES-335. King expressed his love for

his guitar which he used for years, by affectionately calling it Lucille. Les Paul and others were concerned about the short sustaining power and occasional feedback with the amplifier of the semisolid body and worked at improving their pickups to the point where the guitar body could be made of solid, high-density wood. While Paul was still working on his model, Paul Bigsby came up with one that Merle Travis used in 1947, and Leo Fender created his Broadcaster (later called the Telecaster) in 1948. The Gibson company made the Les Paul model in 1952. The solid-body guitar Buddy Holly played, the Fender Stratocaster (first produced in 1954), was an improvement over Fender's earlier models and had a triple pickup. The Fender Telecaster, the Gibson Les Paul, and the Fender Stratocaster all became standard instruments for rock guitarists of the sixties, including Eric Clapton, who used a Gibson Les Paul, and Jimi Hendrix, who used a Fender Stratocaster.

I ever laid eyes on him. Of course, that's kind of freaky too, because I didn't think the Beatles were as good as the Everly Brothers either; you know, I kind of like two-part harmony. "

–Chuck Berry, in a *Rolling Stone* interview (1972)

Musicians with Rhythm and Blues Backgrounds

Fats Domino

Fats Domino (born in 1929) had recorded several hits on the rhythm and blues charts before his 1955 entry onto the pop charts with "Ain't That a Shame." His real name was Antoine Domino, the name "Fats" being given to him as a description of his girth. He was born in New Orleans,

Fats Domino

Listening Guide

"I'm Walkin'"
as recorded by Fats Domino (1956)

Tempo: The tempo is approximately 224 beats per minute, with four beats in each bar.

Form: A four-bar introduction alternates drum thumps on beats one and three with a hand-clapped backbeat.

The musical form is a standard **pop song form** (AABA) in which each A and B period is eight bars long. After a full AABA section with lyrics, an instrumental section follows the same AABA format, and this is followed by another AABA section with lyrics. The ending begins another repetition of the form, but fades out during the second A.

Features: Beat subdivisions are uneven, in a shuffle beat pattern.

The backbeat that was introduced by hand claps continues to be clapped but is also supported by drums once the vocals begin.

Through each A period, the bass repeats a two-bar melodic pattern (in octaves with the guitar) that is notated as follows:

The instrumental section features a growl-toned tenor saxophone solo improvised around the melody of the vocal line.

Lyrics: Walking is symbolic of the singer's attempt to get his girl back.

Billboard pop charts: number four; *Billboard* rhythm and blues charts: number one for six weeks; British hit singles: number nineteen

a center for jazz since before the turn of the century. In the midforties, he met trumpet player and bandleader Dave Bartholomew, who became his producer and co-songwriter. Whether Domino was playing the slow, smooth rhythms of "Blueberry Hill" or the rollicking boogie-woogie style of "I'm Walkin'" (both 1956), his friendly, somewhat understated voice was backed by the honking saxophones in Bartholomew's backup band. Domino had a very long and successful career and was still performing in the eighties. Some basic musical characteristics of Fats Domino's style can be heard in his recording of "I'm Walkin'," for which a listening guide can be found on page 57.

Domino has had many hits on the rhythm and blues charts since 1950. "I'm Walkin'" was his eighth number one hit there and remained at that position for six weeks. It reached number four on the pop charts, displaying his popularity with white audiences as well as African American ones. The pop chart hits continued through 1963, by which time Domino had placed a total of thirty-seven records in the top forty.

For twenty-five years, Fats Domino enjoyed family life in his comfortable New Orleans home, only performing occasionally. He revived his recording career with the release of *Christmas Is a Special Day* in 1993.

Chuck Berry

Chuck Berry (born in 1926) was a guitarist and singer whose style was rooted in blues and rhythm and blues, but whose music was unquestionably rock and roll. He

even defined rock's style and its essential backbeat in both his playing and his lyrics in the 1957 hit "Rock and Roll Music." Berry was born in St. Louis and started playing the guitar as a teenager. The greatest influences on his guitar style were T-Bone Walker and Muddy Waters (whom he met in Chicago in 1955), but his singing style clearly showed the influence of any of a number of white country and western singers. It was partly the fact that he derived his sound from both blues and country roots that made it neither of those, but instead their fusion—rock and roll.

Chuck Berry wrote most of his own material, and he both sang and played lead guitar on his recordings. His songs captured the teenaged spirit through messages that told the world that classical composers could roll over in their graves and get with rhythm and blues ("Roll Over Beethoven," 1956), that his V8 Ford could catch up with a Cadillac Coup de Ville ("Maybellene," 1955), that dancing to rock and roll music can help one survive a day at school ("School Day," 1957), and any number of other subjects of interest to teens. Berry was a terrific poet in addition to a talented guitar player.

Berry's performances were electrifying, often including his famous "duckwalk" (in which he walked across the stage with his knees bent, moving his head forward and back). In his guitar solos, Berry would take a short riff and, with each repetition, dig into the notes more and more to increase the intensity of the sound, creating a rhythm with his melody that soon became a standard rock-guitar sound. He is sometimes referred to as the Father of Rock Guitar because of the great number of guitarists, including Buddy Holly, George Harrison, Keith Richards, and Carl Wilson, who have either copied his style or been greatly influenced by it. An analysis of one of his hit recordings, "School Day," is on page 59. "School Day" hit number three on the pop charts, but it was number one for five weeks on the rhythm and blues charts.

Chuck Berry doing his "duckwalk"

> " I say my style is Carl Hogan, Charlie Christian, T-Bone Walker, and all mixed in with whatever comes through, you know . . . . Like John Lennon says, 'Anything that's chonka, chonka, chonka, chonk is Chuck Berry.' "
> –Chuck Berry, in a *Rolling Stone* interview (1972)

Not all of Chuck Berry's hit recordings followed the classic blues form, but the blues practice of a vocal call

Listening Guide

"School Day"
as recorded by Chuck Berry (1957)

Tempo: The tempo is about 148 beats per minute, with four beats per bar.

Form: The musical form of the twelve-bar blues is followed, but the text does not have the A-section repetition of the blues poetic form.

The recording has seven full choruses of the twelve-bar blues form, the fifth chorus being a guitar solo.

Features: The beats have uneven subdivisions. The drums and the guitar fills play with this shuffle beat.

The bass plays chord roots on the basic beats.

The backbeat is accented, but minimally.

The guitar fills often imitate the vocal line they follow.

With the exception of the fifth (which is instrumental), each chorus ends with a three-beat break in which the instruments stop and the voice sings words that introduce the next chorus. (The first chorus of the form actually begins with the word *school.*)

The piano plays a subtle rhythmic background in a slower triplet pattern called a *hemiola* that is half the speed of the rhythm played by the guitar and drums. The effect of this is very interesting musically. It is most obvious behind the guitar solo in the fifth chorus.

Lyrics: The song is about the burden and drudgery of school, which teenagers can only endure knowing that once school lets out for the day they can enjoy their freedom by dancing to rock and roll music.

Billboard pop charts: number three; *Billboard* rhythm and blues charts: number one for five weeks; British hit singles: number twenty-four

followed by an instrumental response, as heard in "School Day," remained an important element of his style. His use of riffs in his solos was based on the way T-Bone Walker had employed riffs, and he even quoted Walker in some solos. Berry's energetic rhythms came, at least in part, out of Louis Jordan's jumpin' jive.

Berry's energetic music was overshadowed on the pop charts by the popularity of teen idols and girl groups of the late fifties and early sixties. In addition, his career suffered when, late in 1959, he was charged with a violation of the Mann Act (transportation of an underaged woman across a state border for immoral purposes). He went through two trials, resulting in a prison term that lasted from early 1962 to early 1964. When he was released and was ready to record again, Berry was able to make a comeback. His midsixties style picked up right where his earlier recordings had left off—"No Particular Place to Go" (1964), for example, was strikingly similar to "School Day" (1957). Berry's influence on rock musicians was not forgotten, and some of them, including Eric Clapton and Keith Richards, joined him in the concert celebration of his sixtieth birthday in 1986 and the documentary film made at that concert, *Hail, Hail Rock 'n' Roll.* Tangles with the Internal Revenue Service and various other legal problems have plagued Berry in recent years, causing him to perform somewhat less than he had earlier. It still is possible to see him in a live performance from time to time.

Little Richard

An important and influential rock singer and pianist in the rhythm and blues–based rock style of the fifties was Richard Penniman. Born in Macon, Georgia, he began performing at a fairly young age and became known as

Little Richard and his band during the fifties

Little Richard (born in 1932). Little Richard first learned to play the piano at his church, where he also sang gospel music and learned to use such gospel characteristics as vocal slides and embellishments (gospel vocal techniques are discussed further in Chapter 3). These influences remained with him and were used along with the shrieks and moans of his later jump-blues-influenced rock style.

Little Richard wrote (or co-wrote), played piano, and sang on his recordings, which included "Tutti-Frutti," "Long Tall Sally," and "Good Golly, Miss Molly." His piano playing usually had a boogie-woogie bass with chords pounded out above it, but it was the fast tempos and high energy level that made Little Richard's style stand out from that of other jump blues musicians. Sex was his favorite textual subject, and he teased his audiences with his androgynous hairstyle and heavy facial makeup while singing songs with sometimes shockingly graphic or suggestive lyrics. He recorded "Good Golly, Miss Molly" in 1957, and in that year, at the height of his success, Little Richard quit rock and roll to become a preacher. He appeared in England in 1962 on the same bill as the Beatles, who covered some of his hits with Paul McCartney imitating his dramatic vocal style, and in 1964 he attempted a comeback in America. After that, he continued to do occasional rock shows, but devoted most of his time to religious work. An analysis of Little Richard's recording of "Long Tall Sally" appears on page 61. "Long Tall Sally" was Little Richard's biggest hit, reaching number six on the pop charts despite the fact that it was banned in some cities. It was number one for eight weeks on the rhythm and blues charts.

The use of **stop time** in the instrumental parts of "Long Tall Sally" gave the melody a rhythmic punch that has often been used in the blues, rhythm and blues, and blues-based rock music. As is clear in Little Richard's recording, stop time is different from the instrumental breaks in John Lee Hooker's "Boom Boom," discussed earlier, and in Chuck Berry's "School Day," because stop time is a break in which the instruments occasionally reenter with a short chord or note to punctuate the rhythm of the vocal line.

> "You know I used to play piano for the church. You know that spiritual, 'Give Me That Old Time Religion'. . . . I put a little 'thing' in it. . . . I would hear Fats Domino, Chuck Berry, the Clovers, the Drifters, Muddy Waters, Howlin' Wolf, John Lee Hooker, Elmore James, and I admired them, but I always had my little thing I wanted to let the world hear."
>
> –Little Richard

After years of vacillating between rock and religion, Little Richard returned to rock recording in 1986 with a new style he called "message music." The music to such message songs as "Great Gosh Almighty" (1986) still maintained the energy of Little Richard's fifties rock style, but he abandoned his androgynous image for that of a dancing preacher. This return to performing included television commercials and acting roles in several movies, including *Down and Out in Beverly Hills*. Little Richard continues to perform and is often heard both singing and sometimes preaching at charity and other events.

Summary

The beginnings of rock music in blues and rhythm and blues are clear, but exactly which recordings are exclusively in those styles and which are early rock is not. Many recordings of blues and rhythm and blues of the forties are often considered to be rock. The name *rock and roll* was first used to identify rhythm and blues. By the fifties, particular rock styles emerged that were clearly not exclusively rhythm and blues but were something new. That new

Listening Guide

"Long Tall Sally"
as recorded by Little Richard (1956)

Tempo: The tempo is about 176 beats per minute, with four beats per bar.

Form: The musical form of the twelve-bar blues is followed, but, as was generally the case with blues recordings made by rock musicians, the text does not repeat the A section of the poetic form.

The recording has eight full choruses of the blues form.

Features: The piano plays a shuffle beat rhythmic pattern.

The first, second, sixth, and seventh choruses begin with a four-bar instrumental device called stop time. These are not complete breaks for the instruments;

rather, the instruments play a single chord on the first beat of each of the first three bars, and then break for the rest of those bars and the entire fourth bar so the vocal line can be heard alone.

The third, fourth, and fifth choruses are strictly instrumental, with a tenor saxophonist playing an improvised solo employing a "growl" in his tone, effectively imitating Little Richard's rough vocal style.

The eighth chorus is sung and does not use the stop time instrumental beginning.

Lyrics: The singer has caught Uncle John with a loose woman and hopes to have a chance with that woman himself that night.

Billboard pop charts: number six; *Billboard* rhythm and blues charts: number one for eight weeks; British hit singles: number three

music included blues songs that were covered by country musicians such as Bill Haley, Elvis Presley, Buddy Holly, and others. It also included the blues, rhythm and blues, and gospel-based music by such African American artists as Fats Domino, Chuck Berry, and Little Richard, all of whom added country or other influences to their music to make it part of this new sound. In whatever way we want to categorize this rock music of the fifties, it is the music on which the rest of the history of rock music is based.

discussion questions

In what ways were the music and images of these performers rebellious for their time? What would those same performers have to do to maintain their rebellious reputations today? Does Elvis Presley deserve the title "King of Rock and Roll"? What about Bill Haley or Chuck Berry? How did the race of performers affect their popularity, or did race matter to most fans?

The NINETEEN SIXTIES

"We stand today on the edge of a new frontier—the frontier of the 1960s, a frontier of unknown opportunities and perils, a frontier of unfulfilled hopes and threats."

–President John F. Kennedy (1960)

"I draw the line in the dust and toss the gauntlet before the feet of tyranny and I say segregation now, segregation tomorrow, segregation forever."

–Alabama Governor George Wallace (1963)

"The basic heavy beat of the Negroes . . . brings out animalism and vulgarity."

–White Citizens' Council of Birmingham, Alabama

"If they make the Ku Klux Klan nonviolent, I'll be nonviolent. If they make the White Citizens' Council nonviolent, I'll be nonviolent. But as long as you've got somebody else not being nonviolent, I don't want anybody coming to me talking any nonviolent talk."

–Malcolm X (1964)

"I have a dream that my four little children will one day live in a nation where they will not be judged by the color of their skin but by the content of their character."

–Dr. Martin Luther King Jr.

"We demand that no more American youth be sent to fight in a war that is helping neither them nor the Vietnamese people. We have learned lessons from Nazi Germany and will not go along with the aggressive war-making policies of any government, even if it happens to be our own."

–Fifth Avenue Vietnam Peace Parade Committee

"If we ever let the Communists win this war, we are in great danger of fighting for the rest of our lives and losing a million kids."

–Bob Hope on the Vietnam War

The Decade of the Sixties

In many ways, the sixties began with a wave of optimism. The newly elected president, John F. Kennedy (1917–1963), was younger than previous presidents, and many Americans saw him as having an energetic and positive approach to leading the United States ahead of the Soviet Union in both the "missile gap" (there was great fear that the Soviets had more missiles than the United States) and the "space race." He spoke of the cold war as a "long, twilight struggle" for the continued existence of liberty. He said that the United States should "go anywhere" and "pay any price" to win the struggle. One of Kennedy's major goals was putting a man on the moon by the end of the decade. The Soviet Union and the United States were neck and neck in space successes, which made for another serious competition between the two world powers. Some of the most positive news reports of the decade were about accomplishments in space, and, of course, Kennedy's dream of landing on the moon was fulfilled in 1969.

Despite the strong rhetoric, Kennedy had major problems in some of the ways he handled the continuing fight against communism. In 1961, he authorized about

1,500 Cuban Americans to invade Cuba in an attempt to overthrow Fidel Castro's government in what was called the Bay of Pigs invasion. The promised air cover did not show up, and the attempt failed, leaving the U.S. invaders to be killed or taken captive. In the Cuban missile crisis, Kennedy was successful in convincing the Soviets to remove their missiles from Cuba, but the world was moved closer than ever to full-scale nuclear war during the negotiations. Kennedy ended up having only one thousand days in office, not nearly enough to accomplish his primary goals. His assassination in 1963 shocked the world. It also stirred up a controversy about who might have been behind it, and that controversy is still not settled in some people's minds.

White resistance to African American efforts toward increased civil rights provided an undercurrent of protest to the early sixties wave of optimism. Racial segregation was still the norm in many parts of the country. In Greensboro, North Carolina, in 1960, four male African American college students sat down at a lunch counter at an F. W. Woolworth store frequented by whites and ordered coffee. When they were denied service, they got five friends to join them in attempting to order coffee the next day, and more joined them in each day following. Within two weeks, there were groups of African Americans all over the country attempting to order things, check into segregated motels, swim at restricted beaches, and shop at places that had previously not served them. This nonviolent form of protest in which the protesters remained polite and law abiding while getting in the way of business by their sheer numbers was called a "sit-in" and became a popular type of protest for the civil rights movement and other causes, such as the one against U.S. involvement in Vietnam.

The peaceful sit-ins were followed by violent activities as well, however, and they lasted through much of the decade. There were large-scale riots in fifty-eight cities between 1964 and 1967. Deaths and serious injuries resulted. The most serious of the riots were in the Watts area of Los Angeles, California; Newark, New Jersey; and Detroit, Michigan. Dr. Martin Luther King did everything he could to keep the violence at bay while also advocating peaceful demonstrations. By contrast, Malcolm X spoke to the Militant Labor Forum in 1964, saying, "It was stones yesterday, Molotov cocktails today; it will be hand grenades tomorrow and whatever else is available the next day. You should not feel that I am inciting someone to violence. I'm only warning of a powder keg situation. You can take it or leave it." Both Dr. King and Malcolm X were important images to African Americans, and their assassinations, Malcolm X in 1965 and Dr. King in 1968, were followed by further violent reactions in some places.

Alongside the violence and frustrations, the civil rights movement obtained a number of successes on the legislative front. In 1964, Congress passed the Twenty-Fourth Amendment to the Constitution, which outlawed the poll taxes that had kept many African Americans from voting in some places. It also passed the Civil Rights Act of 1964, which forbade discrimination in most public places. The Economic Opportunity Act allowed for equal access to public programs such as Head Start and work-study financial aid programs. In 1965, Dr. Martin Luther King led a voting rights march from Selma to Montgomery, Alabama, which culminated in the passage of the Voting Rights Act. It expanded registration for African American voters and set up federal offices to prevent abuses. In 1967, Thurgood Marshall became the first African American to be appointed to the U.S. Supreme Court. The 1968 Housing Act outlawed discrimination in the sale, rental, or leasing of homes. Throughout the sixties African Americans were elected or appointed to other important offices such as state senates, state governorships, and several federal offices. Their numbers were few compared to the large majority of white citizens holding those jobs, but at least there was the beginning of some African American representation in government.

The sixties were a period of controversy, but the Vietnam War was probably the most controversial subject of all. In past wars there had been clear-cut goals, and it was obvious to all who was on what side. Neither was the case in Vietnam. South Vietnam had gained its independence from France in 1954. U.S. presidents Truman and Eisenhower had both promised to prevent the country from being taken over by the communists in the north and sent in military advisers to oversee the situation and support the promise. President Kennedy sent 16,000 more, giving them orders to train the South Vietnamese to defend themselves. As early as 1961, the elite fighting force the Green Berets was part of the training corps. When it became clear that the South Vietnamese military was not going to be able to fight off the North Vietnamese Army by themselves, Kennedy began to allow U.S. troops to take part in some of the fighting. At that time in the early sixties, the general public opinion about the U.S. presence in the region was positive because fighting off communism was thought to be a good thing. After Kennedy's assassination, President Lyndon Johnson decided to help further stabilize the South Vietnam government by sending more troops and bombing specific targets in North Vietnam. According to a Harris poll in 1964, 85 percent of the nation approved of the bombing. More and more troops were sent in, and the U.S. casualties were getting higher and higher. By 1966, many returning veterans had reported disturbing news about the destruction that the U.S. presence was causing in small Vietnamese villages; the amount of U.S. aid that was going to the black market instead of doing any good for the people; and the ease with which South Vietnamese citizens avoided their own draft with money or by deserting while Americans were dying for their cause. It also became fairly well known that American soldiers were commonly returning from Vietnam with drug problems. Some U.S. veterans reported that they were not allowed to really fight to win, and the restrictions on what they could do caused them to be more targets than soldiers. Domestic responses to the reports led to widespread antiwar demonstrations, particularly on college campuses, and finding ways to avoid the draft developed into an art form. Some young draftees left the country instead of going to Vietnam. The U.S. reason for being there was too unclear, and the casualty rate was so high that many young men saw their entrance into the military as a death sentence.

On the other hand, many Americans continued to support U.S. involvement in Vietnam. Seeing communism as a great threat, many felt that fighting a war to prevent its spread was worth whatever the cost. In any event, the war dragged on, and it continued after the election of Richard M. Nixon in 1968. It was not until 1975 that the U.S. Senate cut off funds to fight the war, and Saigon finally fell. The Vietnam War split the country apart, and it was one that the United States lost. One of the saddest aspects of it was the lack of support the Vietnam veterans received when they returned home.

The decade of the sixties was a time for changes beyond the battles against racism and communism. Biologist Rachel Carson's book *Silent Spring* (1962) warned of the dangers of pesticides such as DDT, and its use was eventually banned or limited as a result. The women's liberation movement was launched with much support after the publication of Betty Friedan's book *The Feminine Mystique* (1963). The book attacked the long-standing idea that women always had to be the homemakers while their husbands could have careers. One important issue was that many companies tended to hire men instead of women who were equally or more competent because they thought that men needed to support their families and women who worked were only adding fat to the family income. It was also common for men to be paid more than women for doing the same work.

All of these varying attitudes had slogans attached to them, and cars in the sixties had more bumper stickers than ever before or since. Some popular ones were "We Shall Overcome," "Black Is Beautiful," "Suppose They Gave a War and Nobody Came," "Make Love Not War," "Support Our Boys in Vietnam," "The U.S., Love It or Leave It," and "Ban the Bra." The hippie movement included young people who wanted to drop out of society and build their own new culture. Psychedelic drugs and extremely casual dress, with Native American–type moccasins, headbands, and lots of beads, became symbolic of the counterculture. The drug-related deaths of such rock stars as Jimi Hendrix (1970), Janis Joplin (1970), and Jim Morrison (1971), as well as the murder at the Rolling Stones' Altamont festival, took much of the optimism out of that movement. For many social commentators, the seventies consolidated the various trends of the sixties.

Chronology Chart

	Historical Events	Happenings in Rock Music
1960	First use of satellite for TV transmission. Sit-ins to protest Woolworth store's refusal to serve African American students in Greensboro, NC. U.S. U-2 reconnaissance plane is shot down in Soviet Union.	Federal Bribery Act outlaws payola to DJs. Elvis Presley out of army. Gene Vincent is injured. Twist and other dance crazes are popularized. Beatles perform in Hamburg. Folk singers popular in coffee houses. *Bye Bye Birdie* first Broadway musical to feature rock music. Motown contracts Stevie Wonder. Eddie Cochran dies.
1961	Kennedy becomes president. Bay of Pigs intervention in Cuba. Amnesty International forms in U.K. Berlin Wall is built. Increase in U.S. military units in South Vietnam.	Surf rock popular on West Coast. Protosoul music by Ray Charles, Sam Cooke, and Motown singers widely popular. Beatles popular at Cavern Club in Liverpool. Bob Dylan performs in New York. Chuck Berry is jailed. Stereo radio is authorized for FM stations.
1962	Cuban missile crisis. U.S. puts astronauts into orbit. First African American student is admitted to University of Mississippi after 3,000 troops stop riots. Rachel Carson's *Silent Spring* inspires environmental studies.	Blues revival bands form in U.K. and U.S. Beatles' first records hit U.K. charts. Bob Dylan releases his first album. Many folksingers change from traditional folk music to protest songs. Folk show *Hootenanny* on ABC TV.
1963	Supreme Court requires counsel for criminal defendants and outlaws use of illegally acquired evidence in courts. Civil rights demonstrations in Birmingham, AL. M. L. King's "I have a dream" speech in Washington, D.C. Kennedy is assassinated. Johnson becomes president.	Nationwide popularity of surf music and Spector's wall of sound. Girl groups popular. Dylan and Baez at Newport Folk Festival. Protest singers at folk coffeehouses. Protopunk "Louie Louie" is released. British press report on "Beatlemania." First cassette tape recorders are sold. Elmore James dies.
1964	Escalation of fighting in Vietnam. Civil Rights Act bans discrimination in voting, jobs, public accommodations, etc. U.S. post office assigns zip codes. M. L. King is awarded Nobel Peace Prize. Warren Commission concludes Lee Harvey Oswald was responsible for Kennedy assassination.	Beginning of Beatlemania in U.S. and British invasion. BMI rejects the Who demos. James Brown begins funk. Kinks popularize guitar distortion, and Beatles use feedback. Moog synthesizer is developed. Jim Reeves and Sam Cooke die.
1965	First walk in space. Johnson orders more bombing of North Vietnam. Civil rights march from Selma to Montgomery, AL. Voting Rights Act passes. Thirty-four die in Watts riot in Los Angeles. Immigration national origins quota system is abolished. Malcolm X assassinated.	Bob Dylan and the Byrds begin folk-rock. Electric twelve-string guitar popular folk-rock instrument. Jefferson Airplane and the Grateful Dead are featured at psychedelic dance halls in San Francisco. Ken Kesey's Acid Test concerts popular. Fuzztone distortion control and first transistor microphones are marketed. Sonny Boy Williamson and Alan Freed die.

1966   U.S.S.R. and U.S. land unmanned crafts on moon. U.S. forces fire into Cambodia and bomb Hanoi. Medicare coverage put into effect. Law against use of LSD passes.

Beach Boys release concept album *Pet Sounds.* Last public Beatles concert. Beatles "Rain" first record to use reverse tape. Garage bands popularize protopunk rebellion. Many radio and TV stations ban drug songs. Light shows are popularized in psychedelic night clubs. Jan Berry and Bob Dylan in serious accidents.

1967   Large antiwar demonstrations in Washington, D.C., New York, and San Francisco. Race riots in Cleveland, Newark, and Detroit. Marshall becomes first African American on U.S. Supreme Court. First human heart transplant operation (in Cape Town, South Africa). Three U.S. astronauts die aboard Apollo 1 craft still on launching pad. Abortions are legalized in Colorado. Microwave ovens are marketed for home use. First 911 emergency phone system is established in New York.

Human Be-In "happening" in San Francisco. FM radio allows for album-oriented rock programming. With release of Beatles' *Sgt. Pepper,* albums begin to take over the popularity of singles. Monaural records beginning to be phased out. Monterey International Pop Festival; the Who and Jimi Hendrix destroy equipment on stage. Proto–heavy metal by Hendrix and Cream. Brian Epstein, Woody Guthrie, and Otis Redding die.

1968   North Koreans seize *USS Pueblo* and crew. Vietnam peace talks begin. Martin Luther King and Robert Kennedy are assassinated. Large outdoor rock festivals popular. Riots at Democratic convention in Chicago. First African American woman is elected to Congress.

Reggae develops from ska in Jamaica. James Brown records "Say It Loud, I'm Black and I'm Proud." Electric Flag records jazz-rock. Dylan and others begin country-rock style. "Bubblegum" music marketed for young and preteens. Moody Blues record with orchestra to begin art rock in U.K. Ralph Nader warns that loud rock music impairs hearing. Iron Butterfly popularizes heavy metal in U.S. Little Walter and Frankie Lyman die.

1969   Nixon becomes president. American lands on the moon. U.S. military to Cambodia. Vietnam peace talks expand; 250,000 march in Washington, D.C., to protest Vietnam War. My Lai massacre of civilians is reported. Manson family murders.

Woodstock and Altamont Festivals. Miles Davis records in fusion style. Elvis Presley, Chuck Berry, the Everly Brothers, Fats Domino, Little Richard, and Jerry Lee Lewis back touring after breaks. The Who performs *Tommy.* John Lennon/Yoko Ono "bed in" for peace. Jim Morrison is charged with lewd behavior in Miami. Brian Jones and Nat King Cole die.

Teen-Styled Rock Music

"Phil Spector, he was everything. There was nothing to compare. He was it. The biggest inspiration in my whole life."

—BRIAN WILSON

By 1960, many of the strongest performers of the energetic rock music of the midfifties had stopped performing and therefore provided no competition for the new pop-rock style that emerged between 1957 and 1960. Carl Perkins remained out of music after the 1956 car accident in which he was severely injured and both his brother and his manager were killed; Little Richard left the music scene to enter the ministry; Jerry Lee Lewis's music was banned because of public disapproval over his illegal marriage to his young cousin; Elvis Presley was serving in the army; Chuck Berry was on trial for a Mann Act violation (taking a woman across state lines for immoral purposes) and later went to prison; Buddy Holly, the Big Bopper, and Ritchie Valens all died in a plane crash in 1959; and Eddie Cochran was killed in the same automobile accident that badly injured Gene Vincent in 1960. It is impossible to say what might have happened had all these performers lived or remained in the music business, but their absence certainly had some effect on the renewed popularity of light, pop-styled music geared to young teens.

It must be noted that at least some of these performers had sensed that pop was an important wave of the future because they had begun to change their styles to fit the pop trend before their careers broke off. Presley had signed with RCA and recorded more pop-styled music than rockabilly, and both Buddy Holly and Eddie Cochran had shifted to a pop style in their last-recorded songs, "It Doesn't Matter Anymore" (Holly in 1959) and "Three Steps to Heaven" (Cochran in 1960). Rockabilly artists Gene Vincent and Ronnie Hawkins did not want to change to this new style and thus left the United States to perform in England and Canada, where rockabilly was still popular.

The Payola Scandal

Payola, or paying for airplay or other publicity, has existed in some form or other since Civil War times. Then, popular vaudeville performers would agree to sing a particular song at all of their shows in return for the reproduction of their photograph on the sheet music for the song. By that arrangement, the songwriter, the publisher, and the performer all benefited when the music for the song sold to the general public. By the late fifties, payola was primarily thought of as payments to encourage programmers to give more radio or television airtime to particular songs. That type of payola was somewhat unfair in that money rather than an honest evaluation of quality or potential popularity was the deciding factor in music that was played. In some cases, there was little chance to get a song played without the payola. Payola was not illegal until after the payola scandal of the late fifties, but it was considered to be a corruption of ethics.

Small, independent record companies benefited from payola by being able to pay for a record's airplay in one town and then make a profit from sales of the record. That money would allow them to move on to other towns

and do the same thing. As a song was heard in more and more places, it had a better chance of really becoming a hit. A hit record benefited the record company, the performer, and the songwriter.

The songwriters were behind much of the scandal of the late fifties; at least it was their representatives who caused the investigation that brought it about. The Copyright Act of 1909 outlined three ways for songwriters to get paid for their work: (1) sheet music sales—the writer usually received a certain percentage of what the publisher made for sale of the music; (2) mechanical fees, which was a small amount of money for each copy of a piano roll or recording of their song that sold; and (3) public performance fees, which involved some amount of money for performances of the song. The publisher of the sheet music paid the songwriter for the sale of sheet music, the company that made the roll or recording paid the writer the mechanical fees, and songwriter organizations formed to collect fees for performances. These different ways of being paid for use of their songs allowed songwriters to receive a good income when songs that they wrote became popular and were often performed.

The American Society of Composers, Authors, and Publishers (ASCAP) was formed in 1914 to collect performance fees and distribute them to their writer and publisher members. ASCAP did not collect the fees from the performers themselves, but it charged annual fees to performance venues such as concert halls, cabaret or dance clubs, restaurants, or other places that had music played for the public. ASCAP devised complicated procedures to estimate which of its members' songs were being played and about how often, and then it paid its members the appropriate percentage of the fees it collected from the venues.

ASCAP was fairly particular about what songwriters it allowed to join and generally excluded blues, rhythm and blues, country, and rock musicians. Because musicians in those styles tended to either write their own or play one another's music, they had no need for the writers in ASCAP, and the tremendous popularity of their songs cut into ASCAP members' overall profits. Broadcast Music, Incorporated (BMI) was formed in 1940 by members of the National Association of Broadcasters who resisted ASCAP's licensing terms and fees for airplay as well as ASCAP's general monopoly on the business. Most rock writers in the fifties and early sixties joined BMI. With the growing popularity of rock music, ASCAP came to resent the competition from BMI and searched for ways to discredit the music it handled. A Special Committee on Legislative Oversight had been formed to investigate accusations of cheating on quiz shows, and in 1958 ASCAP requested that the committee also look into the practice of bribing disc jockeys for airplay. The investigations became known as the payola scandal. The result was that many small record companies that had depended on payola to get any airplay for their recordings went out of business.

Disc jockey **Alan Freed** (1921–1965) fought long and hard against racism by giving music by African American artists as much airplay and performance opportunity as he could, but he had also accepted much payola, and his career sank under investigation. When he was questioned by the committee, Freed had already moved from radio to his own ABC television show called *Dance Party*, which showcased rhythm and blues and rock music. ABC asked Freed to deny all charges made by the committee, but such obvious cases as his name being alongside that of Chuck Berry as a songwriter of Berry's hit "Maybellene" (1955) and others made it obvious that he was guilty and he pled accordingly. Freed lost his television show and was found guilty not only of bribery but also income tax evasion. His alcohol problem worsened, and he died in 1965.

Another important disc jockey who was investigated in the scandal was able to avoid ruin. **Dick Clark** (born in 1929) was the host of the teen dance show *American Bandstand*. The show had been on the air in Philadelphia since 1952 with another host, Bob Horn. Clark replaced Horn in 1956, just in time for the show's syndication to sixty-seven TV stations nationwide. The show brought Philadelphia pop music and dance styles to teenagers all over the country.

American Bandstand did occasionally feature performances by rockabilly and rhythm and blues artists, but it more often spotlighted clean-cut, pop-styled white teen idols such as Pat Boone, Paul Anka, Frankie Avalon, Connie Francis, Fabian, Bobby Rydell, Brenda Lee, and Bobby Vee. The leather-jacketed outfits and rebellious messages of the rockabilly singers who copied the image of Marlon Brando in *The Wild One* had no place on the program. Although *American Bandstand* changed its dress code many times over the years, it always maintained a clean and conservative image. At a time when many leaders of the entertainment industry saw rock music as a threat to the moral base of American society, only shows like *American Bandstand,* with its image of clean-cut kids having fun, were allowed to continue.

Dick Clark did have financial interests in some of the records he promoted on his show and was investigated for payola practices, but he was exonerated when his attorneys showed that he also promoted records in which he had no financial interest. He did have to sell his interests in the music business but was able to continue with the show. One major reason he could continue was that his show was considered by many people in the music industry to be a positive influence on teens, whereas the music that Alan Freed played was considered a corrupting influence.

Teen Idol Pop

American Bandstand served to bring rock music, dancers, and performers to teenage fans, but it was an afternoon program. Ed Sullivan, who had a very popular Sunday evening television variety program designed for family entertainment, realized that he would have to have rock performers on his show in order to attract the teenage part of the family audience. By 1965, in addition to the occasional rock performances on *The Ed Sullivan Show,* ABC TV added a new prime-time rock show called *Shindig* and NBC TV added *Hullabaloo.* In those pre-video and pre-MTV days, these programs served to bring live rock and roll performances into American homes to eager teenage fans.

Most of the singers who became known as "teen idols," particularly the male ones, sang in a style reminiscent of the ballad crooners of the twenties through the forties, whose stars included Perry Como and Bing Crosby. **Pat Boone** (born in 1934) was one of those who became popular singing pop ballads as well as covers of blues or

Pat Boone

commercial audience, and it represented a direction in which rock continued to move for the rest of the decade and well into the sixties. Boone's version of "Tutti-Frutti" can be considered rock, then, but only because of its historical context. The same can be said for much of the pop-rock of the same period.

> **"I had to change some words because they seemed too raw for me."**
>
> —Pat Boone, about his lyrics to "Tutti-Frutti"

> **"The white kids didn't want their mamma to know I was in the house. They'd put Pat on the bed and put me in the drawer."**
>
> —Little Richard, about his and Pat Boone's recordings of "Tutti-Frutti"

The movie and television industry supported the growth in popularity of the clean teen idol image. Pat Boone played teenage roles in the movies *April Love* (1957) and *Journey to the Center of the Earth* (1959). After *American Bandstand* was telecast nationwide and introduced Philadelphia-based teen idols Frankie Avalon (Francis Avallone, born in 1940), Fabian (Fabian Forte, born in 1943), and Bobby Rydell (Bobby Ridarelli, born in 1942) to teenage rock fans, those singers were further popularized by such movies as *Beach Blanket Bingo,* starring Frankie Avalon and Annette Funicello (a former Mouseketeer on *The Mickey Mouse Club*), and many others. Ricky Nelson (1940–1985) was more important to rock music for his rockabilly recordings, but he did have a teen idol image that his appearances on his parents' television show, *The Adventures of Ozzie and Harriet,* introduced to fans. Two of the most successful female singers of the teen idol era were Connie Francis (Concetta Franconero, born in 1938) and Brenda Lee (Brenda Mae Tarpley, born in 1944).

rhythm and blues songs. He made different changes than the rockabilly singers had when he covered the blues because he was not after the energy of rockabilly. His recordings fit his own clean-cut, boy-next-door image. While Carl Perkins and Elvis Presley were tough and threatening to anyone who would dare to step on their "blue suede shoes," Pat Boone wore clean, white buck shoes, which became his trademark. A comparison of Pat Boone's recording of "Tutti-Frutti" with the original one by Little Richard appears on page 72. Little Richard's recording hit number seventeen on the pop charts and number two on the rhythm and blues ones. The recording by Pat Boone made number twelve on the pop charts.

It is obvious throughout Pat Boone's recording that he was trying to imitate Little Richard's rhythmic singing style and vocal inflections, but without capturing Richard's growling tone quality and delivery. Jazz infuences, in the ways the instruments were played in Richard's version, were not used in Boone's recording, with the exception of the tenor saxophone solo, which adds a jazz touch to what is otherwise a pop form of the blues. Many rock fans would argue, and rightfully so, that Boone was not a rock singer at all. Yet when one looks at the many different forms of music that were considered rock in the fifties, it is clear that Boone's version of "Tutti-Frutti" was well within the pop style favored by the white

Most of the teen idol singers were successful more for their visual appeal and in-group identification than for their musical talents. Their natural, though untrained, voices captured the youthful enthusiasm that the style required. On television, in movies, and even in "live" performances, they usually synchronized their lip movements to their recordings (known as lip-syncing) instead of actually singing live. Rarely did any of the singers play musical instruments, other than some occasional simple chording on guitar, and they generally were not songwriters. Paul

Listening Guide

	"Tutti-Frutti" as recorded by Little Richard (1955)	*"Tutti-Frutti"* as recorded by Pat Boone (1956)
Tempo:	The tempo is about 172 beats per minute, with four beats per bar.	The tempo is roughly 176 beats per minute, slightly faster than Little Richard's recording.
Form:	Both the music and the text follow the classic twelve-bar blues form. The recording has eight choruses; the sixth chorus is instrumental, with a tenor saxophone playing the melody, imitating Little Richard's rough vocal inflections.	Both the music and the text follow the classic twelve-bar blues form. The recording has eight choruses; the sixth chorus is instrumental, with a tenor saxophone playing the melody, in an improvised bebop-jazz style.
	The last four-bar phrases of the second, fourth, and eighth choruses are vocal, with stop-time instrumental breaks.	The last four-bar phrases of the second, fourth, and eighth choruses are vocal, with stop-time instrumental breaks.
Features:	Little Richard sings a two-bar introduction of nonsense syllables, giving the listener a taste of his no-holds-barred vocal style, which was often punctuated by octave-leap "oohs."	The introduction imitates Little Richard's, but Boone's voice has a smoother, less rhythmic, more controlled, and "polite-sounding" quality compared to Little Richard's.
	The rhythm section includes piano, presumably played by Little Richard, using even beat subdivisions to offset the uneven divisions of the basic beat, a jazz-style walking bass, and rhythmic punctuation by saxophones.	The rhythm section includes piano, which is most obvious during the instrumental chorus, and a backup vocal group sings "ahs." Beat subdivisions are uneven throughout.
	The drummer gives the backbeat a strong accent.	The backbeat is present, but less obvious than in Little Richard's recording.
Lyrics:	In verses two, four, and eight, Little Richard sings about rocking with Sue (rocking was slang for sexual activity). He also indicates that Daisy knows how to love him too, hinting that he may not be true to Sue.	In verses two, four, and eight, Boone has removed the sexual references. He avoids the reference to rocking, and instead of indicating that he has two girlfriends, he admits that Daisy is tempting to him, but that he remains true to Sue.

Billboard pop charts: number seventeen; *Billboard* rhythm and blues charts: number two for six weeks; British hit singles: number twenty-nine

Billboard pop charts: number twelve

Anka (born in 1941) was the exception. He wrote many of his own hits, and his songs became hits for other artists as well, including "It Doesn't Matter Anymore," which was a hit for Buddy Holly in 1959, "My Way" (1959) for Frank Sinatra, and "She's a Lady" (1971) for Tom Jones. He also composed the theme music for Johnny Carson's *Tonight Show* and several movie soundtracks.

Teen idol song themes were as youthful and wholesome as the performers' images. The delicate balance between happiness and disappointment in puppy love romances and dreams about finding the perfect mate predominated. A few examples are Frankie Avalon's "Venus" (1959), Connie Francis's "Where the Boys Are" (1961), and Paul Anka's "Puppy Love" (1960). Other concerns of young teens were expressed through such songs as Bobby Rydell's "Swingin' School" (1960), but songs about love and temporarily broken hearts prevailed. A listening guide to Frankie Avalon's "Venus" appears below.

Because it featured teen dancers, *American Bandstand* started or spread the popularity of many dance crazes of the late fifties and early sixties. During the fifties, the bop was danced to Gene Vincent's "Be-Bop-a-Lula" (1956) and "Dance to the Bop" (1958), as well as "At the Hop" (1957) by Danny and the Juniors. Dances that were basically variations on the bop assumed animal names, like the Pony, the Chicken, and the Monkey. The Dog and the Alligator were also popular variations on the bop, but they were a bit suggestive and, therefore, not allowed on *American Bandstand.*

Frankie Avalon (1960)

In 1960, a young performer from Philadelphia, Ernest Evans, covered a song called "The Twist," by blues singer Hank Ballard. In search of a stage name, Evans decided on **Chubby Checker** (born in 1941), a not-so-subtle variation on Fats Domino's name. The popularity of the Twist as a dance resulted in more than just a hit record for Checker; it started a craze that continued for the next few years, with more Twist recordings made by Checker and other performers, including the Isley Brothers and Sam

Listening Guide

"Venus"
as recorded by Frankie Avalon (1959)

Tempo:	The tempo is approximately 114 beats per minute, with four beats in each bar.
Form:	The form is based on eight-bar sections. The first eight bars is made up of four bars of a chorus singing "oohs," and then four bars of the singer calling on the goddess Venus. That introduction is followed by two eight-bar verses, one eight-bar refrain, another eight-bar verse, a repetition of the refrain, repetitions of the third verse and the refrain, another eight bars asking Venus to grant

the wish, and a final two bars still calling on Venus.

Features:	The production is very full sounding, including orchestra and chorus with drums. The mood is very gentle and the singer very sincere.
Lyrics:	The singer is so desperate for romance that he prays to the Roman goddess of love for a girlfriend, but he is also rather choosy and details his specifications.

Billboard pop charts: number one for five weeks; British hit singles: number sixteen

Cooke. Other dances popularized by Chubby Checker's songs included the Pony, the Fly, and the Limbo.

When we consider the history of American popular music in the twentieth century, we must include Latin music. In general, Latin rhythms and other Latin musical characteristics have had a much stronger influence on jazz than on rock music, but there certainly have been instances of Latin rock hits. One such case was teen idol **Ritchie Valens**'s (Richard Valenzuela, 1941–1959) hit based on a traditional Mexican dance song, "La Bamba" (1959).

Brill Building Pop

Because pop performers have seldom been songwriters, the burst of popularity of the style created a need for musicians who specialized in songwriting. Many pop-styled hits of the period between 1959 and 1963 were written and published in the Brill Building, located at 1619 Broadway in New York City, or across the street at the headquarters of Al Nevins and Don Kirshner's Aldon Music Company. Influences of gospel, doo-wop, and teen idol music were present in the music produced by these New York–based songwriters. Most of the writers worked in teams, the most famous of which were Howard Green-field and Neil Sedaka, Barry Mann and Cynthia Weil, Doc Pomus and Mort Shuman, Gerry Goffin and Carole King, Jerry Leiber and Mike Stoller, and Jeff Barry and Ellie Greenwich. Sedaka, Mann, and King doubled as performers and sang on the recordings of some of their own hits. Writer/producer George "Shadow" Morton worked with Barry and Greenwich to create short storyline songs like "Remember (Walkin' in the Sand)" and "Leader of the Pack" (both sung by the Shangri-Las in 1964), which were unusual for pop music.

Girl groups such as the Andrews Sisters had been popular from the midtwenties into the fifties and early sixties. They primarily sang swing jazz and then added other styles, including gospel, to their repertoire. In popular music of the early sixties, women still tended to be singers rather than instrumentalists, and many trios or quartets of female singers became popular with teens at that time. Those singers were known as "girl groups." One girl group that placed twelve top ten hits on the pop charts between 1960 and 1963 and who actually did some songwriting—which was also unusual for pop singers of the era—was the Shirelles. The listening guide to their first number-one hit "Will You Love Me Tomorrow?" is on page 75 and serves as a good example of the Brill Building pop sound. Carole King, who remains one of the most successful female songwriters in rock music, and her then husband, Gerry Goffin, wrote the song for the Shirelles.

> "It definitely spoke for women, young women, all over who were wondering if they should 'do it' or not. Will you respect me in the morning? kind of attitude was prevalent in that time."
>
> –Carole King, about the lyrics to "Will You Love Me Tomorrow?"

The Shirelles (ca. 1960)

Listening Guide

"Will You Love Me Tomorrow?"
as recorded by the Shirelles
(1960)

Tempo: The tempo is approximately 138 beats per minute, with four beats in each bar.

Form: After a four-bar introduction, the song has five sixteen-bar periods, each of which is made up of two eight-bar phrases. The overall form of those periods is AABAA. Each A period ends with the question "Will you love me tomorrow?" The first phrase of the last A is instrumental. The ending fades during a final repetition of the title lyrics.

Features: Even beat subdivisions are maintained throughout the recording.

Shirley Alston's solo voice is backed by the rest of the Shirelles in a doo-wop style.

The backbeat is stressed through a drum rhythm with two eighth notes on each second beat and a single accent on each fourth beat through most of the recording.

An orchestral string section plays phrase-ending fills and the lead on the instrumental section.

Lyrics: The singer plans to have sex with her date and is unsure that the relationship will last beyond that night.

Billboard pop charts: number one for two weeks; *Billboard* rhythm and blues charts: number two for four weeks; British hit singles: number four

---

The song "Will You Love Me Tomorrow?" cut right to the heart of one of the most common problems felt by young women faced by the sexual double standard of the era. Another important writer/producer at the Brill Building, Phil Spector, contributed much to the popularity of girl groups during the early sixties.

Phil Spector's Wall of Sound

Many of the Brill Building writers were also competent producers, but few had production skills to compare with those of **Phil Spector** (born in 1940). Spector's productions had such a distinctive effect that his style became known as the *wall of sound.* The term *wall* was descriptive because he used so many instruments, and overdubbed and mixed them so thoroughly, that the result was a massive fortification of instrumental colors and timbres behind the vocals. He did not like to record in stereo because it separated some instruments from others. Spector's productions were generally thick and full, but when he did allow an individual instrument to stand out from the rest, the effect was very colorful, as in the Spanish flamenco-style guitar fills in the Crystals' recording of "Uptown" (1962). He incorporated the natural sound of rain in the background of the Ronettes' recording of "Walking in the Rain" (1964). A standard rock drum set was not enough for Spector's sound. He liked classical music, particularly that of nineteenth-century German romantic composer Richard Wagner, and imitated Wagner's coloristic use of percussion instruments such as chimes, castanets, triangles, timpani, and gongs by adding them to an already full sound. Spector's productions did not sound Wagnerian, but they had more orchestral fullness than earlier rock productions that had used only strings or brass sections. Spector considered his records symphonies for teens.

> **Those records had a Wagnerian power and intensity. Phil got so wrapped up in those recordings. Then everything got bigger, and bigger, and bigger until there was no more record.**
>
> –Brill Building songwriter Ellie Greenwich

Spector worked both in New York and in Los Angeles. He started his own company, Philles (Phil + Les) with Lester Sill, who handled the business arrangements while Spector maintained control of the music. Late in 1962, Sill sold his interest in the company and Spector assumed complete control. With his own company, Spector often contracted singers but

kept ownership of their stage or group names for himself. Because he had the singers under contract and owned the rights to their stage names, Spector could use any combination of singers he wanted and call them the Crystals or Bob B. Soxx and the Bluejeans (two of the group names he owned). He presented Darlene Love (Darlene Wright) with an unnamed backup group whose personnel could change from record to record. The one group he kept as a regular trio was the Ronettes, whose lead singer, Ronnie (Veronica Bennett), he married in 1967. A listening guide to "Be My Baby" by the Ronettes appears below.

Listening Guide

"Be My Baby"
as recorded by the Ronettes (1963)

Tempo: The tempo is approximately 132 beats per minute, with four beats in each bar.

Form: The form is based on eight- and sixteen-bar sections, with a four-bar introduction. The two verses are sixteen bars each and the refrains, during which the title text is repeated many times, are eight bars. There is an eight-bar instrumental section between the second and third repetitions of the refrains. The recording ends by fading out during the final refrain.

Features: The wall of sound background is created by recording and then overdubbing strings, guitars, several keyboards, brass instruments, saxophones, and a variety of percussion instruments. The three Ronettes do not sing in harmony together. Instead, the lead singer, Ronnie, sings the verses alone and the other two singers respond to her with repetitions of "Be My Baby" during the refrains.

The instrumental section has low strings playing the lead melody line.

There is a short break, punctuated by percussion instruments, between the third and fourth refrains.

Lyrics: The female singer promises her undying love and affection to her lover for all of eternity.

Billboard pop charts: number two; *Billboard* rhythm and blues charts: number four; British hit singles: number four.

Phil Spector maintained his reputation for quality, hit-making productions and was asked to sift through hours of tape made by the soon-to-disband Beatles, add backing filler, and produce their *Let It Be* album (recorded in 1969, released in 1970). Both George Harrison and John Lennon had him produce post-Beatles recordings for them, including Harrison's *All Things Must Pass* (1970) and *The Concert for Bangladesh* (1972) and Lennon's *Imagine* (1971). Spector attempted a comeback with productions for Cher and Dion in the midseventies, but he could not recapture his earlier successes. He produced the *End of the Century* album (1980) for the Ramones, giving it a style that made it strikingly different from any of the group's previous recordings. For Spector's wall of sound fans, the new sound represented a positive change for the Ramones, and the album sold well, but to most of the group's long-time fans it was a disaster. The future may see more revivals of earlier rock styles, but for the most part Phil Spector hit his peak of popularity during the pop-styled early sixties. The 1991 boxed set of Spector's work was entitled *Back to Mono* to emphasize the importance of monaural recording in his thick, wall of sound productions. Spector was sentenced to nineteen years to life in prison in 2009 for the shooting death of actress Lana Clarkson.

Influences on the Surf Sound

While pop-rock music from the East Coast was dominated by songs about puppy love and teen dances, West Coast musicians developed their own danceable style known as surf rock. Surf rock was a type of pop music different from that of New York and Philadelphia because its vocals were not based on the old crooner vocal tradition, and surf bands played their own instruments instead of using large studio orchestras. In some ways, in fact, surf bands represented a return to the older rock music played on guitars, bass, and drums, but the surf band image and sound was so light and pop oriented that it is still considered to be part of rock's more pop-oriented phase. Although vocals were an important element of the surf style, instrumental hits became more common in surf rock than in any style that preceded it. Saxophones and electric organs were often used, but the electric guitar was the most common lead instrument. The guitar style that became the foundation of much surf music was based on the styles of Duane Eddy, the Ventures, and Dick Dale.

> " Duane Eddy was the front guy, the first rock and roll guitar god. "
>
> –John Fogerty

Duane Eddy's (born in 1938) distinctive and influential guitar style (called *twangy guitar*) was achieved by plucking the strings of the guitar very close to the **bridge,** where the strings are attached to the body of the instrument. The strings are tightest at the bridge, and plucking them there results in a strong, nasal-sounding attack. Most of Eddy's recordings stressed the use of repetitious lead lines played on the guitar's bass strings, with *vibrato,* or pitch variation, and the studio- or amplifier-produced echo effects gave the guitar a sound that was constantly wavering. It may have been this wavering sound, reminiscent of the motion of water, that led the surf instrumental groups to incorporate it into their styles. Eddy's first hit, "Rebel-'Rouser" (1958), was very much influenced by the energy of gospel music; it used an instrumental form of call-and-response in which Eddy's lead guitar lines were answered by a saxophone. His second hit single, "Ramrod" (1958), was a blues, and "Forty Miles of Bad Road" (1959) had a standard pop-song form.

From Tacoma, Washington, the **Ventures** were among the most important of the early instrumental groups to become associated with the surf image, although they did not actually adopt that image until after other surf groups had copied them. The group consisted of two guitarists, an electric bassist, and a drummer. Duane Eddy's twangy guitar sound was a clear influence on their style. The Ventures became one of the few surf groups to maintain their following through the sixties and beyond; they had several surf instrumental hits and also recorded a version of the theme music for the television program *Hawaii Five-O* (1969). With the help of a large following in Japan, the Ventures were still together and popular when the surf sound experienced a revival in the United States in the early eighties.

The Surf Sound

Dick Dale (Richard Anthony Monsour, born in 1937) was given the title the King of Surf Guitar because he originated an impressive guitar style copied by many surf instrumental groups of the early sixties. From Balboa, California, Dick Dale and the Del-Tones started out using the twangy guitar style of Duane Eddy and the Rebels in such recordings as "Let's Go Trippin'" (1961), which was blues in form though not in style. In his version of the Greek melody "Misirlou" (1961), however, Dale developed a technique based on the tremolo playing used in Middle Eastern plucked-string instruments such as the bouzouki. **Tremolo,** in this case, refers to fast repetitions of a note. Like the Greek bouzouki players, Dale sustained notes by plucking a string up and down very fast with his guitar pick. While continuing that motion, he would slide the other hand up and down the fingerboard, achieving an impressive effect of

The Beach Boys (left to right):
Al Jardine, Carl Wilson,
Dennis Wilson, Brian Wilson,
and Mike Love

speed. To that, Dale added Eddy's twangy style to create a sound often copied by other surf guitarists of the era. The Beach Boys were among the first groups to popularize Dale's style nationally when they recorded cover versions of his hits on their early albums. Dale joined other aging pop artists of the early sixties, Frankie Avalon and Annette Funicello, in the movie *Back to the Beach* (1987), and his 1961 hit "Misirlou" was featured on the soundtrack of *Pulp Fiction* (1994).

Other instrumental surf rock groups that followed the styles of Duane Eddy, the Ventures, and Dick Dale included the Marketts, the Chantays, and the Surfaris. Their hits (not to be referred to as "songs," since there was no singing in them) were often given titles from surfing terminology: the Chantays' "Pipeline" (1963) represented the coiled form of a wave, and even fans who were "side-walk surfers" on skateboards knew what was meant by the Surfaris' "Wipe Out" (1963).

The **Beach Boys** were formed by three brothers, Brian (born in 1942), Carl (1946–1996), and Dennis Wilson (1944–1983), their cousin, Mike Love (born in 1941), and a neighbor, Alan Jardine (born in 1942), in Hawthorne, California. The Wilson brothers' father, Murry Wilson, managed them and, after the success of "Surfin'" (1961), he got them a contract with Capitol Records.

From the beginning of their career, the Beach Boys were more than just a surf rock group. Their guitarist, Carl Wilson, did use Duane Eddy's twangy guitar style and the tremolo style of Dick Dale in many of the group's instrumental recordings, but he also imitated the riff-based sound of Chuck Berry. The group's main writer and producer, Brian Wilson, had been a fan of the jazz vocal group the Four Freshmen and used their group vocal style

and harmonies in many of the Beach Boys' hits. As Wilson learned more about studio production techniques, he came very close to the wall of sound fullness of Phil Spector's productions. Through more than twenty years of recording and performing, the Beach Boys' music developed so far beyond their original surf image that their surf-oriented name came to have meaning only for those who knew their earlier history.

> " We heard 'Day by Day' and I said 'what's that, I love that sound.'. . . I learned everything, all my harmonies, I learned so much from them. "
>
> –Brian Wilson, on hearing the Four Freshmen's vocal harmonies for the first time

One of their early hits, "Surfin' U.S.A." (1963), had the same melody, chord progression, and form as Chuck Berry's hit "Sweet Little Sixteen" (1958), and, although Wilson first claimed writer's credit, probably really believing he had written it, eventually the credit and royalty income was given to Berry. The listening guide on page 79 compares essential musical elements of the two recordings.

A fun way to compare these two recordings and clearly see how closely they match is to sing one of Berry's antecedent phrases and follow it with one of the Beach Boys' consequent phrases, and then try the reverse order. Most who do this will arrive at the conclusion that Berry did, indeed, deserve credit for "Surfin' U.S.A." Wilson may have attempted to keep part of the credit for his new

Listening Guide

	"Sweet Little Sixteen" *as recorded by Chuck Berry (1958)*	"Surfin' U.S.A." *as recorded by the Beach Boys (1963)*
Tempo:	The tempo is about 176 beats per minute, with four beats per bar.	The tempo is about 164 beats per minutes, with four beats per bar.
Form:	The recording begins with a two-bar guitar introduction that ends with vocal pickups leading into the first period of the form.	The recording begins with a two-bar guitar introduction (different from Berry's) that ends with vocal pickups that lead into the first period.
	After the introduction, the song is made up of a series of eight sixteen-bar periods, each of which is based on **antecedent and consequent phrases** that use the same chord progression but have different melodic lines, the second of which sounds more conclusive than the first.	After the introduction, the song is made up of a series of five sixteen-bar periods, each of which is based on antecedent and consequent phrases that closely match those in Berry's recording.
	The first period begins on the word "Boston," and ends with "sweet little sixteen."	The first period begins on the word "ocean," and ends with "surfin' U.S.A."
Features:	Uneven beat subdivisions are used throughout the recording.	Even beat subdivisions are kept most of the way through the recording, but the backup vocals and the organ often relax into uneven subdivisions.
	The drums keep a strong backbeat.	The drums accent a strong backbeat, and the bass drum pounds out each bar's four beats.
	The instruments break for a voice solo in the second and seventh periods and the bars that lead into them.	The second and fourth periods have no breaks, but do change in that the backup vocals repeat a new phrase while the solo vocal line continues its own lyric line.
	After the guitar solo in the introduction, Berry's guitar maintains a riff pattern through most of the recording.	The rhythm pattern of Berry's riff is imitated through most of the recording.
	The fifth period is instrumental and features a boogie-woogie style piano	The fifth period is mostly instrumental featuring an organ solo in the first

(continued)

	solo that is decorated by long and elaborate glissandos.	(antecedent) phrase, and a guitar solo followed by voices in the second (consequent) phrase. The recording ends with four more repetitions of that final four-bar vocal line and then fades out.
Lyrics:	The song is about a sixteen-year-old girl's desire to talk her parents into letting her go out to "rock and roll." The lyrics mention a variety of cities where one could find good rock music.	The song is about surfing and surfers. The singer wishes that everyone in the country had an ocean and could have fun like the surfers in California, Australia, and Hawaii. The cities mentioned in Chuck Berry's song are paralleled by the naming of beaches where the surfing is good.

Billboard pop charts: number two for three weeks; *Billboard* rhythm and blues charts: number one for three weeks; British hit singles: number sixteen

Billboard pop charts: number three; *Billboard* rhythm and blues charts: number twenty; British hit singles: number thirty-five

lyrics, but one can only assume that the two writers agreed with the settlement that was reached.

By late 1963, Brian Wilson had developed into a fine songwriter, and he expanded the Beach Boys beyond beach themes to sing about other teenage interests, such as school spirit and fast cars. Wilson also aided in the writing and production of several popular car- and surf-theme songs for his friends, the vocal duo Jan and Dean.

By 1966, many changes had taken place in Brian Wilson's life. The result was a nervous breakdown that forced him to stop touring. His place onstage was taken at first by Glen Campbell and then by Bruce Johnston. Wilson kept writing, producing, and singing and playing on the group's recordings, however. Without the pressures of touring, he was able to focus his energies on songwriting. In 1966, he put together the Beach Boys' most important album, *Pet Sounds.* The album was not the group's greatest commercial success, but all its songs were connected thematically, and this influenced many rock albums that followed. Such theme, or "concept," albums had existed in jazz and other nonclassical music before with Mel Tormé's *California Suite;* several albums by Duke Ellington including *Perfume Suite* and *Black, Brown, and Beige;* and any number of soundtrack and musical-comedy recordings. Even Phil Spector's *A Christmas Gift to You* (1963) predates *Pet Sounds* as a concept album. But the standard rock albums of the time were simply collections of individual songs with no real connection to each other; it was *Pet Sounds* that sent rock albums in a new direction. That direction included concept albums to follow, including the Beatles' *Sgt. Pepper's Lonely Hearts Club Band* and many other concept albums.

Pet Sounds was a different kind of concept album from its predecessors because the concept, which was not even hinted at in the title, emerged slowly as one song led to the next. In general, the concept was the expression of hopes, dreams, and anxiety about the present and future felt by a young person growing up. The hopes were expressed through the songs "Wouldn't It Be Nice," "Don't Talk (Put Your Head on My Shoulder)," and "I'm Waiting for the Day." Feelings of insecurity were evident in "I Know There's an Answer," "I Just Wasn't Made for These Times," "Caroline No," and "God Only Knows." Wilson's productions on *Pet Sounds* were thick, with many instrumental tracks layered one on top of another, not unlike the wall of sound productions of Phil Spector.

Pet Sounds could be credited for beginning the concept album trend of the late sixties, but without a doubt, it was the Beatles' *Sgt. Pepper's Lonely Hearts Club Band,* recorded the following year, that stimulated other bands to produce concept albums. The Beatles gave subtle credit to the influence *Pet Sounds* had on their *Sgt. Pepper's* album when they put animal sounds and the sound of a galloping horse at the end of "Good Morning." Those sounds were imitative of the dogs barking and the sound of a train rushing past the listener that Brian Wilson had added just after the end of the last song on *Pet Sounds,* "Caroline No."

The Beach Boys followed *Pet Sounds* with "Good Vibrations" (1966), which was a number one hit. A Spector-influenced, complex production that included sound effects made by such nontraditional (for rock music) instruments as sleighbells, and an electronic instrument, the **electro-theremin,** "Good Vibrations" represented a new artistic achievement for Wilson. A listening guide for "Good Vibrations" appears on page 81.

Listening Guide

"Good Vibrations"
as recorded by the Beach Boys (1966)

Tempo: The basic tempo of the recording is approximately 152 beats per minute, with four beats per bar, but the tempo slows to about 138 beats per minute at the end of the D section. The original tempo returns in the last section.

Form: The form is based on eight-bar phrases with an occasional four-bar extension.

Approximately the first half of the recording is made up of clear ABAB sections, each of which includes two eight-bar phrases. The "good vibrations" are sung about in the lyrics to each B section.

The rest of the recording has a less clear-cut formal structure. The C section begins with an eight-bar instrumental section, followed by a four-bar section with the voices holding an "ah" syllable and then singing an eight-bar vocal phrase.

The D section begins with sustained chords on the organ joined by a dampened maraca that establishes a slower tempo. The vocals return with a four-bar phrase played four-and-one-half times with the voices fading out during the third time through the phrase.

A vocal "ah" is followed by a pause after which the original tempo returns for an E section based, in part, on the second phrase of the B section, this time with a very gospel rhythmic feel, followed by eight more bars in which different singers respond to one another with various nonsense syllables. Two different melodies are sung at the same time during the nonsense syllables creating a **polyphonic texture.**

The recording ends with an instrumental version of the first melody in the B section and fades out in the fifth bar.

Features: Uneven beat subdivisions are maintained throughout the recording.

The instrumental background is very thickly produced with a lot of overdubbing to thicken the texture.

In the tradition of Phil Spector's wall of sound, the recording is done in monaural to avoid the separation that stereo would have created.

The drummer is heard softly playing a drum set in the A sections, but the only percussion in the B sections is a tambourine on the backbeats.

An electronic instrument called an electro-theremin is used during the B sections and at the end of the recording to create an oscillating sound that has an almost ghostlike effect.

Lyrics: The singer savors the excitement he feels when he thinks about a particular woman.

Billboard pop charts: number one; British hit singles: number one

Wilson had even greater artistic plans for the album *Smile,* on which he was collaborating with poet/musician/producer Van Dyke Parks, but the album was never finished. *Smiley Smile* (1967), which was released instead, contained only "Heroes and Villains" and a few other songs from the originally planned recording.

Summary

During the late fifties and early sixties, the overall sound of some music called rock and roll changed from the blues and country-based energetic sound of the midfifties to a gentler, pop-oriented sound called teen idol pop. The change happened because songwriters did not like the competition from rock musicians who wrote their own music and because much rock music was recorded on small labels. Also, many parents and others were concerned about the rebellious or sexy lyrics and dances of the fifties that were based on African American blues and rhythm and blues. The songs of the late fifties and early sixties pop style were generally written to appeal to young teens and were marketed in teen movies as well as on the radio. Many of the singers were accompanied by orchestras instead of the guitars, bass, and drums common in much fifties rock, and rock elements such as accenting a backbeat were gone.

By the early sixties, the West Coast surf style had become popular with teens. The surf bands played their own instruments and did not depend on studio orchestras and other effects as did the teen idol pop sound, but the songs were still lighthearted and supportive of a youthful lifestyle. The Beach Boys eventually left the surf style behind and created complex studio-produced records in the style of Phil Spector's wall of sound productions that continued some of the traditions of the teen idol style.

discussion questions

What performers today are more pop than rock but are advertised as rock artists? Are any of them, Britney Spears or Madonna, for example, as far from being rock musicians as Pat Boone was in the late fifties and early sixties?

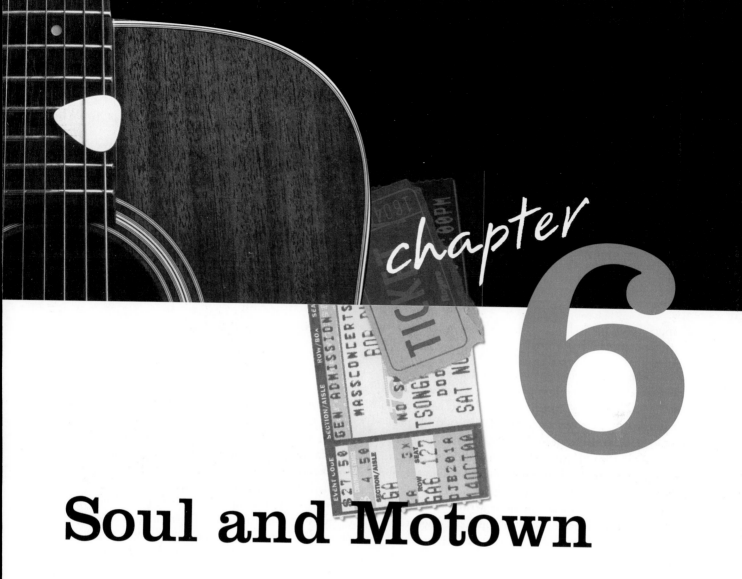

Soul and Motown

"It's a force that can light a room. The force radiates
from a sense of selfhood, a sense of knowing where
you've been and what it means. Soul is a way of life—
but it's always the hard way."
—RAY CHARLES

The infectious beat of rhythm and blues and the exuberance of gospel combined to enhance one another in soul music. With the same impassioned performances gospel singers used in praise of God, soul singers conveyed their messages of human love and relationships. In fact, most of the singers who sang soul were also gospel singers. Their use of melismas added to the melody quick emotional changes ranging from sobbing to shouting and a falsetto vocal quality. These characteristics of black gospel singing also became important qualities in the soul vocal style. The smooth flow of uneven beat subdivisions, the stress on the backbeat, and the energetic horn or sax solos gave soul its gutsy richness. Soul styles varied from one part of the country to another, but all shared a dramatic emotional appeal.

Motown is considered separately from the other soul styles because the company intentionally toned down gospel and blues influences to better reach a large white audience.

Some of that emotional appeal was directly related to the civil rights movement. During the fifties and early sixties, soul music was being written, produced, and performed by people who were very aware that they would not necessarily be welcome to sit in the front of a bus, to attend any school or live in any neighborhood they wanted, or for that matter to purchase a meal in the very restaurant where their music was played on a jukebox. Soul singers, along with other African American performers, would sometimes see their names on a hotel billboard where they were performing but would have to enter and exit by a back door and were not allowed to stay at the hotel as guests. They would have to stay at hotels that catered only to African Americans, and those, generally, were not nearly as well appointed. Until 1965, the singers knew that they would not even be able to vote in some parts of the South. When Aretha Franklin sang out "Respect" (1967), the message was heard as more than just her desire for her man to respect her. She wanted respect from all of her listeners, and she wanted it for other African Americans, not just herself. Throughout the sixties, James Brown used his tremendous appeal to African Americans to cool racial tensions with positive statements of "black pride" alongside admonishments against violence. His song "Say It Loud, I'm Black and I'm Proud" (1968), for example, stressed the need for hard work to obtain the independence he and his people deserved. He carried his message far, touring in both Korea and South Vietnam to entertain American troops.

Some soul styles, particularly those produced in southern cities such as Memphis or Muscle Shoals, tended to include gritty and gutsy vocals and instrumental playing that had much energetic intensity. Northern soul styles from Chicago, Philadelphia, and Detroit were often more refined. The reason for that is probably that most soul singers were trained on black gospel music and the styles of singing in the worship services varied from one part of the country to the other. Of the northern styles, the Motown Company in Detroit stands out as being different from other soul styles in that its music was refined in such a way that it was aimed primarily at white audiences. All of the soul styles had interracial appeal, but Motown particularly tended to stress much more pop- and jazz-influenced, studio-produced sophistication than other soul styles in which the recordings sounded live. That sophistication cut through the image of the television shows that had African Americans portrayed only as servants and instead displayed them as highly refined people. That image helped some white listeners gain a new and more positive image of African Americans and also helped African American listeners have positive role models for their own lives.

The term *soul* did not really come into common usage to describe this style of music until the middle-to-late sixties, but the style was developing in the fifties through the work of such singers as Ray Charles, James Brown, Sam Cooke, and Jackie Wilson. Out of their influences came the many artists discovered and recorded by the Atlantic Record Company in New York, Stax and Volt Records in Memphis, Chess and Vee Jay in Chicago, Motown in Detroit, and Philadelphia International in Philadelphia, to name only the biggest labels. To introduce ourselves to soul there is no better place to begin than with its genius, Ray Charles.

Glaucoma blinded **Ray Charles** Robinson (1930–2004) when he was only six years old. He had already been learning to play the piano, and music gave him a world where sight was not essential. In addition to keyboards, he took up the trumpet, the saxophone, and the clarinet. He also learned to read and write music in

Ray Charles and his orchestra with the Raelettes

braille and studied composition. Orphaned at age fifteen, he made his living by playing music. Dropping his last name to avoid confusion with the fighter "Sugar" Ray Robinson, Ray Charles moved from his home in Greenville, Florida, to Seattle, Washington, where he worked as a singer/pianist much influenced by Nat "King" Cole. Although Charles was one of the few soul singers who never actually performed gospel music in church, he incorporated gospel elements into his rhythm and blues style.

The use of call-and-response, common in gospel style, can be heard in Charles's blues song "What'd I Say" (1959). In its original release, a different version of the same song appeared on each side of the record, the second being a continuation of the first. The more polished rhythm and blues side was a number-one hit on the rhythm and blues charts and number six on the pop charts, but the recording on side two, called "What'd I Say (Part Two)," featured a gospel-styled vocal group responding to Charles's lead vocals. Both recordings were reminiscent of the performance style of blues singer/pianist Clarence "Pine Top" Smith in the twenties. Charles even paid tribute to Smith by quoting some of the lyrics of Smith's "Pine Top's Boogie Woogie" (1928). Charles started his "What'd I Say (Part Two)" with a tribute to another jazz singer, Cab Calloway, who often called out nonsense syllables to which his band (and the audience) responded in imitation. Charles plays an electric piano on both parts of the recording. The listening guide on page 86 discusses "What'd I Say (Part Two)."

An essential part of the talent that sets Ray Charles apart from other soul artists is his ability to synthesize country, rhythm and blues, and jazz styles with gospel music. His band arrangements incorporated elements of country and blues music, and his piano playing owed much to gospel. The storyline texts common in country music were used in some of his songs. In 1962, he recorded two albums of country and country-style songs, *Modern Sounds in Country and*

Western Music (Vols. 1 and 2), on which he covered songs by Hank Williams, Floyd Tillman, and Hank Snow. The single from Volume 1, "I Can't Stop Loving You," proved to be his biggest hit. In the midsixties, after a drug possession arrest, Charles stopped performing and checked into a drug rehabilitation hospital to break his long addiction to heroin. The movie *Ray* (2004) was based on his life.

Sam Cooke (Sam Cook, 1935–1964) began his professional singing career in 1951, when he took the lead vocal role in the established and successful gospel group the Soul Stirrers. He decided to branch out into secular music in 1956 but wanted to avoid the criticism that had been leveled at other gospel singers who "sold out" by leaving pure gospel music. To that end, he used the name Dale Cooke when he recorded "Lovable" (1956). He left the Soul Stirrers, dropped the pseudonym, changed record companies, and in 1957 released "You Send Me." Its success was the beginning of his pop career, as well as the beginning of the influence his light, high, pop and gospel vocal style would have on future singers. Although Cooke was in his middle-to-late twenties when his biggest hits were on the charts, he became a teen idol for young African Americans in much the same sense Dion, Fabian, and Frankie Avalon were for white teens. Cooke's sweet, naive, teen idol image was shattered when he was shot to death in a motel in 1964 by a woman who claimed he had attacked her.

Another musical innovator who started performing simply to make enough money to survive was **James Brown** (1933–2006). By the time he was five years old his mother had left him to be raised by her sister. His father was around from time to time but did not live with him. Brown earned his own money and helped support his aunt by dancing on street corners for tips; the more elaborate his dance steps, the more money he made. The experience could not have been pleasant at the time, but it certainly had an effect on the wild stage antics that later became part of his act. As a youth he sang gospel in the

"What'd I Say (Part Two)"
as recorded by Ray Charles (1959)

Tempo: The tempo is about 180 beats per minute, with four beats in each bar.

Form: The recording begins with eight bars of call-and-response nonsense syllables between Charles and a vocal group. The twelve-bar blues form is used in sections where Charles sings lyrics.

There are no instruments and no particular melody or chords during the eight-bar sections of nonsense syllables, imitative of Cab Calloway's use of call-and-response in the late twenties.

Features: The polyrhythmic effect is less obvious than in the other recording on the record's A side because the piano and percussion are softer.

A vocal group responds to Charles's vocals, taking the place of the horn section in the first recording.

The piano accompanies the voice through the vocal choruses.

The recording begins with what appears to be a continuation of the earlier recording.

Lyrics: The singer is thinking about sex with allusions to dancing. The text of the fourth chorus quotes from "Pine Top's Boogie Woogie" (1928).

Billboard pop charts: number six; *Billboard* rhythm and blues charts: number one

James Brown performs on stage (1965)

Augusta Baptist Church in Augusta, Georgia, and by his early twenties (in the midfifties) he was accepted into the gospel group the Swanees. Not content to stay in the background, Brown became the lead singer. The Swanees changed their name to the Famous Flames when they began to sing nonreligious music.

The first hit song recorded by James Brown and the Famous Flames was the gospel-styled, but thematically secular, "Please, Please, Please" (1956). The recording used the triplet pattern in the piano that was common in gospel, doo-wop, and some rhythm and blues, along with Brown's pleading and emotional vocals. A listening guide to "Please, Please, Please" is on page 87. The recording made number five on the rhythm and blues charts but only number 105 on the pop ones.

Brown's dramatic and energetic vocal embellishments fit well into his wild stage act, which involved rhythmic dance steps, leg splits, and drops to his knees. Brown became deeply involved with his music onstage; he would show the audience that he was giving his all by collapsing on the floor as if from a heart attack during a song, something he had often seen African American preachers in the South do during worship services. In Brown's act, the Famous Flames would then cover his body with a cape and carry him to the side of the stage before he would

Listening Guide

"Please, Please, Please"
as recorded by James Brown and
the Famous Flames (1956)

Tempo: The tempo is approximately 74 beats per minute, with four beats in each bar.

Form: The recording is introduced by Brown's rhythmically free singing of "please" three times. Once the instruments enter and establish a steady beat, the song is composed of six eight-bar periods, all of which follow the same basic chord progression and melodic outline.

Features: Uneven beat subdivisions are maintained throughout the recording.

The drums accent a strong backbeat.

Brown's vocals are full of dramatic melismas and a sense of rhythmic freedom.

Doo-wop influences include the style of the backup vocal group, the triplet patterns played on the piano, and the use of the standard doo-wop chord progression in the fifth and sixth bars of each eight-bar period.

The instruments break at the last two beats of the sixth bar and all of the eighth bar of each period to allow for Brown's solo voice to be heard without accompaniment.

Lyrics: The singer is begging for sex.

Billboard pop charts: number 105; *Billboard* rhythm and blues charts: number five

miraculously recover and finish the song. In some performances, that rejuvenation was sufficient to carry him through encores of attacks and music. For very good reason, James Brown has been called Mr. Dynamite, the Hardest Working Man in Show Business, Soul Brother Number One, the Godfather of Soul, and the Man with All the Names.

With his recording of "Out of Sight" (1964) and "Papa's Got a Brand New Bag" (1965), Brown developed a new style that was more dependent on African-influenced polyrhythms than melody. That style was the beginning of what became known as funk. James Brown's funk style and funk music by later performers is discussed in Chapter 17, "Funk and Disco."

> **Soul was always here, but the form of arrangement, what we called soul, changed with me, because I took jazz and gospel and made it funk, and we started dealin' with it a little different.**
> —James Brown

James Brown delivered sermonlike messages in "Cold Sweat" (1967), "Say It Loud—I'm Black and I'm Proud" (1968), and "King Heroin" (1972). "Say It Loud—I'm Black and I'm Proud" spoke to the very roots of African American pride, encouraging hard work leading to positive achievements for his people. Released the same year that Dr. Martin Luther King was assassinated "Say It Loud—I'm Black and I'm Proud" helped keep Dr. King's message alive. James Brown was publicly praised by Hubert Humphrey (vice president under Lyndon Johnson) for his effective efforts at directing African Americans toward a peaceful movement for equal rights. His music and his messages were meaningful to many white rock fans too, and he traveled to entertain troops in Vietnam and Korea. In "King Heroin," Brown preached to his audience about the dangers of drug abuse. The song was reminiscent of an anti-alcohol song called "King Alcohol," by Oliver Ditson (published in 1843). Because James Brown had grown up poor, with little supervision and direction in a world permeated by drugs, prostitution, and street crime, his songs delivered a musical message that displayed a deep understanding of the problems faced by many of his fans.

Though he always maintained a following with rhythm and blues fans, Brown's pop audience diminished somewhat through the seventies. He was featured in the movie *The Blues Brothers* (1980), and he revived his following with the album *Bring It On* in 1983. In 1985, he performed "Living in America" in the movie *Rocky IV.* Three years later, soul's Godfather was back in the news for some nonmusical activities that landed him in a South Carolina prison for two-and-a-half years. Many rumors were reported, but officially he was found guilty of aggravated assault and resisting arrest. After his release from prison, he was right back on stage to tape a special concert for cable television, which was aired in June of 1991. James Brown has been an influence on both the soul and funk movements, as heard in the music of Sly and the Family Stone and George Clinton's Parliament and Funkadelic.

Memphis Soul

Memphis, Tennessee, had been an important center for developments in rock musical styles since the early fifties when Sam Phillips moved there to record blues singers and, eventually, Elvis Presley and other early rockabilly singers. In the sixties, musicians in Memphis took the gospel-based vocal styles of singers like James Brown and Jackie Wilson and combined them with the energetic rhythm and blues style of Little Richard to create their own brand of soul music. Most of the Memphis soul artists began their careers recording for the Memphis-based record company Stax or its companion label, Volt. Many of the Stax and Volt recordings were later distributed nationally by the Atlantic label.

Memphis soul recordings had a fairly consistent instrumental sound backing the singers because the instrumental group Booker T. and the MGs played on many of the recording sessions, in addition to having instrumental hits of their own. The group was named after their organist/arranger, Booker T. Jones, but the name also served as a tribute to the African American educator Booker T. Washington. "MG" stood for "Memphis Group." The group's guitarist, Steve Cropper, was an important songwriter in the Memphis soul style, often collaborating with others to write several of the biggest hits of the soul movement. Cropper's guitar style added a country flavor to the soul style. The MGs' emphasis on the bass was influential on music to follow, including reggae. Members of Booker T. and the MGs provided the backup band for the Blues Brothers both on tour and in the movie *The Blues Brothers* (1980).

Wilson Pickett (1941–2006) was born in Alabama but moved to Detroit, where he sang gospel music with the Violinaires. In 1959, at age nineteen, he abandoned his gospel-style grunts and shouts to sing rhythm and blues ballads with the Falcons. His old gospel vocal style returned when Jerry Wexler, his producer on the Atlantic label, sent him to record in Memphis. A listening guide for "In the Midnight Hour" is included here. The song was co-written at the recording session by Pickett and Steve Cropper, guitarist in Booker T. and the MGs. It reached number one on the rhythm and blues charts and number twenty-one on the pop charts.

Listening Guide

"In the Midnight Hour" as recorded by Wilson Pickett (1965)

Tempo: The tempo is approximately 112 beats per minute, with four beats in each bar.

Form: The song is comprised of one six-bar instrumental introduction, two seventeen-bar choruses, one eight-bar instrumental section, and two more seventeen-bar choruses.

Features: Booker T. and the MGs provide a guitar, organ, bass, and drums rhythm section to which a horn section with trumpet and three saxophones (alto, tenor, and baritone) has been added.

The bass is played at a higher dynamic level than the rest of the rhythm section, and its constant motion provides a contrast to the sustained notes played by the horns.

The characteristic horn section sound is based on playing of **major chords** in parallel motion.

Even beat subdivisions are maintained throughout.

The drums keep a strong backbeat.

Pickett's black gospel background is evident in his lead vocal.

Lyrics: The singer looks forward to sex around midnight.

Billboard pop charts: number twenty-one; *Billboard* rhythm and blues charts: number one; British hit singles: number twelve

The parallel movement of the trumpet and saxophones in the recording of "In the Midnight Hour" was so commonly used in Memphis recordings that it became known as the "Memphis horn sound." The even beat subdivisions separate the style of the song from most rhythm and blues, but the gospel-influenced vocals make it a good example of Memphis soul. The recording's very active bass line was also characteristic of Memphis soul.

Otis Redding (1941–1967) became the biggest-selling singer at Stax Records. His vocal style was reminiscent of both the aggressiveness of Little Richard and the crooning sound of Sam Cooke, to which he added a tremendous amount of emotional energy. In "Try a Little Tenderness" (1966), for example, he built up tension with his long gospel melismas, gradually increasing the intensity of the song as he moved from one verse to the next. Redding wrote many of his own hit songs, including "Respect," which he recorded in 1965 and Aretha Franklin covered two years later.

Redding's impassioned singing won him a tremendous following in African American communities in the mid-sixties, and his performance at the Monterey Pop Festival in 1967 added white fans to that following. The biggest hit of his career, "(Sittin' on) The Dock of the Bay" (1967), co-written with Booker T. and the MGs' guitarist Steve Cropper, was recorded only three days before Redding and several members of his band, the Bar-Kays, died in an airplane crash in 1967.

Atlantic Records

Co-producers and writers Ahmet Ertegun and Jerry Wexler at the Atlantic Record Company in New York were responsible for much of the success of soul singers Ray Charles, Wilson Pickett, Otis Redding, Aretha Franklin, and many others. Ertegun and Herb Abramson formed Atlantic Records in 1947, some time before the birth of rock-influenced soul music. Some of the early artists represented by Atlantic included blues singer Joe Turner (whose recording of "Shake, Rattle and Roll" is discussed in Chapter 4) and the doo-wop group the Drifters. Eventually the company distributed recordings by a diverse group of bands, including Crosby, Stills, Nash and Young; the Velvet Underground; and Led Zeppelin; but from the late fifties through the sixties, Atlantic was one of the primary distributors of soul music in the United States.

Of course, the sound of any recording will vary greatly depending on the studio and studio musicians used to record it. Atlantic's producers moved their artists from one studio to another depending on what kind of soul sound Ertegun and Wexler had in mind for a particular session. Their own studio was in New York, but when they went down to the Stax Record Studio in Memphis and used the Stax backup bands—Booker T. and the MGs or the Bar-Kays—their productions had much similarity to the tight Memphis sound of Stax's own artists. That sound stressed the electric guitar, an active bass line, and the parallel motion of the Memphis horn sound. Ertegun and Wexler also used the Fame Studios in Muscle Shoals, Alabama, to create a similar southern soul style.

Aretha Franklin was born in Memphis, Tennessee, in 1942, the daughter of a Baptist minister. When she was six, her father moved the family to Detroit, and by the time she was a teenager, Franklin had already spent most of her life singing gospel in her father's church. She was soon traveling to sing at other churches and concert halls, where she met many of the great gospel singers of her time, including Clara Ward, Mahalia Jackson, and Sam Cooke. At age eighteen, she moved to New York and began to record secular songs, including a blues in the classic blues style of Ma Rainey and Bessie Smith titled "Today I Sing the Blues" (1960). Franklin sang her early secular songs with a more restrained approach than she had used for gospel music because her producer from Columbia Records was trying to build her career around a style like that of jazz singer Nancy Wilson. It was not until 1966 that Aretha signed with Atlantic Records. Jerry Wexler took her to Muscle Shoals, Alabama, for a recording session in which he encouraged her to put the energy,

Aretha Franklin (1970)

Listening Guide

"Respect"
as recorded by Aretha Franklin
(recorded in 1966, released in 1967)

Tempo: The tempo is approximately 112 beats a minute, with four beats in each bar.

Form: The recording begins with a four-bar instrumental introduction followed by three ten-bar A sections with vocals, an eight-bar instrumental B section, another A with vocals, and a C section comprised of four four-bar phrases.

The A sections each have three phrases of lyrics. The first two are two bars long and the third is six bars long.

The first phrase of the C section has an instrumental stop time with Franklin beginning her vocal by spelling out the word *respect*.

Features: Even beat subdivisions are maintained by the instruments, but Franklin's vocals sometimes go into uneven subdivisions.

The introduction has the Memphis horn sound of horns playing parallel sustained chords, a guitar playing short riff patterns, and a very active bass line.

The active bass continues through most of the recording.

The drummer maintains a strong backbeat on the snare drum; a tambourine keeps a steady beat.

The backup vocals repeat words out of Franklin's vocal lines, serving to support her message.

The instrumental B section features an improvised tenor saxophone solo.

Lyrics: Franklin uses most of Otis Redding's lyrics that demand respect for the African American community as well as respect from a lover. Franklin's version added the section in which R-E-S-P-E-C-T is spelled out and she asks her man to T.C.B. ("take care of business"), slang for her need to be satisfied by him.

Billboard pop charts: number one for two weeks; *Billboard* rhythm and blues charts: number one for eight weeks; British hit singles: number ten

dramatic delivery, and emotion she had used in gospel performances back into her vocals. After returning to her more passionate gospel style, she had one hit after another, winning her the title "Lady Soul." A listening guide to "Respect," one of Franklin's first Atlantic singles, is above. The recording was number one on both the rhythm and blues and the pop charts.

> **Soul is a constant. It's cultural. It's always going to be there, in different flavors and degrees.**
>
> –Aretha Franklin

The More Commercial Style of Motown

Berry Gordy Jr. (born in 1929) is an African American songwriter from Detroit who saw that the white audience of the fifties had matured to the point that it was ready to accept music by African American performers, but he also recognized that African Americans needed to achieve more than simple acceptance. They needed respect. After the success of the songs "Reet Petite" (1957) and "Lonely Teardrops" (1959), which he had written for Jackie Wilson, Gordy decided to form his own record company. He called his recording studio and record company

Hitsville and then Motown in recognition of Detroit's nickname, the "Motor City." Through the period of racial unrest and riots of the sixties, Motown artists sang of love and other human concerns with which people of all races, religions, and political beliefs could identify. Gordy cultivated in his performers a sophisticated image, helping to bring respect and self-esteem to the African Americans who saw them as role models.

> **"Hitsville had an atmosphere that allowed people to experiment creatively and gave them the courage not to be afraid to make mistakes."**
>
> –Berry Gordy Jr.

In addition to Motown, the company's record labels included Tamla, Gordy, and, after the midsixties, Soul, VIP, Mowest, and Melody. Their music publishing company was called Jobete (for Gordy's daughters, Joy, Betty, and Terry). Most of the performers at Motown during the early sixties lived in the Detroit area and had little or no previous professional experience in music when they auditioned to record for the company. Gordy molded them into a sound and image that he, with his team of writers, producers, and choreographers, created. To that end, he opened a finishing school he called International Talent Management Incorporated (ITM). Gordy hired Maxine Powell, an African American woman who owned the Maxine Powell Finishing and Modeling School, to train Motown's performers to drop the African American modes of walking, speaking, and dancing with which they had grown up and to adopt the sense of grace and style that would be expected of members of the white upper class. Powell told one performer after another that no matter where they performed they were to act as if they were at the White House or Buckingham Palace. Choreographer for the Motown acts was Cholly Atkins. He had been a dancer in a night club act called the Rhythm Pals and then became primary choreographer for groups hired to perform at New York's Apollo Theater before moving on to Motown.

Maxine Powell and others at ITM also oversaw the style of dress Motown artists wore on stage. The sixties were a time when most rock or pop groups dressed in matching outfits, but those outfits were not necessarily very sophisticated. Groups from New York, even African American girl groups like the Dixie Cups, would perform in simple skirts or pants and sweaters. Such casual dress would not be found on a Motown artist, at least not during the sixties. Motown's female acts wore sparkling gowns or other glamorous clothing, and male performers wore suits or tuxedos. Of course, a male singer might take off his coat and loosen his tie during his act, but the effect was still one in which the performer would look appropriate performing at a posh venue. Even the Motown performers' names were chosen to promote the sparkling image. After being hired at Motown, Steveland Morris became Stevie Wonder, the Primes the Temptations, the Primettes the Supremes, the Marvels the Marvelettes, the Four Aims the Four Tops, and the Matadors the Miracles.

Motown's producers used sophisticated background arrangements that often included orchestral string sections along with jazz instrumentation, such as saxophones or brass instruments. Gospel influences were evident through the use of tambourines, staple instruments in African American churches, and call-and-response vocals. A few songs, such as "Money," the early hit by Barrett Strong (1960), were based on the traditional blues progression, but other blues and gospel colorations such as blue notes were rare. Motown productions were aimed at a much larger, mostly white, commercial audience than most other soul recordings of the sixties. Motown arrangements often featured infectious rhythms played to continuously repeating bass lines (ostinatos). Latin rhythms were used in some recordings, such as Smokey Robinson and the Miracles' "Mickey's Monkey" (1963), which was based on a Cuban son **claves beat** (played by wooden sticks tapped together). That rhythm is notated as follows:

Son claves rhythm

The Temptations' "Cloud Nine" (1968) used the polyrhythmic patterns of the Brazilian samba. White musical traditions such as even beat subdivisions and orchestral instrumentation were used as often as African American traditions, assuring that the Motown sound would appeal to the musical tastes of as broad an audience as possible.

In addition to the importance of Motown's singers, writers, and producers, credit for the Motown sound must also be given to Motown's regular backup band, the **Funk Brothers.** The Funk Brothers' background in playing jazz and rhythm and blues made the Motown sound different from previous doo-wop or soul recordings because it pushed them to be more active in their individual parts while not covering the singers. James Jamerson, for example, had no desire to play the two-beat or repetitious cliché bass lines common in previous popular styles of music. He played walking bass lines with chromatic passing tones and syncopated eighth-note patterns that bebop jazz musicians used. What separated his work from that of the bebop jazz school was his use of a Fender electric bass for most of his Motown recordings (jazz musicians were still using the string [upright] bass). Jazz influences are also clear with the addition of vibes, which were sometimes played along with other instruments in unison to add timbre without standing out on their own.

The three guitarists in the Funk Brothers each played their own special role in many of the recordings. Robert White generally filled out the rhythm section with smooth strums of chords on the beats. He used a large hollow-body electric guitar (a Gibson L-5) that provided a mellow but still well-amplified **timbre.** White also became known for his solo tone quality when he used his thumbnail to pluck out melody lines. Eddie Willis added blues-style melodic fills on his Gibson Firebird (solid-body) guitar. Joe Messina played a Fender Telecaster (solid-body) guitar and would concentrate on stressing the backbeat (along with the drummer's snare drum) with fast, percussive strums of chords. In addition, Messina played whatever solo lines the producer requested of him, but stressing the backbeat was his primary function. The three guitarists worked together so much for so long that they could talk over a chart and produce an almost record-ready sound the first time they played it.

The Funk Brothers' leader, Earl Van Dyke, was not always the only keyboard player on a session. He often played on an acoustic Steinway (four-foot) piano, and Johnny Griffith was sometimes called in to add parts on a Hammond organ and James Gittens on organ or vibes. Many Motown recordings also used out-of-the-ordinary percussion effects. The Supremes' hit "Baby Love" (1964), for example, begins with the sound of several people stomping out the beat on plywood boards. Tambourine and conga drums were also used from time to time for their own special effects.

Because Motown productions were musically complex and most of the performers were untrained in music until they began to sing for the company, writers and producers were needed. William Smokey Robinson (born in 1940) was a singer who had written songs for his group, the Matadors, in 1957. Berry Gordy Jr. heard them just as he was beginning to look for talent to start his record company, and with a new name, the Miracles, they became one of Motown's first important groups. Robinson sang lead with the Miracles and also wrote and produced for many of Motown's other acts, including the Marvelettes, Marvin Gaye, Mary Wells, and the Temptations. He eventually became vice president of Motown Records. He left Motown in 1990.

Female groups were very popular during the early sixties. Most of the groups produced in New York sang very light, pop-styled songs designed for a teenage, or even preteen, audience. Motown's girl groups included the Marvelettes, who recorded primarily to please a young age group, and the Supremes, who generally sang about love and lost relationships to a slightly more mature audience. Another girl group at Motown, Martha and the Vandellas, had a more aggressive and gospel-oriented style than was typical for the company's female vocalists. Each of these groups had many successes, but the Supremes, with their very refined sound and image, outpaced the others in number of pop chart hits.

The prolific songwriting team Holland-Dozier-Holland, who wrote almost every hit the Supremes recorded, maintained a certain consistency from one song to another. Their compositions used almost no backbeat but instead maintained a constant and steady pulse played by bass and tambourines. The baritone saxophone was a favored instrument for solo spots. The instruments usually maintained even beat subdivisions, but lead singer Diana Ross's solos added a gospel touch through the use of uneven beat subdivisions and embellishments at phrase endings. Holland-Dozier-Holland used a variety of song forms besides the standard AABA, and they copied arrangers' tricks dating back to dance band styles of the 1940s. One such trick was the use of a portion of the song's refrain as an introduction, as in "Stop! In the Name of Love" (1965). "Baby Love" (1964) even changes key, something somewhat rare in pop-rock music. The Supremes' songs often repeated the introductory melody (the **hook**) over and over at the end, bringing a feeling of completeness to the composition.

By the late sixties, Motown performers had realized Berry Gordy's dream and become as popular with white audiences as black ones. Even so they still often suffered the same indignities as did other black artists when touring in parts of the South.

The Motown company and its productions changed somewhat through the years. The rather regimented soul and pop hits from the early to middle sixties gave way to prefunk influences and the increasing use of electronic instruments in the late sixties and through the seventies. In 1971, Berry Gordy Jr. moved his entire operation to Hollywood in order to add films to Motown's list of productions. The Supremes' former lead singer, Diana Ross, became a very successful film star with *Lady Sings the Blues* (1972), in which she portrayed jazz singer Billie Holiday, and *Mahogany* (1975).

The **Temptations** were one of Motown's most popular male groups. Gordy gave them their seductive name; they had previously called themselves the Elgins and then the Primes. They signed in 1962, but it took two years before

Listening Guide

"My Girl"
as recorded by the Temptations (1965)

Tempo: The tempo is about 112 beats per minute, with four beats in each bar.

Form: The song has seven eight-bar sections, with a four-bar introduction repeated as an extension after the third section.

The fourth section is instrumental but includes vocal responses.

Features: The instrumental introduction begins with two bars of a rhythmic bass pattern using even beat subdivisions, followed by two bars of an ostinato pattern repeated throughout the recording.

The guitar line in the introduction (and later in the recording) serves as an example of Robert White's distinctive thumbnail-plucked solo sound.

The backbeat is introduced with finger snaps and then taken over by the drums.

The very polished production includes an orchestral string section and a brass section that plays fills.

The vocal group responds to lead singer David Ruffin, but the vocal style is more pop than gospel.

Lyrics: The song is about how fulfilled the singer feels when he is with his girl. The song was a male expression of love that responded to an earlier Motown recording, Mary Wells's "My Guy" (1964).

Billboard pop charts: number one; *Billboard* rhythm and blues charts: number one for six weeks

their recordings achieved any commercial success. As was often the case, Gordy experimented quite a bit before he found just the right combination of writers and producers for their performing act. Smokey Robinson proved to be the Temptations' most successful writer and producer on their early hit recordings, and Norman Whitfield after the midsixties.

A listening guide for their hit song "My Girl" (1965), the structure of which was based on the eight-bar phrase lengths commonly used at Motown, is included here. The song had a polished, thick background that included the large number of instruments heard in other pop-oriented productions of the early to middle sixties. It was number one on both the pop and rhythm and blues charts.

The Temptations' musical style changed in several ways throughout their career. Their lead vocalist was tenor Eddie Kendricks until baritone David Ruffin took over the solos, beginning with "My Girl" in 1965. The depth and resonance of the baritone voice changed the group's overall sound. Ruffin left the group for a solo career in 1968 and was replaced by another baritone, Dennis Edwards. Up to that point, the group's music had followed the Motown tradition of pop universality, but the most dramatic change occurred when Ruffin departed. Norman Whitfield, who became their sole producer in 1967, had been listening to the polyrhythmic funk styles of James Brown and Sly and the Family Stone and decided to try to emulate it for the Temptations' recording of "Cloud Nine" (1968).

Although the song "Cloud Nine" made clear references to drugs on one level, its message reached beyond that. It described the very poor economic conditions under which many youths in African American ghettos were raised, in an attempt to show why some turned to drugs for escape. Lyrics of that type would never have been allowed at Motown during the early sixties, when the entire organization was centered on themes that reflected respectable universality, but Gordy let the company change with the times.

Most of the time, Gordy maintained complete control over the careers of his musicians, and few were able to gain control of their own work. One of the first to earn the freedom to write and produce his recordings was **Stevie Wonder** (born in 1950). Blind from birth, Steveland Morris (his father's last name was Judkins) spent his childhood playing a number of musical instruments, including harmonica, bongo drums, and piano. He began to record as "Little Stevie Wonder" for Motown's Tamla label at age twelve. Wonder recorded some studio-produced songs, but his first hit was his live-performance recording of "Fingertips (Part II)" (1963). Wonder's blindness and gospel-style voice earned him a reputation as a young Ray Charles.

When he turned twenty-one years old in 1971, Wonder renegotiated his contract with Motown so that he would have complete control of his recordings. He got married, moved to New York, and made some significant changes in his writing and production styles. The changes were influenced by many of the same funk stylings that Norman Whitfield used in his productions for the Temptations in the late sixties. With the album *Music of My Mind* (1972), Wonder began to incorporate more gospel, jazz, and rhythms with origins in Africa and Latin America into his compositions. He overdubbed his own singing and playing of most of the instruments on his recordings and grew fond of the tonal capabilities of the **synthesizer.**

Berry Gordy Jr. liked having a child star like Little Stevie Wonder at Motown, but, as was bound to happen, Wonder soon outgrew that image. Wonder was nineteen years old when Michael Jackson (1958–2009) and his four older brothers signed with Motown, and the young Jackson quickly became the company's new child star. Gordy teamed himself with others to write and produce songs for the **Jackson Five,** and, as befit their child-star image, their music was very pop-oriented and geared to teen and preteen fans. The Jacksons' father had managed their career before they came to Motown, and he continued as their manager after they signed with Gordy's company. He was aware that Stevie Wonder had been allowed to produce his own music, and when he was refused control of his sons' productions, he decided the group should leave Motown. They signed with the Epic label in 1976 and, after a lawsuit filed by Motown, changed their name to the Jacksons. The group's membership had changed slightly because Jermaine Jackson stayed at Motown, having married Gordy's daughter, Hazel. The Jacksons remained a group of five, however, because the family's next-youngest male member, Steven Randall (Randy) Jackson, joined to take his brother's place. In later years, their little sister Janet also entered the music business. Michael and Janet Jackson's very successful solo careers are discussed in Chapter 19, "MTV."

The jazz and soul style of Ray Charles was a great influence on soul singer **Marvin Gaye** (Marvin Gay, 1939–1984). A preacher's son from Washington, D.C., Gaye had been singing gospel music and playing the organ since his youth. Berry Gordy Jr. heard Gaye with the Moonglows while they were on tour in Detroit and invited him to record as a soloist for Motown. Soon after joining the Motown family, Gaye also joined the Gordy family by marrying Anna Gordy, Berry's sister. Gaye was a tenor, but he had a wide vocal range and the stylistic range to sing such gospel-styled songs as "Can I Get a Witness" (1963), as well as smooth love songs, like his duet with Tammi Terrell, "You're All I Need to Get By" (1967).

Marvin Gaye at the "What's Going On" session (1971)

Without a doubt, Marvin Gaye's most important statement to the world was "What's Going On" (1971). The song was written by Motown staff composer Al Cleveland and Renaldo "Obie" Benson of the Four Tops. When Gaye sang it he found that the song's message expressed the turbulence in his own life at the time, making his performance the best work of his career. The problems in his life included the recent cancer-related death of his singing partner, Tammi Terrell, his marital problems with Berry Gordy Jr.'s sister, his stressful relationship with his preacher father, and disturbing letters he received from his brother who was fighting in Vietnam. Beyond those personal issues, however, Gaye knew that the song spoke to many about the casualties and lack of success in the Vietnam War as well as some of the violence connected with the civil rights movement. The song is a desperate plea for peace among all mankind. As Gaye expressed his feelings, "I knew I'd have to find peace in my heart." At first, the Motown Company did not want to release the song; they were more interested in "commercial" hit productions. Gaye pressured them by refusing to record anything more until it was released. Ironically, the song quickly became a commercial hit, reaching number two on the pop charts for three weeks and number one on the rhythm and blues charts for five weeks. The same-titled album followed and was also very successful. A listening guide appears on page 95.

After a long career with Motown, Gaye left the label in 1982. He was in the middle of a comeback when

Listening Guide

"What's Going On"
as recorded by Marvin Gaye (1971)

Tempo: The tempo is approximately 102 beats per minute, with four beats in each bar.

Form: The form is based on a series of four-bar phrases, most of which vary the same basic melody to fit the text. The melody changes with the section that references "picket lines," drawing the listener's attention to the text about the antiwar and civil rights demonstrations of the time. After several repetitions of "What's going on?" there is a twelve-bar break during which the instruments play and Gaye scat sings words and phrases such as "right on" into the mix. The four-bar sections of text continue after that break, including a repetition of the phrase about picket lines. The end of the recording is an extended instrumental section, again, with Gaye's scat singing and repeating the question about what is going on. The recording ends with a fade out.

Features: The recording opens with party-like conversation and then four bars of instrumental introduction before Gaye's solo voice enters.

Gaye's vocals are accompanied by a very thickly arranged orchestra that includes the Funk Brothers and a group of backup singers.

The electric bass and drums stand out in the instrumental accompaniment.

A subtle backbeat is played by the drums, and clapped by the backup singers toward the end of the recording.

Lyrics: The song is a general plea for peace and understanding in a time of sorrow and unrest.

Billboard pop charts: number two for three weeks; *Billboard* rhythm and blues charts: number one for five weeks

---

he was shot and killed by his father in 1984 after an argument.

> " Isn't the artist's real job to learn from nature? Instead of churning out pop hits, shouldn't the truly talented among us be listening to the flutter of a butterfly's wing? "
>
> –Marvin Gaye

The Motown Company was sold to MCA Records in 1988. Stevie Wonder and others continued to record on the Motown label into the nineties. Jermaine Jackson switched labels to Arista for his later recordings.

Summary

Soul was a tremendously popular style of music that had its roots in the gospel and rhythm and blues styles of the fifties. It spread out into several styles in different parts of the country during the sixties and continued to be popular and influential in later decades. Most soul singers began their careers by singing black gospel music, and they carried their emotional intensity from gospel into the secular themes of soul songs. Most of the singers maintained their gospel stylings, but the basic style of soul recordings varied depending on the producers' choices of instrumentation and instrumental arrangements. The most important record companies to promote soul were Chess and Vee Jay in Chicago, Stax and Volt in Memphis, and Atlantic Records in New York.

The Motown Company recorded more for a large, white, pop-oriented audience than had other soul record companies. They toned down the gospel influences with the goal of reaching more people with their appealing, positive image and style. Berry Gordy Jr. finally allowed a few songs about the poverty, injustice, and political tensions of the time through the release of the Temptations' "Cloud Nine" (1968) and Marvin Gaye's "What's Going On" (1971).

discussion questions

In what various ways did soul music and its performers affect the civil rights movement? Civil rights leaders tended to admire James Brown much more than other great soul or Motown artists. What are some of the likely reasons for that?

chapter 7

The British Invasion: The Beatles versus the Stones

"We idolized the Beatles, except for those of us who idolized the Rolling Stones"
—HUMORIST DAVE BARRY

By 1964, most American rock fans had all but forgotten the raw backbeat of rockabilly and blues-based rock styles of the fifties. Songs about puppy love sung by teen idols and girl groups accompanied by thickly arranged studio orchestras had dominated the sound of rock music for several years. Even rockabilly's originator, Elvis Presley, had long since dropped his rebellious James Dean image and had become a movie star who sang more pop ballads than rock. In November 1963, the American spirit of optimism was crushed by the shocking assassination of President John F. Kennedy. All these factors created a void that made the country's young music fans ready for something new. The sound that captured their attention came from Britain.

Like America, Britain had different musical styles centered in various parts of the country. London was the hub for groups whose music and image were identified with youth subcultures such as the Mods and Rockers (musically, Mods liked "modern" music; Rockers preferred rockabilly and older rock styles), but the city's music fans also supported groups that played American blues and rhythm and blues. The Rolling Stones started out as a rhythm and blues band but soon found more commercial success with a style that combined rhythm and blues with other styles of music.

Rock groups from the northern industrial city of Manchester and its seaport neighbor, Liverpool, had a less serious connection with these subcultures and were generally not interested in the blues or rhythm and blues, instead tending toward a simple, folk-based music called **skiffle,** and later rock music by Buddy Holly. The sound of groups from Liverpool and Manchester was referred to as "Mersey beat," after the name of the river that flows through Liverpool and near Manchester. Skiffle used simple chords that young guitarists could master with little practice and it required little more than the guitar, or sometimes a homemade bass and strumming on a washboard. The simplicity and rhythmic fun of skiffle made it popular among young people throughout Britain because it allowed every young person to be a musician.

The two primary bands to first invade America were the Beatles and the Rolling Stones. The Beatles played music influenced by skiffle and Buddy Holly and the Crickets, both of which were popular in the Beatles' hometown of Liverpool. Their image was clean-cut and their personalities displayed an appealing sense of humor. In one early interview after arriving in America they were asked, "How do you find America?" John Lennon quickly replied "Turn left at Greenland," which is exactly what planes do when flying from England to America. That, of course, was not the answer the interviewer expected. Early in their career, the Beatles wore matching suits that were distinctively tailored, often with colored trim instead of lapels. They wore heeled boots that soon became popular, called "Beatle boots." At the time, most American rock groups dressed alike, but the Beatles' styling looked English. Their hair was long by American standards, but still clean and neat.

The Rolling Stones, on the other hand, gave up on the idea of wearing matching outfits and wore much more casual clothing on stage than was standard for the time. Their image was deliberately cultivated as the "nasty" opposite of the Beatles, and they played rhythm and blues much more like the music of Bo Diddley than Buddy Holly. As Mick Jagger said in a 1964 interview, "If people don't like us, well that's too bad. We're not thinking of changing, thanks very much. We've been the way we are for much too long to think of kow-towing to fanciful folk who think we should start tarting ourselves up with mohair suits and short haircuts." In real life, members of the Beatles and the Rolling Stones became friends with one another, and they shared much the same "rock star" lifestyle. In fact, the Rolling Stones' second hit record was "I Wanna Be Your Man," which John Lennon and Paul McCartney gave them to record. On the B side of the single, however, was another song that was true to the image the Rolling Stones were creating for themselves and very much unlike anything that the Beatles would have recorded in 1964. "Stoned" was a twelve-bar blues that was mostly instrumental with Jagger uttering intoxicated vocal comments at the end of each chorus.

The public divergence between the Beatles and the Rolling Stones was so obvious that many baby boomers defined themselves by which band they liked better. However, most fans, regardless of allegiance, liked both.

The Beatles

In Liverpool in March 1957, **John Lennon** (1940–1980) acquired his first guitar and soon formed a skiffle group called the Quarry Men, named for his school, Quarry Bank High School. In July of that year, while performing with the group at a local church picnic, he met **Paul McCartney** (born in 1942), who was soon asked to join the group; he and Lennon also began to work occasionally as a duo called the Nerk Twins (sometimes spelled "Nurk"). The Quarry Men changed their name to Johnny and the Moondogs and invited **George Harrison** (1943–2001) to join them. All three played guitar and sang, which was sufficient for skiffle, but a drummer and a bass player were needed to play the rock music that most interested them. Stu Sutcliffe, a friend Lennon had met at art college, was not a musician, but Lennon persuaded him to use the money he received after selling some artwork to buy a bass guitar. Owning a bass qualified him to join the Moondogs. Drummer Tommy Moore was also enlisted, and the group's name was again changed, this time to the Silver Beatles; by 1960 it became simply the **Beatles,** partly to echo the insect name of Buddy Holly's Crickets. The deliberate misspelling gave them an eye-catching name, and "beat" suggested not just the musical term but the social rebellion of the American Beat movement.

By late 1960, the Beatles had a new drummer, Pete Best, and the group had become good enough that they were hired to perform in clubs in Hamburg, Germany.

Their repertoire consisted mostly of covers of songs by American artists Chuck Berry, Little Richard, Buddy Holly, Gene Vincent, and others. After several trips and many long hours playing in Hamburg, they returned to Liverpool and played at the Cavern Club, a popular spot for teenagers. The group lost Sutcliffe during a trip to Hamburg in 1961 when he decided to stay there with his German girlfriend and work as an artist; he died of a brain hemorrhage not long afterward. The Beatles chose not to replace him, so McCartney switched from guitar to bass, giving the group the same basic instrumentation as the Crickets, with Harrison on lead guitar, Lennon on rhythm guitar, McCartney on bass, and Best on drums.

The Beatles had gotten to know singer Tony Sheridan, who had also been performing in Hamburg, and Sheridan asked the group to accompany him on his German recording of "My Bonnie" (1961). They were billed as the Beat Brothers on the recording, but when it was sold in Liverpool, their fans knew it was the Beatles. When the recording of "My Bonnie" was requested at a Liverpool record store, the manager of the store, Brian Epstein, was impressed enough to go to the Cavern Club to hear the Beatles. Epstein was wealthy, interested in the music business, and looking for a new creative job, so he offered to manage the group's career, and the Beatles soon agreed. One of the first demands Epstein made was that the group clean up its leather-jacketed Rocker image and wear neat, matching suits and shorter hair.

After several record companies rejected the group's recordings, Epstein finally got the Beatles a contract with

(left to right) Paul McCartney, John Lennon, and three fans.

EMI, where they were assigned to the Parlophone subsidiary and producer **George Martin** (born in 1926). Martin had no previous experience with rock music but had produced light classical music and comedy records by Beyond the Fringe, Spike Milligan, and Peter Sellers. Martin's background in the classics led to the use of string quartets and other classical instrumentation on some of the Beatles' recordings. His comedy work had involved considerable experimentation with **musique concrète** sound effects, which he used later on the Beatles' *Sgt. Pepper's Lonely Hearts Club Band* album (1967). Musique concrète was a French term for the electronic manipulation of natural sounds on tape, a technique used at the time by many avant-garde classical composers to create new sounds.

Before the Beatles' first session, George Martin told Lennon, McCartney, and Harrison that, while Best might be satisfactory for their Cavern Club bookings, he wanted to use someone else for recording. The Beatles decided that Best had to go, and to replace him, they hired **Ringo Starr** (Richard Starkey, born in 1940, nicknamed for his habit of wearing rings), the drummer for another Liverpool group, Rory Storm and the Hurricanes, whom the Beatles knew from bookings in which the groups had shared the billing. In September 1962, the Beatles reentered the studio to record their first single, "Love Me Do," backed with "P.S. I Love You." George Martin did not know Ringo's abilities, so he hired studio drummer Andy White for the session. As it turned out, they recorded a

version of "Love Me Do" with White on drums (and Ringo on tambourine), and a version with Ringo on drums. Both versions were used: the one with White drumming was released on their first album, *Please Please Me* (1963), and the other, with Ringo drumming, was released as the single.

Throughout 1963, the Beatles' popularity escalated in Britain, but EMI's American label, Capitol, had no interest in releasing the group's recordings because they felt their sound would not suit American tastes. Certainly, the 1963 release of *Introducing the Beatles* on the Vee Jay label had not sold enough to indicate the group's potential in the United States. Finally, in January 1964, a large publicity campaign accompanied Capitol's reluctant release of the album *Meet the Beatles,* a slightly different version of the group's second British album, *With the Beatles.* The single taken from the album, "I Want to Hold Your Hand," was an immediate hit on the American charts. By February 1964, when the Beatles arrived for their first visit to America, thousands of fans followed them everywhere they went. Their televised performances on *The Ed Sullivan Show* brought them into the homes of teenagers across the country. Beatlemania had begun, opening the American pop charts to a great number of British groups and bringing about what became known as the British invasion. A listening guide to the Beatles' first American hit is on page 101. "I Want to Hold Your Hand" was a number-one hit on the British pop charts for five weeks in

The Beatles on The Ed Sullivan Show (1964)

Listening Guide

"I Want to Hold Your Hand" by the Beatles (1964)

Tempo: The tempo is about 132 beats per minute, with four beats per bar.

Form: After three eighth-note pickups and a four-bar introduction, the song follows an AABABA form. Each A section is composed of eight bars and a four-bar refrain. The B sections are eight bars with a three-bar extension. The final A is extended by another repeat of the refrain.

Features: The beat pattern in the introduction creates an interesting effect by placing a stress on the third eighth-note pickup, making that half-beat sound like a **downbeat** (first beat of a bar). It is not until the vocals enter that the actual downbeat becomes clear.

Beat subdivisions are even throughout the recording.

The drums maintain a traditional, danceable rock backbeat.

The instrumentation is based on that of the Crickets: electric lead and rhythm guitars, electric bass guitar, and drums.

The instruments all function as accompaniment to the vocals, with no instrumental solo sections.

In several places, a hand-clapped rhythmic pattern creates an interesting polyrhythmic effect.

Lyrics: The singer uses the simple act of hand holding to demonstrate a deeper connection with his beloved.

Billboard pop charts: number one for seven weeks; British hit singles: number one for five weeks

1963 and number one on the American pop charts for seven weeks in 1964.

> **"The greatness about Paul and John being songwriters was they had a style, but the style was continually changing."**
>
> —George Martin

The Beatles were special among rock groups of the sixties because their music progressed from one album to the next as their experience and musicianship grew. They started out playing covers of songs by Chuck Berry, Little Richard, Carl Perkins, and others, and their early compositions showed these influences as well as those of American pop and soul styles. Lennon and McCartney wrote most of the group's hits, more often separately than in collaboration, though they frequently asked each other for advice on particular sections of songs. Their most popular early efforts were lighthearted love songs like "She Loves You" and "I Want to Hold Your Hand." They did their share of studio experimentation in the early days too, using feedback in the introduction to "I Feel Fine" in 1964.

The Beatles met Bob Dylan in 1964. At that point in Dylan's career, he was a folksinger with three albums out and a growing reputation as a writer of effective protest songs. An example of an early Dylan song that had a much deeper meaning than the types of songs that the Beatles had been writing was "Blowin' in the Wind" from *The Freewheelin' Bob Dylan* (1963). Dylan's recording of the song was sung in a traditional folk style not unlike the music of Woody Guthrie. The more commercial folk group Peter, Paul, and Mary recorded a version of it that was a number-two hit on the pop charts in 1963. That song asked listeners to think about death, war, and the lack of freedom allowed some people. The Beatles' song lyrics matured after their early communications with Dylan. Some reported that Dylan introduced the Beatles to marijuana as well, but since that drug was illegal, the musicians did not openly admit to it. Dylan's songwriting, acoustic guitar playing, and general folk style influenced much of the Beatles' work in the middle and late sixties.

The Beatles' music had many outside influences, but they also had a tremendous amount of direct influence on other musicians at every point in their career together. Twelve-string guitars had long been used in American folk music, but when George Harrison appeared playing a Rickenbacker electric twelve-string in the Beatles' first movie, *A Hard Day's Night* (1964), many other guitarists copied its wonderful, jangling sound. The British band the Searchers and Roger McGuinn of the American folk-rock group the Byrds became particularly well known for the sound.

The Beatles' music can be divided into three periods: (1) the pop-influenced love songs discussed earlier; (2) the Dylan-influenced introspective period; and (3) a period in which they concentrated on studio production techniques to produce such songs as "Tomorrow Never Knows" (on *Revolver*, 1966) and the entire *Sgt. Pepper's Lonely Hearts Club Band* album (1967).

> **"Dylan's influence on Lennon is perfectly obvious. He wrote more personal songs. He dug deeper into his own self such as Dylan had been doing."**
>
> —Journalist Al Aronowitz

The album *Rubber Soul* (1965) showed Harrison's increasing interest in Indian culture and music, which led him to learn to play the sitar. The instrument added a new color to their arrangements. The lyrics of many of the songs on this album contained deeper meanings than their earlier works had. Lennon's "Norwegian Wood (This Bird Has Flown)" was a cryptic story about an affair he had fallen into, and in "Run for Your Life" he spoke of the commitment he expected from a lover. McCartney wrote about the need for depth in a relationship in "I'm Looking Through You." The group had not stopped performing love songs, but they wrote of love in broader terms than they had previously. The use of "love" in "The Word" (1965), for example, was much more complex than the simple statement made in "She Loves You" (1964). As an example of the tremendous changes the Beatles' music underwent after their recording of "I Want to Hold Your Hand," compare that listening guide with the listening guide to "Norwegian Wood" on page 103.

The 1966 American albums *Yesterday . . . and Today* and *Revolver* contained songs such as "Nowhere Man" and "Eleanor Rigby," which searched for meaning in life, and "Taxman," which criticized government control over people's pocketbooks. The Beatles had progressed far beyond their formative, imitative early style and had put themselves at the forefront of creativity in rock music. They had also become tired of touring, and their compositions had become too complex to perform effectively onstage. So, in August 1966, the Beatles performed their last concert

Listening Guide

"Norwegian Wood"
as recorded by the Beatles (1965)

Tempo: The tempo is based on a waltz rhythm of three beats in each bar, with the primary accent only on the first of those three beats, or the downbeat. The approximate tempo of the waltz measures is 60 beats per minute.

Form: The form is based on eight-bar phrases ordered as AAAABB[1] AAAABB[1] AAA. (B[1] is like B except that it ends differently.) The first two A phrases are instrumental, the first featuring solo acoustic guitar and the second with that guitar joined by the sitar. The seventh, eighth, and last (eleventh) A phrases also feature the sitar with the guitar.

Features: The vocals are sung gently, creating an almost dreamy effect.

The primary accompaniment instruments are acoustic rhythm guitar and the sitar, which is featured in the second A of the introduction, in the other instrumental sections, and at the ends of vocal phrases. The bass and tambourine add subtle support to that accompaniment.

The sitar stands out from the other instruments because of its ability to bend notes much more than can be done on a guitar.

Lyrics: The song tells a story through suggestion, leaving much to the listener's imagination. The obvious points of the story are that the singer was invited into a girl's room where the two sat on the floor, drank wine, talked, and presumably went to bed together (although the singer claims to have slept in the bathtub). The girl had gone to work in the morning so the singer sat alone and enjoyed watching a fire. The relatively long and dreamy sitar solo after the suggestion of going to bed and the similarity between the words "Norwegian wood" and "knowing she would" caused much speculation and excitement for young listeners.

---

together, in San Francisco, and began to concentrate even more on their efforts in the recording studio.

> **So here you have classical elements of real musicianship, classical elements of world weariness, coming at the height of fame of a popular, bubblegum, rock and roll group introducing high intelligence into universal lyric poetry. That's quite a high advance.**
>
> —Beat writer Allen Ginsberg, about the Beatles

With the help of their producer, George Martin, the group recorded an album that became one of the masterpieces of rock music, *Sgt. Pepper's Lonely Hearts Club Band* (1967). All of the music on the album was planned around a single theme or concept—an idea influenced by the Beach Boys' *Pet Sounds* album from the previous year, but *Sgt. Pepper* went a step further. Rather than simply grouping songs with lyrical relationships, they made them part of a musical whole, a concert in a circuslike atmosphere complete with audience noises and whirling circus organ sounds. The lyrics for "Being for the Benefit of Mr. Kite!," in fact, came directly from a Victorian poster advertising a circus performance. Despite the lightness of McCartney's "Lovely Rita," many of the songs expressed

The Sitar

As is the case in many large countries, musical traditions vary in different areas of the land. Such is the case in India, where instruments and practices common in the north are different from those in the south. Musicians in both the north and the south use plucked-string instruments with fretted fingerboards. The instrument used in southern Indian classical music is called the vina, and its northern counterpart, the sitar. It was the sitar that first came to the attention of rock musicians in the middle sixties, primarily due to the commercial success of concerts given by sitarist Ravi Shankar. It was Shankar who taught Beatle George Harrison to play the instrument.

The sitar has a very distinctive sound when compared with any instrument of European origin because its frets are metal bars positioned almost an inch above the wooden fingerboard. That amount of space allows the player to bend the strings much further away from the pitch than would be possible on a guitar. The **microtones** created by that type of string bending contribute to the sitar's unusual timbre. Another sound that is characteristic of the sitar is the constant humming of a set of **sympathetic strings** set under the plucked strings. They are called sympathetic strings because they are not plucked but instead vibrate in sympathy with the strings above them that are played. The sound created by the sympathetic strings is called a **drone,** or

sustained tone. Most modern sitars have four or five melody strings and two or three additional drone strings. The frets are movable in order to be made to fit whatever key is required by a particular **raga,** or Indian melody. The body of the sitar is a pear-shaped gourd and on some sitars (not the one pictured here) the instrument's sound is enhanced by a resonator gourd at the top of the instrument's neck.

George Harrison and Ravi Shankar with an Indian sitar (1975)

the loneliness mentioned in the album's title. The Beatles had been influenced by the psychedelia of their time, and references to the illusions created by psychedelic drugs were evident in "Lucy in the Sky with Diamonds" (which fans took to represent the drug LSD), "Within You Without You," and "A Day in the Life." The album used musique concrète techniques on "Being for the Benefit of Mr. Kite!," for which Martin cut up a tape recording of a steam calliope and spliced the pieces of tape together (some were spliced in backward), for a background that sounded like what might be heard at a circus. Along with using other nontraditional sounds on the album, the Beatles put some animal noises at the end of "Good Morning, Good Morning," recalling the sound of the barking dogs at the end of the Beach Boys' *Pet Sounds* a year earlier.

By the time the Beatles recorded *Sgt. Pepper,* their music, lyrics, and production techniques had developed

far beyond what they had done only three years earlier. The listening guide to "A Day in the Life" on page 105 points out the complexity of their later work.

As the Beatles attempted to expand their awareness of the world and human relationships through transcendental meditation and experiments with drugs, the four individuals were growing apart both personally and artistically. Their manager, Brian Epstein, who had been instrumental in keeping them on a single path for many years, died of a drug overdose in 1967. The group continued to record, but the unity of their earlier days was gone. Their short television film *Magical Mystery Tour* (1967) and its subsequent album had some thought-provoking moments, but did not come up to the standard set by the *Sgt. Pepper* album. Their next effort, *The Beatles* (1968, often called the "White Album" because of its unadorned white cover), exemplified the individuality of the group members. Lennon had Japanese American artist Yoko Ono add vocal sound effects

Listening Guide

"A Day in the Life"
by the Beatles (1967)

Tempo: A tempo of about 76 beats per minute, with four beats per bar, is maintained throughout the recording. The B sections, however, stress a double note beat to the point that the tempo can be heard as 152 beats per minute.

Form: The recording flows out of the previous album cut. An eight-bar introduction is made up of four bars of solo acoustic guitar and then four bars with the guitar joined by bass and piano. The basic formal structure is AAABA, with sections of unequal lengths and long extensions and sound effects before and after the B section (which is sung by McCartney). The A sections are nine and ten bars long, and the B section is ten (or twenty, if counted at 152 beats per minute) bars long.

Features: Even beat subdivisions are maintained throughout the recording.

The drums add support and rhythmic color to the various sections of the recording but do not maintain a steady, traditional beat or backbeat.

The instruments include strummed acoustic guitar, electric bass, piano, drums, and, in a few places, a forty-piece orchestra. To create the sound mass between the third A and the B section, four recordings of the orchestra were mixed to have the effect of a 160-piece orchestra.

The recording ends with a long extension of an echo of the final piano chord.

Lyrics: The song begins with John Lennon's combining a variety of images to paint a collage of post–World War II British life and his own experiences of it. It begins with an allusion to the suicide of a prominent person, juxtaposes that with a reference to newsreel footage of World War II, then segues to Paul McCartney's section about an ordinary life that includes drug use. It cuts back to John Lennon, singing about an almost Monty Pythonesque image of absurdity that includes counting potholes and imagining them fitted into London's Royal Albert Hall.

on "Birthday" and "The Continuing Story of Bungalow Bill," and Harrison had Eric Clapton play lead guitar on "While My Guitar Gently Weeps." A variety of musical styles were also evident on the album. McCartney parodied the Beach Boys' vocal group sound on "Back in the U.S.S.R." and borrowed Dylan's acoustic folk style for "Blackbird." Ringo contributed "Don't Pass Me By," a country-styled composition. Lennon also experimented with **tape loops** on "Revolution 9" and wrote sentimental ballads such as "Julia," in memory of his late mother, and "Good Night," to his five-year-old son, Julian. Lennon divorced Julian's mother, Cynthia, in 1968 and began his personal and musical relationship with Yoko Ono. The pair released their own album, *Two Virgins,* about the same time the group released *The Beatles.*

The last album the Beatles recorded was *Abbey Road* (1969). Side one of the album had a variety of unrelated, individual songs, but side two centered on the theme of the group's impending breakup, and some rather subtle musical devices were used to help express that theme. "She Came in Through the Bathroom Window" related one of the many problems that had beset the group on tours—crazed female fans attempting anything and everything in order to get at them. "You Never Give Me Your Money" was a reference to the lawsuits group members had filed against each other over the business problems of their

The Beatles and their producer during the "All You Need Is Love" session (left to right): Paul McCartney, John Lennon, Ringo Starr, George Martin, and George Harrison

Apple Corporation. From the time Brian Epstein died, Paul McCartney felt that the burden of holding the group together had fallen on him, and his song "Carry That Weight" hinted at those feelings. During "Carry That Weight," the musical theme from "You Never Give Me Your Money" was reprised, reminding the listener of the group's legal battles and suggesting that the weight had become too much and that McCartney had given up his efforts to keep the group together. This idea of using a melody to remind the listener of a theme expressed earlier in a musical work has often been used in classical music, particularly in operas, in which a melody or melodic fragment (called a *leitmotif* in opera and an *idée fixe* in symphonic music) represented a particular character or mood. *Abbey Road* closed with "The End," in which McCartney, Harrison, and Lennon each took turns playing guitar solos and Ringo played a drum solo. "The End" was followed by silence and then a short song about the Queen of England. The Beatles were finished as a group.

> " Life is what happens while you are making other plans. "
>
> –John Lennon

Each of the Beatles pursued his own career during and after the group's breakup. John Lennon married Yoko Ono, and the two worked in tandem on various projects, including a number of efforts to support the cause of peace. They moved to New York and made recordings separately and together, Lennon often using Phil Spector as his producer. (Spector was the producer brought in to sift through the Beatles' *Let It Be* tapes and produce the *Let It Be* album, which was released after *Abbey Road* though it was recorded earlier.) In December 1980, one of the most tragic ironies in rock history occurred when

Lennon, who had always stood for peace, was shot to death by a "fan" outside his New York apartment.

Paul McCartney also married an American, Linda Eastman, but they made their home in Britain. He recorded the solo album *McCartney* (1970), and he and his wife recorded *Ram* (1971) before they formed the group Wings, which was enormously successful in the seventies.

George Harrison wrote and recorded albums of his own and also became very involved in movie production for Handmade Films, where he often worked with members of the British comedy troupe Monty Python. Ringo Starr pursued his own career as a singer and actor and occasionally played drums on recordings made by the other ex-Beatles. Harrison and Starr played together on several of Harrison's albums, including the successful *Cloud Nine* (1987). Harrison died of cancer in 2001. In 1989, Ringo put together what he called his All-Starr Band.

The American press, particularly when introducing the Beatles in 1964, portrayed them as good, clean, fun, nice guys. Yes, they had hair that was a bit long by American standards, but after all they were English so they could look a bit different. The Rolling Stones, on the other hand, were given the image of "bad guys." The Beatles dressed in matching suits, a look that the Rolling Stones resisted at all costs. The Beatles sang songs about love or dancing, and the Rolling Stones sang covers of blues and rhythm and blues songs. Right from the beginning, the British invasion was led by these two diverse bands.

The Rolling Stones

The **Rolling Stones** of the two-thousands is not a rhythm and blues band, but the Rolling Stones of the early sixties was one of Britain's best. Their bohemian lifestyle was shocking to most conventional Britons, but then they

The Rolling Stones in 1964 (left to right): Bill Wyman, Brian Jones, Mick Jagger, Charlie Watts, and Keith Richards

never cared to appeal to the conventional. They played an expressive, like-it-or-go-to-hell brand of rhythm and blues, and because both the music and their rebellious image appealed especially to young audiences, they attracted untold numbers of blues fans. They became one of the longest-lived groups in the history of rock music. In the course of their career, they veered away from rhythm and blues in most of their original compositions, but their concerts continually revived their roots.

Two members of the Rolling Stones, **Mick Jagger** (born in 1943) and **Keith Richard** (born in 1943), had attended the same primary school. (Keith's name had been mistakenly spelled "Richards" enough times that he eventually adopted the final "s" himself.) Although they lost contact with each other for ten years, they had both become blues fans after hearing Muddy Waters perform in England in 1958. When they ran into each other again in 1960, they began to work together, joining various blues groups in London. In 1962, they formed the Rolling Stones, naming their group after the "rolling stone" that represented a tough and independent man in blues songs like "Rollin' Stone" and "Mannish Boy" (both recorded by Muddy Waters).

The original Rolling Stones included singer/harpist Mick Jagger, guitarist Keith Richards, guitarist **Brian Jones** (1942–1969), pianist Ian Stewart, and other musicians who played with them off and on during their first year. In December 1962, **Bill Wyman** (William Perks, born in 1936) was added on bass, and in January 1963, **Charlie Watts** (born in 1941) joined as drummer. When Andrew Oldham was signed as their manager, he chose to remove Stewart from the official group roster, although Stewart did continue to do occasional work with the band throughout their career until his death in 1985.

Although they started out playing rhythm and blues, most of the Stones' more popular early recordings were covers of songs by other rock artists. Their first hit in

England (1963) was a cover of Chuck Berry's "Come On"; their second was "I Wanna Be Your Man" (1963), by Lennon and McCartney; and their third was a 1964 cover of Buddy Holly's "Not Fade Away." As the listening guide for "Not Fade Away" shows, the Stones' recording did not follow Holly's style at all. They turned the pop-rockabilly song into rhythm and blues. The listening guide on page 108 is a comparison of the two recordings. The Stones' version was a number-three hit on the British pop charts and number forty-eight on the American charts.

By 1964, the Beatles had become well known internationally, and the Stones followed along, gaining a reputation as the Beatles' nasty opposites. American teens preferred the Beatles at first, but the Stones soon won a large following. After all, rebellion had long been part of the history of rock and roll music.

> "The mayor of Denver once sent us a letter asking us to come in quietly, do the show as quietly as possible and split the same night, if possible. . . . They might entertain the Beatles, but they wanted to kick us out of town."
>
> –Keith Richards

The music that most closely influenced the style of the group's first three American-released albums was that of rhythm and blues and blues-rock artists Chuck Berry, Bo Diddley, Willie Dixon, and Muddy Waters, some of whose songs they covered. The Stones also covered "Route 66," which had been a hit for Nat "King" Cole in the forties and was recorded by Chuck Berry in 1961, but instead of imitating Cole's or Berry's vocal style they

Listening Guide

	"Not Fade Away" *by Buddy Holly (1957)*	*"Not Fade Away"* *by the Rolling Stones (1964)*
Tempo:	The tempo is about 184 beats per minute, with four beats in each bar.	The tempo is about 208 beats per minute, with four beats in each bar.
Form:	Each stanza has eight bars, with one line of lyrics in two bars, a guitar response to the line lasting two bars, followed by two more bars of lyrics and another two bars of guitar response.	The basic form of the original is followed, except that the stanzas are kept at eight bars each, where Holly used occasional extra bars in instrumental sections.
Features:	The drums keep a soft Bo Diddley beat (notated in Chapter 2).	The feel of the Bo Diddley beat is present, especially with the use of maracas, which were common in Bo Diddley's own recordings. The tambourine adds a black gospel feel.
	The backbeat is present but not prominent. Instrumental stop time is used (only the drums continue) during Holly's lead vocal lines.	The backbeat is not prominent. There is no stop time; all the instruments keep the rhythm going behind Jagger's vocal lines.
	A vocal group (probably not the Crickets) imitates some of the Bo Diddley beat kept by the drums with punctuations on beats two and four, and then beats two and three of the two-bar instrumental responses.	The beat pattern sung by the vocal group in Holly's recording is kept by the harmonica, but the use of blue notes changes the style from one of clean, crisp pop to include some blues color.
Lyrics:	Holly sings the lyrics as if he were politely informing a girl that she was eventually going to be his lover.	Jagger's vocal tone, singing Holly's same lyrics, sounds much more demanding— even arrogant—in his pronouncement that the girl will soon be his.

Billboard pop charts: number forty-eight; British hit singles: number three.

roughened the sound to be closer to that of their old favorite, Muddy Waters.

Of the blues revival groups, the Rolling Stones became the most popular in America. In addition to blues recordings by Muddy Waters and others, the Rolling Stones covered American soul and Motown songs on their early albums. When they appeared in the concert movie *The T.A.M.I. Show* (1964), they followed soul artist James Brown; to anyone watching the movie, it becomes clear that the types of dance routines that later became a regular part of Mick Jagger's stage performances can be traced to Brown's influence. The influences of soul music were apparent in Jagger's and Keith Richards's own songs, an early example of which was "(I Can't Get No) Satisfaction" (1965). A listening guide to "(I Can't Get No) Satisfaction" is on page 109.

Andrew Oldham knew that groups who depended on outside songwriters would not remain popular as long as

Listening Guide

"(I Can't Get No) Satisfaction" as recorded by the Rolling Stones (1965)

Tempo: The tempo is approximately 138 beats per minute, with four beats in each bar.

Form: After an eight-bar introduction, the song begins with a sixteen-bar refrain, which begins with the lyrics of the title, "(I Can't Get No) Satisfaction," sung twice. That refrain is followed by a verse that totals eighteen bars but is made up of sixteen bars of text extended by a break in the vocals just before the end. The break is two bars of just drums and tambourine. Two more sets of refrains and verses follow. The end is an extended refrain that fades out.

Features: The opening riff is two bars long and played four times through before the vocals begin. The riff sounds much like it is played by a saxophone, but the sound is instead played on a guitar through a Gibson Maestro fuzzbox to help intensify and sustain the sound.

The bass joins the guitar riff at the second bar (halfway through the riff), and the drums, tambourine, and acoustic guitar join on the second playing of the riff. The riff does not repeat during the refrains, but it does repeat during the verses.

The drums play a steady beat with little accenting of the backbeat. The fourth beat of most bars is accented by the tambourine, giving the effect of a backbeat.

Lyrics: The song *feels* like it's about sex, particularly the references to "girly action" and "making" girls, as well as the title theme itself (the singer is lamenting a dry spell in his love life). The underlying theme is a dislike of consumer culture as it is exemplified by commercial advertising. After all, the joke is on the singer. He is a rock star, "doing this and signing that," who *still* is sexually frustrated despite the cultural messages that his life should be perfect if he buys the right stuff.

Billboard pop charts: number one for four weeks; *Billboard* rhythm and blues charts: number nineteen; British hit singles: number one

---

those who wrote their own songs, so he pushed the group to improve their songwriting skills. Their earliest efforts included ideas contributed by all group members, and rather than credit all of them, they made up the name "Nanker-Phelge" to use for that purpose. Jagger and Richards developed writing skills as a team, and their songs gained much more commercial success than the group's cover records had.

An obvious change in the Rolling Stones' musical style came about when Jagger and Richards began to write more of their own songs. *Aftermath* (1966) was the group's first all-original album. Rhythm and blues and soul roots were still evident, but cultures other than those of African Americans were also being explored. The Indian sitar, played by the group's most versatile musician, Brian Jones, added a new timbre on "Paint It Black." The sitar, also used by the Beatles during the same time period, was in vogue for many rock groups, both American and British. In addition to the sitar, other nonstandard (for the Stones) instruments used on *Aftermath* were the dulcimer (played by Jones on "Lady Jane"), harpsichord, and marimba (played by Jones on "Under My Thumb"). Reflecting the macho image they had maintained since early in their career, both "Stupid Girl" and "Under My Thumb" enraged anyone sensitive to women's issues.

The album *Their Satanic Majesties Request* (1967) was musically experimental, particularly on the part of Brian

Jones, who had become intrigued with the possibilities afforded by the use of electronic instruments. He played a **mellotron** (*mel*ody + elec*tron*ics) on "2000 Light Years from Home." The influence of drugs can be heard in some of the Stones' wandering, unfocused instrumentals, which conveyed a feeling of time expanding. The psychedelic artwork on the cover of *Their Satanic Majesties Request* was reminiscent of other drug-influenced albums that were being put out in San Francisco during the same period. Both the cover and the musical experimentation on the album were also reminiscent of the Beatles' *Sgt. Pepper* album, which was released earlier the same year. The Stones had experienced problems with the authorities because of their use of drugs. In England the group's fans believed the title of the album was inspired by the fact that the drug arrests of various group members had kept them from touring freely—British passports contained a line that began "Her Britannic Majesties . . . Request."

" He was a cat who could play any instrument. "

–Keith Richards, about Brian Jones

The Stones' *Beggars Banquet* album (1968) was released five months later than planned because of controversy over the cover the group wanted to use. Once again, they demonstrated they would do anything to challenge society's standards of acceptability, on their album covers and in their songs. "Street Fighting Man" sang of fighting in the streets in much the same way that the American Motown group Martha and the Vandellas had sung of dancing in the streets. Motown's goal was to encourage a peaceful movement toward racial integration and equality, but the Stones cultivated the image of macho fighters. Again experimenting, Brian Jones provided distorted sounds on the recording of "Street Fighting Man," playing an Indian tamboura.

Beggars Banquet proved to be the end of Brian Jones's participation with the Rolling Stones. Although by some accounts he had been asked to leave because his drug use had gotten out of hand, he announced he was quitting the band to explore other musical directions. He never had an opportunity to do any experimenting on his own, however: He went to sleep while sitting alone in his swimming pool and drowned in July 1969. Mick Taylor (born in 1948), from John Mayall's Bluesbreakers, replaced Jones as the group's second guitarist.

Another tragedy hit the Rolling Stones that same year. While on a very successful American tour, they decided to give a free concert at the Altamont Speedway in California. Woodstock had been such a successful rock extravaganza that the time seemed right for another large outdoor gathering of rock fans. To avoid calling in uniformed guards their fans would resent, the Stones followed the advice offered by San Francisco's Grateful Dead and hired members of a motorcycle gang, the Hell's Angels, to handle security for the event. A young African American man, Meredith Hunter, was stabbed to death in front of the stage by "security officers"; the stabbing was recorded during the taping of *Gimme Shelter,* a documentary about the Stones' tour. This much-publicized incident at Altamont certainly lessened the positive attitude toward rock festivals that the success of Woodstock had engendered.

" The Dead told us, 'It's cool. We've used them for the last two or three years.' "

–Keith Richards, about the decision to hire the motorcycle gang the Hells Angels to police the Altamont festival

Although the Rolling Stones started their musical life as a blues band, by the early to midseventies they had become one of the most eclectic groups in rock and roll. By that time, almost all their recordings were original compositions by Jagger and Richards, and the team had learned to assimilate many of the existing styles of popular music. On their *Sticky Fingers* (1971) and *Exile on Main Street* (1972) albums, "Sister Morphine" was styled after American folk ballads; gospel-style call-and-response vocals were used on "I Got the Blues" and "Tumblin' Dice"; and "Dead Flowers," "Moonlight Mile," and "Loving Cup" could have been mistaken for American country, even hillbilly music. The rhythm and blues style of the group's past was evident in "Shake Your Hips," which used blues harmonica, and the guitar in "Casino Boogie" played the old single-chord rhythm and blues style. Both British and American folk and country styles were evident on the *Goat's Head Soup* (1973) and *It's Only Rock 'n' Roll* (1974) albums, and the title cut of the latter used a rhythm and blues beat. Motown's influence was not forgotten with the cover of "Ain't Too Proud to Beg," the Temptations' hit from 1966.

In 1975, Mick Taylor left the group and was replaced by Ron Wood (born in 1947), who had previously worked with the Faces and the Jeff Beck Group. As varied as the Rolling Stones' musical styles had become, the album *Black and Blue* contained a new surprise in the form of African and Jamaican elements. "Hot Stuff" was based on rhythms and vocal devices that could be heard in modern-day Kenya and Tanzania and "Cherry Oh Baby" was a cover of a reggae song by Eric Donaldson. The giant-selling album

The Rolling Stones in 1989 (left to right): Ron Wood, Mick Jagger, Keith Richards, and Bill Wyman. Charlie Watts is in the background.

Some Girls (1978) and its hit, "Miss You," showed that the group did not remain untouched by the disco dance craze of the time. "Miss You" was a number-three hit on the British pop charts and number one on the American charts. The listening guide appears on page 112. *Emotional Rescue* (1980) continued with disco influences, but also included a Jamaican ska rhythm in "Send It to Me" and a country style in "Indian Girl." The albums *Tattoo You* (1980) and *Undercover of the Night* (1983) contained a combination of both funk and country-styled tunes. On *Dirty Work* (1986), "Too Rude" used a reggae rhythm and bass line.

> " 'Miss You' is an emotion, it's not really about 'a' girl. To me, the feeling of longing is what the song is."
>
> —Mick Jagger

The band took a short break while both Jagger and Richards recorded solo albums during the late eighties, but the Rolling Stones were back on the road for a massive tour to promote their *Steel Wheels* (1989) album. That tour was followed by other band members recording solo albums and the long-expected announcement that Bill Wyman was leaving the band. It took almost two years for a replacement to be found. The new bassist was Darryl Jones, a young African American who had previously worked with jazz trumpeter Miles Davis and also played on Sting's album *The Dream of the Blue Turtles* (1985). The album that followed, *Voodoo Lounge* (1994), won a Grammy award for 1994s Best Rock Album.

The recorded output of the Rolling Stones from 1962 through the early two-thousands gave their fans quite an aural-cultural tour through a number of international musical styles, as well as several different period styles, ranging from early British folk to early American country blues to current styles. Borrowing the music of other peoples and other times served to broaden the group's own style. But no matter what style of music they played, or whose recording they covered, they always remained, unmistakably, the Rolling Stones.

Summary

The year 1964 was the beginning of a British invasion that never really came to an end. The first two major bands to gain the affections of American fans were the Beatles and the Rolling Stones. In many ways, the two represented two different kinds of music and had two different images. The Beatles, at least early in their career, played lighthearted

111

Listening Guide

"Miss You"
as recorded by the Rolling Stones
(1978)

Tempo: The tempo is approximately 112 beats per minute, with four beats in each bar.

Form: The form is based on an almost hypnotic repetition of a four-bar phrase with pickups. The repetition of that phrase is broken only once by two four-bar contrasting phrases. The contrast occurs in the phrases with lyrics that ask why the singer's "baby" is waiting so long.

There are four instrumental sections: (1) the instrumental introduction is three phrases long; (2) a one-phrase (four-bar) instrumental with soft vocal responses follows the pair of contrasting phrases; (3) a two-phrase (eight-bar) instrumental occurs five phrases later and features a tenor saxophone solo; (4) the recording concludes with three phrases that feature a harmonica solo and then fade out.

Features: Beat subdivisions are generally uneven, except for the drums, which maintain even subdivisions.

The drums maintain a very steady pulse on each beat, sometimes evenly accenting each beat and other times alternating the accents with a strong emphasis on the backbeat. The regular pounding of the beat is very much part of the dance-oriented disco style.

The vocals are the primary attraction of the recording. Jagger changes his voice in many ways—from soft, subtle begging to an effective imitation of African American "jive talk" as he mimics a friend's voice on the phone.

Lyrics: The singer is so obsessed by how much he misses the person to whom the song is directed that he cannot do anything but think about that person.

Billboard pop charts: number one; *Billboard* rhythm and blues charts: number thirty-three; British hit singles: number three

---

love songs, most of which were original, and dressed in matching suits. They were polite and entertaining when interviewed by American reporters, and they captured the hearts of many American teens. The Rolling Stones, on the other hand, refused to comply with the standard sort of matching dress that was generally expected of bands at the time and chose to display a "bad boy" image. They also based much of their music on that of American blues, rhythm and blues, and early rock music.

The Beatles' music progressed throughout their time together to include elements of Bob Dylan's folk style and poetic lyrics, psychedelic music, Indian music, and new techniques of studio production. The Rolling Stones' music progressed as well. They had not originally considered themselves to be songwriters, but their chart-topping hits only happened once they began to record original

songs. Those songs were influenced at times by rhythm and blues, American country music, soul music, and eventually, reggae. The Beatles broke up, and each pursued his own career, whereas the Rolling Stones remained together with a few personnel changes. Both bands had tremendous influence on other rock bands to follow them.

discussion questions

What was it about the American social, political, and musical situations in the early sixties that made the country so ready for invasion by the British bands? Were the Beatles and the Rolling Stones so great that they could have taken over the U.S. charts any time, or was it mostly a case of good timing that they became so popular so quickly?

chapter 8

The British Invasion Continues and America Reacts

"I think with guitar smashing, just like performance itself, it's a performance, it's an act, it's an instant, and it really is meaningless."

—PETE TOWNSHEND OF THE WHO

113

The Mersey Sound

Like the Beatles, most of the groups from Liverpool and Manchester used a lead guitar, rhythm guitar, bass guitar, and drums. The origin of that instrumental combination lay in American rockabilly of the fifties, except that in most rockabilly the lead guitarist played a hollow-body electric instrument, the rhythm guitar was a steel-strung acoustic, and the bass was an acoustic (string) bass. Buddy Holly had been among the first to use a solid-body electric guitar for his lead playing, and his rhythm guitarist used an electric, though hollow-bodied, rhythm guitar. His bassist played a standard string bass much like that used by other rockabilly groups. Many British groups whose music was influenced by Holly and by rockabilly updated the instrumentation by using electric bass guitar instead of the large acoustic instrument. Although some Mersey groups occasionally added piano—or, as in the case of Gerry and the Pacemakers, orchestral string sections—to their recordings, the Mersey sound depended heavily on guitars.

From Liverpool's neighboring city of Manchester, the **Hollies,** formed in 1962 by singer Allan Clarke and singer/guitarist Graham Nash, chose their name to identify themselves with Buddy Holly. Although their music did not reach America until the release of the single "Bus Stop" in 1966, their popularity allowed them to stay together through much of the seventies and attract attention when they regrouped in the eighties. Graham Nash left in 1968 because he wanted the group to record his "Marrakesh Express" instead of Dylan covers for the album *Words and Music by Bob Dylan* (1969). Nash's song ended up being an early hit (1969) for his new group Crosby, Stills and Nash.

The most commercially successful group from Manchester was **Herman's Hermits,** started by singer/guitarist/actor Peter Noone. They were first known as the Heartbeats but changed the name to make use of Noone's nickname, Herman. Between 1965 and 1967, Herman's Hermits had many American hit singles, most of which were directed at a younger audience than that of the Beatles. Like the Hollies and other Mersey groups, the Hermits played guitars, bass, and drums. Herman's boy-next-door image was not unlike that of Buddy Holly, except that Herman's music had a less serious tone than Holly's. In fact, some of Herman's songs were very funny. "I'm Henry VIII, I Am" (1965), for example, did not refer to England's former king, but instead to a woman who marries only men named Henry; the singer is her eighth husband.

The Mods

London is such a large city that it had room for many different trends in rock music. The blues- and rhythm and blues–styled rock groups like the Rolling Stones, the Yardbirds, and the Animals had the following of one group of fans, while others preferred the clean-cut sound and image of the Dave Clark Five, Peter and Gordon, and Petula

The Kinks in 1971 (left to right): Dave Davies, Mick Avory, Ray Davies, and John Dalton

Clark. The Kinks had formed as part of the blues revival, but their experimentation with distorted sound effects led them away from their traditional blues orientation. The youth subculture known as the **Mods** (or Modernists) had short hair, wore trendy suits, and rode motor scooters (rather than "real" motorcycles). Groups from London during the midsixties with Mod followings included the Small Faces, the Who, and, to some degree, the Kinks.

As was the case with most other bands of the British invasion, the **Kinks** started out by playing covers of fifties rock hits. Their first recording was a cover of Little Richard's "Long Tall Sally" (Little Richard in 1956, Kinks in 1964). Ray Davies realized that to establish and maintain a career they should concentrate on writing their own material and develop their own distinctive sound, which

began by slitting their amplifier speaker to get the distorted **fuzztone** for their powerful hit "You Really Got Me" (1964). At a time when most rock singers were using their music to express feelings of love, or in many cases lust, Davies sang about being "Tired of Waiting for You," wanting a girlfriend to "Set Me Free" (1965), and coldly asking women "Who'll Be the Next in Line" (1965).

The popularity of the Kinks' hit "You Really Got Me" caused widespread interest in the fullness and roughness of fuzztone. Eventually, fuzz boxes were sold, allowing musicians to use the sound whenever they wanted to without having to cut their speakers. A listening guide to the song that stirred up the interest in fuzztone appears below. "You Really Got Me" was number seven on the American pop charts and number one on the British ones.

Listening Guide

"You Really Got Me"
as recorded by the Kinks (1964)

Tempo: The tempo is approximately 138 beats per minute, with four beats in each bar.

Form: The recording begins with a four-bar introduction that consists of four statements of the one-bar guitar riff that continues to repeat throughout the recording. The drums enter in the third bar.

The introduction is followed by three twenty-bar sections, with a ten-bar instrumental section between the second and third sections. Each of the twenty-bar sections follows the form AABC. The A and B phrases are each four bars long and the C phrases are eight bars long. The instrumental section is based on two-and-one-half repetitions of A.

Features: Even beat subdivisions are used throughout the recording.

The drums maintain a strong backbeat, and a tambourine supports the tempo by playing on each beat.

The guitar uses fuzztone created by a cut speaker cone.

The riff pattern begins with a half-beat pickup and then plays three beats, ending with a half-beat rest.

Abrupt key changes occur between sections. Section B is one whole-step higher than A, and C is another fourth higher than B (a fifth higher than A). The pitch of the riff changes along with the key changes. Each new section begins in the original key and then changes key in the same places as did the first section.

An interesting effect is created by shifting the vocal accents from the way the lyrics would normally be spoken (even in England). Instead of accenting "you" and "got" in "you really got me," Davies accents "really" and "me."

Lyrics: The singer is so enraptured by his girlfriend that he is practically sick.

Billboard pop charts: number seven; British hit singles: number one

By late 1965, Davies began to expand his lyrical range to comment cynically on other people's values and lifestyles in his lyrics, losing his pop following in the process but gaining a faithful entourage of "Kink kultists." "A Well Respected Man" (1966) was the first of many songs he wrote about people he saw as lacking the creative energy needed to rise above society's dictates, people who were content to live boring existences simply by fitting into a socially acceptable mold. Davies made effective use of repetition in his music to express the monotony of the life his lyrics depicted. In some ways, "A Well Respected Man" took a dig at the London Mods, many of whom were among the Kinks' most ardent fans. He further insulted the subculture for its penchant for trendy fashions in "Dedicated Follower of Fashion" (1966).

The **Who** came to rock music from a background in early jazz styles. Teenage banjo player **Pete Townshend** (born in 1945) and trumpeter **John Entwistle** (1946–2002) formed a **trad jazz** band (traditional jazz, meaning New Orleans– or Chicago-styled Dixieland) called the Scorpions in 1959. Townshend's parents were musicians and taught him some of the basics of music and its notation. Townshend taught himself to play a number of instruments, including guitar, accordion, piano, and drums, in addition to the banjo. Entwistle had picked up the guitar when he heard the twangy guitar sound of Duane Eddy but decided to set it aside to play bass when Townshend started playing guitar.

Entwistle met **Roger Daltrey** (born in 1944) in 1962. Daltrey had played some skiffle guitar and then graduated to lead guitar with his own band, the Detours. Entwistle joined the Detours as bass player and soon brought in Townshend to play rhythm guitar. Daltrey fired the group's singer, Colin Dawson, to become both lead guitarist and lead vocalist. Along with drummer Doug Sanden, the Detours began to play at various clubs in London.

In 1963, at the suggestion of a friend, they changed their name to the Who, and decided to look for another drummer because Sanden was not experimental enough for them. **Keith Moon** (1947–1978), who had been playing drums for a British surf group called the Beachcombers, asked for a chance to sit in with the Who. On that occasion, Moon played with such energy that he broke the bass drum pedal; and though the destruction of instruments had not yet become a part of the Who's act, they were impressed by Moon's aggressive playing and made him their new drummer.

In 1964, the Who signed with manager Pete Meaden, who had some ideas about molding a group image from having worked for Andrew Oldham, the Rolling Stones' manager. Meaden was a Mod and set about to change the Who's style to appeal to Mods. He had them rename themselves the High Numbers, get their hair cut, and dress themselves in trendy suits. The Motown sound was very popular with Mods, so he had them increase that part of their repertoire and eliminate the older Dixieland and surf styles. The High Numbers' stage performances were improving, with Townshend, Daltrey, and Moon each competing for the audience's attention. Townshend strummed powerful guitar chords, his arm revolving in complete circles, Daltrey twirled his microphone around, and Moon thrashed at his drums as violently as possible.

Film directors Kit Lambert and Chris Stamp became interested in the High Numbers because they were looking for a band to use in a film on rock music. Only a short

The Who (left to right): John Entwistle, Roger Daltrey, Keith Moon, and Pete Townshend

television film was made, but Lambert and Stamp became the group's managers. Out of fear that the name the High Numbers would soon become dated, the group returned to calling themselves the Who. With some inspiration from the choppy guitar rhythms of the Kinks, and with session player Jimmy Page on rhythm guitar, the Who recorded their first hit, an original song by Townshend called "I Can't Explain" (1965). This was soon followed by the single "My Generation," and the Who were on their way to international stardom. The recording, which is one of their most remembered today, only reached number seventy-four on the American pop charts although it was number two in Britain. A listening guide, is included here.

Although Daltrey's stuttering of the lyrics to "My Generation" was connected with the fact that the hyper and sometimes amphetamine-taking Mods had a reputation for being inarticulate, the Who was slowly in the process of dropping their Mod image. After "My Generation" was a hit in Britain, the Who recorded a short version of the song called "My Favorite Station" to advertise a new program for BBC's Radio One. The Who followed that advertisement with others for such things as Coca-Cola. Their experience with the recording of rock-based radio ads was the basis for choosing advertising as the theme in their first concept album, *The Who Sell Out* (1967).

The Who were not widely popular with many rock fans in the United States until after their 1967 performance at

Listening Guide

"My Generation"
as recorded by the Who (1965)

Tempo: The tempo begins at approximately 192 beats per minute, but it varies somewhat through the recording and slows down gradually at the end. There are four beats in each bar.

Form: After a four-bar introduction, the form is based on twenty-bar periods, most of which are made up of five four-bar phrases that end with the words "my generation" (or an instrumental version of the melody previously sung with the words). The last two times those periods are played they are extended to be longer than the earlier ones. The first period begins with the words "people try" and the second period begins with "why don't."

Features: Uneven beat subdivisions are used through most of the recording.

The drums maintain a strong backbeat throughout most of the recording.

The first four four-bar phrases of each period have a solo vocal line in the first

two bars and then a group vocal response in the next two, ending with the words "my generation."

The third period is instrumental, with electric bass improvising around the solo vocal melody and guitar taking the place of the group vocal responses.

Daltrey stutters and stammers on the solo vocal lines, often causing slight variations in the tempo of the music accompanying him.

The music abruptly changes key by moving up one whole step, later a half step, and then another whole step. The key changes happen just after the third (the instrumental) period, in the fifth bar of an instrumental extension of the fourth period, and during the long final extension.

Lyrics: The song is an outcry for rebellious youths who want to be free to do as they please and don't ever want to be like "old" people.

Billboard pop charts: number seventy-four; British hit singles: number two

the Monterey Pop Festival, by which time their attention-drawing antics had grown into the complete destruction of guitars, amplifiers, microphones, and drums on stage. During their chaotic stage performances, John Entwistle kept the music going as long as possible, standing beside the wreckage. He never seemed to care to draw audience attention to himself but concentrated on his playing while the rest of the group put on the visual show. Because the band had only one guitarist, and Townshend was more a rhythm guitarist than a lead player, Entwistle developed his bass technique to enable him to play lines that often functioned as both lead and bass.

The Who's next American hits were "Happy Jack" and "I Can See for Miles" (both 1967). Townshend began to consider the possibility of expanding beyond the standard pop format of two- to three-minute songs and writing a rock **opera,** beginning with the ten-minute "mini-opera" he had written for the album *Happy Jack* (1967). "Rael" had been planned as a mini-opera on *The Who Sell Out,* but too much was cut from the original by the time the album was pressed. Finally, in 1969, the Who produced a double-album-length opera about a boy who turned deaf, dumb, and blind after being traumatized by his violent home life, but whose talent for playing pinball eventually brings about a miraculous healing and return to the world of sight and sound. *Tommy* proved to be an artistic and commercial breakthrough and was hailed as a powerful stage piece, although the group rarely performed it in its entirety. The entire opera became known worldwide through the 1975 film *Tommy,* directed by Ken Russell. A new, live version of *Tommy* hit Broadway in 1993.

Townshend intended to follow *Tommy* with a science fiction concept album for which he had experimented with sounds produced by a synthesizer and sequencer. He abandoned the story idea, but his innovative and distinctive synthesizer effects were featured on the album *Who's Next* (1971) and its hit single, "Won't Get Fooled Again." In that song Townshend expressed disillusionment about the effectiveness of protest movements at a time when many movements were ending and were being reevaluated by those who had participated in them. The Who's Mod association returned for their next rock opera, *Quadrophenia* (1973), based on the long-standing controversy between the Mods and the Rockers. Six years later the opera became a film directed by Franc Roddam.

The last Who album Keith Moon lived to record was *Who Are You* (1978). In September 1978, Moon died of an overdose of Heminevrin, an anti-alcoholism sedative, combined with an excess of alcohol in his system. A movie tribute to the Who's career with Moon, called *The Kids Are Alright,* was released in 1979.

Needing a new drummer, the Who chose Kenney Jones (born in 1948), a friend of theirs from another London-based Mod band, the Small Faces (later called the Faces). There was no point in Jones's trying to imitate the wild playing of Keith Moon. Moon had such an individualistic style that he was virtually impossible to imitate. Instead Jones, a competent and powerful drummer in his own right, brought his own musical personality to the group. Along with a change of drummer, the group added keyboard player John "Rabbit" Bundrick to their new sound. Bundrick was from Texas but had been a studio musician in England, playing on albums by Free and other bands since the early seventies.

Having overcome the loss of Moon, the group lost its enthusiasm for touring when eleven concertgoers were trampled to death in a rush of thousands of fans at Cincinnati's Riverfront Coliseum in 1979. Concert promoters had sold tickets at a single price, with no reserved seats (called festival seating), and before the doors were all opened, they started playing recordings by the Who, making fans think the concert had started. All of this caused a desperate stampede. The group went onstage not knowing about the tragedy. After they were informed about it, they did not want to continue their tour, but they feared that if they canceled they might never want to tour again. Bass player John Entwistle died the night before their 2002 tour, but they replaced him and the tour went on, as did another tour in 2006. The Who continue to tour with only two original members, Pete Townshend and Roger Daltrey.

British Blues Revival Bands

American jazz and jazz-related popular music had intrigued the British since ragtime music by Scott Joplin reached England through published sheet music. During the early decades of the twentieth century, a number of American jazz soloists and groups toured Britain, as well as the rest of Europe, creating quite a furor over the new music, which, in some ways, gained greater acceptance in Britain and Europe than in America, where it too often was considered the primitive product of an inferior people. The development of the recording industry, too, helped to bring American music to the attention of the rest of the world. Groups imitating those on the American recordings sprang up all over Europe, and jazz became an international music with its roots in African American culture.

American rock and roll became popular in England during the late fifties. Although some American performers did tour in Britain, the English soon produced their own soloists and groups who patterned themselves after various American originals. On the heels of Elvis Presley, Gene Vincent, and Eddie Cochran came their British imitators, Tommy Steele, Billy Fury, and Joe Brown. When American rhythm and blues and rockabilly styles were superseded by the blander, dance-oriented style popularized on *American Bandstand,* some British fans turned to the pop rock of Cliff Richard and Marty Wilde. Those who could not relate to that pop style became disillusioned with rock and abandoned it for the older, gutsier type of music in which fifties rock was rooted—the blues.

British musician **Chris Barber** started a band in 1954 that played trad jazz, skiffle, and country blues at clubs in London. As Barber's following grew, musicians who had played with him left to form their own groups. By the early sixties, blues clubs had sprung up all over the city. Among the more successful bands were Cyril Davies Rhythm and Blues All-Stars (formed in the late fifties), Alexis Korner and Cyril Davies Blues Incorporated (formed in 1961), the Rolling Stones (formed in 1962), John Mayall's Bluesbreakers (formed in 1963), the Spencer Davis Rhythm and Blues Quartet (formed in 1963, later renamed the Spencer Davis Group), the Yardbirds (formed in 1963), and the Graham Bond Organisation (formed in 1963). In addition to making many cover recordings of American blues songs, these British groups wrote original material based on the blues style.

Most of the British blues covers were not sanitized and countrified versions of the blues originals, as were those made by white artists in America during the fifties. The British covers of the early sixties, although often not exact copies, were as close to the style and feel of the originals as they could get, including the use of bottlenecks and string-bending techniques on the guitar. Some of the covers added more interesting and active bass or lead guitar lines than were heard in the original recordings; the tempos varied, with some covers slightly faster than the originals and some slower; and at times some modifications were made in melodies. But the important point was that these covers did not involve changes in the basic character of the music. The British were not covering the blues in order to make commercial hits. They were playing the blues out of a real love, respect, and enthusiasm for the music. Some of the groups did indeed go on to commercial success through more pop-oriented music, but even then their styles retained the influence of their earlier experience with the blues.

In the early fifties, Cyril Davies played banjo in a trad jazz band, but as he became more attracted to pure blues he concentrated on singing and playing the harp. With guitarist Alexis Korner, Davies formed the amplified blues group Blues Incorporated, which became the training ground for many blues-styled rock artists, including drummers Charlie Watts and Ginger Baker, singer Mick Jagger, and bassist Jack Bruce.

As a group that started out playing the blues and rhythm and blues, the Rolling Stones were exceptional in having stayed together for so long with so few membership changes. It was more typical for musicians of blues revival groups of the sixties to move from one band to another quite often. The blues was such a distinct musical style, with its own musical language and such well-established formal traditions, that it was very easy for musicians to walk on stage and perform with others with whom they had never worked before. Blues musicians improvised much of what they played, and as long as the improvisations followed the traditional twelve-bar harmonic progression, or some variant of it, and as long as the musicians listened and were responsive to each other, whatever they played would fit together. Clearly, some combinations of players worked better than others, but part of the joy of playing an improvised music such as the blues lay in the musical give-and-take among the musicians.

An even more important group that functioned as a training ground for many a blues-rock musician was **John Mayall's Bluesbreakers.** The group was formed in 1963, and throughout its existence Mayall's singing and harp, guitar, and keyboard playing remained faithful to the blues tradition. Many of his Bluesbreakers left to form commercial rock groups, but their experience in playing the blues continued to influence their rock styles. Among the rock musicians who worked with the Bluesbreakers early in their careers were guitarists Eric Clapton, Mick Taylor, and Peter Green; bassists John McVie, Jack Bruce, and Andy Fraser; and drummers Keef Hartley, Aynsley Dunbar, and Mick Fleetwood. John Mayall was sometimes called the Father of the British Blues because of the Bluesbreakers' importance to the blues revival.

Spencer Davis had sung and played both guitar and harp only as a hobby when he formed the Spencer Davis Rhythm and Blues Quartet, renamed the Spencer Davis Group, in 1963. Singer/guitarist/keyboardist Steve Winwood (born in 1948) and his brother Muff, a bassist, had played in trad jazz bands until they joined with Davis to form his blues band. The group's hit recordings "Gimme Some Lovin'" and "I'm a Man" (both written by Steve Winwood) were made in 1967 and featured Steve Winwood as the singer. After the Spencer Davis Group broke up, Steven Winwood formed and recorded with Traffic, worked with Eric Clapton in Blind Faith, and later had a solo career in which he blended his blues background with jazz, folk, and even classical music.

One of the best examples of a blues musician moving from one group to another was singer **Rod Stewart** (born in 1945). After a bit of experience singing folk music on street corners, Stewart sang and played blues harp with several groups in the London clubs. With his rough-edged vocal sound, he was able to capture the vocal quality of the African American bluesmen. Blues groups with which he performed and recorded during the midsixties included the Hoochie Coochie Men (with Long John

Baldry), the Aynsley Dunbar Retaliation (with Jack Bruce of Cream and Peter Green of Fleetwood Mac), and Shotgun Express (with Peter Green and Mick Fleetwood of Fleetwood Mac). By 1967, Stewart was becoming less of a blues purist, and he began singing nonblues rock music in his bluesy style. He joined the Jeff Beck Group, after which he went on to the Faces (formerly the Small Faces) and then established a successful solo career.

Another British singer who patterned his vocal style after the sound of African American blues and rhythm and blues singers was **Eric Burdon** (born in 1941). He had been an art student in Newcastle upon Tyne until he became involved with the blues, the popularity of which had spread from London to his hometown in the north of England. He joined the Alan Price Combo as lead singer in 1962. Keyboard player Price and his group had been playing blues and rhythm and blues since 1958. With Burdon, the group became a popular club attraction with such a wild stage act that their fans began calling them the **Animals,** a name that stuck with them.

The Animals covered many American blues and rhythm and blues songs by Bo Diddley, John Lee Hooker, Fats Domino, and Chuck Berry. Not only was Burdon very good at imitating the tonal quality of the African American bluesmen, but Alan Price did an impressive imitation of Bo Diddley's distinctive guitar style on his electric organ. The Animals also did nonblues songs, such as the American folk song "House of the Rising Sun" (1964), and with that and their original songs they became less a blues group and more a rock group with a style that was rooted in the blues.

Another in the lineup of British blues bands was the **Yardbirds,** formed in London in 1963. Their lead guitarist, Anthony "Top" Topham, was replaced by **Eric Clapton** (born in 1945) after the group had been together for only four months. The Yardbirds started out playing covers of American blues recordings and gained a following at some of London's blues clubs. When blues singer/harpist Sonny Boy Williamson No. 2 (Rice Miller) visited London in December 1963, he chose the Yardbirds to be his backup group. Only two months after those performances with Williamson, the Yardbirds were in a studio making a professional recording that led to a contract.

"Those English boys want to play the blues so bad, and that's just how they play it—so bad."

–Sonny Boy Williamson after working with the Yardbirds

For the next year or so, the Yardbirds covered tunes by John Lee Hooker, Bo Diddley, Howlin' Wolf, Sonny Boy Williamson, Willie Dixon, and Chuck Berry. But with

the success of the Beatles and other British groups in America in 1964, most members of the group decided to stop playing the blues and try a more commercial style of music. The idea worked, and they achieved pop stardom in 1965 with "For Your Love," but they paid a price. Eric Clapton, the most blues-loving of the Yardbirds, refused to play guitar on any more pop recordings and left the group. To replace him, they first approached **Jimmy Page** (born in 1944). Page had earned a great deal of respect as a blues guitarist who could play almost any form of popular music, including the Yardbirds' new commercial style, but he was so successful as a studio musician that he was not looking to join a group as a regular member. Tours would have caused him to lose studio jobs. Page recommended **Jeff Beck** (born in 1944), who had been playing with a rhythm and blues band called the Tridents, and shortly thereafter Beck joined the Yardbirds.

Musically, Beck turned out to be a good choice. The Yardbirds were developing a commercial, psychedelic stage act, and Beck eagerly joined in by playing his guitar behind his head and experimenting with amplifier **feedback.** He also made frequent use of string bending, a technique that was not exclusively a part of the blues tradition; it was often employed on the sitar and other Indian stringed instruments. Beck even used his technique to imitate the sound of the sitar in the Yardbirds' recording of "Heart Full of Soul" (1965).

Although Beck was a fine musical addition to the group, he turned out to be undependable in other ways. His performances were inconsistent, sometimes requiring the other group members to fill in for him when he was not paying attention to what he was supposed to be playing. He would even miss concerts, choosing instead to be with his girlfriend. In need of a new player to stimulate himself and mollify the group, Beck asked Jimmy Page to join so the two of them could play lead guitar together. Page finally did join the Yardbirds, playing lead guitar alone in Beck's absence and sharing the spot when Beck was there. Beck finally quit the group in 1966 to form his own band, leaving Jimmy Page as the sole lead guitarist. When the other members left, Page put together a new group called the New Yardbirds. That group stayed together for a long and successful career as Led Zeppelin. Musically, Led Zeppelin was an important link between the blues and heavy metal. Their music is discussed in Chapter 13, "Hard Rock and Heavy Metal."

Clapton remained closely tied to the blues for most of his career. Before joining the Yardbirds in 1963, he had played with two rhythm and blues groups, the Roosters and Casey Jones and the Engineers. Upon leaving the Yardbirds, he joined John Mayall's Bluesbreakers and played with them fairly regularly for just over a year, from April 1965 to July 1966. The Bluesbreakers' frequent personnel

Cream in 1967
(left to right):
Jack Bruce, Ginger
Baker and Eric
Clapton

changes gave Clapton an opportunity to work with a variety of blues musicians. He particularly liked Jack Bruce's (born in 1943) bass playing, and when Ginger Baker (born in 1939) sat in on the drums one night, Clapton asked the two of them to join him to work as a trio. At that time, they intended to play the blues in small clubs and did not foresee the tremendous success they would have as **Cream.** The group made its debut in 1966 at the Windsor Festival in England, where they brought their blues-styled songs and brilliant improvisations at a high volume to a rock audience that was ripe for the experience.

> " When you come down to it, it
> was one guy who was completely
> alone and had no options, no
> alternative whatsoever other
> than to sing and play to ease his
> pain. That echoed what I felt in
> many aspects of my life. "
>
> –Eric Clapton

Cream's 1968 recording of Robert Johnson's "Cross Road Blues" (1936) was a successful link between the old country blues and the new blues-based rock. Although the members of Cream obviously loved the rough quality of Johnson's style, they did not copy it in their recording, which they retitled "Crossroads." Johnson had played with the rhythmic freedom out of which the blues form had developed (as pointed out in the discussion and

listening guide to Johnson's recording in Chapter 2). Cream's more modern audience, however, required the sort of polish and formalism to which they had become accustomed. Cream was also made up of three very technically proficient instrumentalists, and where Johnson used his guitar primarily to accompany his singing, Cream displayed their talents through six all-instrumental choruses of the twelve-bar form. A listening guide to Cream's recording of "Crossroads" is on page 122. The recording hit number twenty-eight on the American pop charts; it did not chart in England.

Other British covers of the late sixties included the Jeff Beck Group's recordings of Willie Dixon's "I Ain't Superstitious" and "You Shook Me"; Cream's recordings of Dixon's "Spoonful," Robert Johnson's "Four until Late," and Howlin' Wolf's "Sittin' on Top of the World"; and Led Zeppelin's recordings of Dixon's "I Can't Quit You Baby" and "You Shook Me." A comparison of any of these recordings with the original versions reveals that the late-sixties British blues groups remained less faithful to the old styles than their early-sixties predecessors had.

After just over two years together, Cream disbanded. They felt they had made the musical statement they had gotten together to make, and all three wanted to move on to other experiences. Clapton and Baker formed a new group with Traffic's keyboardist/singer Steve Winwood and Family's bassist Rich Grech. The new group, Blind Faith, was short-lived, putting out only one album, *Blind Faith* (1969).

After Blind Faith broke up, Clapton worked with a variety of groups for short periods of time, including

121

Listening Guide

"Crossroads"
as recorded by Cream (1968)

Tempo: The tempo is about 138 beats per minute, with four beats in each bar. It is quite a bit faster than Robert Johnson's recording, which was about 88 beats per minute.

Form: The instrumental introduction is a full twelve-bar chorus; Johnson's introduction was less than four bars.

Cream maintains the traditional twelve-bar blues form throughout and does not employ Johnson's addition of beats and bars.

The entire recording has eleven choruses of the blues. The first, fifth, sixth, eighth, ninth, and tenth are all instrumental. The instrumental solos are improvised with a sense of freedom, while still remaining connected to the blues harmonic form.

Features: The drums accent the backbeat through most of the recording.

Clapton uses a solid-body electric guitar with fuzztone and low-tension strings to allow for more sliding and bending of notes than Robert Johnson did on his guitar.

Bruce plays riff patterns and also jazz-influenced long walking lines on the bass.

Lyrics: The lyrics are basically taken from Robert Johnson's song "Cross Road Blues," with the addition of one chorus (the third that has lyrics in Cream's recording) from another song by Robert Johnson, "Traveling Riverside Blues." That new chorus is repeated after two instrumental choruses. The additional lyrics outline the singer's plans to take his rider to Rosedale to a **barrelhouse** (a bar or honky-tonk), indicating that he is secure, free, and has his own transportation, in sharp contrast to the subject of Johnson's "Cross Road Blues," who is poor and is ignored by people who pass him on the road.

Billboard pop charts: number twenty-eight

Derek and the Dominos, a group that included American southern-rock guitarist Duane Allman. The name "Derek" was a combination of the names Duane and Eric, and the two guitarists shared lead guitar lines in much the same way that Allman and Dickey Betts had in Allman's own group, the Allman Brothers Band. Derek and the Dominos recorded "Layla" (1970), one of Clapton's greatest musical and personal statements, inspired by his infatuation with Beatle George Harrison's wife, Pattie (whom Clapton later married and divorced). The lyrics to "Layla" included a quote from Robert Johnson's "Love in Vain."

Personal depression led to a heroin habit that kept Eric Clapton from being an active performer during much of 1971 and 1972. He managed to kick the habit with the help of the Who's Pete Townshend, who organized and played with Clapton in *The Rainbow Concert* (January 13, 1973). The concert, which also featured guitarist Ron Wood, Steve Winwood, and Rick Grech, turned out to be Clapton's much-needed comeback. From that point on, Clapton worked as a soloist, with a variety of musicians serving as his backup band. In many ways, his later style became more commercial than he would ever have allowed back in his Yardbird days, but the influence of the blues continued to color his music. His career hit a new peak when he was awarded six Grammys in 1993. An additional Grammy was awarded to Clapton, this time for Best Traditional Blues Album, for *From the Cradle*, released in 1994. Clapton gave further tribute to "King of the Delta Blues," Robert Johnson, by recording his songs on *Me and Mr. Johnson* (2004). Clapton continues to tour.

"**This is me in terms of my musical identity today—where I came from and what I mean.**"

—Eric Clapton, about his 1994 album From the Cradle, *on which he recorded songs by Robert Johnson, Elmore James, and Willie Dixon*

Listeners who know seventies music better than that of the sixties might think of **Fleetwood Mac** as a pop group. In their early years, however, Fleetwood Mac included several veterans of other blues revival groups in England. Mick Fleetwood had played drums for various blues groups from the early to the midsixties, and he and guitarist Peter Green met bassist John McVie while they were all members of John Mayall's Bluesbreakers. Fleetwood, Green, and McVie were joined by guitarist/singer Jeremy Spencer to form Peter Green's Fleetwood Mac in 1967. The name "Fleetwood Mac" combined the names of Fleetwood and McVie. They recorded covers of songs by Robert Johnson, Elmore James, and Howlin' Wolf, as well as blues-styled originals by Peter Green and Jeremy Spencer.

While Fleetwood Mac was beginning its career, Christine Perfect was developing a career of her own. Between 1967 and 1969, she was the pianist/singer for the blues group Chicken Shack. While with that group, Perfect married John McVie of Fleetwood Mac. Although she claimed to have been tempted to settle down and make a career as a housewife, she changed her mind when she won the *Melody Maker* poll as Female Vocalist of the Year in 1969. She organized her own band, called Christine Perfect, but by 1970 the inevitable happened—Christine McVie joined her husband's group.

During the early seventies, Fleetwood Mac left the blues behind to experiment with more commercial music. The McVies and Fleetwood stayed with the band through various personnel changes and in 1974 moved to California, where they were joined by Americans Lindsey Buckingham and Stevie Nicks. In that form, and after Buckingham's departure, Fleetwood Mac had great success playing country-rock-influenced pop music.

The success of the British blues revival rejuvenated American interest in the blues. For American musicians and rock music fans, the British blues revival had a meaning beyond just the popularity of the music played by British groups. American blues musicians in cities like Chicago had managed to maintain their careers by playing the blues through the late fifties and early sixties, but the rock industry as a whole had not considered their music to be suitable competition for the pop style being marketed to teenagers at the time. Music by blues groups was not given the distribution or airplay it would have needed to gain national popularity, but that soon changed after the British blues hit the American charts.

American Reaction

The British groups that came to America in 1964 had not created any new sounds; they started their own careers by playing music that had originated in the United States. For the most part, however, it was not the music of the sixties that they played, but the blues and rockabilly of the fifties. The British copied Little Richard's vocals, Chuck Berry's lead guitar lines, and Bo Diddley's rhythms. They played the blues, imitating the vocal style of Muddy Waters and the slide guitar style of Elmore James. Their groups played guitars, bass, and drums with the energetic backbeat they had heard in Buddy Holly's recordings. The mere fact that the groups were self-contained, playing their own instruments, made them sound different from the studio-blended, wall of sound slickness that had become typical of early-sixties American rock.

In very general terms, the British invasion groups blew the New York–based pop sound off the American charts, but in so doing, they paved the way for American blues groups, garage bands, and folk-rock performers playing nonpop rock to move from regional to national success. The young Paul Butterfield started his blues band in Chicago a year before any British groups had been heard in America, but he did not initially find commercial success; record company executives did not push for national advertising for the blues until after British groups started scoring blues hits. Following the British successes, raucous garage bands like the Standells copied the Rolling Stones; the Count Five used the distorted sound effects of the Yardbirds and the Kinks; and the Sir Douglas Quintet, formed in Texas, first publicized itself as if it were English.

The Beatles had become idols to American teenagers, and as those teens got older, the Beatles music also progressed to express more mature themes, leaving younger fans behind. American record producers were not about to let the young audience go unsatisfied, so they attracted them by forming the **Monkees.** The Monkees were featured in a television program containing skits imitative of the Beatles' playful antics in the movie *A Hard Day's Night.* The members were chosen from a group of musicians and actors who answered an advertisement announcing the intended formation of the group. Michael Nesmith and Peter Tork were musicians before joining the Monkees; Davy Jones and Mickey Dolenz were actors who had to learn to sing and play instruments while with the group. Jones was British, and his accent aided their connection with the Beatles. At first, the group's producers would not allow any of the Monkees to play on their recordings, but eventually the need for live performances became evident and they worked together as musicians in addition to acting on the TV show.

Garage Bands

Garage bands were so named because most of the bands were made up of untrained musicians who practiced in their garages, producing a raw, unrefined sound. As most of the bands were made up of young people with underdeveloped musical skills, they often covered songs by other groups, but occasionally came up with something original. The idea that anybody who could afford an instrument could be in a band was so appealing that by 1965 garage bands were entertaining (or disturbing) neighborhoods all over the country. The most successful songs were ones that were easy for other bands to cover when they played for junior high or high school dances. Lyrics tended to be very simple, sometimes bordering on raunchy, with stories about girls, partying, and fast cars. A few of the songs dealt with meaningful statements such as the antidrug message in Paul Revere and the Raiders' "Kicks," but those were exceptions rather than the rule. Generally any hint of sophistication in the music or the message would remove a song from the garage band category. Eventually, particularly in Detroit, messages of angry rebellion became part of the sound, and it was that combination of simple, crude, and energetic music with aggressive vocals that became punk in the seventies.

One of the simplest and, at the same time, influential of the early garage band songs was "Louie Louie." "Louie Louie" was written and first recorded by Richard Berry in 1956, but it was the **Kingsmen**'s recording that was a number two hit and made it one of the most often covered songs of the era. It had all the necessary elements for garage band music: it was simple and repetitious, and the way the Kingsmen's singer, Jack Ely, slopped through the lyrics lent an air of promiscuity. The belief that the song was too risque was so prevalent that the recording was banned in some places. A listening guide to "Louie Louie" is included here.

The two-bar ostinato that serves as the basis of "Louie Louie" has much in common with that of "La Bamba." This is not surprising in that the song's writer, Richard Berry, was playing in a Mexican band (Ricky Rivera and the Rhythm Rockers) in Los Angeles when he wrote "Louie Louie" in 1955. Richard Berry was African American, but the primary musical influence on this particular song and his own recording of it seems to be more from his work with Mexican music than with African American styles.

Because so many garage band musicians were untrained in music and inexperienced as writers, it was common for garage bands to have one lucky hit but be unable to follow it with anything that equaled its success. Some of the garage bands who made their names on a single hit record included the Premiers, Cannibal and the Headhunters, the Castaways, the Standells, the Leaves, the Syndicate of Sound, Count Five, the Music Machine, the Seeds, and ? and the Mysterians. One band that did not fall into that

Listening Guide

"Louie Louie"
as recorded by the Kingsmen
(1963)

Tempo: The tempo is approximately 126 beats per minute, with four beats in each bar.

Form: The recording begins with a four-bar introduction with a one-beat pickup.

The song is structured around a two-bar chordal ostinato that repeats throughout.

The vocal phrases are four bars long (two repetitions of the ostinato).

The instrumental section is sixteen bars long (eight repetitions of the ostinato).

Features: The drums keep even beat subdivisions, but uneven subdivisions are used in the vocals, the guitar solo, and occasionally the electric piano.

The drums maintain a strong backbeat.

Lyrics: The Kingsmen's recording of this song is famous for its inaudible vocals, but the little that can be understood sounds very much like a sloppy version of the lyrics in Richard Berry's original recording. Using Berry's recording as a guide, the singer has been sailing on a ship for three nights and days thinking constantly about the girl that is waiting for him. He is haunted by the smell of the rose in her hair and plans never to leave her again once she is back in his arms.

Billboard pop charts: number two for six weeks; British hit singles: number twenty-six

Paul Revere and the Raiders

category was **Paul Revere and the Raiders,** who cashed in on the idea of fighting British bands for the attention of fans by wearing pseudo–Revolutionary War costumes. Paul Revere was the name of the band's keyboard player, but the group's leader was their singer and saxophonist, Mark Lindsay. Paul Revere and the Raiders had many top-forty hits even into the seventies. A listening guide to one of their early hits, "Kicks," which reached number four on the pop charts is below.

American Blues Revival

The blues had been essential to rock music through most of the fifties, but it gave way to the sounds of teenage pop singers and dance music between 1959 and 1964. The smooth rhythm and blues style of Fats Domino and some doo-wop groups managed to stay on the pop charts through the early sixties, and some dance music such as "The Twist" (1960) followed the blues form (without its style, in the case of Chubby Checker's hit recording), but many blues-based rock musicians from the fifties either stopped performing at the end of the decade or continued with less commercial success.

Listening Guide

"Kicks"
*as recorded by Paul Revere
and the Raiders (1966)*

Tempo: The tempo is approximately 132 beats per minute, with four beats in each bar.

Form: After a four-bar introduction, the form is structured as ABCDABCDCC, with C having the same lyrics each time and serving as a refrain.

The A, B, and C sections each have eight bars.

The first D section has four bars. The second D has eight bars.

Features: Even beat subdivisions are maintained throughout the recording.

The backbeat is not stressed.

The two-bar guitar riff that begins the recording and repeats through each A section is played on a twelve-string electric guitar and is reminiscent of earlier recordings by the folk-rock group the Byrds. Another, lighter textured guitar riff appears in each D section.

The bass enters in the third bar of the introduction, playing a short ascending and then descending riff that is repeated through each A section. The bass adds an insistent feel as it pulsates the basic beats during the first six bars of the C sections and then pounds out an eighth-note pulse on the last two bars of each C section.

Lyrics: Drugs can't fill the girl's emptiness and will lead to her eventual destruction.

Billboard pop charts: number four

American rock promoters were not interested in the blues until after the midsixties, when British covers of American blues recordings became popular in the United States. The British versions captured much of the vitality of the original recordings and sparked an American blues revival as young American blues groups were finally offered recording contracts. New blues groups formed, and they not only recorded in such blues centers as Chicago but also made the blues an important part of the psychedelic sound of San Francisco during the late sixties, the jazz-rock sound in many different parts of the country, and the southern-rock movement of the seventies.

One young American singer/harpist who was attracted to the blues during the early sixties was **Paul Butterfield** (1942–1987). Living in Chicago, he had the opportunity to hear such blues legends as Muddy Waters and Howlin' Wolf, and in 1963 he formed the Paul Butterfield Blues Band with guitarists Elvin Bishop and Mike Bloomfield. The band found success in blues clubs in the Chicago area and, by 1965, had a record contract. After their second album, *East-West* (1966), failed to gain the attention the group had sought, Bloomfield left to pursue a solo career; he died of an accidental drug overdose in 1981. Bishop went solo in 1968. The Butterfield band experimented with soul and other styles, finally breaking up in 1972. Butterfield continued to perform and record until his drug-related death in 1987.

From Los Angeles came the blues revival group **Canned Heat.** The group had originally formed as a jug band to play a rural form of the blues, with someone blowing and humming into a whiskey jug in place of a bass instrument. Jug bands had a style related to country blues, but with the renewed popularity of urban blues, Canned Heat decided to replace the jug with amplified instruments playing in a rhythmic, boogie-woogie-based style. Their performance at the Monterey Pop Festival in 1967 put them in the spotlight as an important new rock band. Some of their songs, such as "On the Road Again" (1968), did not follow a blues form but instead were based on a single chord with the blues feel implied through the use of string bending and blue notes. "Going Up the Country" (1969) was a traditional twelve-bar blues, and its commercial success earned them a place at the Woodstock Festival in New York in the summer of 1969.

Women were generally the most important of the early classic blues singers, and the rock singer whose interest in the blues was most clearly stimulated by women's blues recordings was **Janis Joplin** (1943–1970). Joplin's favorite singers were Bessie Smith (see Chapter 1) and Willie Mae "Big Mama" Thornton (see Chapter 2), and although Joplin eventually sang music other than the blues, she never lost the dramatic delivery she had learned from listening to Smith and the gutsy, throaty Thornton. After moving to San Francisco from her home in Port Arthur, Texas, Joplin

joined the newly formed folk-blues group Big Brother and the Holding Company, and, with them, stole the show at the Monterey Pop Festival in 1967. Some of the songs she recorded with Big Brother and the Holding Company included "Down on Me" and "Piece of My Heart."

By 1968 Joplin decided she was tired of singing with a group that used only guitars, bass, and drums, and she left Big Brother and the Holding Company to form the Kozmic Blues Band. The group, which included organ, bass, and drums, plus the jazz-band sound of a **horn section** (brass instruments and saxophones), recorded "Try (Just a Little Bit Harder)" in 1969, then broke up in 1970. Joplin's last recordings, including "Cry Baby" and "Me and Bobby McGee" (the latter written by Joplin's friend, Kris Kristofferson), were made with another band she had formed, the Full-Tilt Boogie Band, which included organ, electric piano, guitar, bass, and drums. Joplin was planning to get married and make other major changes in her life when she died of a heroin overdose in October 1970.

Many other blues-based rock guitarists of the sixties experimented with the use of feedback between the guitar and amplifier, but none used it with as much control and psychedelic flash as **Jimi Hendrix** (1942–1970). Like Janis Joplin, Hendrix made the blues one of the most

Jimi Hendrix in concert

important ingredients of late-sixties American rock but did not live to carry that style into the seventies. Hendrix taught himself to play the guitar by copying the recordings of Muddy Waters, Chuck Berry, and B. B. King.

> " The two middle strings he'd be playing as a rhythm guitar . . . and the two top strings he'd be playing lead on at the same time and singing . . . extraordinary command of the guitar. "
>
> –Chas Chandler, about Jimi Hendrix

Raised in Seattle, Jimmy Hendrix (the "Jimi" spelling came later) served in the army for two years, but was discharged because of a back injury he sustained in a parachute jump in 1961. His release from the army left him free to pursue his love of music. At times using the stage name Jimmy James and at others calling himself Maurice James, Hendrix began working with various groups in nightclubs and bars. By 1964, he had moved to New York City and quickly gained a reputation that enabled him to work behind some of the most popular performers of the day, including Sam Cooke, Ike and Tina Turner, Wilson Pickett, Little Richard, and even B. B. King. He formed his own band, Jimmy James and the Blue Flames, in 1965. Chas Chandler of the Animals heard the group in 1966 and was so impressed that he talked Hendrix into leaving the group and moving to London to form a new band. The Jimi Hendrix Experience was formed as a trio, with Hendrix playing a fiery lead guitar, and two English musicians, bassist Noel Redding and drummer Mitch Mitchell, ably backing him. Their recordings of "Hey Joe," "Purple Haze," and "The Wind Cries Mary" were successful in England before the group ever appeared in front of an American audience.

Hendrix's reintroduction to his homeland came when the Jimi Hendrix Experience played the Monterey Pop Festival in 1967. Hendrix brought the group's performance to a memorable conclusion when he "sacrificed" his guitar by setting it on fire. The flaming guitar act did not become a regular part of Hendrix's performances, however, because it was too distracting (and expensive). He preferred to concentrate on playing the blues, or blues-styled rock music. He influenced many of the guitarists who followed him. A listening guide to Hendrix's traditional blues, "Red House," is included here.

> " He took blues from the mud of the Mississippi delta to Venus. "
>
> –Eric Burdon of the Animals, about Jimi Hendrix

Listening Guide

"Red House"
as recorded by the Jimi Hendrix
Experience (1967)

Tempo: The tempo is approximately 66 beats per minute, with four beats in each bar.

Form: The recording has five choruses of the twelve-bar blues. The introductory first chorus and the fourth chorus are instrumental.

Features: Uneven beat subdivisions are used throughout the recording.

The drums maintain a very strong backbeat.

The sound of bass on the recording is played on a hollow-body electric guitar with the bass turned up.

Hendrix's guitar plays the fills and is featured during the instrumental choruses. He bends single and double strings, adds vibrato by shaking his finger that holds down the string, slides from one note to another, and varies his tone by using the wah-wah pedal in different ways.

Lyrics: The singer is disappointed on finding that his girlfriend has moved away while he was in jail and compensates by going after her sister.

After dissolving the Experience in 1968 Hendrix moved to New York, where he built the Electric Ladyland Studio to make experimental recordings with various musicians, including guitarist John McLaughlin. Hendrix organized various groups to back him at such concerts as the Woodstock Festival in 1969. He toured a little in early 1970, but in September of that same year he choked to death in an unconscious state after taking an overdose of barbiturates.

The original home of the blues was not Chicago but the South, and the American blues revival's greatest successes of the seventies were recorded by southern bands and musicians like the Allman Brothers Band, ZZ Top, Jimmie and Stevie Ray Vaughan, guitarist Johnny Winter, and his brother, keyboardist/saxophonist Edgar Winter. The music played by these and other southern-rock musicians was not exclusively a blues-rock style; it combined the blues with other southern music styles, including country, jazz, and gospel. The blues-influenced styles of these and other southern bands are discussed in Chapter 11, Country and Southern Rock.

Summary

The music played by British groups at the beginning of the British invasion was based on American music to which the British added their own themes and styles. Merseybeat groups such as the early Beatles, Gerry and the Pacemakers, the Hollies, and Herman's Hermits were much influenced by Buddy Holly and the Crickets.

The rock music of London was influenced less by Buddy Holly and more by the blues and the tastes of the Mods and the Rockers, the young subcultures prevalent at the time. The Who, and to a lesser degree the Kinks, started out as Mod bands. While most American teens did not relate to British subculture connections, they could appreciate the Kinks' criticisms of modern society and the Who's rough display of energy on stage.

The blues was the basis for most rock music of the early and midfifties, but while it was not being marketed to teens in America, the British were in the process of discovering it. By 1963, blues clubs had become popular in London, and the young blues groups that played in them carefully copied the styles of such performers as Muddy Waters, John Lee Hooker, and Howlin' Wolf. Some of the

most important British blues performers whose music became popular in America during the midsixties included John Mayall's Bluesbreakers, the Rolling Stones, the Animals, the Yardbirds, and Fleetwood Mac.

With their "invasion" in 1964, the British had taken hold of the American rock audience so quickly and completely that American record companies, promoters, and musicians responded in a variety of ways. Many young American musicians formed bands that imitated some of the most popular British groups. The American group, the Monkees, was formed for a television show patterned after the Beatles' movie, *A Hard Day's Night* (1964).

The term *garage bands* came into use to describe bands whose recordings sounded live, as opposed to the lush studio-produced groups popular in America during the early sixties. One of the most successful and long lasting of the garage bands was Paul Revere and the Raiders, who were still performing in the early two-thousands.

The success of British blues bands proved the blues had new appeal for young American audiences, opening the doors to recording careers for the Paul Butterfield Blues Band, Canned Heat, and Janis Joplin, as well as other American blues musicians. American blues guitarist/singer Jimi Hendrix had moved to England to make his first blues-based rock recordings but returned to the United States to continue his career.

By the seventies the blues had become a significant element in the South with the music of such bands as the Allman Brothers Band and ZZ Top. They and many other seventies blues or blues-rock bands continue to record and tour into the early two-thousands.

discussion questions

During the late sixties, some people said that the British saved rock and roll. If true, what did they save it from? Would the postinvasion U.S. styles of garage bands and the blues revival bands have become popular without the popularity of the British bands?

chapter 9

Folk, Folk-Rock, and Singer/ Songwriters

" The tradition of folk music was always political. . . .
Folk music became the liturgy of the consciousness of
change in America. "

—PETER YARROW OF PETER, PAUL,
AND MARY

The sixties were a decade of turmoil. The civil rights movement and the Vietnam War were two causes of much concern to young people, particularly those of college age. Activities related to the civil rights movement were often in the news, and many optimistic young people of all races strongly believed that all human beings deserved equal rights and opportunities. By about 1967, the Vietnam War was a great concern to most young people because young men were required to register for the draft once they turned eighteen. Most young people had friends or relatives who were or had been in Vietnam, so most had some sense of the experience even if they did not go themselves. Many antiwar protests took place on college campuses. Student strikes, reading the names of the dead over school loudspeaker systems, and large-scale demonstrations were common during the late sixties. Since folk music was often political and generally took positions against racism and war, it was the music of choice on many college campuses.

Folk Music

American folk music, like the folk music of most of the world, grew out of what was essentially an oral tradition—songs passed from one performer to another by rote. Unlike most art music, in which the composer plans and notates every interpretative nuance, the melodies, lyrics, and rhythms of folk songs were often changed as each new performer adapted a given song to his or her personality and performance style. Sometimes changes occurred as the result of a performer's faulty memory, but quite often changes were made intentionally so that old songs would speak to the concerns of new and different audiences. In other situations, particularly once written collections were published, traditional songs were performed very close to the way the singer had heard them done by another artist, but the folk singer or instrumentalist was not obliged to re-create an earlier performance exactly.

Folk music and performance traditions varied from one part of the United States to another because the music was based on songs and dances people of different cultures brought with them from their homelands. Many of these settlers maintained their Old World songs and musical traditions as a connection with their cultural roots. Of particular importance to our discussion because of its influences on rock music of the sixties was the British-derived folk music from the Appalachian mountain region stretching from West Virginia to New York. The ballads, fiddle tunes, and dance melodies of that era can be traced directly back to comparable English, Scottish, and Irish music of Elizabethan times. Instruments used by American folk musicians, such as the fiddle, the acoustic guitar, the string bass, and the recorder, had been used in Scotland and Ireland hundreds of years earlier and

were brought to the New World by settlers. Both the language of some of the songs and the types of chord progressions used to accompany them often reflected their sixteenth- and seventeenth-century origins.

Musicologists **Charles Seeger** (1886–1979), John A. Lomax (1872–1948), and **Alan Lomax** (1915–2002) researched, analyzed, notated, and recorded a large number of folk songs from the Appalachians. Seeger traced the often minute changes that had taken place through the passing of songs from one performer to another through the years and published his findings in scholarly studies, one of which was *Versions and Variants of the Tunes of "Barbara Allen"* (1966). Seeger's work was used by his son, **Pete Seeger** (born in 1919), who sang and played guitar and banjo, performing many of the songs his father had researched as well as composing new songs. Both John A. and Alan Lomax recorded and collected folk music for the Archives of the Library of Congress and published collections of the songs they recorded, such as *Folk Song U.S.A.* (1947).

Most folk music was primarily vocal, and instruments were used to accompany singing, but instruments such as the fiddle and the recorder supplied lead fills much as the fiddle did in hillbilly music. Like traditional bluegrass country groups, folk singers avoided using electric instruments or drums, even after they were common in other kinds of music. In addition to using the British instrumentation, American folk groups borrowed instruments such as the five-string banjo from country traditions.

Pete Seeger started the **Almanac Singers** in New York in 1941, and, just as the folk group the Hutchinson Family Quartet had done a hundred years earlier, the Almanac Singers took traditional folk melodies and performed them with new texts that stressed the social and political concerns of their time. The Hutchinson Family Quartet had sung about mid-nineteenth-century issues, such as the destructiveness of alcohol within the family, the need to abolish slavery, and women's right to vote. The Almanac Singers sang out for the development of strong labor unions, civil rights, and the need to end war. Most of the group's views were considered left-wing, which tended to limit their audience. They performed at political events such as American Federation of Labor meetings and were much appreciated and remembered by those who shared their political views. Two of their members, Pete Seeger and Woody Guthrie, established solo careers and performed with later folk groups.

In 1948, Pete Seeger, Lee Hays (also of the Almanac Singers), and two other singers formed the **Weavers,** whose harmonized group vocals were a new experience for many American audiences. The group quickly achieved national fame for their energetic and entertaining performances of folk songs such as "Goodnight Irene," "Kisses Sweeter Than Wine," and "On Top of Old Smokey." The Weavers also sang political songs, and their commitment to left-wing causes resulted in their losing some of their following in the early fifties, when members of the group were investigated by the House Un-American Activities Committee. The group temporarily broke up in 1953, unable to find any place to perform. Regrouped two years later, the Weavers continued to perform regularly for another ten years, with periodic reunion concerts afterwards.

Before joining the Almanac Singers, songwriter/singer/guitarist **Woody Guthrie** (1912–1967) had spent years traveling around the country singing on street corners. He sang about his concerns by putting new texts to traditional folk melodies as well as writing new folk-styled songs. Alan Lomax recognized Guthrie's effective expression of his times and recorded a collection of his songs for the Library of Congress. Guthrie served in the Merchant Marines during World War II, and he sang songs that supported the war cause, with "This machine kills fascists" painted on his guitar. By the early fifties, Guthrie was hospitalized with Huntington's chorea, a degenerative disease of the nervous system, and could no longer perform. Among his best-known compositions were "This Land Is Your Land" and "So Long, It's Been Good to Know You," both of which became classics in his own time.

> **" I sing the songs of the people that do all of the little jobs and the mean and dirty hard work in the world and of their wants and their hopes and their plans for a decent life. "**
>
> –Woody Guthrie

Whereas the Almanac Singers, the Weavers, and their individual members were a politically oriented group of folk singers, other singers such as John Jacob Niles and Burl Ives were less so, and they performed traditional folk material for audiences as early as the twenties (thirties, in Ives's case) and for decades after that. They drew a lot of attention, particularly from college students, and by the late fifties and early sixties had inspired many groups to form and perform both traditional and newly written music in folk style. Some of those new groups—the Kingston Trio, Peter, Paul, and Mary, Joan Baez, and others—recorded nationally popular singles, helping to establish a vocal sound favored over rock music among socially conscious college students and influencing folk-rock music of the middle to late sixties.

Bob Dylan

A young follower of Woody Guthrie, Robert Allen Zimmerman, grew up in Minnesota. In high school he played with a rock group called the Golden Chords, but he dropped rock for folk music, accompanying himself with acoustic guitar and harmonica. He sang in coffeehouses while he was in college and began to use the pseudonym **Bob Dylan.** Many have said he chose the name because of his respect for the twentieth-century poet Dylan Thomas, but Dylan has denied this in some interviews. Regardless of the reason for the choice of name, eventually he legally changed his last name to Dylan. He moved to New York, where Guthrie was hospitalized, so that he could get to know the man behind the music and image he admired.

In a conversation that the young Bob Dylan is reported to have had with Guthrie, Dylan asked for advice about writing melodies to go with his songs. According to the book *Bob Dylan: An Intimate Biography* by Anthony Scaduto, Guthrie replied: "Just write. Don't worry where the tune comes from. I just pick up tunes I heard before and change them around and make them mine. Put in a couple of fast notes for one slow one, sing a harmony note 'stead of melody, or a low note for a high one, or juggle the rests and pauses—and you got a melody of your own. I do it all the time." Guthrie's response points out an important characteristic about folk music that the "song" is the text. While a pop songwriter might well begin with a melody and then fill in words to fit it, a folksinger cares most about the message. Of course, both Guthrie and Dylan have written memorable melodies, but both would agree that the words come first.

While in New York, Dylan performed in folk coffeehouses such as the Bitter End and Folk City in Greenwich Village and began to develop a following for his elusive personality and expressive style. He soon attracted the attention of producer John Hammond Sr. of Columbia

Records, who gave him a recording contract. Hammond had earlier been responsible for bringing such important jazz artists as Billie Holiday, Count Basie, and Benny Goodman to Columbia Records and later discovered and signed Aretha Franklin and Bruce Springsteen. Dylan's first album, *Bob Dylan* (1962), contained traditional folk material as well as two original songs that voiced some of his personal concerns—"Talkin' New York," about the beginning of his performing career in the big city, and "Song to Woody," a tribute to Woody Guthrie.

One of the traditional folk songs Dylan recorded was "House of the Rising Sun." As Guthrie had done in his own earlier recordings of songs written from a woman's point of view, Dylan sang the song's traditional lyrics in which the "house" was a bordello and the singer a woman who ruined her life by running off with a drunkard and now had to support herself as a prostitute. Nothing androgynous was intended in a male folksinger's taking a female role; folksingers often chose to sing the traditional lyrics to a song no matter which sex was implied by the text. This practice was not part of the rock tradition, however, and when the British rock group the Animals recorded the song two years after Dylan, they changed the sex role by making the drunkard the singer's father rather than the singer's lover. The Animals' use of amplified guitar, electric keyboard, electric bass, and drums had a much more rock-oriented sound than Dylan's very rural folk style.

Dylan's second album, *The Freewheelin' Bob Dylan* (1963), gave him the protest-singer reputation that Woody Guthrie and others had established for themselves decades earlier. From that album, "Blowin' in the Wind," a hit when recorded by Peter, Paul, and Mary, became a popular statement of support for both peace and racial equality. "Masters of War" and "A Hard Rain's a-Gonna Fall" contained strong antiwar statements. A listening guide to Peter, Paul, and Mary's recording of "Blowin' in the Wind" is below.

Listening Guide

"Blowin' in the Wind"
as recorded by Peter, Paul,
and Mary (1963)

Tempo: The tempo is approximately 78 beats per minute, with two beats in each bar.

Form: The form is based on eight-bar phrases, put together into verses, each of which contains four phrases. In each verse, questions are asked in the first three phrases, and the fourth phrase explains that the answer to all of the questions is "Blowin' in the Wind."

Features: In true folk tradition, the three singers are accompanied by acoustic instruments, in this case, two guitars and a string bass.

The recording begins with an eight-bar instrumental introduction that establishes a very smooth and gentle rhythmic flow.

The string bass plays on the beats, often with pickups added before them.

The three singers vary the timbre of their voices by sometimes all singing together, sometimes Mary singing alone, and sometimes Peter and Paul singing without Mary.

Lyrics: Wind is perhaps Dylan's most famous image, generally symbolizing the spirit of the times—what is sometimes called the "Zeitgeist" or "time spirit." Political commentators often quote Dylan's line from the song "Subterranean Homesick Blues": "You don't need a weatherman to know which way the wind blows." "Blowin' in the Wind," which was written in 1962 during the height of the antinuclear "ban the bomb" movement but before the escalation of the Vietnam War, foreshadows both the civil rights and antiwar movements in the immediate years to come.

Billboard pop charts: number two; British hit singles: number thirteen

Singer/guitarist Joan Baez aided Dylan's career by recording some of his songs and adding him to her tour in 1963. His fame was spreading fast among folk fans, but his national exposure would have been greatly aided by a television appearance. He was invited to appear on *The Ed Sullivan Show* but refused because he was not allowed to sing his song "Talkin' John Birch Paranoid Blues." Of course, he could have chosen other songs, but the statements he wanted to make were much more important to him than the fame afforded by television exposure. Dylan finished out the folk period of his career with two more albums, *The Times They Are a-Changin'* and *Another Side of Bob Dylan* (both 1964). The former contained protest songs that spoke out for civil rights and antiwar causes; the latter was less folk-oriented and expressed feelings about his personal life and relationships.

Dylan's music and much of his audience changed in 1965, when he shocked his folk-purist fans by walking on stage in front of the Paul Butterfield Blues Band, with their drums and electric instruments, at the Newport Folk Festival. Ever since the Animals had turned "House of the Rising Sun" into a rock hit, Dylan knew there was a potentially large audience for rock-style performances of folk songs. The album *Bringing It All Back Home* (1965) introduced Dylan's new rock-based sound, along with folk-styled material, and it was the rock-styled "Subterranean Homesick Blues" (1965) that became his first hit single. "Mr. Tambourine Man" was less popular when Dylan did it in his folk style on that album than when it was covered with rock instrumentation by the Byrds. The combination of folk and rock styles heard in Dylan's "Subterranean Homesick Blues" and the Byrds' recording of "Mr. Tambourine Man" was the beginning of an entirely new genre of rock music—folk-rock.

> **"It's a psychological investigation into the nature of consciousness itself, into the nature of identity . . . the tradition of the minstrelsy, the trickster hero which has been a persona of Dylan all the way through."**
>
> –Allen Ginsberg, about Dylan's "Mr. Tambourine Man"

Dylan continued in a rock-oriented style, touring with a former rockabilly band, the Hawks (they did not use that name while with Dylan). Despite his change of musical style, Dylan had not abandoned the folk tradition of using music to make social statements. Many of his songs contained rather obscure and cryptic messages that left room for interpretation by the listener, but a basic statement often emerged from his textual ambiguity. "Like a Rolling Stone" (1965), for example, generally described the transient value of wealth and material comfort. Exactly what caused the rich girl to whom he directed the song to lose her money and social standing could be any of several things, possibly heroin addiction or prostitution, but the point of the song was made no matter how the listener interpreted the details. Many fans may have liked Dylan's next big hit, "Rainy Day Women #12 & 35" (1966), because of its allusions to getting "stoned" on drugs, but the constant references to people being stoned (in a literal sense), people who were simply trying to live normal, unfettered lives, expressed his concerns about civil rights and the plight of African Americans in the

Joan Baez and Bob Dylan (1963)

United States. One can also hear the song as Dylan's commenting about being "stoned" by critics no matter what he does.

After suffering severe injuries in a motorcycle accident, Dylan spent the rest of 1966 recovering and recording tapes at home with his backup band. Those tapes were eventually released on *The Basement Tapes* (1975), although a bootleg version of the album surfaced as early as 1969. With Dylan still recuperating, his backup band decided to record and tour on their own, calling themselves simply the Band.

When Dylan began to record on his own again, he ignored the large-scale concept-album trend that had become popular among rock bands. Although he had been known to borrow ideas from others, Dylan was never one to latch onto popular musical trends. He even ignored the rock-oriented direction of his own hits and returned to the folklike simplicity of his earlier recordings, this time with country influences, in the albums *John Wesley Harding* (1968) and *Nashville Skyline* (1969). Again, Dylan was at the forefront of a new style; this time it was country rock.

For the next few years, Dylan worked with various country-rock musicians, including members of the Byrds and singer Doug Sahm (of the Sir Douglas Quintet). He contributed soundtrack music for, and acted in, the movie *Pat Garrett and Billy the Kid* (1973). "Knockin' on Heaven's Door," from that movie, was Dylan's biggest hit of the seventies. Dylan became a fundamentalist Christian in the late seventies, and albums like *Slow Train Coming* (1979), *Saved* (1980), and *Shot of Love* (1981) reflected his newfound religious position. His album *Infidels* (1983), while not actually questioning religious beliefs, employed more ambiguous language in referring to them.

" **Well, everybody has got their own truth. What works for one man is fine as long as it works for him. If I was searching, it was just to get down to the root reality of the way things really are, to pull the mask off. My thing was always to pull the mask off of whatever was going on.** "

–Bob Dylan, about his conversion to Christianity

The song "Union Sundown" from *Infidels* represented a return to social and political concerns, pointing out

how American labor unions had been undermined by the widespread availability of cheap foreign goods that greedy, unfeeling people purchased to avoid paying the price of goods made by workers who received good wages and benefits. In a manner similar to that used in pro-union songs by the Almanac Singers during the forties, in which unions were portrayed as the solution to the needs of the working class, Dylan's song pointed out some of the negative effects of modern-day American materialism.

Dylan's continuing concern for social and political issues caused him to become involved in many fund-raising campaigns during the middle eighties, including the "We Are the World" recording and the Live Aid and Farm Aid concerts. Throughout his career, Dylan changed the course of the history of rock music more than once. His middle-sixties move from traditional folk music to folk-rock sparked a new trend and then again a few years later, he stimulated the development of country rock. Official credit for those accomplishments and others was finally awarded him by the music industry when, in 1986, he was given the Founders Award by the American Society of Composers, Authors, and Publishers (ASCAP). In 1988, Dylan was inducted into the Rock and Roll Hall of Fame.

As every "real" Dylan fan knows, bootleg recordings of everything from live concert performances to studio out-takes are very easy to come by, and the desire to hear rare songs, as well as many different versions of popular ones, is irresistible. There is no hiding that fact, and Dylan and his record company have always been aware of it as are other performers whose work is often released in the same illegal way. Bootlegs are a problem for the performer, not only because he does not receive royalties from their sale, but because the performer and producer have no control over the quality of the recordings or the choices of material the recordings include. While other people in the industry try to ignore the problem and hope it will go away, Dylan made a straight and honest attack by releasing *Bob Dylan, The Bootleg Series, Volumes 1–3 (rare & unreleased) 1961–1991* in 1991. That collection not only included songs that had never been released legally before, but it also included recordings that had never been available on bootlegs before, winning at least part of a music business versus fan battle for Dylan himself. Dylan returned to his roots in traditional folk music for the albums *Good as I Been to You* (1992) and *World Gone Wrong* (1993). Both old and new fans welcomed him at Woodstock '94 and then on "MTV Unplugged" later the same year. Bob Dylan continues to record and tour into the early two-thousands. His album *Together Through Life* (2009) hit number one the first week of its release, making Dylan, at age 68, the oldest artist to have an album debut at the top spot.

Folk-Rock Music

Bob Dylan's "Mr. Tambourine Man" was folk-styled music when he sang it, but it became folk-rock when recorded by the **Byrds.** The Byrds were formed by musicians who had previously belonged to other folk groups. Their leader, singer/guitarist Roger (Jim) McGuinn, bought an electric twelve-string guitar in order to imitate the accompaniment style he had heard both the Beatles and the Searchers employ. The result was not simply a copy of the British sound; it instead became one of America's most effective responses to the British invasion. "Mr. Tambourine Man" was the group's first recording, for which uncredited studio musicians were hired to record most of the instrumental parts; the track also featured McGuinn's distinctive twelve-string guitar and the rest of the members of the Byrds singing in close, folk-style harmony. A comparison of the folk recording by Dylan and the number-one pop chart hit recording by the Byrds is on page 136.

The Byrds followed "Mr. Tambourine Man" with another Dylan song they turned into folk-rock, "All I Really Want to Do" (1965), and a Pete Seeger composition, "Turn! Turn! Turn!" (1965), the lyrics of which came from the Old Testament book of Ecclesiastes.

The Byrds' music moved further from folk music toward psychedelic rock with their recording of "Eight Miles High" (1966). The song, written by McGuinn and the Byrds' other guitarist/singer, David Crosby (David Van Cortland), had lyrics that were interpreted to refer to the effects of psychedelic drugs. Both writers denied it vehemently, explaining that the lyrics came from a fear of air travel, but nevertheless it was banned by many radio stations. Frequent personnel changes plagued the Byrds during the late sixties, and they were joined by country guitarist/singer/songwriter Gram Parsons for the album *Sweetheart of the Rodeo* (1968), which influenced the development of country rock.

The members of a New York City folk band called the Mugwumps (a term that meant political fence-sitters or politically uncommitted people) separated into two folk-rock groups, the Lovin' Spoonful and the Mamas and the Papas. The Mugwumps' lead guitarist/singer, Zal Yanovsky, started the Lovin' Spoonful with singer/guitarist/harmonica player John Sebastian, who had done some recording with the Mugwumps. The Lovin' Spoonful took their name from the title of a song by blues singer Mississippi John Hurt.

Soon after Sebastian and Yanovsky left to form the Lovin' Spoonful, the Mugwumps broke up. The group's singers, Denny Doherty and Cass Elliot (Ellen Naomi Cohen), went their separate ways for a short time but met again in California in 1965. Doherty had formed the New Journeymen with husband-and-wife duo John and Michelle Phillips. Elliot joined their group, and they changed the name to the **Mamas and the Papas.** John Phillips wrote most of their songs, praising California in "California Dreamin'" (1966) and tracing the group's history back to their Mugwump connection in "Creeque Alley" (1967).

Paul Simon and Art Garfunkel became famous for their folk-rock music, but originally they sang songs that Simon wrote while they were in high school in Newark, New Jersey, during the midfifties. Using the names of the cartoon characters Tom and Jerry, they performed their first single (which copied the vocal-duo style of the Everly Brothers), "Hey, Schoolgirl" (1957), on *American Bandstand.* After graduation, they lost touch with each other. Simon attempted to establish himself as a teen idol under the pseudonym Jerry Landis but later returned to folk music, performing in New York coffeehouses. His old partner rejoined him five years later to record a folk album, *Wednesday Morning, 3 A.M.* (1964), this time using their real names, **Simon and Garfunkel.** The

The Byrds (left to right): David Crosby, Chris Hillman, Gene Clark, Michael Clarke, and Roger McGuinn

Listening Guide

"Mr. Tambourine Man" as recorded by Bob Dylan (1965)	"Mr. Tambourine Man" as recorded by the Byrds (1965)
Tempo: The tempo is about 168 beats per minute, with four beats per bar.	The tempo is about 122 beats per minute, with four beats per bar.
Form: The recording begins with a four-bar instrumental introduction.	The recording begins with a four-bar instrumental introduction.
There are ten different verses of varying length; the first two repeat several times, functioning as a refrain.	Only four of Dylan's verses are sung; the first two are repeated at the end.
Features: The lead line is sung by Dylan alone.	The Byrds sing the refrain in close harmony; McGuinn sings the verses alone. The second voice is sometimes heard above the melody, in the style of country music.
The instrumentation includes strummed acoustic guitar, electric guitar accents on beats one and three, and no bass or drums. A harmonica plays lead during instrumental sections.	The instrumentation includes twelve-string electric guitar, electric bass, tambourine, drums, and a thickly layered background.
There is no accent on the backbeat.	A strong backbeat is played by both the drums and the tambourine.
The recording lasts five minutes and thirty seconds.	The recording lasts two minutes and fourteen seconds.
Lyrics: Conventionally seen as a drug song with Mr. Tambourine the dealer, the song weaves a series of surrealistic (dreamlike or drug-induced) images, generally connected by the themes of sandy desolation and ancient ruin.	The hints about drug use remain, but the song is much shorter and missing many of Dylan's images.

Billboard pop charts: number one; British hit singles: number one

album included traditional folk songs, songs by Bob Dylan, and some Simon originals, all recorded with only acoustic instruments to accompany their singing. Soon after the album's release, while Simon was traveling and performing on his own in Europe, the producer of the album, Tom Wilson (who also produced Dylan's *Bringing It All Back Home* album [1965]), took it upon himself to overdub electric guitars, bass, and drums on the album cut "The Sounds of Silence" and release it as a single. The single became a folk-rock hit before either Simon or Garfunkel even heard about the production changes. Having witnessed the success possible through the combination of folk and rock styles, Simon and Garfunkel reunited to record a folk-rock album using the new version of "The Sounds of Silence" as the title track. A listening guide is on page 137.

Art Garfunkel and Paul Simon (1966) on *The Ed Sullivan Show*

Listening Guide

**"Sounds of Silence"
as recorded by Simon and Garfunkel
(1965)**

Tempo: The tempo is approximately 108 beats per minute, with four beats in each bar.

Form: The song has five verses, most of which are fifteen bars long. The melodies are basically the same in all verses, but variations are made to fit lyrics. A one-bar instrumental introduction precedes the first verse. The fourth verse has an additional two-beat bar added between bars twelve and thirteen. An additional three bars finish off the song.

Features: The recording begins with electric guitars imitating the folk-style picking patterns (the player's right hand picks across the strings, rather than strumming them together) from the earlier recording of the song. It is not until the second bar of the second verse, on the word "alone," that the drums and electric bass guitar join in, changing the sound from "folk" to "folk-rock."

The drums accent the backbeat in a rock fashion, but not so loudly that it gets in the way of the gentle flow of the song.

Simon and Garfunkel sing in harmony throughout the song.

Lyrics: The singer assumes the role of an Old Testament prophet, relating a divine vision about how the people have gone astray by following the false god of modern commercial civilization, resulting in general alienation and inauthentic human relationships.

Billboard pop charts: number one for two weeks

Although most of the music by such folk-rock groups as the Lovin' Spoonful and the Mamas and the Papas consisted of light and simple love songs, Paul Simon's introspective songs introduced an additional depth to folk-rock music. Bob Dylan had followed the folk tradition of using music to raise social consciousness of political and social causes, but he was not alone in that endeavor. Several other folk and folk-rock singers expressed concerns over the same issues Dylan had—issues like the Vietnam War and the civil rights movement. Phil Ochs (1940–1976) and Tom Paxton (Thomas Richard, born in 1937) were both singer/songwriters in the Woody Guthrie tradition who performed in New York coffeehouses. Ochs's songs such as "Talking Vietnam" (1964) and "Draft Dodger Rag" (1965), and Paxton's songs "A Thousand Years" and "Talking Vietnam Pot Luck Blues" (both 1968), put the two singers in great demand to perform at many antiwar demonstrations. Another writer, Philip "P.F." Sloan, composed "Eve of Destruction" (1965), which was recorded by ex–New Christy Minstrels singer **Barry McGuire** (born in 1935). The song questioned the ethics of war and racial inequities in a society that claimed to be based on biblical morality. A listening guide is below.

Fifteen-year-old singer/songwriter Janis Ian (Janis Eddy Fink, born in 1951) made one of the era's most poignant statements about racism in "Society's Child (Baby I've Been Thinking)" (1967), in which she accused hypocritical parents and teachers of preaching equality while at the same time being intolerant of interracial relationships.

Whether the cause was war or racism, some marches and gatherings of protesters turned violent when police riot squads arrived. After a demonstration turned into a riot on Los Angeles's Sunset Strip, the Buffalo Springfield's

Listening Guide

"Eve of Destruction" as recorded by Barry McGuire (1965)

Tempo: The tempo is about 118 beats per minute, with four beats in each bar.

Form: The six-bar introduction begins with two bars of timpani imitating the sound of bombs, followed by four bars of strummed acoustic guitar.

The song has four verses, the first two of which are ten bars long and the third and fourth are fourteen bars. There is a refrain between the verses and at the end. The refrain also varies in length, being ten bars the first and second times and twelve after that.

The final refrain has an added bar during which there is a ritard.

Features: Even beat subdivisions are maintained throughout the recording.

Strummed acoustic guitars provide most of the accompaniment.

The drummer maintains a strong backbeat in the refrains.

Harmonica is used at the ends of refrains.

McGuire sings the verses with speech-like inflections, using a very gruff, forceful vocal timbre.

Lyrics: Seldom are lyrics so directed at news events from a particular time, in this case, the summer of 1965. Events then did seem to be building to a climax of destruction, with border skirmishes on the Jordan River, civil rights marches, and violent backlash in Selma, Alabama, and an ongoing cultural evolution in what was then called "Red China." The singer also mentions a four-day Gemini space mission that briefly diverted attention from the more threatening developments of the summer.

Billboard pop charts: number one

singer/songwriter Stephen Stills wrote what became an anthem of the protest movement, "For What It's Worth (Stop, Hey What's That Sound)" (1967). The group disbanded after a little over two years together, but many of their members continued to be important in both folk- and country-rock styles, writing and singing about the serious issues of the day. Stephen Stills formed Crosby, Stills and Nash; Neil Young had a solo career, but also worked with Crosby, Stills, Nash and Young as well as his own band, Crazy Horse; Richie Furay and Jim Messina formed the country-rock band Poco.

Crosby, Stills and Nash began singing together casually at a party at Mama Cass Elliot's home in Los Angeles in 1968. David Crosby had stopped working with the Byrds, Stephen Stills was freed by Buffalo Springfield's breakup, and Graham Nash had grown tired of working with the Hollies, who refused to record his "Marrakesh Express." He

left them, and the song became the first of many hits by the trio Crosby, Stills and Nash. The pleasing vocal group arrangements gave their recordings a distinctive style. All its members were writers, providing the group with a wide range of original material. They had all had at least some experience in both folk and country music, and with the development of country rock during the late sixties, they incorporated some of its elements into their music.

Neil Young joined the group in 1969 and **Crosby, Stills, Nash and Young** performed at Woodstock. Although the group did not concentrate solely on protest songs, they were affected by the violence that erupted during the anti-war movement. "Ohio" (1970) was Neil Young's lament over the shooting death of four students during a demonstration at Kent State University. The listening guide included here discusses that recording. "Ohio" reached number fourteen on the pop charts.

Listening Guide

"Ohio"
as recorded by Crosby, Stills, Nash and Young (1970)

Tempo: The tempo is about 80 beats per minute, with four beats in each bar.

Form: The eight-bar instrumental introduction begins with a solo guitar playing a repeated pattern used later in the recording. The drums join at the third bar and the bass and lead guitar enter at the fifth bar.

After the introduction, the song follows an ABCABCA form, in which the A verses are four bars long, the B choruses are eight bars long, and the C instrumental sections are partially based on chords from the A sections.

Features: Even beat subdivisions are maintained throughout. Near the end of the recording, the drummer builds the intensity by accenting four even subdivisions to each beat.

A rock backbeat is maintained by the drummer.

The bass plays on beats one, three, and four almost constantly through the recording.

The four singers are in unison during the first vocal section, then split into three-part harmony with a fourth part coupled at the **octave** (that is, the highest and the lowest voices sing the same melody an octave apart while the two other voices fill in chord tones between them).

Lyrics: The lyrics are about an antiwar demonstration at Kent State University in Ohio, at which four students were shot to death by the National Guard sent to the campus by the state's governor.

Billboard pop charts: number fourteen

Crosby, Stills, Nash, and Young in 1970 (left to right): Stephen Stills, Graham Nash, David Crosby, and Neil Young

Crosby, Stills, Nash and Young began to work on solo careers in the early seventies, but the members regrouped, sometimes in pairs or trios, to perform or record together in the years to follow.

Singer/Songwriters

In contrast to the tendency of folk singers of the sixties to sing about topical or political matters, in the late sixties and beyond some folk singers turned inward to communicate very personal experiences and feelings about their own lives and relationships through their songs. This style was called singer/songwriter to stress that the singer was the songwriter. Such very personal songs also tended to set up a close communication between the singer/songwriter and the listener, making this style lastingly popular. One such singer/songwriter who is still active as a performer is James Taylor.

James Taylor

James Taylor (born in 1948) was a singer from Boston, Massachusetts, who, like so many others, moved to New York to play in folk coffeehouses. He went to London, where he worked with producer Peter Asher, a singer from the British duo Peter and Gordon. After one unsuccessful

James Taylor (2002)

140

album there, Asher and Taylor both moved to Los Angeles, where Asher produced Taylor's introspective *Sweet Baby James* album (1970). Many of the songs on the album were written by Taylor while he was institutionalized to recover from heroin addiction.

His first big hit (number three) on the pop charts was "Fire and Rain" from the *Sweet Baby James* album. A listening guide to that song is below.

Taylor became friends with other important singer/songwriters such as Carole King, Joni Mitchell, and Carly Simon (to whom he was married from 1972 to 1983). Taylor sometimes played guitar on their albums and the others would play piano or sing backup on his albums. Carole King gave him her song "You've Got a Friend" to record in 1971 and his recording hit number one on the pop charts. The 1977 album *JT* was enormously successful, reaching number four on the album charts. As his career continued, he had other hits in the top forty and toured often, straining his home life.

Joni Mitchell

A singer/songwriter from a more strictly folk background, **Joni Mitchell** (Roberta Joan Anderson, born in 1943) performed with her husband, folksinger Chuck Mitchell, before divorcing him and establishing her own solo career. Raised in Saskatoon, Canada, she developed a distinctive rural-folk vocal style in which she changed her tone quality at different pitch levels. She learned to play the piano, which was helpful to her as a songwriter, but usually accompanied herself with folk-style acoustic guitar or

Listening Guide

"Fire and Rain"
as recorded by James Taylor

Tempo: The tempo is approximately 76 beats per minute, with four beats in each bar.

Form: A four-bar instrumental introduction is played on an acoustic guitar and a piano joins at bar three.

Each of three verses is eight bars long.

A chorus (same text each time it is sung) follows each verse. The first two choruses are eight bars long with a one-bar instrumental extension.

The final chorus is extended a full eight bars with Taylor adding short vocal phrases based on the text of the chorus.

The recording ends by fading out in the seventh and eighth bars of the final extension.

Features: The mood is gentle and plaintive, expressing very sensitive feelings about the subjects in the text.

A bowed string bass is added at the beginning of the first verse and continues on through the recording along with the guitar and piano.

Drums enter at the first chorus and continue on playing a soft backbeat.

Lyrics: Many people take the lyrics to this song too literally and assume that the entire song is about a friend of Taylor's who died in a plane crash. According to interviews with Taylor, the three verses refer to three different things. The first is his reaction to the death of a friend, although he has never said publicly what his relationship was with that friend or how the friend died. The second verse is about his return to America with an aching body, desperate to overcome his drug problem. The third verse's reference to flying machines in pieces was not about a plane crash, but about the breakup of his first band The Flying Machine.

Billboard pop charts: number three; British hit singles: number forty-two

Joni Mitchell (1976)

mountain dulcimer. Some of her songs, including "Both Sides Now" (Judy Collins in 1968) and "Woodstock" (Crosby, Stills, Nash and Young in 1970 and Matthews' Southern Comfort in 1971), became hits for others. In addition to being a successful songwriter and performer, Mitchell was an artist, and many of her own albums, as well as those recorded by friends, featured her paintings on the covers.

Mitchell's debut album was released in 1967, but it sold slowly. It was a difficult time to begin a career as a folk singer because so many folk protest singers already had well-established careers. The seventies were ready for Mitchell's personal style, however, and "Big Yellow Taxi" (1970) gave her the start she needed. Through that song, Mitchell expressed ideas many listeners could relate to. In general, she sang about the human tendency to recognize the value of the things and people around them only after they are no longer there. The song included examples from nature and the ways in which urban development removed it from people's lives, and the loss of her husband, who drove away in a "big yellow taxi." Mitchell's feelings about her divorce and ex-husband resurfaced in other songs, including "The Last Time I Saw Richard"

Listening Guide

"Help Me"
as recorded by Joni Mitchell (1974)

Tempo: The tempo is approximately 168 beats per minute, with four beats in each bar.

Form: After a four-bar introduction, the song is constructed of four verses, with instrumental extensions after each one, in an AABA format.

At the end of each extension the jazz instrumental group plays a vamp pattern that leads into the next section of lyrics.

The A sections all begin with the words "help me."

Features: The introduction is played by Mitchell strumming her acoustic guitar. The drums enter at bar four.

The L.A. Express jazz group provides the instrumental accompaniment to Joni Mitchell's vocals and strummed acoustic guitar. Their instrumentation is saxophone, guitar, keyboards, bass, and drums. A female vocal group also inserts responses to Mitchell's vocal lines.

Mitchell's vocals often freely sing around the steady beat played by the rhythm section, particularly at the ends of verses when she sings about loving her freedom.

Lyrics: A female singer laments her tendency to chase after bad men who have no intention of sticking around, but ends the song with the suggestion that she herself really does not want a permanent relationship either.

Billboard pop charts: number seven

(1971). Trying a more commercial style on her next album, *Court and Spark* (1974), provided Mitchell with the biggest hit single of her career, "Help Me." A listening guide is on page 142.

> " I've known Joni since I was eighteen. We met in one of the coffeehouses. . . . What an incredible talent she is. She writes about her relationships so much more vividly than I do. "
>
> –Neil Young, about Joni Mitchell

Mitchell followed that success with some experimental use of unusual (for rock or American folk music) instruments. For example, on *The Hissing of Summer Lawns* (1975), she used stick-beaten drums from Burundi, Africa. She had worked with a jazz group, the L.A. Express, for some concerts and recordings in 1974, and went back to a jazz-influenced style for a live album with jazz bass virtuoso Jaco Pastorius and guitarist Pat Metheny in 1976. Mitchell returned to a pop style in her work in the eighties.

Mitchell performed on stage very few times during the eighties and nineties, but she continued to write and record. Her songs on such albums as *Dog Eat Dog* (1985) concentrated less on her personal life and relationships and more on social and political issues. She also continued her work as an artist, and her paintings and photographs have been displayed in galleries around the world.

Summary

American folk music comes from the songs and dances of people from various different parts of the world who settled in the United States. The folk music from which folk-rock developed in the sixties came primarily from the British Isles. The songs were often ballads that told stories about people and their relationships and activities. Performers of traditional folk music sing the old songs in what is close to their original versions, but some singers also wrote new songs that related to political or other issues of concern to them. When folk music is political, it tends to embrace such progressive or left-wing causes as support of labor unions and civil rights. The American civil rights movement and the Vietnam War were both causes of the sixties that folk and folk-rock musicians used as themes for their songs. Folk-rock music is folk music that is performed with such "rock" instruments as electric guitar, electric bass guitar, and drums. Traditional folk music avoids amplification and drums.

Singer/songwriters of the seventies tended less toward political issues and more toward the expression of personal thoughts and interests than had most folk-rock singers of the sixties. The messages they communicated were sometimes quite individual and introspective and at other times more universal. Whatever the message, the singers effectively reflected the sentiments of large numbers of people, and the style remained popular into the early two-thousands. The communication of thoughts and ideas between the musician and the listener has always been part of folk music, and the singer/songwriters who came from the folk tradition stressed this.

discussion questions

Is folk music at its best when expressing controversy and hard times, or is it music for all time? Why were young adults listening to Bob Dylan instead of pop or soul music during the early sixties? Why were traditional folk musicians offended when Dylan began to use amplified instruments? Is acoustic folk music more "authentic" and folk-rock too commercial to also be heard as authentic? Frank Zappa criticized singer/songwriters for being too personal and too quick to dump their problems and feelings on their listeners, who are already burdened with their own problems. Is the widespread popularity of music by singer/songwriters an indication that he was wrong, or did he make a valid point?

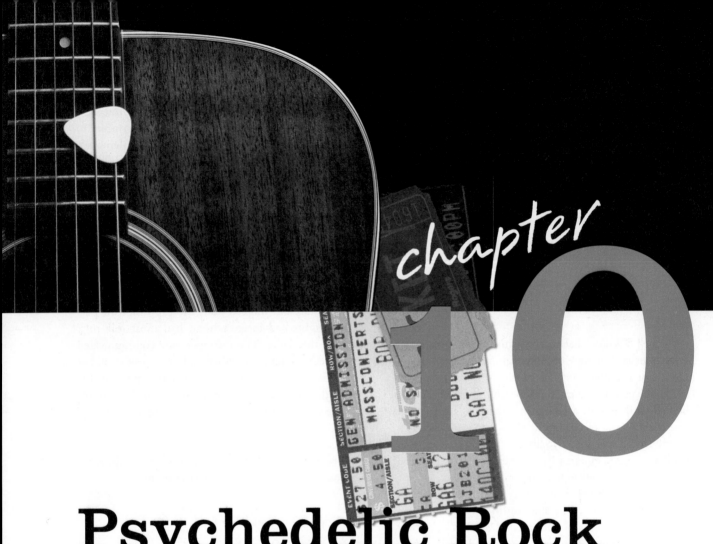

Psychedelic Rock

" LSD is Western yoga. The aim of all Eastern religion, like the aim of LSD, is basically to get high; that is, to expand your consciousness and find ecstasy and revelation within. "
—DR. TIMOTHY LEARY

"The nature of outer life is activity. Inner life is all silent and quiet. At this quiet end is absolute being, nonchanging, transcendental bliss." –Maharishi Maresh Yogi

The late sixties was an era of experimentation and innovation in rock music and the cultural values it expressed. Many of those values had been influenced by the work of such writers and poets as Allen Ginsberg (1926–1997), Jack Kerouac (1922–1969), and Gregory Corso (1930–2001). Known as the **Beats** (and their followers as "beatniks"), from the word *beatific* (meaning blissfully happy), Ginsberg, Kerouac, Corso, and others decided that inner peace could only be achieved by one who was completely free from the artificial constraints of society. In the case of Ginsberg, personal freedom required that, among other issues, society accept homosexuality. He maintained that America's claim of being "the Land of the Free" was simply not valid. He saw America as a hypocritical, oppressive society in which some citizens were despised and legislated against because of their rejection of conventional morality and their choice of nontraditional lifestyles. In order to force his point, he wrote in crass and exhibitionistic language, drawing attention to his point of view. Ginsberg influenced the thinking of many of his generation, as well as numerous members of the psychedelic counterculture of the late sixties and the androgynous leaders of the glitter movement that followed. Drugs, particularly marijuana, and Eastern meditation were often used by the Beats and their followers to increase awareness.

The desire for freedom expressed through the Beats' writings was an attempt to duplicate the sort of creativity and individuality they heard in improvisations by jazz musicians. The bebop jazz played by Charlie "Bird" Parker, Dizzy Gillespie, and Thelonious Monk during the forties, as well as the bebop-influenced **cool jazz** styles of Miles Davis, Gerry Mulligan, and Chico Hamilton in the fifties, were all an integral part of the movement. Bebop and cool jazz were both generally played by small groups of musicians that included from one to three lead instruments and a rhythm section of guitar or piano, bass, and drums. At times, particularly in some of Gerry Mulligan's groups, the rhythm section would include only bass and drums. With so few musicians, written arrangements were not necessary. A song title or even just a chord progression along with a key center and someone counting to establish a tempo was all that the musicians needed to begin an improvisation that could continue as long as the musicians or the audience wanted. Individual solos would become almost conversational, as one player would take off on a line that would respond to—and perhaps imitate and then move beyond—what another soloist had played. In this and other ways, the music was both very free and very personal. Beat writers tried to capture that same expressive intimacy and uninhibited sense of free rhythmic flow in their works. By the midsixties, psychedelic rock musicians would also use a great deal of free improvisation.

At times the Beats and their followers gathered in coffeehouses to perform and listen to readings of their works, and the interrelationship of the writing style with music led to readings that were accompanied by live jazz. In such situations, the music would accompany the reading or enter responsively at the ends of lyric phrases. Either way, the arts of music and poetry were melded for personal and free expression. Many of the Beats' works were written in an almost casual style to capture that sense of improvisation experienced in the live performances.

The Beat movement started in New York, but after Lawrence Ferlinghetti (born in 1919) moved to San Francisco and established the City Lights Bookshop, City Lights Press publishing company, and *The City Lights Journal,* all of which featured works by Ferlinghetti and many of his like-minded friends, he convinced Ginsberg, Kerouac, and Corso to join him there. San Francisco was attractive because it had (at the time) fairly lax enforcement of drug laws, good cheap wine, and a number of citizens who were ripe for new experiences. The Beat movement suffered criticism from literary societies in both New York and San Francisco, and the Beat writers' works did not even gain acceptance as literature until the seventies. Conservative critics believed the poets to be dangerous to the basic fabric of society and, in reviewing their works, generally blasted them unmercifully. Some of the writers were still in San Francisco, or had left and returned, to be part of the psychedelic counterculture centered there during the sixties.

Just as some of the Beats wrote about their political views, many young people of the middle to late sixties were also very involved in making political statements and in fact some psychedelic music reflected those views. As discussed in the opening section, "The Nineteen Sixties," many eighteen-year-old men were forced to enter the military and fight in Vietnam because of the draft. The death rate among these men was so high that college campuses across the country had many different types of student demonstrations against the war. Some even went so far as to "take over" campus administration buildings.

The San Francisco Sound

Political and social issues of the middle to late sixties, such as the Vietnam War and the civil rights movement, brought attention back to many of the criticisms of American culture that had earlier been expressed by the Beat writers. Even to young people who had never read the Beat writers, it seemed that concepts of love, freedom, and individual worth did not hold the importance they should, and that their parents and society in general had become money-grubbing and materialistic. A wish to return to basic human values led to the development of a new culture, or counterculture, in such cities as San Francisco. Referred to as *hippies* or *flower children,* this new group stood for peace, free love, and nonmaterialism. They often stood out from the rest of the community by wearing loose, casual clothing decorated with beads and other ornaments, sporting long hair, and maintaining a lifestyle that often centered on communal sharing of possessions.

The use of mind-altering **psychedelic drugs** such as LSD (lysergic acid diethylamide, also called acid) had also become common within the subculture, giving the name psychedelic rock (or acid rock) to the music favored by San Francisco's hippies. LSD was not declared illegal until late 1966, so it was often readily available at parties and concerts. The effects of the drug included a feeling of timelessness, increased physical and visual sensitivity, unreal and rather dreamlike connections between thoughts, and vivid hallucinations. Musicians tried to re-create these effects in their music, generally through long instrumental improvisations on one or two repeating chords, often involving one musician responding to what another had just played.

The philosophy of existentialism, developed originally by Soren Kierkegaard (1813–1855) and further expanded by Jean-Paul Sartre (1905–1980), influenced the alienation from society embraced by the Beats and the hippie counterculture. Existentialism itself has been interpreted in a variety of ways, but for the hippies it became an attitude that stressed the importance of freeing the individual from the hostility of the outside, tradition-bound world. Once individuals were free, they had no need to be restrained by the expectations of others, and so could act as their own mood or personal beliefs dictated. They were required, however, to take responsibility for their actions, according to the tenets of existentialism. The young hippies who adopted an existential philosophy felt free, even obligated, to drop out of the world of their parents and to refuse to fight in Vietnam. Those who did not sign up for the draft, or who did sign up but refused military service, had to choose whether to be jailed or to leave the country—not knowing if they would ever be allowed to return. Those decisions were faced by many who had made the existential choice of refusing to follow the dictates of society.

The freedom felt by the hippie generation was celebrated at the "First Human Be-In" in San Francisco's Golden Gate Park in January 1967. Beat poets Allen Ginsberg and Gary Snyder read to the crowd, and the music for the program was played by Quicksilver Messenger Service, the Grateful Dead (or, as they were known, the Quick and the Dead), and Jefferson Airplane. The national exposure the event received attracted many like-minded people to San Francisco, and the summer of 1967 was dubbed the "summer of love" by those who attended

the many other outdoor concerts and "love-ins." The First Human Be-In also paved the way for other large rock festivals during the next two years, many of which featured San Francisco bands, in Monterey and Newport (California) and in other parts of the country as well, including Miami, Atlanta, Atlantic City, and Lewisville (Texas), and also for the well-publicized Woodstock Festival in New York.

> **"I think it's the scene this area has that makes it attractive to musicians, and that's why a lot of them moved here. That freedom, that lack of competition, the fact that you aren't always having to battle and you can really get into what playing music is all about."**
> –Jerry Garcia, about San Francisco

No group of musicians mastered the techniques of extended improvisations better than the **Grateful Dead,** a name founder Jerry Garcia (1942–1995) claimed to have discovered in an ancient Egyptian prayer. Garcia was a guitarist and bluegrass banjo player who earlier had led a group called Mother McCree's Uptown Jug Champions, with guitarist Bob Weir and keyboard/harmonica player Ron "Pigpen" McKernan. They changed their name to the Warlocks when they switched to electric instruments in 1965 and were joined by bassist Phil Lesh and drummer Bill Kreutzmann. In the same year, they became known as the Grateful Dead and joined other San Francisco–based bands for free concerts and acid parties, as well as more formal

Members of the Grateful Dead: back-up singer Donna Godchaux, Bob Weir, Phil Lesh, and Jerry Garcia

gatherings in clubs and auditoriums. Eventually they moved to Ashbury Street, which bordered Golden Gate Park and which became the base of operations for most members of the hippie counterculture in San Francisco.

The Grateful Dead and other San Francisco bands such as Big Brother and the Holding Company played at "acid tests" (parties where LSD was available very inexpensively) organized by writer Ken Kesey. The three-day version of an acid test, held January 21–23, 1966, drew thousands of fans and the attention of news media. Light shows were part of many such events. Often the lights were shined through water with colored oils floating on it. The slow, rhythmic moving of many different shapes soon became the standard for the era, as were lava lamps that had similar slow motion and changing shapes.

Musically, the Grateful Dead's commercial recordings displayed the group's ability to blend country, folk, blues, and Latin influences with rock, but they generally failed to capture on vinyl the excitement of their live performances. When the band decided to give their fans an album recorded live, they could not resist calling it *Live Dead* (1970). The double album contained several of the long improvisations for which the group had become famous.

The entire first side was one composition, "Dark Star," a continuous improvisation. A listening guide to that recording is below.

Long instrumental improvisations like "Dark Star" were not commercial because they had little appeal for the rock listeners who wanted short, catchy songs they could sing along with. Such recordings could never fit on a 45 rpm record and were not suitable for AM radio. The same could be said for much of the music played by the Grateful Dead and other psychedelic groups. The radio, however, was still the essential medium that allowed music to reach large audiences. The changes in the music and demands of its fans finally brought about changes in rock radio itself.

Several members of the Grateful Dead were as much at home in country music as they were in rock, and this background was evident on their *Workingman's Dead* and *American Beauty* albums (both 1970). The music on these albums departed from the psychedelic freedom of *Live Dead* by basing the songs on more organized arrangements. A listening guide to "Uncle John's Band," from *Workingman's Dead* is on page 149. The recording reached number sixty-nine on the pop charts.

Listening Guide

"Dark Star"
as recorded by the Grateful Dead
(1970)

Tempo: The speed of the beat at the beginning of the recording is about 88 beats per minute, with four beats per bar, but the tempo varies as the improvisation progresses.

Form: The form is **through-composed** in that it does not have regular sections that repeat or contrast but instead is a continuous spinning out of musical ideas that are probably improvised.

Features: The recording begins in silence, with the volume gradually being turned up after the group has begun playing. Instruments come in one at a time, beginning with bass and guitar, then the drums lightly touching the cymbals; rhythm guitar is added, then organ and maracas.

Harmonized vocals near the final cadence sound as if they had been worked out in advance; the rest of the piece was probably improvised.

The recording lasts over twenty-three minutes.

Lyrics: The recording is mostly instrumental with short phrases of lyrics sung about six minutes into it and then again at the end. Both lyric sections suggest visual effects one might see when watching a "dark star" crash. Reflections and diamonds are parts of the images.

AM versus FM Radio

Before the late sixties, rock music had been played mainly on commercial AM stations, stations that maintained their financial support from advertisers who required they play only songs from the top ten or top forty in order to appeal to the largest possible number of listeners. **AM** (amplitude modulation) **radio** was a system that could carry sound far beyond a line-of-sight distance but was often full of static and, at that time, could not be transmitted in stereo. The **FM** (frequency modulation) **radio** system had been invented during the thirties but did not come into regular commercial use until the sixties when the advantages of static-free, high-fidelity stereo sound became more important than the drawbacks of FM's limited range, line-of-sight transmission. At first, FM stations received funding to broadcast classical music because of listeners' demands for improved sound quality, and soon a number of subscriber-supported stations appeared. Finally, FM stations airing rock music went into operation and became the primary vehicles for the dissemination of psychedelic rock and other "underground" music that AM radio stations ignored.

In San Francisco, it was former top-forty AM disc jockey Tom Donahue who decided to reject the pop-station format and start an FM psychedelic radio station that aired extended album cuts and featured new and noncommercial bands. Eventually, the superior sound quality of FM led to its adoption by an increasing number of commercial stations.

Listening Guide

"Uncle John's Band"
as recorded by the Grateful Dead
(1970)

Tempo: The tempo is approximately 132 beats per minute, with four beats per bar for most of the recording. Rhythmic interest is added when the fourth and eighth bars of each A section are shortened to only three beats. The instrumental D section also varies the beat pattern by alternating four- and three-beat bars.

Form: The recording begins with an eight-bar introduction comprised of two bars of a single strummed acoustic guitar, two bars of two strummed acoustic guitars with bass, and then four bars of those instruments with another acoustic guitar playing a lead line.

After the introduction, the recording continues in sections of varying lengths as follows: AABCCAACBDCB.

Each A section is sixteen bars (the fourth and eighth of which have only three beats) with lyrics followed by a two-bar extension.

Each B and C section is made up of eight four-beat bars. The second C and D are both instrumental. The C section functions as a refrain with repeated lyrics.

The instrumental D section is based on a rhythmic pattern that plays a seven-beat pattern (one four-beat bar followed by one three-beat bar) seven times before going back into the four-beat pattern of most of the rest of the recording.

(continued)

The last C section is preceded by silence and sung a cappella (without instrumental accompaniment).

The second and final B sections have the same lyrics as the C refrain.

The recording ends with an extension of the last B, which fades out.

Features: Even beat subdivisions are followed throughout the recording.

A backbeat is played softly on a wood block in parts of the recording but not stressed in most places.

Strummed acoustic guitars and electric bass provide the main instrumental

accompaniment with additional color added by such Latin percussion instruments as **guiro,** maracas, claves, and conga drums.

The harmonized group vocals include two voices above the main melody.

Lyrics: The lyrics stress virtuous living and ask the listener to go with the singers to visit "Uncle John's Band" by the riverside so that Uncle John can take them home. If one sees a Christian baptism as going home, then Uncle John can be seen as John the Baptist.

Billboard pop charts: number sixty-nine

By 1970, the Grateful Dead's psychedelic mixture of country, blues, and whatever else they were in the mood to play attracted a following of "dead heads," whose way of life was to go from one Dead concert to another, selling food, posters, jewelry, and other wares. During the seventies, the band experienced several personnel changes and even disbanded from 1974 to 1976, but their popularity remained constant with their hard-core fans. Even through the yuppie era of the eighties, with its electronically sophisticated new wave and new age sounds, fans experienced a time warp at Grateful Dead concerts, which offered them a nostalgic return to the psychedelic sixties. Their music continued to embody the attitudes and

spirit of the psychedelic rock era three decades after its heyday.

For many, that era came to an abrupt end with the death of Jerry Garcia in August of 1995. Surviving Grateful Dead members did not deny that they might decide to play together again, but said that they did not feel right about continuing under the same name without Garcia. After several solo projects, the remaining band members regrouped and performed as "The Dead."

One of the most commercially popular psychedelic bands was **Jefferson Airplane.** Formed by singer Marty Balin and guitarist/singer Paul Kantner in 1965, the group first played folk-rock but soon changed their sound

Jefferson Airplane (1967)

to one with a harder edge. Balin sang in harmony and alternated leads with Signe Anderson (formerly Signe Toly), until she left and was replaced by Grace Slick (formerly Grace Wing). After Slick joined, Balin continued to share the vocal roles, but it was Slick's dramatic voice and stage appearance that became the hallmark of the sound and style of Jefferson Airplane. Two songs she had previously recorded with her earlier group, the Great Society, "Somebody to Love" and "White Rabbit" (both 1967), emerged as statements of the hippie counterculture's beliefs in free love and drugs when Jefferson Airplane recorded hit versions. "Somebody to Love" served as a suitable theme song for 1967's summer of love in San Francisco.

"White Rabbit" was based on Lewis Carroll's story "Alice's Adventures in Wonderland" (1865) and *Through the Looking Glass* (1871). The strange, dreamlike manipulation of the physical world Alice experienced in Wonderland was recalled in the song, which was banned in some cities for its drug implications; it made reference to a world that changed after Alice took pills and ate mushrooms. Musically, the song was interesting because it did not follow a standard pop song form with repeated verses. It started with a soft beat and quiet mood that gradually intensified, without obvious seams, to a high-energy ending. An exotic touch was added by the use of the Phrygian mode (a sixteenth-century mode composed of the natural notes from E to E, often used in flamenco music) and bolero-influenced rhythm patterns. A listening guide to "White Rabbit" is included here.

Much of Jefferson Airplane's music was commercial because it consisted of short, single-length songs with vocals and a rock backbeat, but they also employed the long improvisations favored by other groups of the era. Although their roots were in folk-rock, the Airplane made recordings in many other styles, the most experimental of which involved the avant-garde (for the time) use of electronic sound effects in "Chushingura" (1968). They also made general statements about the hippie culture through songs like "Crown of Creation" (1968), which stressed the need for loyalty among the members of the counterculture, calling outsiders "obstructionists."

Listening Guide

"White Rabbit"
as recorded by Jefferson Airplane (1967)

Tempo: The tempo is approximately 104 beats per minute, with four beats in each bar.

Form: The song is constructed in five twelve-bar sections, the first of which is instrumental, and the last has an extension during repetitions of the final line of text.

Features: The recording opens with a soft, regular beat played by the bass. The drums enter at the third bar and the guitar at the fifth bar.

The recording gradually gets louder from the soft bass at the beginning to Grace Slick's almost screaming repetitions of "Feed your head" at the end.

Spanish flavor is added by a bolero rhythm and the use of Phrygian mode, which is often used in flamenco music.

Lyrics: The imagery is drawn from Lewis Carroll's *Alice's Adventures in Wonderland* and *Through the Looking Glass,* in which Alice chases a white rabbit, falls down its hole, becomes very small when she drinks an unknown liquid, and then grows very large when she eats a cake. The references to a hookah smoking caterpillar, a mushroom, a chessboard, the White Knight, the Red Queen, and the Dormouse are also from those stories. The fact that a hookah is a traditional way of smoking hashish and the way in which the song creates a general sensory disorientation of space and time both give it a clear connection to the drug culture of the late sixties.

Billboard pop charts: number eight

"Volunteers" (1969) identified the counterculture as a social revolution.

The blues was well represented in the psychedelic rock movement through the noncommercial songs and instrumentals by the Quicksilver Messenger Service, as well as by the attention-riveting vocals of **Janis Joplin** with her bands Big Brother and the Holding Company (1967–1969), the Kozmic Blues Band (1969), and the Full-Tilt Boogie Band (1970). Steve Miller had been a guitarist/singer in blues revival groups in Chicago during the midsixties, and he moved to San Francisco in 1966 to form the Steve Miller Blues Band. After their 1967 performance at the Monterey Pop Festival, they removed the word *blues* from their name, and as the Steve Miller Band expanded their style in more commercial directions.

Psychedelic Rock beyond San Francisco

Venice Beach in Los Angeles became a gathering place for southern California hippies. Allen Ginsberg and other Beats often appeared for poetry readings in its several coffeehouses. Of the psychedelic bands formed in Los Angeles, the **Doors** was the most important. The group chose their name as a shortened version of *The Doors of Perception,* a book by Aldous Huxley (1894–1963) about the influences of drugs. The phrase was previously used by William Blake (1757–1827), although in his case it did not refer to drugs. The Doors were formed by keyboard player Ray Manzarek (born in 1939) and poet/singer Jim Morrison (1943–1971), both of whom had studied filmmaking and saw their dramatic stage performances as the

The Doors (left to right): Ray Manzarek, Robbie Kreiger, John Densmore, and Jim Morrison

door through which they would bring new awareness to their fans. Other members were guitarist Robby Krieger (born in 1946) and drummer John Densmore (born in 1944), who had both belonged to the Psychedelic Rangers.

> "Poetry appeals to me so much—because it's so eternal. As long as there are people, they can remember words and combinations of words. Nothing else can survive a holocaust, but poetry and songs."
>
> –Jim Morrison

For most of the Doors' songs, Morrison wrote poetry that Krieger set to music. Their favorite song themes were influenced by Beat poetry. The Beats' interest in both sex and drugs, for example, could be heard in "Light My Fire" (1967), which was based on an almost hypnotic repetition of the organ theme along with sexually suggestive and drug-related lyrics. When the Doors were invited to perform on *The Ed Sullivan Show,* they were allowed to perform "Light My Fire," but Morrison had to promise to take the word *higher* out of the lyrics and change it to something that would not be taken as a reference to drugs. He broke his promise and sang the word loudly and clearly, and because the show was aired live, it could not be cut by the producers. A listening guide to "Light My Fire" is on page 153. It was number one on the pop charts for three weeks.

The Doors gained a great number of fans across the country between 1967 and 1969, but they were unable to go on the long concert tours those fans craved because of Morrison's chronic abuse of drugs and alcohol. He had become completely undependable on stage, being so careless about his language and actions that he was eventually arrested for public obscenity and indecency. His arrest for lewd behavior in Miami in 1969 caused a break in the group's professional activities because Morrison had to attend the court proceedings on the matter. Although the judge dropped the charges for lack of evidence that Morrison had actually exposed himself on stage, the negative publicity surrounding the case hurt the band's commercial image and promoters were hesitant to hire them.

After the Miami incident, Morrison changed his stage persona. He threw out his leather pants in exchange for more conservative dress, gained weight, and grew a beard. He also became more introverted and detached from the rock star image he had previously affected. The Doors continued to record and to perform occasionally in concerts, but Morrison began to look for solace more in his

Listening Guide

"Light My Fire"
as recorded by the Doors (1967)

Tempo: The tempo is approximately 126 beats per minute, with four beats in each bar.

Form: After a five-bar introduction, the form is structured as ABAB and an improvised instrumental section 145 bars in length, then ABAB and an extension.

The A sections are eight bars long and the B sections are seven bars long.

The long instrumental section features the organ for the first seventy bars, the guitar with organ accompaniment for the next seventy bars, and then a repeat of the five-bar introduction. The musical basis of the improvisation is a one-bar, two-chord ostinato (repeating pattern).

The B sections function as a refrain and have the same lyrics each time.

The lyrics to the third A section are a repetition of the second A, and the lyrics to the fourth A are a repetition of the first A.

The recording ends with an extension based on the B section followed by a repeat of the instrumental introduction.

Features: Even beat subdivisions are maintained throughout the recording.

The drums keep a strong backbeat in the B and the instrumental sections, but they accent the backbeat more softly in the A sections.

The bass lines are played on the organ.

Lyrics: The singer asks a girl to help him get as high as possible. Both sex and drugs are hinted at as part of the trip.

Billboard pop charts: number one for three weeks; British hit singles: number forty-nine

poetry and film experiments than in music. Finally, after the completion of the *L.A. Woman* album (1971), he took a break and moved to Paris to rest. He died of a heart attack while he was there.

With Morrison's death, the Doors were reduced to an instrumental trio. They tried to continue as such but disbanded to pursue solo projects. In 1978, they released the album *An American Prayer,* which contained their music dubbed over Morrison's recitation of his poetry. The mystique of Jim Morrison continued well after his death. The Doors' music enjoyed a resurgence in popularity in the late seventies and early eighties, to the point that their albums sold better during this revival than when they were first released. Oliver Stone revived their memory again with his movie *The Doors* (1991).

Ray Manzarek and Robby Krieger decided to ring in the new century with a return of the Doors. Original

drummer John Densmore refused to be involved in the project, but it moved ahead without him. The new group was first called the Doors of the 21st Century, and they tried out various different singers and drummers. By 2007, the members included lead vocalist Brett Scallions, Phil Chen on bass, and Ty Dennis on drums. That group toured in 2009 under the name Ray Manzarek and Robby Krieger of The Doors.

Despite the importance of San Francisco and Los Angeles for their counterculture enclaves, California had no monopoly on the psychedelic movement. Similar events were happening in many parts of the United States and in England. Jimi Hendrix had moved to London to start the **Jimi Hendrix Experience,** and Hendrix's blues-based but psychedelic-influenced guitar style became the model for other guitarists for years to come. The Jimi Hendrix Experience debuted in the United States at California's Monterey

Pop Festival in 1967 and many U.S. tours followed. Hendrix had always admired Bob Dylan's music, and his psychedelic version of Dylan's "All Along the Watchtower" became Hendrix's first top-twenty hit in the United States and his biggest pop chart hit. The listening guide compares Hendrix's recording to the original by Dylan. Dylan has said he liked what Hendrix did with the song, and he even made some changes in his own live performances because of Hendrix's influence.

The Jimi Hendrix Experience broke up in 1969. Hendrix moved back to the United States and worked with a variety of musicians, often including Experience drummer Mitch Mitchell. Hendrix's performance of the "Star Spangled Banner" was a highlight of the Woodstock Festival in 1969. Just through his playing of the national anthem, Hendrix managed to make statements that supported the feelings and attitudes of the hippie counterculture. Between bits of melody Hendrix broke off to make his guitar sound like bombs were going off, a reminder of the fact that the Vietnam War still raged on, and after the melody where the words "land of the free" would be sung, his guitar line took a dive from a very high to a very low

Listening Guide

	"All Along the Watchtower" as recorded by Bob Dylan (1968)	*"All Along the Watchtower"* as recorded by Jimi Hendrix (1968)
Tempo:	The tempo is about 126 beats per minute, with four beats in each bar.	The tempo is about 116 beats per minute, with four beats in each bar.
Form:	The lyrics and instrumentals fall into eight-bar sections, but the basis of the musical form is a two-bar chord progression with a descending bass line. Both the chord progression and the bass line repeat throughout the recording. (This form is called a **passacaglia** in classical music.)	The form of Dylan's recording has been followed, except Hendrix extends one of the instrumental sections from eight to thirty-two bars, and he adds an extension with vocal comments to the ending.
Features:	Even beat subdivisions are maintained throughout the recording.	Even beat subdivisions are maintained by the instruments, but the vocals occasionally relax into uneven subdivisions.
	The eight-bar instrumental introduction includes two bars of strummed acoustic guitar, two bars of that pattern with harmonica, and then four bars with electric bass and drums. Those instruments are the only ones used in the recording.	From the beginning to the end the instrumental background is a thick texture created by rhythm guitar, keyboard instruments, electric bass, two drums, and congas.
	No backbeat is accented.	The drums and tambourine play a very strong backbeat.
	Dylan plays the harmonica during the instrumental sections.	The instrumental sections are used to feature Jimi Hendrix's distinctive and colorful guitar style.

(continued)

	Dylan plays his harmonica to fill between his vocal phrases. His guitar supplies the only accompaniment.	Hendrix plays his guitar to fill between his vocal phrases. Other instruments play the accompaniment.
Lyrics:	The central image is of an a ancient walled city, with high towers rising over the walls to allow guards to see enemies approaching from afar. The "watchtower" is an allusion to the Biblical accounts of coming destruction of walled cities; the singer thus adopts the persona of a prophet, like Ezekiel or Jeremiah ("the hour is late"). Cities are traditional symbols of civilization; this city is caught in its own absurdities. Outside forces are now coming to challenge the "city." The reference to the howling wild cat recalls the poet W. B. Yeats's famous line about a rough beast slouching toward the archetypical ancient walled city, Jerusalem.	Dylan's lyrics are kept the same and even amplified through the repetitions of bits of phrases at the end of the recording.

Billboard pop charts: number twenty; British hit singles: number five |

note as if to say those words did not ring true. Hendrix died the following year, but the influence he had on other rock guitarists and the psychedelic movement in general continued on.

Other blues revival groups like Cream and even the Beatles were greatly influenced by the psychedelic movement. Pink Floyd was a psychedelic group in the beginning of their career, but after 1967, when their writer/guitarist/singer Syd Barrett left, they became much more important as a progressive rock group than as a psychedelic one. The music of Pink Floyd is discussed in Chapter 14, "Progressive and Glitter Rock."

expressed an in-group identity inspired by the Beat writers and attempted to provide a drug-influenced mood and atmosphere to aid escape from the outside world. Whether the music had the country and folk roots of jug band music; the commercial flair of Jefferson Airplane; the blues roots of Janis Joplin or Jimi Hendrix; the dramatic stage performances of the Doors; or the combination of styles played by the Grateful Dead, psychedelic rock shared the favorite themes of its fans and was musically influenced by their fascination with the effects of psychedelic drugs.

Summary

Psychedelic rock was not a single style of music but rather the music of the peace-and-love-minded counterculturists grouped in San Francisco as well as in other parts of the United States and England. Psychedelic rock music

discussion questions

Psychedelic drugs were used, at least in part, during the sixties to help the user "drop out" of a society that she or he disapproved of. What do young adults do today when they disapprove of the government or society in general? Is music used to express that disapproval?

The NINETEEN SEVENTIES

"We remember the napalm and the phosphorous bombs that rained on peasant villages, leaving burnt bodies and blackened holes where once there was family life. . . . We also remember more than 58,000 Americans who lost their lives."

–The Vietnam Peace Twenty-fifth Anniversary Committee

"I have never been a quitter. . . . [To] leave office before my term is completed is abhorrent to every instinct in my body. . . . [B]ecause of the Watergate matter I might not have the support of the Congress that I would consider necessary. . . . I hereby resign the Office of President of the United States."

–President Richard M. Nixon

"I . . . do grant a full, free, and absolute pardon unto Richard Nixon for all offenses against the United States."

–President Gerald R. Ford

"Throw away your belief system, tear yourself down, and put yourself back together again."

–Werner Erhard, The Founder of est (Erhard Seminars Training)

In many ways, the seventies were a consolidation of the trends of the sixties. Sixties hippies had long hair and casual to outrageous ways of dressing while living a lifestyle that included "free love," but it wasn't until the seventies that beards, mustaches, long hair, and casual dress became commonly acceptable. It also wasn't until the seventies that freer sex became more acceptable in terms of unmarried couples openly living together, college dorms becoming coed, contraceptive sales being encouraged, and abortions being made legal. In some parts of the country, the sale of contraceptives was against the law until the *Griswald v. Connecticut* case in 1967. That was one of several cases that opened the door to *Roe v. Wade* (1973), which legalized abortion nationwide. The Vietnam War created a tremendous amount of controversy in the sixties, but it wasn't until 1975 that U.S. troops were finally pulled out of South Vietnam and the South Vietnamese capital, Saigon, fell to the northern communists. Many South Vietnamese refugees fled to the United States.

On some issues the seventies not only continued trends of the sixties but also gave new expression to them. The civil rights movement had stressed the need for integration and equality. The seventies saw the stress on racial issues become one of celebration of racial differences. African Americans and others displayed their pride in African roots by wearing "afro" hairdos and clothing with African prints. The popularity of funk music such as that by James Brown and Sly and the Family Stone illustrated that movement. Other groups also began to look to their ethnic heritage with a renewed sense of independence. More than three hundred Native Americans took over Alcatraz Island in San Francisco Bay for nineteen months in 1969, and then others protested to demand Indian sovereignty and treaty rights at Wounded Knee, South Dakota, in 1973. Hispanic Americans developed bilingual programs in schools. More and more Asians had been entering the United States since the loss of the Vietnam War, and they began settling into their own communities and starting their own businesses. Some of those businesses affected America's food tastes with great numbers of new Vietnamese, Szechuan, Hunan, Indian, and other restaurants. All of these racial groups gained further recognition through a variety of ethnic studies courses and departments in colleges and universities nationwide.

Movies and television shows also supported ethnic pride through the production of a variety of shows. The eight-night television series *Roots,* based on Alex Haley's book of the same title, dramatized the horrors of slavery. African Americans were portrayed as having moved up to a "deluxe apartment in the sky" on *The Jeffersons* while their bigoted former neighbors, Archie and Edith Bunker, remained totally middle class, proudly moving nowhere on *All in the Family.* Freddie Prinze's *Chico and the Man* gave Hispanic Americans a show with which they could identify. The movie *The Godfather* began with the son of a proud Italian American mob family repudiating his family's ways and ended with his carrying on the old family traditions.

The Watergate scandal brought down President Richard M. Nixon and intensified a general mistrust in government. That scandal began in 1972 after burglars were caught breaking into the Democratic National Headquarters at the Watergate Hotel. The cover-up that followed included President Nixon's ordering the CIA to stop an FBI investigation, hush money being paid to the burglars, Nixon aides being caught lying under oath, Nixon's firing a special prosecutor, and the resignation of the attorney general and the associate attorney general. All these events took the news media months to uncover, creating a real national drama. Finally, President Nixon resigned his office. His vice president, Spiro T. Agnew, had already resigned in disgrace over other issues, and Nixon chose to appoint Gerald R. Ford

to be his successor. Ford immediately pardoned Nixon for all wrongdoing. While that whole series of scandals did spread the mistrust much further than it had been felt before, it wasn't the beginning of that feeling in any way. There had been a general lack of trust in American institutions and leaders since the race riots and antiwar protests of the middle sixties, at least among many of the protesters. To go back even further, the Beat writers expressed a number of complaints about the government in the fifties.

President Ford's pardon of Richard Nixon might have been a primary factor in his failure to be elected president. His successor as president, Jimmy Carter (inaugurated in 1977), also became infamous for a controversial pardon—a limited pardon to Vietnam protesters who had "dodged" the draft and were living outside the United States. Without that pardon, they would have been arrested and jailed for reentering the United States. Carter also aided the veterans of the war with a new jobs program. An Arab oil embargo had created energy shortages in 1973, and long lines at gas stations resulted. President Carter tried to limit U.S. dependency on foreign oil with a National Energy Policy that offered various different incentives for reduction in use of oil products. Sale of solar-powered water heaters, added insulation for homes and other kinds of buildings, as well as a concentration on the development and popularity of more economic automobiles resulted. Through the seventies, the general well-being of the environment was an issue of great concern for many Americans, and March 21 was chosen to be celebrated as Earth Day.

Carter's biggest problems as president were in the economy. Property taxes had risen far beyond what many homeowners could afford, and California's 1978 revolt (called Proposition 13) to lower current taxes and limit future increases to them was followed in almost half of the other states. Additionally, Carter could not control inflation and increasing interest rates. By the fall of 1979, inflation had led to a recession and the end of Carter's chance of winning reelection. Energy prices had increased and oil was in short supply, creating gas rationing and, again, long lines at service stations.

Some Americans tried to escape the social and economic pressures of the decade by living alternative lifestyles. Some in communes and others in their own homes tried to do without cars, grow their own organic foods, and concentrate on building new awareness and spirituality. Some who could afford it went to the Esalen Institute in Big Sur, California, to experience and gain training in massage, yoga, tai chi, and est (Erhard Seminars Training). The goals of est were to cause trainees to throw away beliefs, tear themselves down, and then put themselves back together again. They were to experience "the world as it is without the intercession of human understanding." Several additional types of New Age groups used other methods to help their followers "discover themselves." By the middle to late seventies, some who were not necessarily part of the New Age danced to disco music to escape.

Women's rights advocates were disappointed that the Equal Rights Amendment (ERA) that Congress passed in 1972 failed to be ratified by enough states to become law. The National Organization for Women (NOW) that had formed in 1966 gained members and influence during the seventies. Various kinds of aid became available to women during the seventies through the establishment of battered women's shelters, rape crisis centers, and abortion clinics.

Through most of the seventies, women were generally thought to be less capable of competing with men in athletic events. The arrogant male tennis pro Bobby Riggs challenged any woman to attempt to match him. When female tennis pro Billie Jean King took his challenge and then beat him, she not only won the cheering respect of women nationwide, but she became an example that eventually led to a 1978 law that gave women's sports parity with men's, at least in terms of educational funding.

Just as racial and ethnic differences were being seen as something to be celebrated, sexual differences were escaping traditional molds. A gay rights movement that began in the sixties gained much attention and support during the seventies. Among the images for gay men were "macho" looks that included leather outfits, tight jeans, Levi jackets, and very short hair. Disco music was popular among many gays, and such bands as the Village People became popular with songs like "Macho Man" and "In the Navy."

Sometimes the seventies are referred to as the "Me Decade," a term coined by writer Tom Wolfe. When he used that description he was looking at the many examples of extreme self-indulgence he saw among Americans, including much of the openness about sexual freedom that had gotten to the point of partner-swapping parties, the common use of illegal drugs to increase "awareness," as well as what he saw as self-centered thinking behind est and other New Age attitudes. Apple Computer head Steven Wozniak tried to change that attitude by funding the "Us Festivals" in the early eighties.

Rock music had always been a combination of several different protorock music styles, but it diffused more than ever during the late sixties into new seventies styles that combined rock with other types of music. Country and southern rock combined rock and blues with characteristic country sounds that included the distinctive qualities of banjo, mandolin, and fiddle. Jazz-rock and fusion both put specific jazz elements together with rock in new ways to create new styles. Progressive rock put orchestras, orchestral instruments, or other avant-garde classical elements together with rock instrumentation and style. Hard rock and heavy metal began to develop away from their origins in the blues revival and became much more aggressive and powerful. Punk brought rock down to its basic roots and pounded anger at society. Funk and disco offered colorful escape while singer/songwriters looked into their own lives and shared personal thoughts and feelings with their fans. Through and after the seventies, rock music was just as diverse as American society in general.

Chronology Chart

Historical Events	Happenings in Rock Music
1970 National Guard kills four students at Kent State University, Ohio, at antiwar demonstration. Antiwar demonstrations cause the closing of U.S. colleges and universities. U.S. signs cease-fire agreement in Vietnam. SALT talks begin. First Earth Day celebration. Portable electronic calculators are marketed.	Nationwide, city councils and police fight to ban rock festivals. Folk-rock popularity gives way to more intro-spective singer/songwriter style. Allman Brothers Band establishes southern-rock style. Santana records Latin-rock style. Jimi Hendrix and Janis Joplin die.
1971 U.S. Mariner 9 orbits Mars. Eighteen-year-olds given the right to vote. Pentagon papers on Vietnam War are publicized. Food and Drug Administration establishes the Bureau of Prod-uct Safety.	Glitter rock emerges, led by David Bowie and Marc Bolan. Protopunk poet Patti Smith performs in New York. Philadelphia Int. Record Co. forms. Berry Gordy Jr. moves Motown to L.A. Jim Morrison, Duane All-man, and Gene Vincent die.
1972 Leakey and others find 2.5-million-year-old hominid skull. SALT I is signed. Nixon visits China. U.S. combat troops leave Vietnam. Strategic arms pact between U.S. and U.S.S.R. Watergate break-in. ERA is sent to states for ratification. Bombing resumes in Vietnam after impasse in peace negotiations.	Underground FM radio gains popularity over AM. Oldies radio stations play fifties hits. Country and south-ern rock increase in popularity.
1973 Watergate hearings on national TV and radio. Airlines begin regular screening for weapons. Abortion is legalized nationwide. Vietnam peace pacts are signed, North Vietnam releases U.S. prisoners, last troops leave, military draft ends. Henry Kissinger is awarded Nobel Peace Prize. Vice President Agnew resigns.	Reggae becomes popular in U.S. The Everly Brothers break up. AM and FM radios standard in new U.S. autos. Pink Floyd releases *Dark Side of the Moon*. New York Dolls release debut LP. The group Television formed. Jim Croce, Bobby Darin, Gram Parsons, and Barry Oakley die.
1974 Impeachment hearings open against Nixon; Supreme Court orders release of Nixon tapes; Nixon resigns presidency. Ford becomes presi-dent and pardons Nixon. Patty Hearst is kid-napped. National Guardsmen who shot students at Kent State are acquitted.	New York punk by Patti Smith, Television, the Ramones, and the New York Dolls popular at CBGB's. Cass Elliot, Nick Drake, and Graham Bond die.
1975 Attempt on life of President Ford. 140,000 refugees from South Vietnam are flown to U.S. U.S. and U.S.S.R. spacecrafts link in space. VCRs commercially available. Patty Hearst is arrested.	Government begins new probes into payola practices. Sex Pistols form in U.K. Blondie, Devo, and Talking Heads form in U.S. Disco becomes popular in gay and black clubs in New York. Twelve-inch singles are released to limited market. Louis Jordan, Bob Wills, and T-Bone Walker die.
1976 U.S. bicentennial celebrations. U.S. soft landing on Mars. Race riots in South Africa. Home computers are marketed. North and South Vietnam unite as a socialist republic. Twenty-nine die from mysterious legionnaire's disease.	Liverpool's Cavern Club closes and sells pieces of stage to fans. Punk becomes stronger movement in U.K. than in U.S. Sid Vicious starts pogo dance craze. Lasers are used by the Who in concert. Highly synthesized disco gains wide popularity. Phil Ochs, Howlin' Wolf, and Keith Relf die.

1977   Nobel Peace Prize is awarded to Amnesty International. U.S. is involved in Nicaragua. Carter becomes president. Panama Canal treaty is ratified. Conditional amnesty given to draft evaders. Energy Department is established.

1978   First test-tube baby is born in U.K. U.S. and China establish a diplomatic relationship. Humphrey-Hawkins Bill passes Congress to help reduce unemployment.

1979   Nuclear accident at Three Mile Island. Ninety hostages (including sixty-three Americans) are taken at U.S. embassy in Iran.

New York disc jockeys use dubbing vocals. Some punk bands commercialize and develop new wave. Tape sales increase to 26 percent of recorded music on market. Elvis Presley, Marc Bolan, and members of Lynyrd Skynyrd die.

Sex Pistols break up. Dead Kennedys form. Bee Gees' brand of disco is popularized through movie *Saturday Night Fever*. Blondie adds disco to punk style. 45 rpm picture disks are sold. Keith Moon and Terry Kath die.

No Nukes concert and film. UNICEF concert at U.N. General Assembly. Eleven fans die at Who concert in Cincinnati. Revival of old rock styles. Sony Walkman first sold. Sid Vicious, Lowell George, and Maybellene Carter die.

Country and Southern Rock

"Dylan is going to influence anybody that is close to him, I think, as a writer, some way or another. He's a powerful talent."
—JOHNNY CASH

chapter

11

162

Bob Dylan had always been a fan of country artists like Hank Williams Sr. and Hank Snow, and his interest in playing country music may have been renewed by his performances with the Hawks (formerly the backup band for rockabilly singer Ronnie Hawkins) during the midsixties. To record *Nashville Skyline,* Dylan went to Nashville (where he had recorded *Blonde on Blonde* in 1966 and *John Wesley Harding* in 1968) and included country musicians Charlie Daniels and Johnny Cash on the sessions. Much of the music on *Nashville Skyline* exhibited a fairly standard country and folk-rock instrumentation—strummed acoustic guitars, electric lead guitars, electric bass, honky-tonk piano, and drums, with the occasional use of pedal-steel guitar, which added more country flavor.

These two Dylan albums, along with Gram Parsons and the International Submarine Band's album *Safe at Home* (1967), the Byrds' *Sweetheart of the Rodeo* (1968), and the Flying Burrito Brothers' *The Gilded Palace of Sin* (1969), helped forge the style known as country rock, the latter three albums sharing a common element: Gram Parsons.

Country Rock

Gram Parsons (Cecil Conner, 1946–1973) wrote songs and played the guitar with the International Submarine Band until 1968, when he joined the Byrds, a folk-rock group from Los Angeles, and convinced them to do a country album. Parsons' goal was to combine country music with rock, but in many ways the album that resulted, *Sweetheart of the Rodeo* (1968), was more of a country album with occasional rock influences than a real melding of country and rock styles. The most rock-oriented cut on the album was "One Hundred Years from Now" (written by Parsons). It was rock-oriented because it followed a four-beat metric pattern, used a strong backbeat, and had background instrumentals that, at times, almost obscured the lead vocals, something country musicians generally avoided. Other songs, like "Pretty Boy Floyd" and "You're Still on My Mind," had a rock beat, but the strong bluegrass influences in the former and the honky-tonk style of the latter made it difficult to call them rock. "Blue Canadian Rockies," "Hickory Wind," and "Christian Life" were all in triple meters, common for country, but unusual for rock. Although the album was not the synthesis of country and rock styles that later groups would perfect, it was an important influence on many of those groups.

Parsons left the Byrds after refusing to tour in South Africa because of his opposition to apartheid. In 1968, he and former Byrd Chris Hillman formed the Flying Burrito Brothers, a group that included the country timbre of pedal-steel guitar, a strong rock backbeat, and Everly Brothers–influenced vocal harmonies. Parsons quit the Burrito Brothers in 1970 and was joined by singer Emmylou Harris (born in 1947) on his solo albums, *GP* (1972) and *Grievous Angel* (1973). The exposure Harris gained through her appearances on Parsons' albums and concert tour helped her establish a career in country and country-rock music. An important pioneer of the country-rock sound, Parsons died in 1973; though the cause of death was never established, a combination of drugs and alcohol was evident in the autopsy. Groups and individuals who followed his lead in developing country-rock music remembered Parsons through newly written song tributes and covers of his compositions.

Linda Ronstadt has sung in a number of different styles, including country and country rock, and she chose backup musicians well. For her country album *Linda Ronstadt* (recorded in 1971, released in 1972) her band included guitarist/singer Glenn Frey, guitar/banjo/mandolin player and singer Bernie Leadon, bass player/singer Randy Meisner, and drummer/singer Don Henley. After working together on Ronstadt's album, they decided to form their own band, the **Eagles,** and soon became one of the most important and successful country-rock bands to come out of southern California in the seventies. The Eagles played a more complete fusion of country and rock musical styles than most previous country-rock groups. Their recording of "Take It Easy" (1972) used a rock beat, but the sound of a five-string banjo playing continuously in the background gave it a definite country flavor. The strummed acoustic guitar on their recording of "Best of My Love" (1974) made it sound like folk-rock, but the electric guitar fills were country-styled. "Lyin' Eyes" (1975) was rock music with the country timbres of electric bass, electric guitar fills, honky-tonk piano, and mandolin, as well as storyline lyrics. A listening guide for "Lyin' Eyes" appears on page 164. "Lyin' Eyes" was a number-two hit on the pop charts. It was the Eagles' biggest hit on the country charts at number eight and one of many international hits for the band.

The Eagles (ca. 1974) performing live (left to right): Randy Meisner, Glenn Frey, Don Henley, Bernie Leadon, and Don Felder

Listening Guide

"Lyin' Eyes"
as recorded by the Eagles (1975)

Tempo: The tempo is approximately 132 beats per minute, with four beats in each bar.

Form: The song is basically made up of eight-bar verses with a repeating chord progression, except the sections that include the words "lyin' eyes" serve as a refrain made up of two eight-bar phrases followed by one six-bar instrumental phrase.

An eight-bar instrumental introduction is followed by six eight-bar verses with lyrics, the twenty-two-bar refrain, four eight-bar verses, another refrain, six eight-bar verses, and the refrain again with repetitions to extend the ending.

Features: Steel and twelve-string guitars play fills between the singers' phrases.

The drums maintain an even beat subdivision with a subtle accent on the backbeat.

Honky-tonk piano can be heard in the background.

The electric bass guitar plays on beats one and three, as was standard in two-beat country bass rhythms, but the bass player in this recording adds notes on the second half of beat two and sometimes also after beat four, notated as follows:

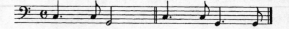

Lyrics: The theme of the infidelity of a younger mistress or wife of an older man she now finds unattractive is an old one; it is found in folk songs and opera. Here, the main idea is that the woman cannot hide her infidelity because her eyes give her away.

Billboard pop charts: number two for two weeks; *Billboard* country charts: number eight; British hit singles: number twenty-three

The country direction of their music changed somewhat in 1976 when guitar/banjo/mandolin player Bernie Leadon quit and was replaced by rock guitarist Joe Walsh. The change did not harm their commercial appeal, and they continued to place songs such as "Hotel California" (1976) and "Life in the Fast Lane" (1977) at the top of the pop charts. In the early eighties, the group broke up to allow Frey and Henley to pursue solo careers. By 2007 the Eagles were regrouped by Frey, Henley, Walsh, and Timothy Schmit. They released the album *Long Road out of Eden* (2007) on their web site and in limited stores. It debuted at number 1 and was the basis of the music on their tour in 2009.

> "I'm a songwriter. . . . As a songwriter you try to aim high: Does it have a memorable melody? Does it have words that you like to sing? Do you like the way it sounds?"
> –John Fogerty

In northern California, **Creedence Clearwater Revival,** led by brothers John and Tom Fogerty, took rock music and flavored it with country or rockabilly guitar fills and country-influenced lyrics to create their own brand of country rock. Without the stand-up bass and acoustic rhythm guitar sound of country music, they still managed to capture the energy of rockabilly. Except for occasional covers, such as "Suzie Q" (1968) by rockabilly singer Dale Hawkins, most of their songs were written by **John Fogerty** (born in 1945). Country lyrical themes that stressed love for the southern landscape and personal pride in the face of hard economic conditions were evident in "Born on the Bayou," "Green River," "Fortunate Son," and "Down on the Corner" (all 1969). Country stylings could also be heard in their live concert repertoire, including "Tombstone Shadow," with its country guitar fills, and "Don't Look Now," with country guitar and two-beat bass lines.

Creedence Clearwater Revival broke up in 1972, but John Fogerty began to experiment with overdubbing techniques and made a number of recordings on which he played all the parts—guitar, bass, keyboards, and drums. He used his own name for rock recordings made by that method, but used the Blue Ridge Rangers name for his recordings of traditional country songs. As the Blue Ridge Rangers, he had hit singles beginning with Hank Williams' "Jambalaya (On the Bayou)" in 1973, but it was not until his *Centerfield* album in 1985 that he returned to the attention of his old rock fans and created a new following for his music. After years of lawsuits between him and his old record company as well as with former CCR members, Fogerty overcame the problems and expressed a love of life in his new album, *Blue Moon Swamp,* in 1997.

In the two-thousands, John Fogerty used his music and tours to back political causes. His 2004 album, *Déjà Vu (All Over Again),* attacked the Iraq War as another Vietnam with many American lives lost for no reason. He actively supported Democratic candidate John Kerry in the 2004 presidential campaign against George W. Bush. On another front, 2004 turned out to be good for Fogerty's songwriting rights. His old record company, Fantasy Records, with whom he had had several legal battles and to whom he had to give up royalty rights to many of his old CCR songs, was bought by new owners who attracted him back to the company with the restoration of his royalties. His 2007 album, *Revival,* was nominated for a Grammy Award. He performed with a variety of old friends in 2008 and 2009, recording with some of those friends on individual songs, including Bruce Springsteen and Don Henley and Timothy Schmit of the Eagles under the name The Blue Ridge Rangers Ride Again.

In 1995, two of Fogerty's old bandmates from CCR formed their own band, Creedence Clearwater Revisited. They have had much success performing the old hits on tour and continued their career into the twenty-first century by adding new material to their repertoire.

Once the combination of country and rock music was popularized by rock musicians, country musicians themselves began to use rock rhythms and instrumentation in their performances. Some of the country performers who have recorded in a country-rock style include Johnny Cash, Kris Kristofferson, Nicolette Larson, Dolly Parton, Kenny Rogers, Leon Russell (who recorded country music under his real name, Hank Wilson), Wanda Jackson, Waylon Jennings, and Loretta Lynn. From Springfield, Missouri, the Ozark Mountain Daredevils recorded old-style hillbilly string-band dance music and country-pop-rock albums through the middle and late seventies. The Amazing Rhythm Aces in Knoxville, Tennessee, played a combination of blues, bluegrass, country, and rock music that could best be characterized as country rock. Country rock was not a classification in which performers necessarily remained throughout their careers. It was often a style many country and rock musicians played from time to time before moving on to other styles.

> "Pop and rock have just changed their name to country."
> –Neil Young

Many consider country rock a seventies style that has stayed alive only through the continued work of the original artists, but the Illinois group Uncle Tupelo (formed in 1987 and disbanded in 1994) and its offshoots Wilco and Son Volt (both formed in 1994) were drawing crowds of new, young fans to their lively interpretations of country rock in the nineties. The new bands play music influenced by Hank Williams, Neil Young, and others while also updating their sounds with punk influences. For fans of country rock, the popularity of these bands offers hope for a continuing revival of the style in the future.

Southern Rock

Many southerners have long considered their region to be almost a separate country, set apart from the rest of the United States. One expression of that philosophy came through southern rock, which was generally an aggressive music played by musicians who projected a very macho, stubbornly independent, outlaw image. The movement began around 1968, at about the same time as country rock, when the **Allman Brothers Band** started playing music that combined elements of blues, soul, and country.

The Allman Brothers Band moved from their home in Florida to Macon, Georgia, to record at the Capricorn Records studio. The two lead guitarists, Duane Allman and Richard "Dickey" Betts, as well as the two drummers, Jaimoe Johanny Johanson (John Lee Johnson) and Butch Trucks, gave the group a distinctive sound. The twin lead guitars created a sound that was thick and full compared to the usual single lead guitar in most rock. In the song "Trouble No More" (written by M. Morganfield, aka Muddy Waters) from the group's first album, the introduction and some guitar fills in the instrumental choruses featured the two lead guitars playing in octaves. In other instrumental sections of the recording, the two lead guitars used a technique often employed in jazz when two musicians improvised together, **trading twos,** meaning that the soloists alternate, each playing two-bar phrases ("twos") that give the effect of a musical conversation between them. The lines played by the lead guitarists in the Allman Brothers Band were not typical country lines, but were closer to the long, expressive guitar lines common in the blues tradition.

In October 1971, when the group was right at the beginning of a successful and influential career, Duane Allman died in a motorcycle accident. *Eat a Peach* (1972) contained three tracks that had been recorded before Duane's death, but for the remainder of the album the twin lead sound was changed to that of a single lead guitar. Missing their trademark guitar style, Gregg Allman, originally the group's keyboard player, hired Chuck Leavell to play keyboards so that Allman could join Dickey Betts on lead guitar and revitalize the band's unique guitar style. Eventually other guitarists were added so that Gregg Allman could concentrate on keyboards. A listening guide to "Ramblin' Man" from the album *Brothers and Sisters* is on page 167. "Ramblin' Man" was the Allman Brothers Band's only top-ten hit, reaching number two on the pop charts.

"Duane and Gregg were students of the urban blues. Their thing was like a real honest, truthful chilling delivery of that music, whereas Oakley and I . . . would

The Allman Brothers Band (2007) in concert at the Beacon Theatre in New York City (left to right): Gregg Allman, Butch Trucks, Warren Haynes, and Derek Trucks.

Listening Guide

"Ramblin' Man"
as recorded by the Allman Brothers Band (1973)

Tempo: The tempo is approximately 176 beats per minute, with four beats in each bar.

Form: The basic structure is made up of sixteen-bar choruses of two eight-bar periods each.

The lyrics to the first chorus serve as a refrain and are repeated several times, with choruses of new lyrics and sixteen-bar instrumental sections between repetitions.

Features: The recording begins with a solo lead guitar line that is then repeated by honky-tonk-style piano, followed by the Allman Brothers' trademark twin lead guitar sound.

The twin drums maintain an evenly subdivided beat with a strong backbeat that often has both halves of the second beat accented, notated as follows:

A tambourine keeps a steady half-beat (eighth note) rhythm throughout.

The recording has a western-swing-influenced fullness and style.

Guitar solos often lapse into uneven beat subdivisions, giving them a swing style that contrasts with the basic beat of the accompaniment instruments.

Lyrics: The lyrics stress a theme common in southern rock, in which the male singer makes it clear that he must be free and avoid being "tied down" to one woman.

Billboard pop charts: number two

> try to take a blues tune and, instead of respecting the sacredness of it, we would go sideways with it. . . . We gave each other a new foundation.
>
> –Dickey Betts, guitarist in the Allman Brothers Band

Legal and personal problems caused the Allman Brothers Band to break up in 1976, and individual members pursued solo careers. In 1978, members of the original band, including Gregg Allman, appeared in concert with Dickey Betts's band Great Southern and a new album, *Enlightened Rogues* (1979), followed. The reunion was not to last, however, but fans in the eighties and nineties have had opportunities to hear offshoot bands such as the Dickey Betts Band or the Gregg Allman Band as well as occasional regroupings of the Allman Brothers Band. In the early two-thousands, the Allman Brothers Band was still touring extensively with only three original members, Gregg Allman, and their two drummers, Butch Trucks and Jaimoe Johanson.

The twin lead guitar and twin drum sound of the Allman Brothers Band was imitated by many groups in the South, including the **Charlie Daniels Band.** Charlie Daniels was an eclectic country musician who played hillbilly fiddle, electric guitar, and slide guitar. His song "The South's Gonna Do It (Again)" exemplified the southern pride of the entire southern-rock movement as well as any single piece of music could, even to the point of including in the lyrics names of many well-known performers of the style (also mentioning the state or city where each

Listening Guide

**"The South's Gonna Do It (Again)"
as recorded by the Charlie Daniels
Band (1975)**

Tempo: The tempo is approximately 176 beats per minute, with four beats per bar.

Form: An instrumental introduction made up of two eight-bar periods is followed by twelve choruses of twelve-bar blues, the third, fourth, fifth, sixth, ninth, tenth, eleventh, and twelfth of which are instrumental.

Features: The hillbilly-style fiddle introduction uses stop time with drum accents. The fiddle is joined by a steel guitar, then by bass and drums.

The bass plays a shuffle rhythm pattern (uneven beat subdivisions).

The drums strongly accent the backbeat.

The first chorus is played in a honky-tonk style.

Some of the instrumental sections contain multiple fiddle parts.

A boogie-woogie bass pattern is played by both the bassist and the pianist.

The recording ends with a jump blues riff pattern, reminiscent of Louis Jordan's style of the forties.

Lyrics: The theme exudes pride in the South and in music from the South. Various popular southern rock musicians and bands are named along with their home city or state.

Billboard pop charts: number twenty-nine

originated). In addition, in the music itself Daniels managed to incorporate several southern musical styles, both black and white in origin, including hillbilly, honky-tonk, boogie-woogie, and the blues. The different styles were brought out in various sections of the recording. The listening guide points out those styles. "The South's Gonna Do It (Again)" was number twenty-nine on the pop charts. It did not make the top 100 on the country charts.

A genuine love for the South and its music led Daniels to organize an annual concert in Nashville called the *Volunteer Jam Concert.* Starting in 1974, the concerts have continued with enormous success and goodwill among the country, rock, and country-soul musicians invited to perform. Live albums and television programs have been recorded at these concerts.

Daniels's most popular recording was "The Devil Went Down to Georgia" (1979), a novelty song based on the old myth of the devil as a musician with whom great

players competed in musical duels. Daniels also tended toward political statements in his songs from time to time (common in rock, but rare in country), and while it was generally more common for rock musicians to take liberal stands, his were often rather conservative. Daniels continued to record and tour during the eighties and nineties, often using his music to express his opinions about America's treatment of Vietnam veterans, bringing drug dealers and other criminals to justice, and various other subjects. His 1994 album, *The Door,* was his first gospel album. During the two-thousands, Daniels has made many guest appearances with such contemporary artists as Kid Rock and Hank Williams Jr.

In 1970, the Texas-based power trio **ZZ Top** began building a career that lasted well beyond that of many southern bands. Guitarist/singer Billy Gibbons had played with the psychedelic band Moving Sidewalks when that band's single, "99th Floor," was popular in the South. They once opened for the Jimi Hendrix Experience, and

Gibbons took advantage of the opportunity by watching the way Hendrix controlled distortion and fuzztone in his solos. After Moving Sidewalks broke up, Gibbons enlisted bassist Dusty Hill and drummer Frank Beard, both of whom had previously played in the Dallas band American Blues. ZZ Top's first album, *The First Album* (1970), was not an immediate hit, but it did set them up for a successful tour and later recordings. Their career was built on the following they gained through their tours and album sales more than on hit singles.

> " We have not only been fans of the blues for a long time, but we've really tried to study and deliver it with some kind of forceful feeling. "
>
> –Bill Gibbons of ZZ Top

ZZ Top's hit single "Tush" (1975) followed the twelve-bar blues form and had bottleneck guitar solos during the instrumental sections. The band frequently used images of the Southwest during their concerts in the seventies, not only in their music but also in the cactus, snakes, and cattle with which they often shared their stage. The band took a three-year break during the beginning of the eighties and finally entered the new decade with the hit singles "Gimme All Your Lovin'" and "Sharp Dressed Man" from their album *Eliminator* (1983). The album title referred to a 1933 Ford automobile, and their rustic cowboy image had been exchanged for one built around fast

modern cars and mock designer jumpsuits. ZZ Top toured with Aerosmith in 2009.

Hank Williams Jr. (born in 1949), the son of famous country singer and songwriter Hank Williams (1923–1953), was a country musician who appreciated the way southern rock synthesized the styles of country and rock music. He had always disliked the stereotyped characterizations that often separated musicians and fans of the two styles, so he decided to record an album with members of some of the bands he liked. The result was *Hank Williams Jr. and Friends* (1976), which included Charlie Daniels, Chuck Leavell (from the Allman Brothers Band), and Toy Caldwell (from the Marshall Tucker Band). In later years, Hank Williams Jr. returned exclusively to his career in country music, making no further efforts to reach out to a rock audience.

Of all southern-rock bands, **Lynyrd Skynyrd** most completely captured the national rock audience. The name was a respelling of Leonard Skinner, a high school teacher who had criticized the members of the group for having long hair. From Jacksonville, Florida, the group played hard rock music with the Allman Brothers Band's characteristic twin lead guitar sound, which Lynyrd Skynyrd turned into a triple lead. Not denying the influences the Allman Brothers had on them, the group's first album, *Pronounced Leh-Nerd Skin-Nerd* (1973), included "Freebird," written and recorded to honor the late Duane Allman.

Though none of the group members were from Alabama, Lynyrd Skynyrd wrote "Sweet Home Alabama" as a retort to Neil Young's songs "Alabama" and "Southern Man," in which Young (a Canadian) had dared to depict

Lynyrd Skynyrd (left to right, back row): Leon Wilkeson, Artimus Pyle, Allen Collins, Leslie Hawkins, Gary Rossington, Ronnie Van Zant, Steve Gaines, Jo Billingsley; (front): Billy Powell, Cassie Gaines

Listening Guide

"Sweet Home Alabama"
as recorded by Lynyrd Skynyrd (1974)

Tempo: The tempo is approximately 100 beats per minute, with four beats in each bar.

Form: The structure is based on repeating eight-bar periods, with occasional four-bar instrumental sections between some of the periods.

A simple three-chord progression is followed in each four-bar phrase.

Features: The drummer maintains a strong back-beat with even beat subdivisions.

A female vocal group sings responses to the lead singer, Ronnie Van Zant, in a black-gospel-influenced style.

The single lead guitar is often joined by two other lead guitars, creating the sense of fullness of the Allman Brothers' twin lead guitar sound.

The piano plays in a honky-tonk style.

Lyrics: The song displays pride in the South (affectionately personified as "she") in putting Neil Young down for singing songs with lyrics that reminded listeners about southern stereotypes and a racist past. It mentions the time when Alabama governor George Wallace resisted the racial integration of the University of Alabama, but follows that statement with boos. It goes on to make it clear that the singer has no problem with Republicans having broken into the Democratic Headquarters at the Watergate Hotel, however.

Billboard pop charts: number eight

---

southern stereotypes. In places, the lyrics to "Sweet Home Alabama" boo Alabama's governor George Wallace, who had blocked the entrance to the University of Alabama to keep the first two African American students from entering. That happened in 1963, but it was an event that many people still associated with Alabama. The song goes on to say that Watergate, the scandal surrounding the Republican break-in at the Democratic National Headquarters that caused Nixon to resign the presidency, does not bother the singer. The listening guide outlines characteristics of country, gospel, and rock music in Lynyrd Skynyrd's recording of "Sweet Home Alabama." The recording reached number eight on the pop charts.

> **" I was into ZZ Top and Skynyrd really heavy, which sounded like Hank [Williams], Sr., through Marshalls to me. "**
>
> –Mike Estes, guitarist with several southern rock bands

In October 1977, en route from a show in South Carolina to one in Louisiana, their chartered plane crashed, killing lead singer Ronnie Van Zant, guitarist Steve Gaines and his sister, backup vocalist Cassie Gaines, and badly injuring other band members. Back performing in 1980, two of Lynyrd Skynyrd's guitarists formed the Rossington-Collins Band and rerecorded "Freebird" without vocals as a tribute to Ronnie Van Zant. The popularity of Lynyrd Skynyrd's music lasted through the ten years after their crash, and the surviving members, including guitarists Gary Rossington and Ed King, keyboardist Billy Powell, bass player Leon Wilkeson, and drummer Artimus Pyle, formed a new version of Lynyrd Skynyrd with Ronnie's brother Johnny Van Zant as lead singer, and new members Randall Hall on guitar and female backup singers Dale Rossington (Gary Rossington's wife) and Carol Bristow. Another original member, guitarist Allen Collins, would have joined the group and did make an appearance at some concerts, but he was unable to play because of injuries he suffered in an automobile accident in 1986. The new band released the album *Legend*

(1987), which included several B sides of old singles and recordings that had been left unfinished by the original band. Although Allen Collins died in 1990, the rest of the revival band continued to work together into the middle nineties, and Johnny Van Zant also had some success as a solo artist. In 2009, Lynyrd Skynyrd recorded the album *God and Guns* and continued to tour.

Molly Hatchet and .38 Special were two other southern bands (from Jacksonville, Florida, like Lynyrd Skynyrd) that followed the multiple lead guitar sound of the Allman Brothers Band and Lynyrd Skynyrd. Molly Hatchet named themselves after a legendary southern prostitute known as Hatchet Molly, who reputedly castrated her clients. They played highly amplified, guitar-heavy music that was as tough as the image their name gave them. With a sound almost closer to heavy metal than to country, they remained popular as a touring band through the late seventies and into the eighties. .38 Special had connections with Lynyrd Skynyrd that were more than just musical. Donnie Van Zant, the brother of Ronnie and Johnny Van Zant of Lynyrd Skynyrd, was their singer. In true Allman Brothers fashion, they had two lead guitarists and two drummers.

Summary

Country influences on rock music of the early sixties were limited to pop songs recorded by singers whose background experience and style were rooted in country music traditions. Nonpop country styles returned to rock music during the late sixties. Some characteristics of country music that influenced that style included lyrical themes that told stories or expressed love of a rural lifestyle, two-beat bass patterns, even beat subdivisions, occasional waltz (triple meter) rhythm patterns, using lead instruments to fill space between singers' phrases instead of playing through them, and the use of country instruments such as the steel guitar.

Solo performers such as Bob Dylan and groups such as the Byrds and Buffalo Springfield had established careers in folk-rock during the midsixties and effectively combined their folk styles with characteristics of country music to create an early form of country rock. With the exception of some recordings by the Band, which was made up of musicians from Arkansas and Canada, country rock was generally a western style popularized by such singers and groups as the Eagles and Creedence Clearwater Revival.

While country rock was becoming established as an important and popular style in the West, musicians in the southern states had begun to combine country music and rock to create an often aggressive, always proud style known as southern rock. The Allman Brothers Band was among the first of the bands to define the style with their twin lead guitars and twin drums instrumentation, which influenced the instrumental makeup of the Charlie Daniels Band, Lynyrd Skynyrd, Molly Hatchet, and .38 Special. Southern rock generally included other southern styles such as blues, gospel, and jazz, in addition to country and rock music.

Both country rock and southern rock were very popular during the seventies, and many of the bands playing those styles survived into the eighties. Even rockabilly, a style that had lasted only a short time during the fifties, returned to rock charts in the eighties. Country music was a basic ingredient in the development of rock music during the fifties, and country music is bound to remain of importance to rock as long as rock remains a viable musical style.

discussion questions

Many southern bands proudly identified with cultural aspects of the former confederate states of the southern United States. Are there other regions in the United States that have music that similarly represents the region? Is the southern identity residue from the Civil War, or are there other reasons for it?

12

Jazz-Rock Styles

"My main thing is to create and not to compare. . . . I don't wanna be like I used to be years ago. . . . Stravinsky never wrote anything the same way."
—MILES DAVIS

In a variety of ways, jazz has always been a part of rock. The blues was important to the development of both jazz and rock, but because jazz started early in the twentieth century it had already evolved into a number of different styles before rock came on the scene. Various jazz styles influenced rock in different ways at different times. Early rock music by Bill Haley and the Comets, for example, was influenced by both big-band jazz and the blues. Haley's western swing style combined country music and jazz, and many of his rock recordings were western swing–styled blues covers. The blues became rockabilly when performed by country musicians such as Elvis Presley, Carl Perkins, and Jerry Lee Lewis, who sped up the tempos, changed lyrics, and added country-style instrumental sections. Jazz instruments such as the saxophone were used to play jazz-style improvisations in the bands that backed early rock performances by many African American artists, from Little Richard in the fifties through the many soul, Motown, and funk musicians of the sixties and later.

Most rock music has some characteristics that came from jazz, but the terms *jazz rock* and *fusion* did not refer to just any combination of jazz and rock music. They were particular styles that developed during the late sixties. **Jazz rock** combined the horn section sound of swing dance music, as played by most of the big bands of the forties and fifties, with a rock rhythm section and rock beat. It almost always used vocals, an element more essential to rock than to jazz. **Fusion** was a somewhat experimental jazz style that made use of rock instrumentation and took some rhythmic and melodic patterns from rock. Fusion was primarily an instrumental music; when vocals were included they were usually not given any more prominence than the instrumental solos. Jazz rock tended to be more closely related to rock, whereas fusion maintained clear connections with its jazz roots.

Small-group jazz styles, including most performances of the blues, centered on the practice of improvisation, but the large swing bands could not have so many instrumentalists improvising at the same time and, therefore, played from written arrangements. Individual instrumentalists were allowed to improvise solo choruses accompanied by part or all of the band, but most of the music played by swing bands was predetermined by an arranger who, in effect, established a band's style. Typical instrumental groupings commonly employed in jazz-style big bands included a rhythm section consisting of piano, acoustic or amplified guitar, string bass, and drums; a brass section (trumpets and trombones); and a woodwind section (saxophones, whose players often doubled on related instruments such as clarinets and flutes). These combinations of instruments grew to be so commonly associated with jazz that when rock styles such as soul and funk used horn sections of brass instruments or saxophones, they automatically created a link with jazz.

Defining exactly what constitutes jazz music or jazz style is not an easy task. Improvisation is, of course, an important element, but even without it jazz can exist. Jazz style is a "feel," as a jazz musician would term it—an approach to the melodic and harmonic material that is unique to the idiom. And, as Duke Ellington maintained, "It don't mean a thing if it ain't got that swing." Jazz arrangements, no matter how carefully notated, cannot be effective without the infusion of musical instincts that jazz musicians bring to a performance. Jazz players sense how long to dwell on a note, when to bend it, what notes to accentuate and which ones merely to suggest, what liberties to take with the beat, and any number of other, often subtle techniques of jazz interpretation. A well-written arrangement in jazz style, if put in front of musicians whose background is only in, say, symphonic music, would not "swing," but would sound stilted and stiff. The players would certainly be proficient enough as instrumentalists, but they would not have the necessary background and experience to convincingly produce stylistic jazz.

Rock music likewise developed its own instrumentation, phrasing practices, and "feel" that, when mixed with elements of jazz to create jazz rock or fusion, were emphasized or de-emphasized depending on the backgrounds and interests of the musicians. Even the standard types of improvised solos are different in rock than in jazz. Rock solos tend to stay within a single scale or **mode,** whereas jazz solos more often include nonchordal tones and move from one mode to another, creating harmonic complexities with the chords played by the rhythm section. Rock guitarists will even stay within notes of a particular finger pattern rather than move to avoid repeated patterns. Rock solos also tend to be less rhythmically complex than jazz ones. Jazz soloists often set up rhythmic patterns that contrast with that of the accompaniment. Even the number of notes and the speed at which they are played is often different between rock and jazz. Rock solos are often very fast, flashy, and continuous, whereas silence is as important as the playing of notes in jazz. Certainly, Miles Davis's trumpet style serves as a perfect example of the use of silence as a musical element.

Jazz rock often took fairly conventional rock forms and simply enhanced them with a horn section playing jazz-inflected arrangements. Fusion often included rock-styled solos played on amplified instruments using distortion and feedback, as well as various types of synthesizers that had become standard rock equipment by the late sixties. Jazz rock was pretty easily understood as rock music, and because the horn sections had been used in rock styles like Memphis soul and James Brown's rhythm and blues, they did not sound foreign. Fusion, on the other hand, was often barely recognizable as rock, and much of it seemed further from standard rock styles than jazz rock was from swing band styles.

Jazz Rock

Much jazz rock of the late sixties was played by former blues revivalists who added sections of brass or woodwind instruments to their rock instrumentation. One of the earliest of the jazz-rock bands was the **Electric Flag,** formed in 1967 in San Francisco by guitarist Michael Bloomfield, who had played with the Paul Butterfield Blues Band in Chicago the year before, and singer Nick Gravenites. The Electric Flag consisted of a rhythm section that included keyboards, bass, and drums, and a horn section, including trumpet and two saxophones, a tenor and a baritone. The group had several personnel changes and disbanded after only a year and a half together, but their commercial success sparked other musicians to create their own jazz-rock bands.

In Chicago in 1967, guitarist/singer Terry Kath and clarinetist/saxophonist Walter Parazaider decided to form a jazz-rock band, calling it the Big Thing. The group consisted of a horn section—trumpet, trombone, and saxophone—backed by a rock rhythm section of guitar, keyboards, bass, and drums. Most of the members of the group were also singers and group vocals were often featured in their recordings. They changed their name to Chicago Transit Authority before recording their first self-titled album in 1969, but, because of objections from city officials, shortened their name to **Chicago** for future work. Chicago's early recordings captured the energy and spontaneity of a jazz band and included jazz-style improvisations by individual group members, but they eventually attracted a larger audience by recording in more of a pop style. Chicago released an all new studio album, *Chicago XXX,* in 2006 and continued to tour.

Singer/keyboard player Al Kooper had recorded with the Royal Teens during the late fifties, had played sessions with Bob Dylan in 1965 (for Dylan's *Highway 61 Revisited* album), and had been a member of the Blues Project. Kooper liked the idea of combining rock and jazz instruments and styles and, in 1968, formed his own jazz-rock band, **Blood, Sweat and Tears.** Although the group's personnel changed often through their career, Blood, Sweat and Tears always maintained a strongly brass-oriented sound. The first version of the band included two trumpeters, both of whom doubled on fluegelhorn (a trumpet-like instrument with a larger, conical bore that gives the instrument a fuller and mellower tone), and a trombonist who doubled on recorder. Other instrumentalists included an alto saxophonist, a keyboardist who doubled on both flute and trombone, a guitarist, a bassist, and a drummer. Based in New York, the band played music by many of the city's best-known writers, including Harry Nilsson, Gerry Goffin and Carole King, and Laura Nyro, as well as arrangements of classic songs, like Billie Holiday's ballad

"God Bless the Child" (Holiday in 1941; Blood, Sweat and Tears in 1968).

Kooper left soon after the first album and was replaced by a very distinctive bluesy voiced singer from Surrey, England, David Clayton-Thomas. The listening guide on page 176 points out some of the main jazz influences in Blood, Sweat and Tears' popular recording of "Spinning Wheel," from the first album Clayton-Thomas recorded with the band, *Blood, Sweat and Tears* (1968). The recording was number two on the pop charts for three weeks. It reached number five on the rhythm and blues charts.

Some of the rhythmic complexities of well-arranged jazz-band music are represented in "Spinning Wheel," particularly in the way tempo and metric shifts are used. As is generally true of big-band jazz, some solo instruments are given time to improvise—most notably the bebop-style trumpet solo in the instrumental passage after the third A section—but the overall organization of the music was carefully planned in advance. The use of even beat subdivisions through most of the song is a characteristic of rock music, not jazz.

Blood, Sweat and Tears' dynamic singer, David Clayton-Thomas left the group for a couple of years in the early seventies but found that he was less successful as a soloist. His return was stressed by renaming the band Blood, Sweat and Tears Featuring David Clayton-Thomas. One version or other of the group stayed together through the eighties and into the nineties but with so many personnel changes that no original members (Clayton-Thomas not having been part of the original band) remained. Blood, Sweat and Tears continues to tour in the two-thousands.

Blood, Sweat and Tears in concert

Listening Guide

"Spinning Wheel"
as recorded by Blood, Sweat and Tears
(1968)

Tempo: The tempo is about 96 beats per minute with four beats in each bar, but the speed doubles during the instrumental section that precedes the last A section. The last A section returns to the beginning tempo.

Form: The form of the song has a returning A section that is eight bars long. The first A section begins when the singer enters and gradually introduces new instruments one by one, with a cowbell added in the third bar, drums in the fourth, and a tambourine in the fifth.

The second A section is followed by an eight-bar refrain with a ten-bar extension.

The refrain, or B section, is followed by another A.

Features: The recording begins with a **crescendo** (increase in volume, or loudness level) of the horn section followed by the horns playing a single bar (four beats) of a **sixteenth-note** (four notes in each beat) rhythmic pattern.

Even beat subdivisions are maintained throughout the recording, except during the improvised trumpet solo.

Each A section has an instrumental stop time in the seventh bar; the last A has the stop time in both the seventh and the eighth bars.

During the repetitions of the A sections, the horns punctuate the rhythm by playing chords where the drums are accenting the beat, sometimes (but not always) the backbeat.

After the third A, there is an extended instrumental section with a trumpet solo in a bebop jazz style.

The last A (after the instrumental section) repeats the lyrics of the third A, and it is followed by a metric shift in which the half beats of the basic tempo become accented in patterns of threes, creating a temporary change to a $\frac{9}{8}$ meter.

The new meter breaks into a playful improvisation by a recorder, a flute, and an alto saxophone, with a muted trumpet accentuating the second and third notes of the triple patterns.

The recording ends with the sound of maracas shaking and band members making casual comments about the quality of the recording.

Lyrics: The song uses the image of a spinning wheel to compare life to the experience of gambling (as in wheel of fortune, roulette wheel), suggesting that life is governed by fate; however, that view is opposed with the biblical reference to the "straight and narrow" highway. It is not clear that the singer finds that road too restricting because the references to direction and reflection are ambiguous.

Billboard pop charts: number two for three weeks. *Billboard* rhythm and blues charts: number five

Fusion

The jazz-rock style of the Electric Flag, Chicago, and Blood, Sweat and Tears was more rock or, in the case of Chicago's later work, pop music influenced by jazz than it was any sort of equal combination of jazz and rock. A more jazz-styled music with rock influences was created by jazz trumpeter **Miles Davis** (1926–1991) in the mid- to late sixties. Called fusion (though not by Davis), the style was further developed by musicians who worked with Davis and later formed their own bands.

From as early as the midforties, Davis had been playing bebop with such performers as alto saxophonist Charlie Parker, bassist Charles Mingus, and drummer Max Roach. With some help from arranger Gil Evans, Davis recorded the innovative album *Birth of the Cool* (1949, released in the midfifties), which sparked the development of the cool-jazz style that was popular with the Beat writers of the fifties. Through the late fifties and midsixties, Miles Davis led a number of ensembles, in which the personnel often changed, and experimented with the music, replacing traditional scales and progressions of chords with different, often startling, melodic and harmonic structures.

> **"I'll play it first and tell you what it was later."**
>
> –Miles Davis

Miles Davis

In 1968, Davis began to add rock elements to his music. Among these rock elements were the use of (1) an evenly subdivided rock beat in the drums; (2) bass patterns involving short repeated lines (ostinatos) that functioned to give the music a simpler sense of organization; and (3) instruments commonly associated with rock such as electric piano, electric guitar, and electric bass guitar (Davis had rarely used guitar in his previous recordings). Most jazz styles that Davis had played in the past maintained a rhythmic flow of uneven beat subdivisions—the swing feel—that jazz inherited from its roots in the blues. Jazz bass lines were rarely as repetitious as those in rock, but tended more toward long walking bass patterns; and jazz groups were still using acoustic basses long after rock groups had switched to electric bass guitars. By the time Davis recorded the albums *In a Silent Way* and *Bitches Brew* (both 1969), he had begun to use heavy rock-styled drum patterns. The listening guide to "Miles Runs the Voodoo Down" (page 178) from the *Bitches Brew* album serves as an example of Davis's innovative fusion style.

Miles Davis continued to incorporate elements of rock music into his recordings in the seventies, even to the point of altering the tone quality of his horn. He added electronic devices like those used by Jimi Hendrix and other rock guitarists to reproduce tonal variations in his trumpet sound similar to what was heard in hard rock and heavy metal guitar styles. A number of musicians who played on *Bitches Brew* and other fusion albums with Davis put together fusion bands of their own. Guitarist John McLaughlin assembled the Mahavishnu Orchestra, keyboardist Josef Zawinul formed Weather Report (with saxophonist Wayne Shorter), keyboardist Chick Corea (who played on "Miles Runs the Voodoo Down") started Return to Forever, and keyboardist Herbie Hancock formed the jazz-funk Headhunters.

Another musician who developed an interest in fusion was rock guitarist **Carlos Santana** (born in 1947), who branched out from the Latin-based rock style of his own band to record the album *Love, Devotion, Surrender* (1973), on which he collaborated with fusion musicians, including McLaughlin, keyboardist Jan Hammer, and drummer Billy Cobham, all members of the Mahavishnu Orchestra.

Santana returned to his own band and continued to play fusion, often hiring musicians who had earlier worked with Miles Davis, including keyboardist Herbie Hancock, drummer Tony Williams, and saxophonist Wayne Shorter (the soprano saxophone soloist on "Miles Runs the Voodoo Down") to record with the band. Santana had some commercial successes during the seventies and early eighties, but he returned to the top of the charts with "Smooth," from his 1999 album *Supernatural.* "Smooth" was number one on the pop charts for twelve weeks.

Listening Guide

"Miles Runs the Voodoo Down" as recorded by Miles Davis (1969)

Tempo: The tempo at the beginning and end of the recording is about 116 beats per minute, with four beats per bar. The beat is intentionally sped up and slowed down again very gradually as the intensity builds and relaxes. The tempo of much of the middle section is about 126 beats per minute.

Form: No standard form with repeated sections is followed throughout the recording, although Davis's use of a returning **motive** (short bit of melody) gives the effect of formal unity.

Features: Even beat subdivisions are maintained throughout the recording.

Jazz instruments used include trumpet, soprano saxophone, bass clarinet (though not typical in jazz), acoustic bass, and drums (three set drummers and one auxiliary percussionist).

Rock elements include two electric pianos, electric bass guitar, electric lead guitar, and the use of distortion.

John McLaughlin's electric guitar playing includes rhythmic punctuations similar to those used by guitarists in funk bands led by James Brown or Sly Stone, as well as a rock-style solo about one-third of the way through the recording.

No standard type of chord progression is followed; the track is based on a single chord to which individual soloists add **chord extensions** and **nonchordal tones.** The bass players play repeated rifflike (ostinato) lines.

Many of the solos used the **dorian mode** (natural notes from D to D), which differs from a major scale because it has lowered third and seventh degrees.

Distortion in the guitar and keyboard increases as the intensity builds and the tempo quickens.

The texture is thickened by dense polyrhythms behind the soloists. Polyrhythms over a single chord are perhaps influenced by James Brown's or Sly Stone's funk style, but Davis's rhythms are less repetitious than theirs because more instruments are involved.

The thick texture creates a full, almost hypnotic, effect.

Lyrics: The instrumental recording has no vocals.

One of the more rock-oriented of the fusion bands was formed as the **Dixie Grits** by southern-rock guitarist Steve Morse and bassist Andy West while the two were in high school. Attending college was not important to Morse until he heard a performance by classical guitarist Juan Mercadel. Mercadel demonstrated so much technical facility and control of his instrument that Morse decided to study with him at the University of Miami at Coral Gables, Florida, where Mercadel was on the faculty. The Dixie Grits remained together, but after the other members left, Morse joked that he and West were the "dregs" of the Grits, and they chose to name their next band the Dixie Dregs.

The University of Miami had a leading jazz program, with such fusion musicians as guitarist Pat Metheny and bass guitarist Jaco Pastorius teaching workshops. Having studied composition there in a curriculum that included both classical and jazz, and combining this with his rock experience, Morse wrote arrangements for the **Dixie Dregs** that had them playing a variety of musical styles, from Allman Brothers–style blues rock to fusion. In addition to a keyboardist, a bassist, and a drummer, their lineup included Allen Sloan, who played electric violin and doubled on other instruments, and Morse, who played guitar, guitar synthesizer, and banjo. Their all-instrumental debut album, *Free Fall* (1977), displayed a fusion style reminiscent of some work by Weather Report and the Mahavishnu Orchestra, with funk rhythms and a rock drumbeat, while also showing their southern roots in one cut that was a hoedown featuring Morse playing banjo. The band shortened its name to the Dregs in the early eighties and broke up shortly thereafter. Morse later formed a trio called the Steve Morse Band, in which he played organ and synthesizers in addition to fast, heavy-metal-style guitar.

Walter Becker and Donald Fagen from Steely Dan

Other Jazz Influences on Rock

Pianist Donald Fagen met guitarist/bassist Walter Becker while they were students together at Bard College in Annandale-on-Hudson, New York. Both jazz lovers, they experimented with jazz, pop, and rock styles in various bands they organized with friends while at college. Fagen, a self-proclaimed beatnik, had a penchant for the inventive types of chords and chord progressions used in jazz, some of which he incorporated into his own compositions. After doing some writing for other performers, Fagen and Becker decided to form their own band, **Steely Dan,** to have more control over their compositions.

Steely Dan started out as a foursome and later grew to six members; but by 1974, all the regulars except Fagen and Becker had left the group, partly because of their leaders' reluctance to tour. Fagen and Becker disliked life on the road and basically had lost interest in merely re-creating their recorded performances for concert audiences. As songwriters they were perfectly happy to be rid of the pressures of touring, and for recording they enjoyed the new freedom to use whatever musicians they wanted for any given session. Guitarist Jeff "Skunk" Baxter and singer/keyboardist Michael McDonald, for example, were brought in for the *Pretzel Logic* album (1974); they later joined the Doobie Brothers.

Some influences of jazz could be heard in Steely Dan's earliest albums, which included compositions ranging from pop rock to country rock to amalgams of several styles, but jazz inflections became more important as time

went on. A listening guide to "Rikki Don't Lose That Number" from *Pretzel Logic* appears on page 180.

Two tracks on *Pretzel Logic* served as tributes to jazz greats. Alto saxophonist Charlie Parker was the inspiration for "Parker's Band." And Fagen and Becker did more than simply pay tribute to Duke Ellington and his jazz orchestra in "East St. Louis Toodle-oo"; they covered Ellington's own 1927 recording very closely, copying the notes and phrasing of the original, though at the same time updating the sound by using electric guitar (with effects) and pedal-steel guitar as solo instruments where Ellington had used muted trumpet and saxophone.

Fagen and Becker continued to call on well-established jazz and fusion musicians for their later albums, some of whom included alto saxophonist Phil Woods (for "Doctor Wu" on 1975s *Katy Lied*), tenor saxophonist John Klemmer (for "The Caves of Altamira" on *The Royal Scam* in 1976), and tenor saxophonist Wayne Shorter (for the title cut on *Aja* in 1977). In 1978, jazz bandleader Woody Herman paid Fagen and Becker a tribute when he asked them to supervise recordings that his own Thundering Herd big band was going to make of several Steely Dan compositions. Herman, a reed player, singer, and bandleader since the thirties, had become interested in jazz-rock styles and had added a number of jazz-rock arrangements to his band's repertoire. Becker and Fagen spent most of the eighties apart, each pursuing solo careers. Then in 1993 they regrouped an eleven-member version of Steely Dan to play their hits on a very successful U.S. tour. They continued to tour in the later nineties. Steely Dan won a Grammy for Best Album for *Two Against Nature* in 2000. After spending some time on solo projects, Steely Dan reunited for tours in 2008 and 2009.

Listening Guide

"Rikki Don't Lose That Number" as recorded by Steely Dan (1974)

Tempo: The tempo is about 120 beats per minute, with four beats in each bar.

Form: The form begins with a six-bar introduction, followed by an A section (made up of one eight-bar and one seven-bar phrase), a B section (refrain—also one eight-bar and one seven-bar phrase, but with a different melody from that in A), a four-bar instrumental section, another A, another B, an extended instrumental, a partial A (only the seven-bar section), another B, and then a six-bar ending in which the title lyrics are repeated.

Features: Even beat subdivisions are used throughout the recording.

A marimba-like instrument plays an ad-lib introduction, and then acoustic piano, bass guitar, and drums enter and establish a relaxed Latin beat pattern for a six-bar introduction. The pattern played by the bass is a direct "quote" from "Song for My Father" by jazz pianist/composer Horace Silver.

The rhythm section returns to the Latin feel the first time the singer sings the refrain (beginning with the words of the title); this time the feel is even more "Latin" because of the Latin syncopation in the rhythm, which varies the backbeat from what the listener expects to hear. A bell tree adds a shimmering effect several times.

Lyrics: The singer adopts the persona of the tempter, who is trying to persuade Rikki to reconsider his or her decision not to engage in a "wild time," probably a reference to doing drugs. The lines suggest something more sinister than sex, and the mentions of the tempter's friend, "slow" motion, and a certain part of town suggest connections with the drug underworld.

Billboard pop charts: number four; British hit singles: number fifty-eight

Summary

Of the many ways jazz has influenced rock music, only those styles specifically called jazz rock and fusion were discussed in any detail in this chapter. Blues, blues revival, soul, and funk-rock styles also used jazz instruments played with jazz phrasing and style. The jazz rock of the late sixties was, for the most part, brought about simply by combining jazz band horn sections with a rock band instrumentation of electric guitar, electric keyboards, electric bass guitar, and drums.

When Miles Davis's groups added rock elements to their jazz styles (in some cases avant-garde jazz), they united jazz's harmonic richness with the driving power of rock instrumentation and amplification. The result was not pure jazz and not pure rock, but fusion. Davis's late sixties album *Bitches Brew* included several musicians who went on to form their own fusion bands. Depending on the backgrounds and inclinations of the musicians in the group, some of these fusion groups attracted a large rock following; others appealed primarily to jazz audiences.

The jazz influences on such rock musicians as Donald Fagen, Walter Becker, and others were primarily demonstrated in their decision to use jazz musicians for their backup bands and for their recordings. The result was not jazz, but then it was not intended to be jazz. It was rock with the sensitivity and harmonic complexity of jazz, and a style that gained the attention of many appreciative fans who did not care about labels or categories but who simply wanted to listen to expressive and interesting music.

discussion questions

Miles Davis started two important styles of music, cool jazz and fusion. He said that he tried new things to keep from repeating what he had done in the past. Is that how most new artistic ideas come about? Do any current bands use jazz instrumentation such as a horn section?

Hard Rock and Heavy Metal

" *As its detractors have always claimed, heavy-metal rock is nothing more than a bunch of noise; it is not music, it's distortion—and that is precisely why its adherents find it appealing.* "
—LESTER BANGS, ROCK CRITIC

Hard rock and heavy metal are loud, powerful, and aggressive styles that developed out of the sounds of such blues revival bands as the Rolling Stones, Cream, and the Yardbirds, with further influences from the Who and the Jimi Hendrix Experience. Although a certain amount of overlap existed between the styles of hard rock and heavy metal, they remained fairly separate, with hard rock maintaining closer connections with its blues and folk-rock roots. Hard rock singers were generally as capable of singing ballads as they were of singing loud, heavy-rock songs, while heavy-metal singers concentrated on screaming often-obscured lyrics to audiences caught up more in the power of the sound than with any meaning in the words. Hard-rock bands often included acoustic guitars played in the strummed or plucked patterns used in folk music, sometimes updating their sounds with the addition of synthesizers, whereas heavy-metal bands generally used the electric guitar, bass, and drums instrumentation used by the Jimi Hendrix Experience, Cream, and Led Zeppelin. (Heavy-metal bands did sometimes vary their sound by using acoustic instruments, but that was the exception, not the rule.) Heavy metal also often included highly amplified and seemingly uncontrolled sound. It was aggressive and macho, frequently stressing rebellious attitudes of young men who felt caught between boyhood freedoms and society's expectations of manhood, to the point of employing symbols of death and destruction to appeal to their aggressions as well as to upset their parents and other authority figures. Hard-rock bands, on the other hand, usually sang songs that more often expressed themes about love and human relationships. Perhaps for that reason, female performers were successful in hard rock while heavy metal remained male dominated. By the nineties, the terms *hard rock* and *heavy metal* were being used interchangeably.

Distortion and feedback were characteristic of both hard rock and heavy metal. Distorted amplification was probably first recorded by Link Wray in "Rumble" (1958), for which Wray poked a pencil through the speaker of his amplifier to achieve the effect. The Kinks copied that sound by cutting into a speaker cone with a razor blade for their recording of "You Really Got Me" (1964). Not long after that, various electronic distortion devices were developed to enable musicians to produce and control these effects by the use of foot pedals, such as the fuzzbox the Rolling Stones used in "(I Can't Get No) Satisfaction." Feedback between the guitar and amplifier—not an artificial effect, but achieved simply by striking a guitar note or chord and then holding the instrument in front of the amplifier—was used by several British groups during the midsixties, including the Beatles at the beginning of "I Feel Fine" (1964), the Who in "My Generation" (1965), and the Yardbirds in "Shapes of Things" (1966). It soon came into common use in hard rock and heavy metal.

The effects of distortion and feedback used in some hard-rock and most heavy-metal music were enhanced through the guitarists' use of **power chords.** Power chords are not traditional chord structures such as those used in most rock music. Instead, they are just two bass notes that are the interval of a perfect fourth or a perfect fifth apart: for example, G on the sixth string played with C or D on the fifth. Power chords can be rhythmically pounded or sustained—either way they add much to the heavy depth and weight of the metal sound. Many heavy-metal groups would also sometimes tune their instruments down as much as a half or whole step for a deeper and heavier timbre.

Early Influences

The powerful British blues revival trio Cream formed to play Chicago blues classics like Willie Dixon's "Spoonful" (1966) and Muddy Waters's "Rollin' and Tumblin'" (1966) but changed their style to include distortion and extended improvisations like those by the Jimi Hendrix Experience. On Cream's *Disraeli Gears* album (1967), the song "Sunshine of Your Love" was organized around a blues-derived element called a **bass riff** (a relatively short, low, repeated melody), a device that became a basic characteristic in hard rock and heavy metal to follow. As played by Cream's bassist, Jack Bruce, the repeated riff gave the recording an almost hypnotic effect that provided a footing from which the voice, lead guitar, and drums could freely improvise without causing the music to lose its unity. The importance of the riff was stressed by the voice that often paralleled it. Another characteristic of Cream that influenced a lot of hard rock and heavy metal was the bottom-heavy sound created by Ginger Baker's use of two bass drums, a sound clearly represented in "Sunshine of Your Love" (listening guide appears on page 184). "Sunshine of Your Love" reached number twenty-five on the British pop charts and number five on the U.S. ones.

Cream and other psychedelic-influenced blues revival bands of the late sixties became essential links between the blues and the hard-rock and heavy-metal styles of the seventies. Cream used parallel lead and bass guitar lines in "Sunshine of Your Love," as had the Jimi Hendrix Experience, to create a very thick, full, powerful reinforcement of the riff. Heavy-metal bands later copied this technique.

Hard Rock

The pubs in London were the birthplace of the hard-rock sound in Britain, beginning with Free, which was formed in 1968. The members of Free had come from the blues revival groups Brown Sugar, John Mayall's Bluesbreakers, and Black Cat Bones. In one of their most popular recordings, "All Right Now" (1970), Free's blues roots were evident through their use of a riff in the introduction, but they did not maintain it as the central theme of the song as most heavy-metal bands of the time would have done. The guitar used heavy distortion effects and the drums maintained a very strong backbeat, characteristic of most hard rock.

Singer Paul Rodgers and drummer Simon Kirke continued their careers with another hard-rock band, Bad Company, which used Free's riffs, distortion, and strong backbeat, but not the loud, rebellious themes or uncontrolled sounds of heavy metal. By the late seventies, the group had begun to experiment with synthesizers and updated their sound with new-wave influences, such as the throbbing, repeated-note pulse on each half beat played by the bass in "Rock and Roll Fantasy" (1979). Bad Company took a four-year break from 1982 to 1986 and then regrouped with a new singer, Brian Howe. They were still recording in the nineties, with only drummer Simon Kirke and guitarist Mick Ralphs remaining from their original lineup. Paul Rodgers recorded a solo album after leaving Bad Company and then sang in Jimmy Page's group, the Firm, in the middle eighties. Rodgers returned to his blues roots in the early nineties and joined Queen in 2004 and continued to work with them until his departure in 2009.

Many American hard-rock groups formed during the late sixties and early seventies as the style became popular with fans who wanted to hear stronger rock than the music by singer/songwriters of the period, but who found heavy metal too hostile and theatrical. Steppenwolf was formed in 1967 by Canadian musicians with backgrounds in blues, country, and folk-rock—all styles that influenced most hard-rock music. Steppenwolf's recording of "Born to Be Wild" (1968) contained the words "heavy metal" (in reference to a motorcycle), and although Steppenwolf's music did not fit completely into the heavy-metal mold that was in the process of taking shape, the song gave the style a name. Steppenwolf followed "Born to Be Wild" with many other recordings, but that song title stayed with them on later albums *Reborn to Be Wild* (1977) and *Born to Be Wild—A Retrospective* (1991). Their membership changed many times with guitarist/singer John Kay (Joachim Krauledat, born in 1944) as the only original member who lasted into the early two-thousands.

Heart evolved out of a group called the Army that was formed in Seattle in 1963. The Army passed through many style and personnel changes before turning to hard rock in 1972. Sisters Ann and Nancy Wilson had both been folk and folk-rock singer/guitarists before joining Heart, and that background was evident in their early Heart recordings such as "Crazy on You" and "Magic Man" (both 1976). A listening guide to "Magic Man" is on page 185.

Heart's membership changed often, and the Wilson sisters' folk roots gradually disappeared. Eventually, their sound in the late eighties was almost as aggressive as many

Listening Guide

**"Sunshine of Your Love"
as recorded by Cream (1967)**

Tempo: The tempo is about 116 beats per minute, with four beats in each bar.

Form: The formal structure is four repetitions of a twenty-four-bar blues form. The form is simply a twelve-bar blues in which each section is twice the normal length. (Instead of four bars of the initial chord in the first A section, there are eight; instead of two bars of the next chord as the first half of the next A section, there are four; and so on, except that some single-bar chords are added to the eight-bar B section.)

Features: A bass riff is the most important bit of melody in the recording; it not only repeats throughout most of the recording, but it is also paralleled by the guitar and the beginning of the vocal melody. The riff is played four times as an introduction to the first chorus. (The chorus begins when the voice enters.) The riff is notated as follows:

The guitar and bass are in octaves using even note subdivisions. (The arrow over the F note indicates that the players bend their strings while playing it, producing a blue note about halfway between F and F#.)

The riff is two bars long and is based on a single chord, requiring it to be played through four times on the single chord during the first A section of each chorus (eight bars). The riff changes pitch to fit the next chord for two repetitions of the riff (four bars). It returns to the first pitch level for two more repetitions on the last four bars of the second A section.

The beginning of the B section varies the normal blues progression, playing single bars of chords not usually part of the blues structure before ending the chorus. Because the riff is two bars long, it would not fit that new-chord-in-each-bar progression and is omitted during the endings of the B sections.

The third twenty-four-bar chorus is instrumental, with the riff continuing on the bass and with the guitar as the solo instrument. The guitarist, Eric Clapton, quotes from the song "Blue Moon" at the beginning of his guitar solo. (Quoting from standards or well-known melodies while improvising is a sort of game for musicians, and a way to keep listeners on their toes.)

Baker uses two bass drums to produce a heavy, throbbing pulse, uncharacteristically accenting beats one and three of each four-beat bar and playing softly on the backbeats.

The recording ends with a long extension of the last musical idea at the end of the fourth chorus and then fades out.

Lyrics: The lyrics begin by expressing the anticipation of spending the night with a lover. Later, the singer rhapsodizes about the experience and says he wants it to continue.

Billboard pop charts: number five; British hit singles: number twenty-five

Listening Guide

"Magic Man"
as recorded by Heart (1976)

Tempo: The tempo is approximately 100 beats per minute, with four beats in each bar.

Form: After a four-bar instrumental introduction, there are three verses of ten bars, each followed by one with twelve bars. That is followed by a four-bar instrumental section and another verse of eighteen bars that extends the text "try to understand." A very long instrumental follows with a twelve-bar verse using "ahs" instead of lyrics, and then comes the second verse with lyrics returning at the end of the recording.

Features: The basic rhythm section that includes guitar, electric bass guitar, and drums repeats a two-bar pattern throughout most of the recording.

The drums keep a regular, but not overly emphasized backbeat.

Occasional solos by electric guitar or synthesizer play during instrumental sections.

Lyrics: This is a story of a charming older male who whisks a young girl—the song suggests she might be underage—off her feet and takes her to live with him. For her, the relationship seems predestined, but her mother worries the girl remains under the man's "magical" powers. The end of the relationship is not clear, but it seems that she might be being exploited.

Billboard pop charts: number nine

Heart (left to right): Mark Andes, Ann Wilson, Nancy Wilson, Denny Carmassi, and Howard Lesse

heavy-metal bands on some recordings, although still without the wild theatrics of the genre. Heart continued to tour in the two-thousands.

British Heavy Metal

British heavy metal often used riffs as the basic structural element of the music. The riffs were usually played by the bass, and often started on high notes and ended on low notes, giving a very heavy, powerful effect. Just as in Cream's "Sunshine of Your Love," the riffs would drop off during instrumental improvisations that took place somewhere near the middle of the recording and then would return to reintroduce the vocals. The central concern of the British groups was power.

Group names, such as Black Sabbath and Judas Priest, and album covers and posters with symbols of witchcraft and death shocked some parents into believing the music was satanic and would be the end of anything positive in their children's lives. The young fans, of course, reveled in their parents' aversion to the music, just as Elvis Presley fans had in 1954 and Rolling Stones fans had in 1964; but these fans also realized that the songs were more often about the fear, not the worship, of evil. The fans could enjoy the power of the music, horrify their parents, who they felt did not understand them anyway, and indulge themselves in fantasies that represented an aggressive confrontation of things people fear most—evil and death.

Led Zeppelin was of great importance to the development of heavy metal. The group was formed by musicians who had been part of the British blues revival, and they continued to play covers of songs by blues artists like Howlin' Wolf and Willie Dixon. In their early music, they often used bass riffs not unlike those in Cream's "Sunshine of Your Love." As one example, "Dazed and Confused," from their first album, *Led Zeppelin* (1969), used a long, slow, descending bass riff.

Long instrumental improvisations, often played by Led Zeppelin, were a direct outgrowth of psychedelic music's efforts to give the listener the feeling that he or she was experiencing eerie connections of thoughts and images, as if in a drug-induced state, stretched out without a perceptible measure of the passage of time. The return of the bass riff was intended to bring the listener back to the real world.

Lead singer Robert Plant had sung many blues songs in the past, and bits of lyrics from them often crept into his singing with Led Zeppelin. Chicago blues writer Willie Dixon sued Led Zeppelin for using his song "You Need Love" as the basis of their "Whole Lotta Love." Dixon obtained an out-of-court settlement and used part of the money to form the "Blues Heaven Foundation," an organization that aims to help blues writers receive royalties due them when others use their material. A listening guide to "Whole Lotta Love" is on page 187.

Led Zeppelin continued to use bass riffs as the foundation of many of their later recordings, but it did not remain the prominent characteristic of their style that it had been in 1969. The riff they used in "The Immigrant Song" (1970), for example, was short and more rhythmic than melodic. Led Zeppelin's music of the late sixties also helped to define other characteristics of heavy metal, with Robert Plant's screeches and moans as part of his dramatic vocal delivery, and also with new guitar sounds, such as Jimmy Page's drawing a violin bow across the strings of his guitar.

Led Zeppelin in 1973 (left to right): Robert Plant, John Paul Jones, and Jimmy Page.

Listening Guide

"Whole Lotta Love"
as recorded by Led
Zeppelin (1969)

Tempo: The tempo is approximately 168 beats
per minute, with four beats in each bar.

Form: There is an eight-bar instrumental
introduction, three eighteen-bar verses,
an eight-bar refrain that is sung between
the verses, and much unstructured
freestyled improvisation.

Features: The instrumental introduction
features a distorted guitar riff that is
repeated much the way riff patterns
repeat in late sixties and early seventies
heavy-metal music. That riff leads into
the first verse, is played during the
refrains, and repeated to end the
recording.

The refrain repeats the text "Wanna
Whole Lotta Love" four times, and
follows each of the verses.

The second refrain is followed by a very
free psychedelic-styled improvisation in
which the drums keep a steady beat, but
everything else creates a frenetic amount
of building passion. Jimmy Page plays an
electronic instrument called a **theremin**
to create distorted sounds that slide
around in varied and irregular rhythms.
Robert Plant's vocals range from moans
to screams. Eventually, the drums introduce a guitar solo that has drum and
bass punctuations.

The third verse and refrain follows that
free-form section, and then Plant's voice
sings alone in a free rhythm to which an
echo of this voice has been added.

The freedom of the earlier improvisation
returns with more vocals, but not a
complete verse, and repetitions of the
riff bring the recording to a conclusion.

Lyrics: The overly amorous singer wants to
tutor (or "school") the object of the
song in various sexual activities.

Billboard pop charts: number four

By the early seventies, the group had expanded their early heavy-metal sound by incorporating music based on Celtic folk traditions, as in their song "The Battle of Ever-more" (1971). Their most popular recording, "Stairway to Heaven," was never released as a single but was included on the group's untitled 1971 album (often referred to as *Led Zeppelin IV* or *Zoso*). It began with a melody reminiscent of English Renaissance music played by a guitar and the sound of recorders (woodwind instruments of the flute family popular in England during the sixteenth century), but later the song developed the power and form of blues-based heavy metal.

Many of Led Zeppelin's performances during the seventies included acoustic sets. The acoustic music provided fans with a sense of intimacy with the band, who knew that every note they were hearing was being played and not filled in by feedback or other electronically created sounds. Sometimes the acoustic sets were performed with band members sitting down, closer to the audience and seeming much more vulnerable than they did standing in dramatic poses and dominating the stage with a sense of power.

Led Zeppelin broke up after John Bonham's alcohol-related death in 1980. Guitarist Jimmy Page worked on a number of projects after the breakup of Led Zeppelin. The former singer for Free and Bad Company, Paul Rodgers, joined him to record two albums with the Firm, and seven years later Page was joined by the former singer for Deep Purple and Whitesnake, David Coverdale, for the album *Coverdale/Page* (1993). Robert Plant spent that same time recording solo albums with a variety of backup musicians. Plant and Page worked together as the Honey-drippers in 1984, and Page contributed a guitar solo to "Tall Cool One" for Plant's album *Now and Zen* (1988). Some of Led Zeppelin's old favorite songs were included on the album *No Quarter: Jimmy Page and Robert Plant Unledded* (1994), which was recorded with the London Metropolitan Orchestra. They also recorded with an Egyptian ensemble, musicians from Marrakech, as well as other musicians playing folk and rock instruments. Keyboard/bass player John Paul Jones was working with Diamanda Galás at that time and recorded the album *The Sporting Life* (1994). Page, Plant, and Jones added John Bonham's son, Jason, to play drums with them at a tribute concert for Ahmet Ertegun in 2007, but hopes for further reunion concerts remain only rumors.

Black Sabbath took the hypnotically repetitive bass riff idea of Cream and Led Zeppelin and led British heavy metal into the seventies. Like the Who, Cream, and Led Zeppelin, Black Sabbath had one lead guitarist, a bassist, and a drummer to back their central attraction, vocalist **Ozzy Osbourne** (John Michael Osbourne, born in 1948). The listening guide to "Paranoid" outlines some important characteristics of seventies heavy metal. The song was Black Sabbath's only top-ten hit in Britain; it reached number sixty-one on the U.S. pop charts.

Black Sabbath began to soften their dark-power-centered image and record occasional ballads, such as "Changes" from the *Volume 4* album (1972), a song based on a waltz pattern that featured piano and mellotron in place of heavy guitar, bass, and drums. They also used acoustic guitars on "Laguna Sunrise" (1972). Despite the title and witchcraftlike symbolism on the cover of the *Sabbath, Bloody Sabbath* album (1973), the group began to drift away from their earlier demonic image. As often happens when a group changes a very strong, well-established style or image, their popularity began to decline, particularly in Britain. Osbourne quit Black Sabbath in 1978, and they became a group that other singers used as a springboard into

Listening Guide

"Paranoid"
as recorded by Black Sabbath (1970, released in 1971)

Tempo:	The tempo is approximately 164 beats per minute, with four beats in each bar.
Form:	The form is based on four-bar phrases that are paired into eight-bar periods. After an eight-bar introduction, the periods follow the pattern ABACBABB BABAA. All of the A periods have two phrases of vocals except the final one, which is instrumental. The B periods are instrumental and often function as vamps in that they do not feature a contrasting melody but rather maintain the basic beat and bass riff in preparation for the next entry of another vocal A period. The third and fourth B sections feature guitar solos. The C period has a new melody and vocals in which the singer asks for help.
Features:	Even beat subdivisions are kept by the drums and bass, but the voice and guitar subdivide the beat unevenly.
	The most prominent feature is the pounding of the bass drum and electric bass guitar on each beat.
	The drums accent a strong backbeat.
	Bass riff patterns repeat through much of the recording.
	Fuzztone is used in the guitar solo instrumental.
Lyrics:	The song's main themes are mental illness and an inability to experience happiness. Together these combine to make the singer a spiritually lost soul whose brain is its own private hell.

Billboard pop charts: number sixty-one; British hit singles: number four

Black Sabbath and Ozzy Osbourne (1973)

fans. He disgusted many parents with such acts as biting the head off a live dove and urinating on the Alamo while on tour in Texas, but the publicity he received from those activities just increased his appeal to his fans. Eventually, he paid for his perverse antics when he bit the head off a bat a fan had thrown onstage in 1982 and had to undergo a series of painful rabies shots after the show. Osbourne was greatly criticized for his song "Suicide Solution" and was sued by parents who blamed the song for their own son's death, though Osbourne claimed it was actually an antialcoholism song written after the alcohol-related death of AC/DC's singer, Bon Scott, in 1980. Osbourne won the lawsuit. Osbourne rejoined Black Sabbath in 1997 and continued to work with them into the two-thousands.

> "The backlash from the suicide suits has been that bands are more apt to use these types of lyrics to draw attention to themselves. . . . I never sat down to write lyrics with the intent that anyone should kill themselves. I feel very sorry for those kids. But why can't you sing about suicide? It's a thing that really happens."
>
> –Ozzy Osbourne

solo careers. Ronnie James Dio, formerly with Elf and Rainbow, sang with Black Sabbath before forming Dio; and ex–Deep Purple singer Ian Gillan joined Black Sabbath before forming the Ian Gillan Band. Only guitarist Tony Iommi remained with Black Sabbath throughout the group's career. The other two original members, bassist Terry "Geezer" Butler and drummer Bill Ward, left and returned several times. The original band members reunited to perform at the 1985 *Live-Aid* concert in Philadelphia, and they joined Ozzy Osbourne at the end of what was billed as his last tour in 1992. The recording of "I Don't Wanna Change the World" that was made during that tour won Osbourne his first Grammy.

After Ozzy Osbourne left Black Sabbath, he organized his own group, the Blizzard of Ozz. For that group he imported the talented young guitarist and songwriter Randy Rhoads from the California-based band Quiet Riot. While on tour after two successful albums in 1982, Rhoads and members of the band's road crew were in a plane crash, and Rhoads was killed. Rhoads was soon replaced and the tour went on, but Osbourne sorely missed Rhoads as a writing partner.

Osbourne's "wild madman" image was an important ingredient of the appeal he had for his young, rebellious

Deep Purple was a heavy-metal band that almost turned in the direction of progressive rock, or art rock. During their first few years, the group's progressive elements were emphasized by the keyboard playing of classically trained Jon Lord. The band's guitarist, Ritchie Blackmore, added his psychedelic-influenced blues riffs, creating a successful combination of the styles. By 1969, Ian Gillan's vocals and Ritchie Blackmore's guitar style led the band toward the newly developing heavy-metal style, while Lord pulled in the art-rock direction by writing a concerto for the band to perform with the Royal Philharmonic Orchestra at London's Royal Albert Hall. (**Concertos** are compositions in which an orchestra plays with a featured soloist or small group.) Despite the critical acclaim they received after performing the concerto in 1969, the band's next efforts moved away from art rock and further in the direction of heavy metal. Like most British heavy metal, their music was blues influenced and riff-based. Often, as in "Smoke on the Water" (1972), the riff involved a parallel guitar riff with the bass holding a low pedal note below it.

In 1975, Ritchie Blackmore left Deep Purple and was joined by American musicians from the upstate New York band Elf to form **Rainbow.** Most of Rainbow's music was co-written by Blackmore and other band members, and while former Elf member Ronnie James Dio was with them, the band explored exotic cultures of the past in such works as "16th Century Greensleeves" (1975) and "Gates of Babylon" (1978). Their "16th Century Greensleeves" was quite different from the traditional song "Greensleeves," dating from the Renaissance. Though a sixteenth-century castle was the setting described in the lyrics, and the musical style of that earlier time was suggested by the use of modal harmonies, the melody was not the original "Greensleeves." The music of "Gates of Babylon" was based on melodic themes styled after modern Middle-Eastern scales which, at least to Western ears, had an ancient and foreign sound. The devil was mentioned in the song, as was common for British heavy metal, but with the warning of death to anyone who would dare to "sleep" with him.

After many personnel changes, the members who were in Deep Purple during the early seventies regrouped in 1984 and recorded *Perfect Strangers,* which was well received by their long-faithful fans. Disagreements among band members kept them from recording and touring regularly, although they did manage to get together long enough to record *The Battle Rages On* in 1993. Despite several membership changes, Deep Purple continued on in the two-thousands, releasing new albums *Bananas* (2003) and *Rapture of the Deep* (2005).

Judas Priest, a band that came to symbolize British heavy metal during the eighties, did not tour the United States until the late seventies, even though they had been together, slowly building a following in England, since 1971. For the first three years they were together, they used the most common early seventies heavy-metal instrumentation—a singer, a single guitarist, a bass player, and a drummer. In 1974 they added a second lead guitarist, expanding their powerful sound with their two lead guitarists playing parallel lines, in much the same way the Allman Brothers and other American southern-rock bands of the late sixties and early seventies had. This full lead sound made Judas Priest's debut album, *Rocka Rolla* (1974), noticeably different from the music played by a trio of instruments, which had become standard for early heavy-metal bands. A listening guide to "Victim of Changes" from their second album, *Sad Wings of Destiny,* is on page 191.

The power of this and other recordings by Judas Priest suited their image, which favored the black-leather-jacketed biker look; Halford sometimes even roared out on stage on a Harley-Davidson motorcycle. Marlon Brando popularized leather jackets with his "tough guy" image in the fifties, but Judas Priest added chains and metal to the leather to give a "metallic" twist to their rebellious image. The later album *Screaming for Vengeance* (1982) and its single "You've Got Another Thing Comin'" brought Judas Priest a very large following in the United States.

In 1986, the American press had nonmusical events to report on about Judas Priest when the parents of two teenagers who attempted suicide after listening to the album *Stained Class* (1978) filed suit against the band. One of the teens died in the attempt, and the other was badly injured and died from a drug overdose three years later. The parents alleged that members of Judas Priest put the words "do it" and some backmasked references to

K.K. Downing and Rob Halford from Judas Priest

Listening Guide

"Victim of Changes"
as recorded by Judas Priest (1976)

Tempo: The tempo is about 84 beats per minute, with four beats per bar. The bars are subdivided in halves to the point that a double-time feel is created and the beat sounds twice as fast.

Form: A twelve-bar A section (made up of three phrases of lyrics and two repetitions of the riff) is followed by an eight-bar B (two phrases with riffs), a six-bar instrumental, another A, another B, a C with a new riff, and finally a long, riff-based instrumental.

The beginning riff returns to end the recording, balancing the form.

Features: The drums accent the backbeat very heavily.

The recording begins with electronic sounds, which then give way to the bass riff that continues through much of the song.

More than one riff is used throughout the recording, but each is short (a single bar in length) and repeats over and over before changing.

The vocalist, Rob Halford, often intones on a single note; melody is not lacking in British metal, but it is not the most important element.

Stop time, an effect commonly used in the blues, is used in sections where the instruments fall silent between words Halford sings; they return to support him on certain words.

Lyrics: Two sets of parallel images dominate the lyrics. The first image is of a particular woman who is analogized to bad whisky; she has been unfaithful to the singer and has literally driven him to drink. The second image is that of alcoholism itself, which is (brilliantly) analogized to a woman with whom the singer has a, literally, intoxicating, but ultimately destructive personal relationship. Both whisky and the woman start out with an initial rush of pleasure ("wonderful and beautiful") but then both escape the singer's control.

suicide in the album cut "Better By You, Better Than Me." The court heard no evidence to support the claims of subliminal messages, but it did hear evidence about other problems in the lives of the teenagers and the case was dismissed. After the trial, band members said that if they believed that subliminal messages could affect their listeners, the messages they would choose to put on albums would be ones that would encourage album sales and concert attendance and certainly not ones that could possibly destroy their fans. Judas Priest followed the trial decision with another album, *Painkiller* (1991), after which Halford left the band to form Fight. He later formed Halford. Judas Priest replaced Halford with Tim

"Ripper" Owens, a fan who had been singing in a Judas Priest cover band in Ohio. They released *Jugulator* in 1997 and *Demolition* in 2001. Halford returned in 2003, and two years later the band recorded *Angel of Retribution* (2005) and then *Nostradamus* (2008).

British rock bands had visited Germany regularly during the sixties, and German rock groups often styled themselves after their English counterparts. Two brothers from Hannover, Germany, Rudolf and Michel Schenker, formed **Scorpions** in 1970. They recorded an album, *Lonesome Crow* (1972), with the sibling guitarists following the blues revival tradition of one (Michel) playing lead and the other (Rudolf) playing rhythm. Most of

Scorpions' music followed the riff-based style of British heavy metal, but they also wrote interesting melodic lines similar to those common in American heavy metal. Of the British groups that influenced them, **UFO,** which Michel Schenker eventually joined (changing the spelling of his name to "Michael"), was the most important. UFO had become very popular in continental Europe during the early and middle seventies, although English audiences had mostly ignored them. Schenker left UFO in 1979 to form the Michael Schenker Group. He returned to Scorpions to record *Lovedrive* (1979) but left again to work with other bands. Schenker rejoined the newly reformed UFO to tour during the middle nineties.

The powerful drive of heavy metal required singers to force their voices, sometimes to the point of damage to the vocal cords. After Scorpions' *Animal Magnetism* album (1980), their lead singer, Klaus Meine, could no longer sing and was forced to have surgery to have nodes scraped off his vocal cords. After the surgery, Meine went to Vienna for voice lessons to learn to sing without straining. The training involved techniques similar to those learned by classical singers, but Meine did not turn away from heavy metal, as his vocals on Scorpions' *Blackout* album (1982) clearly demonstrate.

In 1988, Scorpions became the first heavy-metal band to tour in the Soviet Union, and the following year they were invited back to perform in the Moscow Music Peace Festival, this time joined by Ozzy Osbourne and Bon Jovi. The song "Wind of Change" (1991) was about their Russian visits. Again giving tribute to social and political changes, this time in their own country, the album *Face the Heat* (1993) included songs about the reunification of Germany. Scorpions continue to record and tour in the early two-thousands.

Blues- and riff-based British heavy metal had spread all over the world and, by the early seventies, was copied by bands as far away as Australia. One such band, AC/DC, formed in 1973. Brothers Malcolm and Angus Young had moved to Australia from Glasgow, Scotland, in 1963. Their older brother, George Young, was a member of the Easybeats, a pop-rock group that had one international hit, "Friday on My Mind" (1967); Malcolm and Angus wanted to surpass his success. High-voltage heavy metal was the style of music the brothers chose to play, as the name **AC/DC** (alternating current/direct current) indicates.

AC/DC's style developed in the British riff-based tradition; they varied it, however, by using repeated riffs only as introductions and endings, not continuing them during the central part of the song. Sex and violence were their favorite themes, and the group's graphic lyrics kept many radio stations from playing their music. Bleaker, more depressing themes followed the death of the band's heavy-drinking vocalist, Bon Scott, who died early in 1980. Scott was replaced by Brian Johnson, whose powerful vocals gave tribute to his predecessor on the album *Back in Black* (1980).

A rapport between band members and fans was an important element at most heavy-metal concerts, and AC/DC paid tribute to that relationship on their album *For Those about to Rock, We Salute You* (1981). (The title was a paraphrasing of the call the gladiators of ancient Rome gave to the Emperor when they entered the arena to engage in battle to the death: "We who are about to die salute you!") Still recording in the early nineties, AC/DC's album *Razor's Edge* (1990) gave them a top-forty single, "Moneytalks." AC/DC continued to record and tour in the two-thousands, and their tremendous popularity caused the Recording Industry Association of America to declare them the fifth best-selling band in the United States with sixty-nine million albums sold. AC/DC followed that with the release of *Black Ice* in 2008.

Following the dual lead guitar idea brought to heavy metal by Judas Priest, and also adding punk influences, the English band **Iron Maiden** built its image around the theme of death and destruction favored by so many British groups. They named themselves after a medieval torture and execution device that surrounded and then stabbed its victim with multiple spikes, reinforcing this image by using as their symbol a rotting corpse spitting blood. Many of Iron Maiden's song lyrics portrayed medieval and even earlier mythical stories of torture and death, but some also stressed such current issues as the atrocities of war in the twentieth century and the horrors of potential nuclear war. Horrifying their fans' parents, Iron Maiden included a section of the biblical Book of Revelation and its image of "the beast," or the Antichrist, on the album *The Number of the Beast* (1982). Although the main theme projected fear of the beast, the band was still strongly criticized by concerned groups who did not understand this message and feared the influence it might have on young fans. Iron Maiden's first British hit, "Run to the Hills," from *The Number of the Beast* album, was sung from the perspective of Native Americans being slaughtered by European settlers in the United States. Iron Maiden was still recording and touring in the early nineties. They had many personnel changes over the years, with only bassist Steve Harris and guitarist Dave Murray remaining from the original band. The eighties band regrouped, with three guitarists this time, in 1999. They were still recording and touring in the early two-thousands. Not only has Iron Maiden won several Best Band awards in Britain, but their music became known to many new fans through its use in a variety of video games.

The British band **Def Leppard** formed just one year after Iron Maiden and followed the double lead guitar style of Judas Priest. The band members were teenagers when they began working together and signed a recording contract in 1979. They started out touring with well-established, older groups, and their youth helped them win the adulation of young fans. Although they occasionally donned medieval attire, Def Leppard's song texts were generally closer to traditional rock themes about human relationships and the attractions of alcohol rather than the demonic themes projected by other British heavy-metal acts. Musically, they used riffs as introduction themes, but broke away from them through the course of their songs.

Def Leppard's career climaxed with the release of their third album, *Pyromania* (1983), and a long tour followed it. Their career and immediate future were interrupted by a car accident on New Year's Eve that same year when their drummer, Rick Allen, lost his left arm. Allen was determined to continue playing the drums, and the band decided to let him try because they felt Allen was as important to the band as any other member. In 1987, he resumed recording and touring with Def Leppard, aided by an elaborate arrangement of pedals rigged to his drums that allowed him to use his feet to play the beats his left arm would have played. The band was hit with another tragedy when guitarist Steve Clark died in 1991. They chose not to replace him for the recording of their next album, *Adrenalize* (1992), but Def Leppard retained their double lead guitar style by having Phil Collen double track the guitar parts. Clark was later replaced by Vivian Campbell. Def Leppard's next album, *Retro Active* (1993), was a collection of old B sides and covers, but that did not mean that it lacked the hard-edged appeal for which the band was known. It made the top-ten album charts in the United States. Pop influences became part of Def Leppard's new sound on their tenth album, *X* (2002). Back to hard rock, they released an album of cover songs, *Yeah!* (2006), and then followed that with a new studio album, *Songs from the Sparkle Lounge* (2009), and extensive touring.

American Heavy Metal

Heavy metal was not solely a British invention. It developed out of the playing styles of many late-sixties groups, both British and American. One of the first American groups to use heavy metal's distorted guitar sound was **Iron Butterfly,** from San Diego, California. Their recording of "In-A-Gadda-Da-Vida" (1968), which fans took to mean "In a Garden of Eden," was based on a strong, descending bass riff similar to those in British heavy-metal recordings. Unlike those recordings, however, they used an electric organ as their main instrument and added distorted guitar sounds. The seventeen-minute-long original recording of "In-A-Gadda-Da-Vida" broke away from the riff for more than two minutes of drum solo, after which the guitar and the organ played back and

forth in an instrumental call-and-response pattern that served as a break before the bass riff returned. Iron Butterfly recorded several other albums, and their single "Easy Rider" was included on the soundtrack of the film *Easy Rider* (1969). They broke up in the late seventies but have gotten back together from time to time for concert appearances.

In the occult tradition that was central to some metal bands, Vincent Furnier reportedly used a Ouija board to find the name he used for himself and for his band; the board chose **Alice Cooper.** Furnier was from Detroit, but moved to Phoenix and then to Los Angeles to find audiences who would accept the group's unconventional routines, which included live snakes and staged executions. Back in Detroit in 1971, Alice Cooper started out with an androgynous "glam" image but eventually became one of the first American heavy-metal groups to score hit singles. Their music was as loud, aggressive, and distorted as that of British groups, and they used riffs, but the riffs did not serve as the basis of the main melodies as they had in British heavy metal, and their music was often quite melodic and contained more understandable lyrics than

Alice Cooper (1970)

Listening Guide

"School's Out"
as recorded by Alice Cooper (1972)

Tempo: The tempo is approximately 132 beats per minute, with four beats in each bar.

Form: After a twelve-bar introduction, the form is structured: A Interlude B Interlude C Instrumental (based on A) ABCCB with sections of unequal lengths.

Each A section is eight bars long. The first A is followed by a four-bar interlude with no guitar riff and a very strong pounding on each beat.

Each B section is twelve bars long and includes a four-bar vocal phrase that begins with the words "school's out" sung three times through. The B section functions as a refrain. The first B section is followed by a four-bar instrumental interlude.

Each C section is eight bars long and has a lighter instrumental and vocal timbre with children singing the old "No more pencils, no more books . . ." school song.

The first C section is followed by an eight-bar instrumental section based on the A section.

The recording ends with an extension of the last B section, a school bell ringing, and then a descending electronic sound.

Features: Uneven beat subdivisions are maintained throughout the recording.

The backbeat is not stressed.

The two-bar opening guitar riff pattern is played six times in the introduction and then also repeated through each A section. The riff is not heard in the rest of the recording.

After leaving the riff pattern, the lead guitar, using fuzztone, continues playing in the background or plays fills after vocal phrases.

Lyrics: The singer is both forceful and exuberant about the ending of the school term.

Billboard pop charts: number seven; British hit singles: number one

---

British heavy metal. Songs such as "Eighteen" (1971), "School's Out" (1972), and "No More Mr. Nice Guy" (1973) were not full of death-and-destruction themes but were based on subjects close to their young fans' actual experiences. The listening guide to Alice Cooper's "School's Out" is included here. The song was a number seven hit on the U.S. pop charts.

"To us it was a combination of comic books, every RKO horror movie I'd ever seen. We were total students of trivial television . . .

we invented this Frankenstein named Alice Cooper that was really a reflection of that."

—Alice Cooper

Cooper borrowed many of his stage effects from horror movies and was even featured on a 1975 television special called *Alice Cooper—The Nightmare.* After some time playing slightly less aggressive music, Cooper returned to his former strength with the album *Raise Your Fist and Yell* (1987), from which the song "Freedom" made a strong statement against censorship. Cooper's theatrical stage antics finally made it into the movies with his appearances in *Prince of Darkness* (1988), *The Decline of Western Civilization, Part II—The Metal Years* (1988), *Freddy's Dead: The Final Nightmare* (1991), and *Wayne's World* (1992). Alice Cooper continued to tour and record a series of albums with a new backup band in the early two-thousands.

Another loud, passionate musician who emerged during the late sixties was the "Motor City Madman," **Ted Nugent** (born in 1948), who was considerably influenced by Jimi Hendrix. Like Hendrix, Nugent played psychedelic music; in fact, Nugent's act with the Amboy Dukes included many of Hendrix's tricks of controlled screeching feedback sound effects and plucking the guitar strings (or pretending to) with his teeth. When he first started playing, Nugent took guitar lessons where he learned to use all four fingers on his fingerboard hand instead of avoiding the little finger when playing lead, like many self-taught guitarists tended to do. The additional finger allowed for more speed and melodic extensions that would be harder to reach without it, and he did his best to prove his technical superiority by challenging other guitarists to competitions. Nugent also insisted on using hollow-body electric guitars because he claimed their resonance allowed him to enhance his feedback. Ideologically, he differed with many rock musicians and fans of the time because he spoke out against the use of drugs and for private possession of guns. He also became famous for bow-hunting for food and taunting animal rights activists. From the middle seventies through the early nineties, Nugent recorded under his own name with various different musicians singing and playing backup for him. He recorded with Damn Yankees in the early nineties and returned to a solo career in 1995 with *Spirit of the Wild*.

From the northeastern part of the United States, **Aerosmith** formed in 1970 and spent several years imitating the post-blues-revival styles of the Rolling Stones and the Yardbirds. The group did not copy their British predecessors by covering their recordings; Aerosmith's singer Steven Tyler and guitarist Joe Perry co-wrote their own songs. However, Tyler styled his vocals and stage personality after Mick Jagger, and the basic hard and assertive rhythm and blues beat adopted by Aerosmith came from their British counterparts. Like the Rolling Stones, Aerosmith also added folk and country characteristics to their rhythm and blues style. The introduction to "Dream On" (1973), for example, was played on electric instruments but modeled after the types of picking patterns used by folk musicians on acoustic guitar. Later in the recording, hard-rock-style guitar distortion joined the folk-based sound, but the result was still more like a folk ballad played on amplified instruments than a heavy-metal sound. In "Walk This Way," Aerosmith used blues-based riffs and country influences of a very steady, evenly subdivided

beat, with strong accents on the first and third beats of each bar. To that they added drums accenting the backbeat. "Walk This Way" introduced Aerosmith's music to younger fans when the group performed it with rappers Run-D.M.C. in 1986. Band members had a number of private disputes that caused their two guitarists, Joe Perry and Brad Whitford, to leave the group for solo careers, but the original group reunited to record *Pump* (1989). Aerosmith signed a new four-album contract in 1991 and continued to top the charts with hit singles and videos in the nineties. They returned to their roots in the blues revival for their *Honkin' on Bobo* (2004) album. A new studio album and tour were planned for 2009.

Brothers Edward and Alex Van Halen formed the band **Van Halen** in 1974. Their father was a musician who saw to it that they had early classical training in piano. The family moved from Nijmegen in the Netherlands to Pasadena, California, in 1968, and the two teenagers formed a rock band called Mammoth. The band played a repertoire of early heavy metal by Cream and Black Sabbath, as well as soul and funk music by James Brown, at every school dance or backyard party they could. They attracted singer David Lee Roth from the Redball Jets and bassist Michael Anthony from Snake when they regrouped under the name Van Halen. With the production assistance of Gene Simmons from Kiss, they recorded an album that was eventually bought and released by Warner Brothers Records of Los Angeles.

Michael Anthony, Eddie Van Halen, David Lee Roth, and Alex Van Halen.

Musically, Van Halen took full advantage of guitarist Eddie Van Halen's extensive musical training. Although most of that training was as a pianist, as a guitarist he made use of classical techniques such as natural and artificial harmonics (which can be used to play entire melodies) utilized by classical guitarists. He worked out innovative methods to combine slurring and hammering patterns (pulling and hitting the strings instead of plucking or strumming) with both hands on his guitar neck, creating sound effects that were new to rock guitar. At the same time, singer David Lee Roth worked up a stage routine to rival such classic performers as James Brown.

Van Halen's first top-forty hit was a cover of the Kinks' "You Really Got Me." Read the listening guide to Van Halen's recording and compare it with the guide to the Kinks' original recording that was presented in Chapter 8. Van Halen's version of "You Really Got Me" reached number thirty-six on the U.S. pop charts.

By the end of the seventies, Van Halen was touring with Black Sabbath, a band they had copied just a few years earlier, and constantly upstaged the longer-established group. Although Black Sabbath's career managed to survive the inevitable comparisons, it was newer groups like Van Halen that led heavy metal to a revival in the eighties.

Listening Guide

"You Really Got Me"
as recorded by Van Halen (1978)

Tempo: The tempo is approximately 138 beats per minute, with four beats in each bar.

Form: The recording begins with an eight-bar introduction consisting of eight repetitions of the one-bar guitar riff that continues to repeat throughout most of the recording. The drums enter in the fifth bar.

The introduction is followed by three twenty-bar sections with vocals, and a sixteen-bar instrumental section between the second and third sections. Each of the twenty-bar sections follows the form AABC. The A and B phrases are each four bars long and the C phrases are eight bars long. The instrumental section is based on four repetitions of the A section.

Features: Even beat subdivisions are used throughout the recording.

The drums maintain a strong backbeat.

The guitar uses elaborate sound effects including much fuzztone.

The riff pattern begins with a half-beat pickup and then plays three beats, ending with a half-beat rest. It is strongly supported by the bass.

The riff breaks into guitar and/or bass solo lines at the ends of phrases and at the final phrase of the instrumental section.

Abrupt key changes occur between sections. Section B is one whole-step higher than A, and C is another fourth higher than B (a fifth higher than A). The pitch of the riff changes along with the key changes.

An interesting effect is created by shifting the vocal accents from the way the lyrics would normally be spoken. Instead of accenting "you" and "got" in "you really got me," Roth accents "really" and "me." This accenting and most of the lyrics imitate the original recording by the Kinks in 1964.

Lyrics: The singer is so enraptured by his girlfriend that he is practically sick.

Billboard pop charts: number thirty-six

Eddie Van Halen put his keyboard background to use on a synthesizer for "Jump" and the somber-toned "I'll Wait," both from the band's *1984* album. He had used a synthesizer in the background of such earlier recordings as "Dancing in the Street" (1982) but feared that his heavy-metal fans would not appreciate its use as a primary instrument. Van Halen's fans stood by them for the style change, however, and "Jump" became a hit single.

The growing competition for stage dominance between Eddie Van Halen and David Lee Roth finally culminated in Roth's leaving the group in 1985 to pursue a solo career. His replacement, Sammy Hagar, had been the singer in Montrose, a southern California band that had shared bills with Van Halen back in their days as Mammoth. Van Halen's career with Hagar proved to be more successful than did Roth's solo career. Eddie Van Halen quit drinking and changed his image in the nineties, calling himself "Edward" and sporting a new short haircut, and the band played on with the album *Balance* (1995). Fans of the original Van Halen band received a surprise in 1996 when David Lee Roth returned, displacing Hagar as the band's singer. The reunion was not to last, however, and Roth was again removed from the band. Former Extreme singer Gary Cherone took his place. Cherone left after three years to form Tribe of Judah, and rumors spread that Roth might return. Instead, it was Sammy Hagar who rejoined Van Halen in 2004. Hagar's return was short lived, and David Lee Roth replaced him in 2006. When Roth returned, he was the only non–Van Halen member of the band because Eddie's son, Wolfgang, had joined Eddie and Alex as the new bass player.

Heavy-metal fans often wanted to hear their bands "say it like it is" with no holding back for the sake of other people's feelings. Los Angeles–based **Guns N' Roses** certainly fit that bill. Whether or not lead singer Axl Rose said it "like it really is" was much disputed, but the sense of completely carefree personal freedom he portrayed was a major part of his and his band's appeal. Musically, Guns N' Roses fit the old hard-rock category as much as they did heavy metal because it was not uncommon for lead guitarist Slash to use an acoustic guitar for a folk-influenced effect or for the band to add horns, vocal choirs, or synthesized sounds to their recordings. This musical diversity was well displayed on the band's first studio album, *Appetite for Destruction* (1987), which some fans saw as their best. Guns N' Roses disgusted many of their fans by including a song by Charles Manson on their *Spaghetti Incident?* (1993) album. Axl Rose kept the band's name alive through Slash's departure in 1993. Slash was replaced by former Nine Inch Nails guitarist Robin Finck. Slash formed his own band, Slash's Snakepit.

Speed Metal and Thrash

Speed metal combined heavy-metal vocals and fuzztone guitar timbres with the intense, throbbing beat of punk. Just as the term *speed* indicates, the music often included instrumental solos played at breakneck speed. Thrash metal shared many of the characteristics of speed metal, but was angrier and stressed the demonic themes of earlier British heavy metal. With the development of these new styles, the former distinctions between British and American styles, for the most part, dissolved.

One of the earliest bands to synthesize punk's energy with the power of heavy metal was the British band **Motörhead,** formed in 1975. ("Motorhead" is slang for someone addicted to methedrine or speed. Presumably the umlaut was included in the name to make it look exotic or foreign.) Motörhead first performed as the opening act for the Damned, causing them to be pegged as a punk band. Their music was certainly derived from punk, but not simply the British punk style played by the Damned and the Sex Pistols. The flashy guitar solos of the American "Madman of Motor City," Ted Nugent, and the early punk style played by the MC5 and the Ramones also influenced their style. Motörhead's image was the leather-jacketed biker, and their sound was fast, tight, and loud. They soon gained a large British following and served as inspiration for later bands, including Iron Maiden, Guns N' Roses, and many of the American speed-metal bands. After many personnel changes, the only original member left in the nineties was bassist/singer Ian "Lemmy" Kilminster. None of the changes marked a reduction of power, however, and the band was still bursting eardrums at concerts and on recordings in the two-thousands.

Some of the best-known bands to follow Motörhead's fast and loud lead included three California-based bands—**Metallica,** Megadeth, and Slayer. While raw power was an important element in the music played by these bands, their lyrics sometimes portrayed death and destruction as the evils of drug use and war, not unlike the music of folk singers or singer/songwriters of the sixties and seventies. For example, the title track from Metallica's *Master of Puppets* (1986) album served as a powerful statement about the dangers of drug use. A listening guide to that recording is on page 198.

Metallica's bassist, Clifford Lee Burton, was killed in a bus crash while the band was touring in Sweden in 1986. He was replaced by Jason Newsted. Political themes were added to Metallica's next album, *. . . And Justice for All* (1988), and despite very little airplay on radio or video stations it charted in the top ten. Powerful speed-metal bands seldom had the pop-chart success that Metallica experienced. The album *Metallica* (1991) shot to number one the week it was released and contained several top-forty hit

Listening Guide

"Master of Puppets"
as recorded by Metallica (1986)

Tempo: The tempo is approximately 208 beats per minute through most of the recording, but the center C section is half that speed, or about 104 beats per minute. Most bars have four quarter-note beats ($\frac{4}{4}$ meter), but bars with five eighth-note beats ($\frac{5}{8}$ meter) are placed at the ends of phrases in the A section. The B section includes some two-beat bars ($\frac{2}{4}$ meter).

Form: After an extended instrumental introduction, the form follows the following pattern: A B A B C D instrumental extension A B instrumental extension.

The A sections are each made up of five phrases of vocals and one instrumental phrase. Each phrase is made up of three four-beat bars followed by one bar of five half beats ($\frac{5}{8}$ meter). The B sections function as refrains, always beginning with the words "come crawling faster." They begin with four-beat bars, but then change to phrases constructed of four-beat and occasional two-beat bars at the section that begins "master of puppets." The meter is further complicated by the use of quarter-note triplets in that same section.

The instrumental C section is played at half the speed of the rest of the recording and is constructed of asymmetrical bar and phrase lengths that avoid the repetition of a regular metric pattern.

The D section is based on four-bar phrase lengths with four beats in each bar.

Features: Even beat subdivisions are used throughout the recording.

The drums sometimes punctuate individual beats of the bass riff and guitar pattern, but at other times, they fall into a regular rock backbeat.

The guitars and bass generally play together in short, repeated riff patterns.

The intensity of the very fast beat is accentuated by the use of phrases that end with shortened bars because the listener's ear expects to hear the beat and a half that is missing, but instead hears the next phrase enter.

Power chords add depth to the sound.

The instrumental C section provides a break from the intensity of the rest of the recording. The beat is slower and the rhythm guitar plays smooth **arpeggio** patterns around which synthesized lead guitar weaves melodic lines.

The recording ends with band members laughing at their puppet victim.

Lyrics: The singer plays the role of a drug that has gained control of the person to whom the song is directed. He demands to be called "master" and promises to kill his puppet victim.

singles. In 2000 Metallica angered some fans by fighting the trading of their recordings by Napster, but that didn't keep their 2003 album, *St. Anger,* from debuting at the top of the *Billboard* charts and winning them a Grammy award. Metallica followed that success with extensive touring and a new album, *Death Magnetic* (2008).

Thrash metal, another style rooted in both punk and earlier heavy metal, was played by bands like New York's **Anthrax.** Those roots became particularly clear when a speed- or thrash-metal band covered an old song by a punk or metal band. Sex Pistols songs such as "Anarchy in the U.K." and "God Save the Queen," as well as songs by Black

James Hatfield with Metallica (1990)

Sabbath, were favorites that newer bands often covered. Audiences often slam-danced their way through the concerts, just as the Sex Pistols' own fans did a decade or more earlier. The lyrics of original songs by speed-metal or thrash-metal bands were generally directed at an audience of angry and aggressive young people who felt a great sense of alienation from society. This kind of theme was certainly not uncommon for rock music in general, but the anger was more intense in this music than it was in prepunk times.

With the EP *I'm the Man* (1987), Anthrax became the first metal band to add rap vocals to their sound. They continued to develop that style, eventually touring with Public Enemy and then rerecording Public Enemy's "Don't Believe the Hype" with the rappers themselves. Anthrax left Elektra and signed with another label that went out of business. Then their subsequent label did the same thing. They finally signed with Sanctuary Records and released the highly acclaimed *We've Come for You All* album in 2003. After a series of personnel changes, Anthrax has regrouped with a new singer, Dan Nelson, and released a new album, *Worship Music* (2009).

Death Metal

Black Sabbath, Iron Maiden, and other heavy-metal bands from the past painted images of death and the power of the devil or other demons, but to some metal

fans in the eighties and nineties those bands stopped short of creating an image that could really horrify. Modern audiences did not want images that were merely reminiscent of death and evil; some youths became obsessed to the point that they wanted lyrics about real-life murderers and a sense of a "real" presence of Satan. Beginning as an underground movement, albums by death-metal bands such as Death, Possessed, Morbid Angel, and many others first circulated among small circles of teens who had met at concerts or through underground newspapers. By the middle eighties, the death-metal following had grown to the point that albums began to be distributed nationally and some appeared in music stores that were willing to handle them.

One of the most important and influential of the death-metal bands was **Slayer,** formed in Huntington Beach, California, in 1982. They recorded their *Reign in Blood* (1986) album while under contract with Def Jam Records, but the company's distributor, Columbia, refused to allow the album's release. It was finally distributed by Geffen Records, and the fact that it sold enough to make the top 100 on the pop charts indicated that death metal had indeed been pulled out of the underground. The song "Angel of Death" from the *Reign in Blood* album is sometimes cited as an important example of death metal because of its horrible and graphic portrayal of death at Auschwitz during the holocaust. The song's expression of Nazi brutality is one that many non-death-metal fans could understand and perhaps even appreciate, but many listeners would likely object to other lyrics on the album. Never allowing themselves to "sell out" to commercialism, Slayer was still pounding out aggressive depression in the two-thousands.

Death metal was an important influence on the development of grindcore, a style of metal that developed from a combination of thrash metal, hard-core punk, and industrial music. Grindcore is discussed in Chapter 20.

Ironically, the potential for real death from a malignant brain tumor brought death-metal fans together. Frontman of the band Death, Chuck Schuldiner, was diagnosed with the tumor and his health insurance would not cover the recommended treatments. His family paid all they could afford over a period of two years and then such bands as the Red Hot Chili Peppers, Korn, Slipknot, Marilyn Manson, and others donated items for an auction to raise money to save Schuldiner's life. As Slipknot's Corey Taylor said, "Chuck's music was really important to me growing up. So I wanna auction something that's really cool that can hopefully bring top dollar." Schuldiner died in 2001.

Glam Bands

Androgynous hairdos and makeup made a new appearance on heavy-metal stages with such eighties performers as Mötley Crüe (from Los Angeles) and Twisted Sister

Poison in 1987 (left to right): CC DeVille, Brett Michaels, Bobby Dall, and Rikki Rocket

(from New Jersey). The long, full hairdos and makeup and songs about drinking and partying gave heavy metal a new, lighter image than it had had in the past.

Poison had their own hairdresser in their drummer Rikki Rockett (Richard Ream, born in 1961). The band formed in Pennsylvania but relocated to Los Angeles where they became one of the most successful L.A. glam bands during the style's heyday in the late eighties. A listening guide to one of their top-ten hits, "Nothin' but a Good Time," is below. The recording reached number six on the U.S. pop charts.

Poison's commercial success was partially due to their versatility. Another hit from the same album (*Open Up and Say . . . Ahh!*), "Every Rose Has Its Thorn," was a ballad.

Listening Guide

"Nothin' But a Good Time"
as recorded by Poison (1988)

Tempo: The tempo is approximately 130 beats per minute, with four beats in each bar.

Form: The instrumental introduction is composed of a four-bar riff played four times and then extended two more bars. The form is based on eight-bar phrases, although the two phrases that begin with the song title have an additional one-bar extension. Each phrase begins with two eighth-note pickups.

Features: Uneven beat subdivisions are used throughout the recording.

The drums maintain a strong backbeat.

A twenty-four-bar instrumental section ends with the opening riff played twice.

The instrumental section features solo guitar.

Lyrics: The song presents the point of view of someone who resents having to work so hard to get enough money to have a good time.

Billboard pop charts: number six

200

Poison's next two albums also sold well, and the band was still together in the two-thousands, but by that time the elaborate costumes and stage theatrics of both glitter and glam (hair bands) had begun to give way to the growing popularity of alternative groups whose looks and staging generally avoided such glitz.

Summary

Hard rock developed out of the blues revival during the late sixties and shared some of the characteristics of heavy metal, such as loud, distorted guitar timbres and a strong backbeat, but it generally had more commercial appeal than heavy metal. Hard-rock bands often played slow ballads in addition to the hard, driving backbeat of other music in the style, and they also used instruments such as acoustic piano, acoustic guitar, and synthesizers. Hard rock was music that appealed to the many fans who craved loud, danceable rock music, but did not identify with the macho heavy-metal bands, androgynous glitter groups, or punk and new-wave bands of the seventies and eighties. In later years the terms *hard rock* and *heavy metal* came to be used interchangeably.

Heavy-metal music developed out of riff-based blues revival music in which extreme, distorted sound effects were used. The hypnotic repetition of the riffs along with the loud, screeching guitars, power chords, and pounding drums laid down a powerful foundation for songs that stressed fear of death, destruction, or evil. Whether the songs were about mythological beasts or images from horror stories, the music was aggressive and emotionally satisfying to its young, mostly male fans. Even heavy-metal bands whose songs centered on antiwar themes created such rebellious and angry music that people who did not listen closely to the lyrics assumed that the bands were trying to cause violence rather than warn against it.

Heavy metal had undergone many changes by the late eighties. The music played by classically trained musicians in Van Halen and others developed into a highly technical and progressive style of music. Going in another direction completely were the thrash- and death-metal bands that combined punk's anger and violence with heavy-metal riffs and screeching, distorted guitars. Although heavy metal has suffered the criticisms of many who fear the effects the music may have on young and impressionable fans, it has continued to appeal to its followers for a number of years and is certain to spark disagreement among critics and fans for many years to come.

Eighties glam bands added heavy-metal-influenced power to their glittery looks of long hair and makeup. The music and images of glam bands were generally less tough than those of heavy-metal groups, and glam bands often sang songs about drinking and partying.

discussion question

Does the sound of music or the meaning of song lyrics cause listeners to do things they would not otherwise do?

chapter 14

Progressive and Glitter Rock

> "What started to happen in music at this time was more of the well-educated university graduate types were coming in as musicians and band members."
>
> —CHRIS BLACKWELL
> OF ISLAND RECORDS

The first rock album members of the art music community lauded as going beyond the field of popular music into the "higher level" of art music was the Beatles' *Sgt. Pepper's Lonely Hearts Club Band* (1967). That album was extremely important in rock music because it was effectively a concept album that inspired a number of other important bands of the late sixties to create concept albums. To people in the field of **avant-garde** classical music, it was other effects that impressed them about the *Sgt. Pepper* album. Classical composers had been including a sense of randomness in their compositions for some time. In live concert situations, that randomness was often written into the compositions through notes to the performers indicating that they should make some of the decisions about what they played. That caused each performance of a work to be somewhat different from other performances. The idea was to create a sort of "musical happening." This is called *aleatory* in classical music. A recording cannot be aleatoric, of course, because it is going to sound the same each time it is played. The Beatles and their producer George Martin still used the idea of randomness by cutting up previously recorded tapes of instrumental sounds often found in circuses and then splicing them together in an arbitrary way to create circus effects in "Being for the Benefit of Mr. Kite." They had a forty-piece orchestra play whatever the musicians wanted from a low note to a high one four times, and then they overdubbed the sounds to create the orchestral buildup in "A Day in the Life." Both of these ideas were brilliant uses of techniques that classical composers had been using. The *Sgt. Pepper* album also gave a nod to classical traditions by playing the first song again toward the end of the album. This repeat of an earlier idea created a sense of "classical" balance much like the music of such composers as Mozart and Beethoven.

As more rock musicians began to add influences of art music to their rock styles, several new progressive styles developed. The simplest form of progressive rock used instruments normally associated with symphony orchestras, such as violins, violas, and cellos, or wind instruments such as the flute, in addition to the usual rock instrumentation; this was an extension of what producers Phil Spector and George Martin had done earlier. A more complex style was created by musicians who wrote multimovement works, such as those common in classical music, in addition to recording their own versions of classical works themselves. A third, even more experimental progressive-rock style was based on ideas from the works of modern composers of avant-garde and electronic music.

Rock Bands with Orchestras

The **Moody Blues** was formed in 1964 by musicians who had previously played in blues and rhythm and blues bands in Birmingham, England. They did write original songs, but their most popular early recording, "Go Now!" (1965), was a cover of a ballad by American rhythm and blues singer Bessie Banks. By the end of 1967, the Moody Blues had changed some of their personnel and had also modified their sound by incorporating a classical **orchestra,** the London Festival Orchestra conducted by Peter Knight, into their rock arrangements. "Nights in White Satin" (1967, rereleased in America in 1972) was among their most popular recordings made with the orchestra. The listening guide on page 204 is intended to point out musical complexities in the **meter** and form of the piece, as well as the ways orchestral instruments have been combined with the rock guitar, bass, and drums.

Listening Guide

"Nights in White Satin"
as recorded by the Moody Blues (1967)

Tempo: The basic tempo is 52 beats per minute, with four beats in each bar and each beat subdivided into three equal parts. Technically, the time signature is twelve-eight (12/8) and is notated with each of the four slow beats (at 52 per minute) made up of three **eighth notes,** putting twelve of those eighth notes into each bar.

Form: A solo singer sings a four-bar melody (the A section) two times through. The melody is based on an **aeolian mode** (natural notes from A to A), accompanied by the orchestra backing the rock instruments.

The orchestra grows louder for a four-bar B section.

Another two A sections and one B section with a one-bar extension are followed by a twelve-bar instrumental section that features flute, plucked acoustic guitar, and strings with a rock drummer accenting the backbeat.

The instrumental interlude is followed by two more A sections and one B section with an extension.

The recording continues with a dramatic orchestral statement based on the A and B themes (melodies).

Features: The recording begins with a swirl of sound played by the strings, flute, harp, and chimes before the drums enter to establish a beat pattern for a two-bar introduction.

The drums maintain a fairly strong backbeat through most of the recording, but drop out for the orchestral finale.

The recording concludes with the recitation of a poem that conveys the same mood as the rest of the lyrics. (The poem is not included in some shortened versions of the recording.)

Lyrics: Love has disoriented the singer. The theme of endless love letters is used to express a general sense of unrequited love.

Billboard pop charts: number two for two weeks; British hit singles: number nineteen

It was very difficult to work with a large orchestra on a regular basis. Rehearsals had to be organized well in advance, and touring with so many musicians was prohibitively expensive. In order to keep the orchestral sound, the Moody Blues found that they could use an electromechanical instrument, the mellotron, to imitate the orchestra. In fact, the mellotron was used in addition to the orchestra in the recording of "Nights in White Satin." The mellotron supplied them with a variety of electronic effects, such as the wavering of tone on the word *strange* in the recording "Isn't Life Strange?" (1972), in addition to various orchestral timbres. The Moody Blues did from time to time work with orchestral musicians, but they never again added any of those instrumentalists to their regular personnel. They continued to tour into the two-thousands.

The mellotron was soon used by many groups that wanted to add orchestral effects to their rock sound. Among those was **Genesis,** formed in 1966 by singer/flutist Peter Gabriel, keyboard player Tony Banks, bassist/guitarist Mike Rutherford, and guitarist Anthony Phillips. They went through three drummers until Phil Collins joined late in 1970. Phillips left in 1970 and was replaced by Steve Hackett.

During the early seventies, Genesis created multi-movement works with classical overtones for their albums. Elaborate stage acts were also becoming very popular by that time, and Genesis used their music to create a surrealistic, at times even grotesque, fantasy world that they portrayed on stage, with Gabriel as the central actor making many outrageous costume and character changes. David Bowie, Queen, Roxy Music, and other glitter performers were concentrating on theatrical stage performances around the same time and were also using classical instruments and musical forms. As far as the music was concerned, little separated some of the British glitter groups from the progressive-rock groups. It was the glorification and celebration of androgynous sexuality, which was central to glitter but not to progressive rock, that separated the two styles more than any specific musical characteristic.

For one of Genesis's most dramatic productions, *The Lamb Lies Down on Broadway* (1974), Gabriel played Rael, a New York City street punk who goes through a process of self-discovery when he finds himself transported to a surrealistic netherworld. Although Genesis started out as a group of four equally productive writers, Gabriel wrote the majority of the lyrics for *The Lamb,* and his stage performances had become the focal point of the band for much of the audience. When Gabriel decided to leave Genesis in 1975, they were faced with more than the need for a singer. They emerged with a somewhat altered style and image when Phil Collins assumed the double role of lead vocalist and drummer. Collins had a singing voice that was strikingly similar to Peter Gabriel's, and he had a dramatic flair that enabled him to portray some of the characters Gabriel had, though he never attempted to play these roles quite as elaborately as Gabriel. On tours, Genesis added another drummer so Collins could concentrate on singing. The group gravitated toward a more commercial pop sound from the late seventies and into the eighties with several top-ten hits, including the title track to their *Invisible Touch* (1986) album. More successes followed with their 1991 album *We Can't Dance,* which was followed by live albums during the next two years. After an extended break, Genesis regrouped in 2006 and continued to tour.

After leaving Genesis, **Peter Gabriel** (born in 1950) recorded a series of albums, all entitled *Peter Gabriel,* followed by *So* in 1986, which strayed from his interest in science fiction–styled futurism and classical timbres and instead incorporated musical internationalism through the addition of instruments and vocal sounds from Asia and Africa. Gabriel's inclusion of Senegalese singer Youssou N'Dour helped introduce N'Dour to Gabriel's fans, resulting in N'Dour's inclusion on the 1988 Amnesty International tour with Gabriel, Sting, Bruce Springsteen, and Tracy Chapman. Gabriel won a Grammy for Best New Age Performance for his music on the soundtrack for the movie *The Last Temptation of Christ* (1989). His personal life and broken love relationships were the subject of his 1992 album *Us,* which he followed with the live double album *Secret World Live* (1994). Gabriel has worked on many projects during the two-thousands from creating sound for video games to performing at the 2006 Olympic games.

Another rock group to perform with orchestral instruments was **Procol Harum.** They formed in 1966 and gained international success with "A Whiter Shade of Pale." For their studio albums, group members who normally played piano, organ, guitar, bass guitar, and drums added to the studio orchestra by overdubbing such instruments as celeste, marimba, recorder, conga drums, tabla, and tambourine. The group's singer/pianist, Gary Brooker, did most of their orchestral arrangements. After recording five albums with studio orchestras, the group decided that orchestral musicians played their best in live situations, and to capture the brilliance of live performance they recorded *Procol Harum Live: In Concert with the Edmonton Symphony Orchestra* (1971). This project was a success because "Conquistador," which had been ignored when released in 1967, became an international hit when revamped and recorded on the live album. Procol Harum changed membership often, but Brooker, organist Matthew Fisher, guitarist Robin Trower, and lyricist Keith Reid lasted through most of their time together. They disbanded in 1977 and reformed in 1991 and continued to record and tour into the twenty-first century.

A blues revival band from Blackpool, England, in the late sixties, the John Evan Band included singer/flutist/guitarist/saxophonist Ian Anderson (born in 1947 in Scotland, but raised in Blackpool). When the John Evan Band broke up, Anderson decided to form a group of his own, calling it **Jethro Tull** (after the author of an eighteenth-century book on agriculture). At first the group played more blues and jazz than anything resembling what was soon to be called progressive rock; in fact, one of their earliest successful concert performances took place at the British National Jazz and Blues Festival in 1968.

Although jazz continued to be an important part of Jethro Tull's style, their first connection with progressive rock appeared on the group's second album, *Stand Up* (1969), which featured Anderson's flute playing on their recording of the "Bourrée" from the Suite in E Minor for lute by German composer J. S. Bach (1685–1750). Anderson used a distinctive flute technique that included humming or fluttering his tongue while blowing into the flute. While his tone was far from being a traditional classical sound, it had an energetic drive that worked well for Jethro Tull's music. The idea of **flutter-tonguing** and singing into wind instruments had been used by avant-garde classical instrumentalists and composers who were searching for new sounds on traditional instruments. Jethro Tull's recording of the Bach "Bourrée" started out with the original two-part composition, varied rhythmically using uneven beat subdivisions. After the original music was played, the group played variations that exemplified the continuing influence of jazz and blues on their style. In addition to using the flute, which was heard more in classical and jazz music than in rock, many of Jethro Tull's recordings used a synthesizer to add orchestral timbres.

As a lyricist, Ian Anderson used his music to make statements about society and politics. The album *Aqualung* (1971), for example, though not sacrilegious in general terms, contained songs that were clearly critical of organized religion. In later years he spoke out against, among other things, nuclear power and drug abuse. After taking some time off from recording for a period in the mideighties to fish for salmon in Scotland, he regrouped Jethro Tull with a modernized approach to blues-styled rock, adding distorted guitar timbres on his album *Crest of a Knave* (1987), for which the band won a Grammy for Best Hard Rock/Metal Performance. Many of the group's long-faithful fans were happy that they won a Grammy but questioned their inclusion in that particular category. Jethro Tull continued to record and tour in the nineties and early two-thousands, but with less commercial success than it had known in the past. Anderson also works with his other band, Rubbing Elbows.

One of the most popular of the British progressive-rock groups of the seventies was the **Electric Light Orchestra.** Much more of a "rock orchestra" than the Moody Blues had been, the group consisted of traditional rock instruments—electric guitars, bass, and drums—along with a scaled-down version of an orchestral string section. Guitarist/singer/writer Roy Wood and guitarist/keyboardist/writer/singer Jeff Lynne formed the Electric Light Orchestra in 1971. At that time they were still members of the Move, a rock band that had dabbled in many styles from folk to psychedelic rock, but they ended up concentrating more on an orchestral sound and the Move soon disbanded. For the first recording by their new orchestra, *Move Enterprises Ltd. Presents the Services of the Electric Light Orchestra* (1972, released in America as *No Answer*), they used the Move's drummer, Bev Bevan, and two temporary members, one playing several wind instruments, and the other, violin.

An inevitable split occurred between the two writers, Wood and Lynne, because each had different ideas about the musical direction of their new orchestral sound. Wood wanted the rock orchestra to be styled after Phil Spector's wall-of-sound productions of the early sixties, and Lynne wanted to work toward the more classically

oriented productions the Beatles had made with George Martin. Wood finally left the Electric Light Orchestra to form another group, Wizzard, and Lynne gradually molded the Electric Light Orchestra to fit his own plans. His rock orchestra included Lynne on guitar, keyboards, and vocals; a keyboard player who often used synthesizer; a drummer, a violinist, two cellists, and a string bass player. The four members from the string section of an orchestra, a synthesizer to add wind or percussive effects, and heavily overdubbed vocals enabled them to create a thick orchestral and choral sound, played with a rock backbeat. The Electric Light Orchestra developed their stage show into an elaborate space-age extravaganza with a giant spaceship and a laser display as part of the act.

> **"I had the idea for ELO. . . . I thought 'wouldn't it be great to get a band together and instead of advertising for a guitarist, advertise for a French horn player or a cellist 'cause there must be young people around that play those instruments that like rock and roll.'"**
>
> –Roy Wood of ELO

Progressive Rock Based on Classical Forms

Groups that added orchestral instrumentation to what was basically a rock-band setup created an extremely popular form of progressive rock, but not one requiring a great deal of classical training on the part of the rock musicians. Another style of progressive rock was played by musicians with more extensive classical backgrounds. These musicians composed original works in classical structures, but they also recorded their own versions of well-known classical pieces. This is not to say they were writing "classical" music. They were rock musicians playing for a rock audience but adding a rock rhythm section to what was based on a classical work or their own work set in a classically influenced form.

Yes, one of the first and longest lasting of the progressive-rock supergroups, was formed in 1968 by singer/percussionist Jon Anderson, guitarist/singer Peter Banks, keyboardist Tony Kaye, bassist Chris Squire, and drummer Bill Bruford. The members of Yes were interested in creating classically structured music that included full-group vocal harmonies. The group's personnel changed during their career, including at various times guitarist Steve Howe, drummer Alan White, and keyboard players Rick Wakeman, Geoff Downes, and Patrick Moraz. Early in their career, Yes used the synthesizer to add new instrumental timbres and to fill out their sound without the use of an orchestra. However, eventually their music developed around the virtuosic technical skills of its instrumentalists instead of concentrating on synthesized orchestral sounds.

All the members of Yes were competent soloists, and their album *Fragile* (1971)—recorded when the

Listening Guide

"Roundabout"
as recorded by Yes (1971)

Tempo: The basic tempo is about 135 beats per minute, with four beats in each bar, although each A section varies the beat pattern by including one two-beat bar.

Form and Features: The recording opens with a crescendo of sound probably produced by playing a tape-recorded sound backward.

The taped sound dissolves into an acoustic guitar playing **harmonics** and a classically influenced melodic pattern in a free tempo.

At the end of this introduction, the guitar plays a progression establishing the tempo of the song, and a very active bass and the drums enter playing an eight-bar vamp. The vamp pattern continues under the beginning of the vocal line.

The first verse of lyrics is sung to the A section of music, which is ten four-beat bars long, but the regular beat pattern is broken by two-beat bars both at the beginning and at the ending of the verse.

The music to the A section is repeated to the lyrics of the second verse.

The B section follows the two A sections, and it also changes from two-beat to four-beat bars, giving a feeling of complex irregularity to the beat pattern.

The drums maintain a strong backbeat, which remains steady through each two- and four-beat pattern.

After another A and B section, an instrumental section features a bass riff, a synthesizer, and many percussion effects.

When the A theme and vocal line return, a synthesizer plays a repetitious pattern very similar to the minimalistic themes used by modern composer Philip Glass.

The synthesizer pattern continues behind the acoustic guitar, which returns to the theme played in the introduction.

A section of improvisation on the organ is backed by guitar and bass with the drums maintaining a strong backbeat.

The A and B sections repeat and are followed by group vocals, with one group of three singers overdubbed on top of another group of three singers.

The recording ends with a repetition of part of the guitar solo that was played at the beginning. Classical composers also often closed their works with a repetition of a musical idea from the beginning to balance the form.

Lyrics: The lyrics can be interpreted many different ways, but it is helpful to know that roundabouts are English traffic circles, where drivers can change their course of direction if they wish.

Billboard pop charts: number thirteen

group included Anderson, Howe, Wakeman, Squire, and Bruford—had each musician taking a turn as the featured performer on a track, with ensemble playing on other tracks. One of *Fragile*'s full-group tracks, "Roundabout," is discussed in the listening guide on page 207. It reached number thirteen on the U.S. pop charts.

> **"That kind of using the classical structure as a basis to make music, rather than pop music, that's where we were heading when we did *Fragile*."**
>
> –Jon Anderson of Yes

The high level of musicianship of each member of Yes is obvious in their recording of "Roundabout," both in the way the individual instruments are played and in the careful way they play as a group without getting in each other's way. The arrangement is quite complex and is played with the sensitivity one would expect of classical musicians.

Yes followed *Fragile* with other albums using the classical multimovement form called a **suite.** In the eighteenth century, suites (such as the suite for lute whose theme Ian Anderson borrowed for Jethro Tull's recording of "Bourrée") were collections of instrumental pieces based on dance rhythms and forms. Dances themselves were not important to progressive-rock performers or to their general audience, and Yes freely used the title "suite" to identify classically influenced multimovement compositions such as those on their *Close to the Edge* (1972) and *Relayer* (1974) albums.

Yes had essentially broken up by the early eighties but was then reformed by Anderson, Kaye, Squire, White, and a new guitarist from Johannesburg, South Africa, Trevor Rabin. That version of Yes charted a number-one hit single with "Owner of a Lonely Heart" (1983). After several more breaks and personnel changes, Yes was back on tour in 2008.

Another group with constantly changing membership, but no questions about who owned the name, was **King Crimson.** Robert Fripp (born in 1946), a guitarist with a background in both classical music and jazz, was the central and only constant figure in King Crimson, which he formed in 1969. For King Crimson's music, Fripp melded together avant-garde electronics, jazz, and psychedelic effects.

In addition to his work with King Crimson, Fripp experimented with avant-garde electronic sound effects with British composer/producer Brian Eno during the early to middle seventies. They used two tape recorders to develop a sound-delay box that Fripp could use with his guitar, a sound system they called Frippertronics. Fripp had become increasingly interested in experimental electronic work and disbanded King Crimson to have more time to spend on projects of that type during the late seventies.

Fripp reformed King Crimson in 1981, this time with drummer Bill Bruford, formerly of Yes. Their new work drew on some of the musical variety and richness of their past work, as well as incorporating touches of African polyrhythms. One of Fripp's greatest concerns was to avoid the tendency of reverting to older styles and creating, in his words, a "dinosaur" sound. In hopes of maintaining a fresh approach, Fripp outlined rules for the group to follow, based on such ideas as the importance of each musician maintaining musical independence from other band members while still listening carefully and allowing the others' ideas to be heard. Fripp wanted freedom and spontaneity for each of the musicians while still keeping unity within the group sound.

Fripp formed a new version of King Crimson in 1994 with former members guitarist/singer Adrian Belew, bassist Tony Levin, and drummer Bill Bruford, along with new members drummer Pat Mastelotto and Trey Gunn, who played the Chapman stick, a twelve-string instrument that functions as both a bass and a guitar. That band is still touring in the two-thousands.

Many British progressive-rock groups made recordings based on works from standard classical repertoire, but few recorded as many extended classically based works as **Emerson, Lake and Palmer.** Keyboardist Keith Emerson had played with another British progressive-rock group, the Nice, between 1967 and 1970, during which time they arranged and recorded an "Intermezzo" from the *Karelia Suite* by Jean Sibelius (1893) and "America," a medley of themes from Leonard Bernstein's musical *West Side Story* (1957). Guitarist and bass player Greg Lake came to the group from King Crimson, and drummer Carl Palmer had previously played in a number of British rhythm and blues groups, including the Crazy World of Arthur Brown.

Having studied classical piano, Emerson was familiar with Russian composer Modest Mussorgsky's (1839–1881) multimovement piano work entitled *Pictures at an Exhibition* (1874), a musical description of a visit to an art gallery. Individual sections of the music evoked the moods of particular works of art that were on display, and each of those was connected by the "Promenade," which represented the viewer walking from one work to the next. Emerson, Lake and Palmer's *Pictures at an Exhibition* (1971) was the group's own arrangement of some of the sections of Mussorgsky's composition: "Promenade," "The Gnome," "The Old Castle," "The Hut of Baba Yaga," and "The Great

Gate of Kiev," with the addition of new "picture" sections: "The Sage," "The Curse of Baba Yaga," and "Blues Variation," as well as the occasional addition of lyrics written by Greg Lake. *Pictures at an Exhibition* was one of four top-ten hit albums by Emerson, Lake and Palmer. Emerson, Lake and Palmer broke up to work with other bands during the eighties but regrouped in 1991. They broke up again in 1998.

Progressive Rock Influenced by Avant-Garde Trends

While the Electric Light Orchestra and others went from live orchestras to mellotrons to enhance their sound, and Emerson, Lake and Palmer and others played elaborate arrangements of classical compositions, other rock musicians explored more avant-garde compositional styles. Two of the most important twentieth-century styles to influence rock music were **minimalism** and the organization of sound effects not traditionally used in music, both natural and electronic, into musical compositions. Minimalism is also called **systematic music,** and both terms describe the characteristics of the sounds they represent, as the music involves systematically organized repetition of a minimal amount of musical material. The musical material is most often one or more motives (short bits of melody), and the systematic organization usually involves some sort of variation, such as gradual changes in length, melody notes, or rhythms through many repetitions. This style became popular through the works of composers like Terry Riley, Steve Reich, and Philip Glass during the sixties, having originated in part through influences of music from parts of Asia and Africa.

Composer Edgard Varèse (1883–1965) pioneered another important avant-garde style by incorporating non-musical sounds into musical compositions as early as the thirties. He created music he described as "organized sound," including such effects as hammered anvils, sleigh bells, and sirens, along with traditional percussion instruments such as bells and drums of various kinds, in his work *Ionisation* (1931). He later manipulated and organized natural and electronic sounds for his *Poème électronique,* composed for the Brussels World's Fair of 1958.

Among those rock groups who used both minimalism and nonmusical sounds effectively was **Pink Floyd.** A blues-loving art student who played the guitar and sang, Syd Barrett (Roger Keith Barrett) joined with friends from a London architectural school to form the Pink Floyd Sound in 1965. The name was a tribute to two blues musicians from the Carolinas, Pink Anderson and Floyd Council. The group's early repertoire of traditional blues and Rolling Stones–style rhythm and blues was expanded to include wandering psychedelic improvisations and light shows as Barrett became increasingly involved with the use of psychedelic drugs. However, it was the shorter compositions "Arnold Layne" and "See Emily Play" that were their most popular early recordings.

The Pink Floyd Sound shortened their name to Pink Floyd and released their first album, *The Piper at the Gates of Dawn,* in 1967. The album included some of Barrett's most creative experiments in special effects, such as sounds that jumped from the left speaker to the right speaker in "Interstellar Overdrive." On the tour following the album, Barrett's desire to be completely original and, probably more important, his excessive use of LSD, were the source of many problems. He became undependable at concerts, and he refused to lip sync to songs for television appearances. When Pink Floyd returned to Britain, they decided it was necessary to add another guitarist, David Gilmour, even before they had the nerve to fire Barrett. Barrett managed to stay with the group to contribute to "Jugband Blues" and "Remember a Day" on their *A Saucerful of Secrets* album (1968), but he soon drifted away, leaving the group to continue without him. Roger Waters and Richard Wright shared the bulk of the songwriting duties in Barrett's place.

> **Syd's moving out meant that we had to start writing. . . . In fact, his leaving made us pursue the idea of the extended epic and a more classically constructed idea of music.**
> —Roger Waters of Pink Floyd

Pink Floyd continued to include extended psychedelic improvisations with repeated electronic sound effects in their music, and they soon attracted the attention of British movie producers and classical composers who were interested in electronics. The spatial music on some of their albums was recorded for movie soundtracks. Electronics expert Ron Geesin worked with them on the recording of their experimental *Atom Heart Mother* album (1970), and after the album's release, they became the first rock group to be invited to perform at the Montreux Classical Music Festival.

Many experimental classical composers had become interested in the idea of using randomly gathered material as the basis for a sound collage. The Beatles' producer, George Martin, had used the idea when he spliced together pieces of prerecorded tapes as sound effects on the Beatles' *Sgt. Pepper's Lonely Hearts Club Band* album (1967). For their *Meddle* album (1971), Pink Floyd

ROGER WATERS

RICK WRIGHT

NICK MASON

DAVE GILMOUR

PINK FLOYD

Pink Floyd publicity photo
ads 1973

decided to experiment further with the organization of new but randomly produced sounds. "Echoes," which took up one entire side of the album, was made up of bits of material taped by band members who had gone into the recording studio individually and recorded whatever ideas came to them at the moment, without concern for any general scheme, key, chord progression, or other kind of unifying device. The segmentation and organization of the tapes came later when the pieces of tape were put together for the recording. Also from the *Meddle* album, "One of These Days" used Varèse's idea of including nontraditional sounds in a piece of music; it also included some of the repetitious but slowly changing electronic patterns that minimalist composers were using.

Roger Waters (born in 1944), who had become the group's principal writer, wanted to create a concept album out of an idea he had used for the cycle of songs titled "Eclipse," which the band had performed in concert in 1972. The concept came from his own past and his feelings of alienation, depression, and even paranoia over the fact that he had grown up without a father (his father died when his plane was shot down during World War II). After many months of work on the song cycle, it grew into an album that was the longest-lasting success of Pink Floyd's career, *The Dark Side of the Moon* (1973). Beginning and ending with a heartbeat, the album cuts were joined by the insane muttering, screaming, and demonic laughter of the depressed protagonist.

Listening Guide

"Money"
as recorded by Pink Floyd (1973)

Tempo: The tempo is about 120 beats per minute, with seven (or four followed by three) beats in each bar through most of the recording, but in one part of the instrumental section there are four beats per bar.

Form: The form and chord progression are based on the twelve-bar blues in a minor key.

Two twelve-bar A verses are followed by a twelve-bar instrumental section that features a funk-style tenor saxophone solo along with keyboard, bass, and drums.

After the instrumental chorus featuring the saxophone, the beat pattern changes from seven to four per bar, and three twenty-four-bar instrumental sections feature the guitar as a solo instrument. The twenty-four bars continue to follow the blues progression, with each bar of the progression doubled in length.

The seven-beat pattern returns just before the singer returns to repeat the A section.

The four-beat-per-bar pattern returns at the end of the song.

Features: The recording begins with the sounds of old-fashioned cash registers ringing and their change drawers opening. Those sounds fall into the seven-beat pattern that is then picked up by the bass when it enters.

After the bass establishes its pattern, the drums enter, accenting the second, fourth, and sixth beats of the seven-beat pattern. The effect is quite different from a standard rock backbeat that accents beats two and four of a four-beat pattern, because the four-beat pattern allows for exactly every other beat to be accented as one pattern leads into another. With the seven beats in this recording, the accents are placed on every other beat until the final beat number seven (which is not accented) goes to beat one (which is also not accented), resulting in two unaccented beats in a row. Two bars of a standard rock four-beat pattern and two of the seven-beat pattern used in "Money" are notated as follows:

The bass line, which repeats a seven-beat pattern throughout most of the recording, changes to a four-beat pattern during the instrumental section that uses four-beat patterns.

The recording ends with casual conversation that continues into the next album cut.

Lyrics: The lyrics constitute a satirical commentary on money and its effects on people. A sense of sarcasm used in the first half of the song mocks the wealthy. The second half is a vignette of life among the "down and out" underclass.

Billboard pop charts: number thirteen

"Money," a popular track from the album, included the nontraditional musical sounds of rhythmically organized ringing cash registers, but more interesting musically was its rhythmic organization using seven-beat bars. To a non-musician, who most likely would not think to count the beats but would still be used to the feel of the standard rock four-beat bar, the effect of seven-beat sections was slightly, inexplicably discomforting. The seven-beat pattern did break and revert to a standard four-beat pattern during the last part of the instrumental improvisation section, but the seven-beat pattern returned just before the voice reentered. Also important to the overall effect of the recording of "Money" was the constant repetition of a bass line with changing melodic lines above it. A listening guide to the recording is on page 211. "Money" reached number thirteen on the U.S. pop charts.

The Dark Side of the Moon was enormously successful, and planning a follow-up album was difficult. Pink Floyd reminisced about their early relationship with Syd Barrett, who had dropped out of their lives, and the *Wish You Were Here* album (1975) was a tribute to him. Their long-lost member actually appeared in the studio while the group was finishing the recording of the song "Shine on You Crazy Diamond," but he left as quietly as he had entered, unrecognized by his former colleagues. He had been hospitalized for LSD-related mental and emotional problems and was not able to care for himself or work effectively. Roger Waters had not gotten over his own depressed emotional state and used his songs to express his feelings about having lost his father in addition to having lost Barrett. An inflatable airplane that was made to crash in front of the stage during the tour for the albums *Wish You Were Here* and *The Dark Side of the Moon* served as a physical reminder of his father's death.

Waters portrayed human beings as animals when he wrote songs for the album *Animals* (1977). His view of humanity was reminiscent of George Orwell's in his book *Animal Farm* (1945). *Animals* included such songs as "Pigs (Three Different Ones)," "Sheep," and "Dogs." A gigantic inflated pink pig floated in the air above the band during concerts on the *Animals* tour and became a symbol that the group used again in later years.

It was two years before Pink Floyd produced another album, and when *The Wall* (1979) was released, it served as a very personal view into the psyche of Roger Waters. He was pessimistic about every aspect of life in modern society. He found no solace in his relationships with his mother and wife, and he viewed formal education as confining and as inhibiting freedom of thought. That view of education was clearly expressed in the song "Another Brick in the Wall (Part 2)," the music of which was repetitious and (as performed in the movie version) featured a large group of expressionless children singing along. In general, *The Wall* was about a young man who acted out his feelings of alienation by building a wall around himself, only to find that he was susceptible to decay from within and that no meaningful hope for the future existed. On stage, Pink Floyd had a wall constructed between them and their audience during the show. After the wall crashed into a smoky mess, band members wandered through the debris in childlike confusion. The wall set was too elaborate to carry throughout a normal tour and was used only in London, New York, and Los Angeles. A movie called *The Wall* was made in 1982 featuring Bob Geldof (lead singer for the Boomtown Rats) as the lost and unhappy protagonist. Many of the characters' illusions were portrayed through wildly psychedelic animated sequences.

The Final Cut (1983) was Pink Floyd's last album with Roger Waters. Waters's separation from Pink Floyd created a legal war because Waters felt he was the most essential person in the band and the other members had no business continuing to use the name Pink Floyd or the symbol of the floating pig in his absence. The group's album *A Momentary Lapse of Reason* (1987) was very successful, and Waters's old bandmates had become his unwanted competition. Pink Floyd continued on, seemingly not missing Waters at all. Their 1994 album *Division Bell* hit number one on the U.S. album charts, and its instrumental cut, "Marooned," won a Grammy. Pink Floyd essentially broke up in 1996, although they regrouped a few times for concerts in the two-thousands. Keyboardist Richard Wright died in 2008.

For the most part, progressive rock was a British phenomenon, at least when it began in the late sixties. Some American groups, such as the Tubes, performed a theatrical version of progressive rock, but most of their albums were more appreciated by critics than by large numbers of fans. The one American whose work paralleled many of the avant-garde characteristics and experimentation of the British artists was **Frank Zappa** (1940–1993). Zappa played rhythm and blues and rock guitar but became interested in contemporary experimental art music by the composers Edgard Varèse, Igor Stravinsky (1882–1971), and Karlheinz Stockhausen (born in 1928). Varèse was among the first composers to gain acceptance for musical works that included sounds played by nontraditional musical instruments. Stravinsky became known for his dynamic use of complex rhythmic patterns, and Stockhausen had gained much attention for his work with electronics and spatial effects in performance. Although Zappa's music was influenced by many rock and jazz styles as well, the rhythms and timbres of modern art composers often flavored his style.

Frank Zappa (1970)

Zappa gained a reputation for more than just the sound of his music, however; he became, for many, a spokesperson for freedom of expression in a world where people claimed to be free but blindly followed pop trends. Many of Zappa's views about the importance of individual freedom were similar to those of the Beats. With his band of constantly changing members, the Mothers of Invention, Zappa aimed attacks at American notions about "respectability" in such songs as "Plastic People" and "America Drinks and Goes Home." He followed that by taking a stab at the tastes of some of his own fans by mocking the Beatles with an album called *We're Only in It for the Money* (1967). He targeted roles and attitudes he thought lacked substance such as phony conformity among those involved in the hippie counterculture in San Francisco and the gutlessness of the punk movement in Hollywood.

> " I don't know whether doing emotional music is a mark of excellence. That's been one of my downfalls with rock critics, 'cause they all seem to have this feeling that the more emotional it is, the better it is. And that's not my aesthetic at all. "
>
> –Frank Zappa

Zappa liked to tell stories through his music and often varied the sound of the music to fit the story. His first top-one-hundred hit single, "Don't Eat the Yellow Snow," was number eighty-six on the pop charts and a good example of this type of little drama. Zappa's *Apostrophe (')* (1974)

album includes an extended version of "Don't Eat the Yellow Snow." *Apostrophe (')* reached number ten on the album charts. A listening guide is on page 214.

Because Zappa often spoke out for freedom of expression, he opposed any form of censorship. His album *Joe's Garage, Acts 1, 2, and 3* (1979) was an effort to create a rock opera that expressed his hatred of censorship by describing a mythical time when music was declared to be illegal. In 1986, the album *Frank Zappa Meets the Mothers of Prevention* had a "Warning/Guarantee" label suggesting anyone who would curtail freedom of speech was dangerous to society. The label was an obvious dig at parents who had organized a group to require warnings on rock album covers to prevent their children's exposure to objectionable material.

> " Censorship, in effect, is turning the United States into a police state, as far as ideas go. It's not about children learning dirty words. It's about putting a lid on ideas. "
>
> –Frank Zappa

The language Zappa used kept many of his recordings off the radio, but his albums continued to sell well. When he went further than his record company would allow, he formed his own recording company. Even with his own recording studio and record label, however, Zappa still depended on Mercury Records to distribute his albums to record stores. His arrangement with his distribution company was working well until he wrote and recorded the song "I Don't Wanna Get Drafted," which criticized President

Listening Guide

"Don't Eat the Yellow Snow"
(single version)
as recorded by Frank Zappa (1974)

Tempo: The recording has three sections. The beginning tempo is approximately 138 beats per minute with seven beats in each bar. That is followed by a short double-time section (twice the speed of the beginning) with two beats per bar. The last and longest section has a tempo of approximately 46 beats per minute with four beats in each bar.

Form: A one-bar bass riff is played twice as an introduction and then continues to repeat another eleven times with lyric lines inserted at irregular times above it. That is followed by a double-time section made up of two repetitions of a little four-bar (two beats per bar, where each bar is equal to a single beat of the previous section) phrase. The last section is made up of thirty full four-beat bars and then an abrupt interruption after the first two beats of a last bar.

Features: Even beat subdivisions are used throughout the recording.

The sound of wind can be heard during the beginning of the story describing the cold.

Backup group vocals respond at the ends of several of the lead vocal lines.

The short double-time section has group vocals sung in a rapid patter style.

A descending bass line leads into the final section where most of the lyrics are almost spoken.

Most of that last section has a single-bar bass riff repeated, although it varies at times. The drums accent a backbeat through most of it as well. The third bar of that section has a little jazzy trumpet line being played in the background and syncopations in the rhythm section. Short flourishes played by an electric lead guitar, a trumpet, and a horn section respond to various different lyric phrases.

The final section ends abruptly with an interruption played by a marimba and a horn section.

Lyrics: The song is about a dream in which the singer is an Eskimo who defends his seal against a fur trader by rubbing snow with dog urine in it ("yellow snow") into his eyes, blinding him. The fur trader reacts by rubbing a "dog doo" snow cone into the dreamer's eyes, temporarily blinding him. One senses that the story is a metaphor for the coercive way in which members of society treat each other.

Billboard pop charts: number eighty-six

Carter's reinstatement of the military draft, and Mercury Records refused to distribute it. The only way Zappa could think of to get out from under the control of distribution companies was to bypass both the distributors and the record retailers and to accept mail orders directly from his fans. He did just that, calling his new mail-order company Barking Pumpkin. (Many of the Barking Pumpkin albums eventually became available in stores through CBS International.)

Despite his reputation as a rock guitarist and social critic, Zappa's abilities as a composer were taken seriously by others in the classical field, and composer/conductor Pierre Boulez commissioned Zappa to compose a suite of seven dances called *The Perfect Stranger* (1984). The recording was conducted by Boulez and played by musicians from his Ensemble InterContemporain. In 1988, Zappa's *Jazz from Hell* won a Grammy for Best Rock Instrumental in 1987. Zappa spent much of the late eighties and early nineties remastering his earlier works for release on CD and recording new ones. He died of prostate cancer in 1993. Both as a musician and as a social critic, Zappa became successful in many different areas of contemporary music and never failed to make his beliefs and observations clearly understood.

Progressive Rock with Roots in Hard Rock

Within the genre of hard rock, **Rush** was one group that spent much of its lengthy career exploring sounds outside of its Led Zeppelin–based roots. Yet Rush's music remained sufficiently powerful and distortion oriented to still be considered on the outskirts of heavy metal. The Canadian power trio's beginnings lay in the youthful friendship between classical-turned-rock guitarist Alex Lifeson and bass player Geddy Lee. They formed a guitar, bass, and drums trio to play Led Zeppelin and Cream covers at various high school dances and clubs. Neil Peart replaced their first drummer in 1974 and also became their lyricist.

Rush began to separate from their hard-rock roots with their album *Fly by Night* (1975). The music was still loud and heavy, and song themes about the power of evil still connected them with British heavy metal, but they began to use extended classical forms in multimovement works. Such progressive-rock bands as Yes had used classical forms before, but the idea was rare in heavy metal. The most successful example of that structure was "By-Tor & the Snow Dog," for which Canada recognized

Rush with a Juno award, the equivalent of an American Grammy, as best group.

Early in their career, Rush played out science fiction stories through some of their songs and albums. The album *2112* (1976), for example, was built around the theme of one human being battling the forces of a very depersonalized society in the year 2112. They also occasionally used their songs to make social or political statements. "The Trees" (1978) was based on Quebec's efforts to secede from Canada, "Distant Early Warning" (1984) expressed fear about the potential dangers associated with both peaceful and wartime use of nuclear power, and "Nobody's Hero" (1993) was about the AIDS crisis. They began to broaden their sound by adding synthesizer to some of their recordings in the early to middle eighties but left that techno style behind in 1989. Although Rush was best known for theme albums, they did end up with one top-forty hit single on the U.S. charts, "New World Man" (1983). The song reached number twenty-one on the U.S. pop charts and number forty-two on the British charts. A listening guide to that recording is included on page 216. Rush was less active between 1997 and 2002 to allow Neil Peart to recover after the deaths of his daughter and wife. The band returned with *Vapor Trails* (2002) and has continued to record and tour in the early two-thousands.

Glitter Rock

The Beat movement spread to England when the Beat writers' works reached British bookstores. The teenaged David Robert Jones read Jack Kerouac's novel *On the Road* (1957) and was impressed by the book's characters who were able to express their feelings of alienation from the conformist middle-class society that surrounded them. Jones himself felt penned in by a family that included an older half-brother who had a number of emotional and

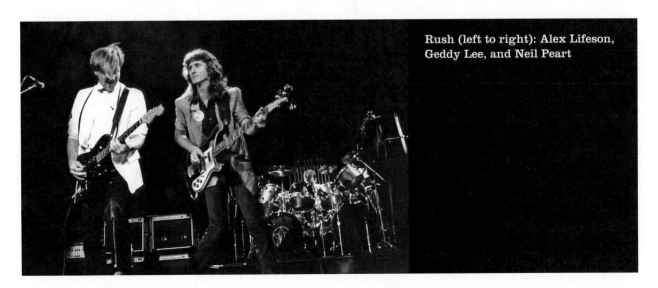

Rush (left to right): Alex Lifeson, Geddy Lee, and Neil Peart

Listening Guide

"New World Man"
as recorded by Rush (1982)

Tempo: The tempo is approximately 160 beats per minute, with four beats in each bar.

Form: A sixteen-bar instrumental introduction is followed by seven sections of unequal lengths. Frequent changes of key keep the sections with similar melodies from forming actual A or B sections, but each section ends with a four-bar instrumental extension or with repetitions of the title text, "New World Man." The first section with vocals includes two lyric lines that begin with "he's a" and "he's got a problem" and is twenty bars long including the instrumental extension with which it ends. That music returns later with vocal lines that begin with those same lyrics but then continue with new lyrics. The next section is twelve bars long, including an instrumental extension. It begins with the words "learning to" the first and third times it is played and the words "trying to" the second time. A third section is sixteen bars long and begins with "he's got to make." Later in the recording a section similar to that begins with "he's not concerned." The recording ends with repetitions of the title text.

Features: Both even and uneven beat subdivisions are used.

The backbeat is accented by the drums.

A single-bar riff pattern played by a synthesizer begins the introduction and continues to repeat through most of the recording.

Other riff patterns one or two bars in length are repeated by the bass at various sections of the recording.

Key changes are frequent, including changes within individual sections.

Lyrics: The song ambiguously embraces the frenetic changes associated with scientific modernity, both celebrating them and expressing a distrust of the new world.

Billboard pop charts: number twenty-one; British hit singles: number forty-two

psychological problems. Thus, the sense of personal freedom demanded by the Beats had great appeal for Jones. Having played saxophone since the age of twelve, Jones began his escape from his family by spending his spare time playing jazz with a band called George and the Dragons. His love of jazz gradually gave way to an interest in rhythm and blues, and by 1963 he was singing with the Hooker Brothers. The Hooker Brothers changed their name to the King Bees, and then to David Jones and the King Bees.

Jones began to frequent London's Mod clubs and left the King Bees to sing with such Mod bands as the Manish Boys and the Lower Third. Allen Ginsberg's demands for acceptance of homosexuality had, along with other anti-establishment movements of the time, sparked a trend of performers wearing androgynous dress in both New York and London. As part of his act, Jones developed such an image, one to which he returned many times during his career. He needed a new stage name after 1966 when the Monkees emerged with their British singer, Davy Jones, and because he wanted his musical art to "cut like a knife through lies," he picked the name Bowie, after the knife. **David Bowie** (born in 1947) was to become one of the first and most influential stars of the glitter movement.

Because of his interest in theater and art (he had also been a commercial artist) Bowie would not simply walk out on stage and sing songs backed by a band. He wanted to create a character for himself and make his performances theatrical experiences. Stanley Kubrick's movie *2001: A Space Odyssey* (1968) and the popular interest in space that was brought on by the American moon landing in 1969

Listening Guide

"Space Oddity"
as recorded by David Bowie (1968)

Tempo: The tempo is approximately 69 beats per minute, with four beats in each bar.

Form: The form is rather complex, with less repetition than in most standard song forms. The introduction is followed by two six-bar A sections, two seven-bar B sections, one six-bar C section, an instrumental section, another B, a five-bar D, another C, and an instrumental ending.

Features: Strummed acoustic guitar gradually increasing in volume is used as an introduction; a snare drum enters, playing a military march beat.

The recording is heavily produced, with a large (or overdubbed) group of string instruments and other orchestral instruments blended into the background. A rhythmically strummed acoustic guitar precedes the instrumental sections.

Electronics and strings playing glissandos give the recording "spacy" sound effects (the string glissandos are the most obvious at the very end of the recording).

The recording does not follow traditional chord progressions in a single key for any length of time; **modulations** (changes of key center) to remote keys add to the effect of instability and the feeling of floating away from home base.

Bowie sings alone but has also overdubbed his voice, producing a duo effect.

Lyrics: The poignant image of an astronaut lost on a space walk separated not only from earth but his own capsule ("tin can"), and helplessly facing his death in the vast void of space, was, interestingly enough, recorded in 1968, before the near disaster of Apollo 13 in which a similar tragedy almost occurred. Not surprisingly, it was a hit in the United States in 1973 after three astronauts were almost lost in space on Apollo 13.

Billboard pop charts: number fifteen; British hit singles: number five and later number one

---

provided the image he was searching for—an astronaut named Major Tom who in Bowie's "Space Oddity" (1969) chose to live in alienation from humanity in space over returning to earth. A listening guide to this recording is on page 217. "Space Oddity" was a number five hit on the British pop charts in 1969 and a number fifteen hit in the United States in 1973. It was back on the British charts as a number one hit in 1975.

Bowie's use of simple strummed acoustic guitar was in contrast with the spacy sound effects of electronic instruments and string glissandos, providing a reminder that the song included characters speaking from both earth and space. His space-age image and sound was one to which he returned during the early seventies with his Ziggy Stardust character, at which time he called his band the Spiders from Mars. In 1980, the astronaut from "Space Oddity" returned in the song "Ashes to Ashes (The Continuing Story of Major Tom)."

> **The chief ingredients were to deviolence the look of Clockwork Orange, evoke the mystery of kabuki and noh theater . . . all I knew it was this otherness, this other world, an alternative reality. . . . I wanted anything but the place that I came from.**
> —David Bowie, about his Ziggy Stardust character

David Bowie

actresses of the forties, wearing an elegant dress, and holding the queen of diamonds playing card in his limp-wristed hand. The glitz and glamour of glitter rock to follow was shaped by that image. The album cover, not surprisingly, was banned in the United States, but the music on the album was very much influenced by the dark, repetitious drone of Lou Reed's New York protopunk group of the late sixties, the Velvet Underground.

In general, defining Bowie's musical style is difficult because he did not adhere to a single style and did not work with a regular band. His music and musicians were always chosen to fit the character he was portraying at the moment. The idea of music being almost secondary to the act itself was at the heart of most glitter rock. The most important component of the genre was the grandiose production that turned rock into theater. Of course, Bowie sometimes did scale down his act to a more conventional musical performance, but it was not then a glitter performance. Whether it was Elton John, Marc Bolan, or Gary Glitter prancing around in sparkling costumes and taunting the audience with whatever sexual images they were displaying at the moment; the art-influenced music of Queen and Roxy Music; the heavy-metal-influenced music of Kiss and Alice Cooper; or in later years, a pop show by Boy George or glam-metal by Bon Jovi, glitter meant one thing—theater.

The British group **Queen** placed itself in the glitter category by virtue of the androgynous implications of its name. Singer Freddie Mercury (Frederick Bulsara),

In 1971 Bowie went beyond androgyny on the cover of the British version of the album *The Man Who Sold the World,* which pictured Bowie relaxing on a day bed with the same sort of hairdo worn by Hollywood movie

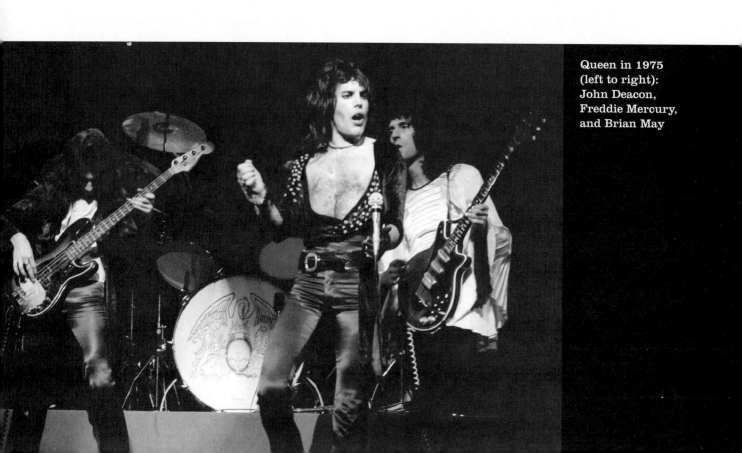

Queen in 1975
(left to right):
John Deacon,
Freddie Mercury,
and Brian May

Listening Guide

"Bohemian Rhapsody"
as recorded by Queen (1975)

Tempo: The tempo is about 72 beats per minute, with four beats per bar in the introduction, but the tempo varies from one section of the recording to another.

Form and
Features: The elaborate group vocals were created by overdubbing the voices of group members Freddie Mercury, Roger Taylor, and Brian May. The soloist, who sings the role of the murderer, is Freddie Mercury.

The mini-opera begins with a cappella group vocals introducing the story and setting the mood in much the way a recitative (sung recitation or dialogue that tells the story) might in a classical opera. The protagonist (Mercury) begins his aria with the second verse of lyrics. He is accompanied by a strong backbeat in the drums that drops out and then reenters. The tempo is slightly faster than the introduction.

Percussion instruments are used to add color to the meanings of the lyrics. Soon after the word *shivers* in the second verse, for example, chimes are used to convey the feeling of shivering.

Although the third verse repeats the melody of the second verse, the rest of the verses change with the dramatic events in the story rather than having the form dictated by standard "song form" types of repetitions.

The fourth verse, or section, is faster than the previous verses (about 144 beats per minute) and uses **antiphonal choruses** (vocal groups that call out and answer one another) to express their positions for and against the release of the murderer. The dramatic way in which one chorus repeats lines just sung by the protagonist is reminiscent of the operetta style of Gilbert and Sullivan.

Heavy bass and distorted guitar sounds add power to the fourth section, in which the murderer begs for his freedom.

The mini-opera ends at a fairly slow tempo (about 80 beats per minute) with a softly sung epilogue about the fact that the drama did not matter that much to the murderer after all. The lyrics and melody heard at the end were used earlier, helping to give a balanced musical form to the piece. The last sound is that of a gong.

Lyrics: The recording is a mini-opera, sung from the perspective of a man who has just committed a murder and confesses it to his mother. One chorus represents a society that begs for leniency and the other a society that wants to get rid of the murderer. Beelzebub (the Devil's sidekick) is ready for him, but the man wants to be free. An epilogue, however, states that ultimately the murderer believes nothing really makes any difference.

Billboard pop charts: number nine and later number two; British hit singles: number one

guitarist Brian May, bassist John Deacon, and drummer Roger Meadows-Taylor were all completing college degrees in fields other than music when they decided to try for rock stardom. They had all done some playing in other groups but did not want Queen to spend years playing in small clubs. Instead, they worked on a demo tape and an elaborate stage act before approaching a record company. When they finally did sell their tape, they were ready for superstardom.

Queen's music was hard rock with heavy-metal-flavored guitar lines, but it also approached progressive rock in its well-crafted arrangements and production techniques. With overdubbed guitar parts and four-part close harmony vocals, they achieved dramatic effects that were unsurpassed in most of the rock music of their time. Their stage show eventually included a touch of the most elaborate genre within classical music with *A Night at the Opera* (1975). From that album, "Bohemian Rhapsody" was a mock operetta ("little opera"), the components of which are discussed in the listening guide on page 219. "Bohemian Rhapsody" was a number one hit in Britain in 1975 and a number nine hit in the United States in early 1976. After being featured in the movie *Wayne's World,* it reentered the U.S. pop charts at number two in 1992.

> **"Freddie always looked like a star and acted like a star, even when he was penniless."**
>
> –Brian May about Freddie Mercury

Queen's music ceased to be so glittery and dramatic during the eighties, and both their hard-rock and classical influences gave way to fifties rockabilly (using Chuck Berry–style guitar lines) with "Crazy Little Thing Called Love" (1980) and the funky "Another One Bites the Dust" (1980). Queen joined forces with glitter star David Bowie for "Under Pressure" in 1981.

As had been the case for many other glitter acts of the seventies, Queen's recordings of the eighties met with reduced success. Their 1991 album *Innuendo* was their last due to the AIDS-related death of their dynamic singer, Freddie Mercury. Remaining group members were joined by stars such as Elton John, David Bowie, and Def Leppard for a memorial concert in 1992. The attention given to "Bohemian Rhapsody" in the movie *Wayne's World* (1992) as well as the release of *Greatest Hits, Classic Queen,* and *Live at Wembley '86* (all 1992) exposed Queen's music to a new, younger audience. Queen reunited in 2004 with a new bass player and added musicians to play guitar and keyboards. Paul Rodgers (formerly from Free and Bad Company) sang, but in order to avoid billing him as Freddie Mercury's replacement, the group was called Queen + Paul Rodgers.

Summary

Progressive rock was so named because it was influenced by styles and characteristics of "art," or "classical," music. It developed out of experimentation during the late sixties in which rock musicians attempted to expand rock from a popular art into one they saw as more elite. Groups such as the Moody Blues, Genesis, Jethro Tull, and the Electric Light Orchestra added orchestral instruments, or synthesized sounds of those instruments, to create a style that was a logical extension of earlier efforts by producers Phil Spector and George Martin. Other groups, such as Yes, King Crimson, and Emerson, Lake and Palmer, were led by classically trained rock musicians who wrote music in the multimovement forms often used in classical music. They also used their groups' rock instrumentation to rearrange and record well-known classical works.

Electronics and sound effects had been used by twentieth-century classical composers, and Roger Waters made use of that idea by incorporating effects such as wind, cash registers, or voices and television laugh tracks into recordings by Pink Floyd. The almost hypnotic effect of constant repetition with subtle variation, developed by minimalist composers Steve Reich and Philip Glass, was also used effectively by Pink Floyd. An American exception in a British-dominated style, Frank Zappa wrote works based on a very free organization of rhythms and polyrhythms much like those used by classical composers.

Whether a progressive-rock group used traditional classical orchestral instruments or electronic or other nontraditional sounds introduced to music by contemporary classical composers, the result was a synthesis of art music and rock music. Critics of the style claimed that the melding of those two dissimilar styles was pretentious, that rock music had its own values without holding itself up against the historical importance of classical traditions. Music listeners disagreed, however, and many forms of progressive rock remained popular with millions of faithful fans all over the globe and continue to be renewed by new bands in the two-thousands. Those new bands are usually referred to as "Prog. Rock" bands.

Sexual ambiguity had been present in rock music before the glitter stars of the early seventies took to the stage with makeup, dresses, and high heels, but it had never before been so blatant. For the purposes of understanding and enjoying the music and the stage shows of the androgynous glitter artists, it did not matter whether the artists were gay, bisexual, or just very convincing actors; the purpose of the music was to enhance the all-important glamorous show. The music of most glitter acts, particularly that of David Bowie, Roxy Music, and Queen, reached beyond the standard rock styles, incorporating other forms of art music that became popular as progressive rock. In a sense, many of the glitter artists' performances themselves became theatrical works of art.

discussion questions

Progressive rock is often called pretentious. Is it? Why does androgyny make some people uncomfortable? To what degree was glitter an expression of homosexuality, and to what degree was it merely rebellion against those who were easily offended by it? Might glitter have reflected or promoted the gay rights movement?

Ska and Reggae

> "*A lot of people expect that reggae has to have a message. Rubbish. Reggae is a beat. You can put a message on top of it, you can put gospel, you can put slackness, you can put on pop. But reggae is a beat.*"
>
> —LLOYD LOVINDEER,
> REGGAE ARTIST AND SOCIAL COMMENTATOR

On his second trip to the New World in 1494, Columbus discovered Jamaica, an island in the Caribbean just south of Cuba. It was then settled by the Spanish, who killed most of the native tribes and brought in African slaves to work the land. The English took it over during the middle of the seventeenth century, and it became part of the British West Indies. The black population grew through several centuries to become the dominant race in a mixture of peoples including indigenous Indians and others originally from various parts of Europe and Asia. By the twentieth century, English had become the principal language of the country, but mixtures of other languages were commonly spoken in small towns outside the main population centers. Jamaica gained its independence from Britain in 1962. The rich mixture of cultures in Jamaica, its closeness to the southern United States—allowing access to AM radio broadcasts—and its historical relationship with Britain all contributed to the development of ska and reggae.

Jamaicans played a type of folk music called **mento,** a slow version of a Cuban-styled rumba combined with African rhythms. The name *mento* evolved from the Spanish word *mentar,* meaning "to mention," referring to the subtle ways their song lyrics, sometimes accompanied by symbolic dance steps, expressed personal complaints or social criticisms. Subtlety was necessary to avoid offending the person or group to whom the criticisms were directed while still getting the point across.

Although European musical instruments were used in Jamaica, mento and other folk music was often performed on homemade flutes and bowed string instruments made out of bamboo. Guitarlike instruments were made from wood with gut strings attached to a resonating gourd. Percussion instruments included drums and rattles of various kinds. Some drums had skins stretched over wooden, clay, or metal chambers, and others were made of bamboo or hollow tree trunks. A coconut shell scraped with a spoon was often part of the percussion section. Because so many languages were commonly spoken in Jamaica, no particular language was exclusively associated with mento. A dialect of English was the most common, and many mento melodies were variants of English folk songs.

During the late forties and early fifties, American rhythm and blues became quite popular in Jamaica, having reached the island by radio and through recordings. Much of the music played by American radio stations during the early sixties, however, had become too pop-styled to suit the Jamaican taste. With radio no longer a dependable source of entertainment, Jamaican disc jockeys set up large sound systems to play the music of performers such as Louis Jordan, Fats Domino, and various doo-wop groups. The disc jockeys played their records from the backs of trucks, creating discothèques out of vacant land in poorer areas of the island. A great deal of competition grew among the disc jockeys, each wanting to attract the largest crowds and make a profit from selling drinks to the dancers. In order to find rhythm and blues records that no other disc jockey had, they traveled to southern cities in the United States like Miami and New Orleans to buy records. The competition was so stiff, in fact, that to keep from revealing details about their new records, the disc jockeys usually even removed the labels.

Ska

As rhythm and blues styles became more familiar to the people of Jamaica, some began to play the music themselves. To the rhythm and blues beat they added characteristics of mento, along with elements of other styles that had reached them by radio, through traveling performers, or on records. A brass style of Cuban origin, reminiscent of that played by Mexican mariachi musicians (but without the exaggerated vibrato of the Mexican players), was sometimes mixed with other styles. Often the Jamaicans would include saxophone solos styled after those in rhythm and blues recordings, or forties jazz- or swing-style improvised solos played on trumpet or trombone. Modern musical instruments were mixed with traditional folk instruments, depending on what was available to a particular group. The style resulting from the combination of all of these musical and instrumental elements was called ska.

Ska combined so many different styles of music that the sound of different groups often varied considerably. The common element was a four-beat pattern based on rhythm and blues, but with some instruments playing a very strong accent on a subdivision (even or uneven) just after each of the four beats. That accent was strong enough to be heard as if it were the main beat, creating a feeling of a delayed beat. For this reason, the ska pattern is often called a *hesitation beat.*

One of the most often recorded instrumental groups was the **Skatalites,** a group that included a brass section made up of four trumpet/fluegelhorn players and two trombonists; a woodwind section of two alto and two tenor saxophonists; and a rhythm section of two guitarists, three keyboard players, one bass player, and three percussionists.

The Skatalites recorded instrumental hits of their own, and backed such vocal groups as the Maytals, the Wailers, and the Heptones. The Skatalites had hits in Jamaica, and their recording of "Guns of Navarone" even made the British charts in 1967.

> **"He [Chris Blackwell] has done so much to make the music of some poor ragged Third World people respected and respectable, just because of how he operates and the breadth of his vision."**
>
> –Makeda, Rastafarian journalist

Records were important in spreading ska's popularity outside of Jamaica. England had communities of people who had immigrated from Jamaica, and ska became popular there. The British often called ska *blue beat* music. "My Boy Lollipop," a record made in Britain by a young Jamaican singer named Millie Small, combined a rock drumbeat with a ska hesitation beat and became a hit single in both Britain and the United States in 1964. "My Boy Lollipop" was produced by Chris Blackwell, a Jamaican of British ancestry who moved to London and used the profit from his hit recording to establish the Island Record Company.

Desmond Dekker (Desmond Dacres, born in 1941 or 1942) knew the future reggae singer Bob Marley when they were teenagers together in Kingston, Jamaica. On Marley's recommendation, Dekker auditioned for Jamaican producer Leslie "King" Kong who helped him organize his

---

The Language of the Jamaican Disc Jockey

Jamaican disc jockeys developed their own set of terms to describe what they did when they played for dance shows. The following list of terms and definitions provides some insight into the disc jockey's techniques. In the early days, the "deejay"/"toaster" and the "selector" duties were performed by the same person. As the practice developed, however, the two jobs were separated so that each person could concentrate on either the record playing or the vocals.

Deejay—The vocalist, also called the toaster.
Dub—From "double"; a recording in which the vocals and some parts of the instrumentals have been removed, usually leaving just bass and drums.

Dub plate—A soft wax record often used by selectors.
Peps—Vocal sounds made by the deejay or toaster to "pep up" a record: "chicka-a-took, chicka-a-took, chicka-a-took."
Rewind—Spinning back a record so that part of it can be played twice in a row.
Selector—The person who plays the records to back up a deejay or toaster.
Toaster—The vocalist, also called the deejay.
Version—An instrumental recording from which the vocals have been removed; sometimes a version also contained newly added instrumental tracks.

backup group, the Aces, and produced his first number-one hit record (in Jamaica), "Honour Thy Father and Mother" (1963). That was the first of many Jamaican hits that eventually gave Dekker the title King of the Bluebeat. His first top-twenty hit in England had the James Bond inspired title "007 (Shanty Town)" (1967). The song was used in the soundtrack of Jimmy Cliff's movie *The Harder They Come* (1972). A listening guide to that recording is included here. "007 (Shanty Town)" was number fourteen on the British pop charts. Dekker's next hit, "Israelites" (1969), was popular in the United States as well as in Britain. His music continued to be popular in Britain through the midseventies. His songs were revived by some of the 2 Tone ska bands in England during the late seventies, and the band the Specials worked with him to record the album *King of Kings* in 1993.

By 1966, ska began to undergo changes in Jamaica. Influences of Memphis soul music by such performers as Wilson Pickett and Booker T. and the MGs brought gospel-style call-and-response vocals and a heavy rhythmic bass line to ska performances. The tempo of the music also slowed down, and the result was a new ska-based style called **rock steady.** "Oh Ba-a-by" by the Techniques and "Rock Steady" by Alton Ellis were both rock steady recordings that became popular in Britain during the late sixties.

Jamaican disc jockeys continued to be the crucial element in disseminating the music to the poor people of Jamaica. Still in competition to outdo one another, and remembering hearing American radio disc jockeys make comments after records had begun playing, Jamaican disc jockeys built on that idea by talking in a rhythmic patter while ska and rock steady records were playing. The practice was called **toasting** when it was no more than rhythmic **patter-talk,** but eventually the talk involved manipulation of the recording during the disc jockey's performance.

Listening Guide

"007 (Shanty Town)"
as recorded by Desmond Dekker
and the Aces (1967)

Tempo: The speed of the beat is approximately 100 beats per minute with four beats in each bar.

Form: After a four-bar instrumental introduction, the song follows the form ABBABB. The A sections are fourteen bars long, and the B ones are eight bars each.

Features: The beat subdivisions are even, keeping the hesitation beat halfway between each two of the primary beats.

The hesitation beats are stressed by a guitarist strumming up (from high to low strings) and a drummer hitting a high-hat on them.

The bass is subtle, generally playing on the second half of the first and third beats (the hesitation beats), the second and fourth beats (the beats that are underlined here: 1 & 2 & 3 & 4 &).

The vocals during three of the B sections are rather fast and rhythmic with slower responses of the words *shanty town.*

The second B section is instrumental.

The general feel of the recording is relaxed and gentle with a concentration on the rhythmic flow.

The recording fades out at the end of the last B section.

Lyrics: Popular movies, specifically the James Bond series and *Ocean's Eleven,* about a group of army buddies planning to rob several Las Vegas casinos, romanticize the life of gang members in a bad area of Jamaica.

British hit singles: number fourteen

It then took the name **dubbing,** because changes were being made in the sound of the recording, and in some cases those changes involved dropping the sounds of some instruments or vocals out of the recording. Dubbing was soon performed in the recording studios as an essential element of spoken patter over a rock steady beat.

Reggae

In 1968, a fast form of rock steady was recorded by the ska group the Maytals in their recording "Do the Reggay." Eventually this new music that had evolved out of ska was called *reggae*. To Jamaicans, reggae meant "the king's music," and the king to whom it referred was Haile Selassie, the emperor of Ethiopia. Reggae groups used modern amplified instruments, including lead and rhythm guitars, piano, organ, drums, and electric bass guitar, along with Jamaican percussion instruments. Bass players usually set up melodic patterns that they repeated throughout most of a piece of music. These patterns involved much syncopation, often avoiding important beats such as the first beat of the bar. In addition to being played loudly, the bass line was often emphasized by having the lead guitar parallel it in octaves. The typical reggae rhythm fell into a pattern of four beats, but unlike ska, it often accented the first and third subdivisions, as had rhythm and blues. Another rhythm and blues element reggae employed was the accented backbeat, a characteristic that made it more easily accessible to rock music fans. The reggae beat differed from the rhythm and blues beat through the use of syncopated bass lines and the influence of other Latin-styled rhythms.

Reggae's infectious beat earned it more commercial success than the earlier musical styles from Jamaica. Reggae song lyrics usually centered on the concerns of the poor and socially downtrodden people who played it. Most reggae performers came from the west side of the capital city of Kingston, on the southeastern part of the island. The poverty and political subjugation of those people was the theme of the film *The Harder They Come* (1972), which starred the young ska and reggae singer Jimmy Cliff (born in 1948). Like the movie, the lyrics of many reggae songs dealt with threats of revolution, a call for people to stand up for their rights, and faith in their god, "Jah," to save them. The term *rudeboys* soon came into use to identify these poor Jamaicans who "rudely" sang or spoke out against their oppressors. Later ska bands and their followers also identified themselves as rudeboys.

The religion practiced by many reggae musicians was Rastafarianism, a name taken from Ras Tafari, the real name of Haile Selassie. Rastafarianism was based in Judeo-Christian theology, using the Christian Bible along with writings by the Jamaican-born African American minister Marcus Garvey (1887–1940) as its texts. One basic belief separating it from Christianity was that Ras Tafari was a messiahlike prince sent by God. Selassie was the emperor of Ethiopia from 1930 until he was deposed in 1974, and many Rastafarians believed it was necessary for them to travel to Ethiopia. Also as part of their religion, Rastafarians were vegetarians, made sacramental use of marijuana, which they called *ganja,* and did not comb their hair, causing it to mat together in a style that became known as dreadlocks.

One of the most influential of the Rastafarian reggae groups was the Wailers. The Wailers originally formed in 1963 as a vocal group whose recordings were accompanied by the Skatalites. Both **Bob Marley** (1945–1981) and Peter Tosh belonged to the Wailers at that time. Members drifted away and the group broke up in 1966, but reunited a year later and began recording again in 1969. To avoid dependence on instrumental groups, some of the singers began to play instruments, and other instrumentalists were added as well. Their Jamaican-produced albums did moderately well in their homeland, but it was not until 1972 when a contract with Chris Blackwell's Island Records was signed that they had a chance at international success. The albums *Catch a Fire* and *Burnin'* were both released in England in 1973. British guitarist Eric Clapton covered the song "I Shot the Sheriff" from *Burnin'* and made Marley's song and its reggae beat an international hit. Clapton's cover drew attention to the Wailers, who began to tour on their own. A listening guide to the Wailers' recording of the song is on page 227.

❝ **Bob [Marley] was a revolutionary with his music. He would never pull a gun, but he would stand**

Bob Marley

Listening Guide

"I Shot the Sheriff"
as recorded by Bob Marley
and the Wailers (1973)

Tempo: The tempo is approximately 96 beats per minute, with four beats in each full bar.

Form: After a two-beat percussion flourish, the form is organized as follows: ABABABAB Instrumental.

The eight-bar A sections are composed of two four-bar phrases that begin with the words "I shot the sheriff" and serve as a refrain.

The B sections are composed of three four-bar phrases followed by a two-beat percussion flourish similar to the one introducing the song.

The final instrumental includes a few vocal statements and is based on a repeated A section.

A fade ending is used.

Features: The beat subdivisions in the A sections are basically even. Both even and uneven beat subdivisions are used in the B sections, often in different instruments at the same time.

A soft backbeat is maintained through most of the recording.

The backup vocalists sing in falsetto.

The B sections are polyrhythmic.

Lyrics: The singer rehearses his legal defense to a shootout. He claims he only shot the sheriff, who bore a personal grudge against him anyway, in reflexive self-defense. Like a lawyer though, he insists on drawing a distinction between the killing of the sheriff, which he admits and for which he claims justification, and a killing of an anonymous deputy, which he claims he did not do.

there before the mic and fire shots . . . and some people didn't like that. "

—Rita Marley

" If I had to describe Bob Marley in a few words, I'd say he was a great lyric writer, a musical genius, and a great leader of men. "

—Eric Clapton

" Being a Rasta is acknowledging the presence of God within you, having an identity. It's a feel . . . we believe in Ethiopia, the Promised Land. . . . Give God thanks and praises. Some call him Allah, Jesus, it's all the same for us. "

—Rita Marley

Marley died of cancer in May 1981. His mother, Cedella Booker, recorded a tribute to him called "Stay Alive" (1981), and his widow and their children continued to keep the Marley name alive with their own successful careers as reggae singers. By the late eighties, Ziggy Marley (born in 1968) had established his own career as a writer and singer, with his siblings backing him as the Melody Makers.

"Reggae music is simple music—but it's from the heart. Just as people need water to drink, people also need music. If it is true music, the people will be drawn to it."

–Ziggy Marley

The Specials (left to right): Jerry Dammers, Sir Horace Gentleman, Neville Staples, Terry Hall, Roddy Radiation, Lynvall Golding, and John Bradbury

Ska and Reggae Influences on Rock

Revolutionary song themes common to reggae drew the interest of British punk bands of the midseventies. Bands such as the **Clash** shared the poor Jamaican people's anger about police and government brutality and took stands against racism. The Clash covered Junior Murvin's song "Police and Thieves" (1977) and incorporated a reggae beat and reggae bass lines into some of their own songs, such as "White Man in Hammersmith Palais" (1978). A British punk band that became interested in the engaging pulse of reggae, though not the political messages behind the music, was the **Police,** who added a reggae beat and ska/reggae melodic contours to the song "Roxanne" (1978) and much of the music they recorded after that. No longer a punk band, the Police continued to write and record their winning mixture of pop, rock, and reggae, led by their singer/bassist/main songwriter, Sting (Gordon Sumner). Their *Reggatta de Blanc* album (1979) (the title literally meant "white reggae") gave them an international hit with the song "Message in a Bottle."

Ska Revival

Ska was revived in the late seventies in Coventry, England, by a former punk band, the **Specials.** In addition to fast-driving punk, the Specials had also played reggae. They tried to combine the two styles in a new way and found that reggae's ancestor, ska, had a much simpler rhythmic pattern than reggae and could be sped up to a punk tempo more easily. The new style merged the pulse and shouted vocals of punk with the hesitation beat of ska. The Specials took a strong stand against racism; the group itself was racially mixed, and that was an important theme of much of their music. They formed their own record company, 2 Tone Records, and released the single "Gangsters" (1979), the commercial success of which established both their group and their company, at least for a few years. The Specials broke up in 1981 and regrouped in 2008.

"Concrete Jungle" was recorded by the Specials for the movie *Dance Craze* (1979). A listening guide to that recording is on page 229.

Madness was another British punk group that added a ska hesitation beat to some of their music. They took their name from the song "Madness" by ska king Prince Buster, a disc jockey in Jamaica in the midsixties, to whom they dedicated their song "The Prince" (1979). Madness's sound was based on the fast ska beat and punk-like drive with shouted vocals that had been started by the Specials, but they also added a rough-toned saxophone playing the lead on most of their recordings, giving them a unique sound. Saxophone often had been used in early Jamaican ska recordings based on American rhythm and blues.

Ska had been a dance music in Jamaica, and the British punk-driven version became popular dance music as well. A movie called *Dance Craze* (1981) featured the music of the Specials and Madness, along with other British ska revivalist groups—the English Beat, Bad Manners, and the Bodysnatchers—and helped to establish the popularity of the style.

By the early eighties, the music favored by skinheads, boneheads, and rudeboys (named after the Jamaican rebels of ten years earlier) was a more intense combination of punk and ska called **Oi!** Not all followers of Oi! were violently racist, although that was the case for some members of the movement. Racist or not, the basic statement behind Oi! was that punk had become mainstream to the point of being overly commercial. Oi! bands such as Cockney Rejects shouted anarchist statements and resisted any hint of commercialism.

Listening Guide

"Concrete Jungle"
as recorded by the Specials (1979)

Tempo: The tempo is approximately 152 beats per minute, with four beats in each bar.

Form: After a fourteen-bar introduction, the recording has seven sixteen-bar sections ordered as follows: ABAB Instrumental AB.

The sixteen bars of each section are made up of four four-bar phrases.

The B sections all begin with the words "concrete jungle" and function as a refrain. The B sections end with the beat pattern used in the introduction.

Features: Beat subdivisions are slightly earlier than even half-beat subdivisions. An organ plays a chord on each subdivision.

The drums keep a strong backbeat.

The introduction is made up of group chanting and rhythmic pounding of a beat commonly used in cheers at sports events.

The vocals are sung in a punk-influenced monotone with occasional pitch changes at phrase endings.

Group vocals are used for emphasis and support the singer's statements that he needs to stay with his mates (friends).

Fuzztone lead guitar is featured in the instrumental section.

The electric bass plays reggae-influenced syncopations in some parts of the A sections but plays on the beats during most of the B sections.

The bass plays melodic octaves during the instrumental section with the lower note on the beat and the upper octave note at the subdivision. This creates an interesting rhythmic pattern that stresses the slightly uneven subdivisions.

A loud sound of breaking glass is heard at the end of the second B section.

Lyrics: The song centers on the horrors of an impoverished urban ghetto somewhere in Britain, where crime is everywhere (including racist groups who attack people of color, hence the reference to "The National Front"). In this artificially dark and hard-edged "jungle," physical light becomes synonymous with safety, if not salvation.

Many postseventies ska bands based their style on the postpunk styles of the British 2 Tone movement a decade earlier, but this time the movement was not limited to one record label or, for that matter, even to one country. By the eighties, ska bands were popular all over the United States and in various parts of Europe, including West Germany, Italy, France, Holland, the Basque areas of Spain, and, of course, England. As was also true of songs by the 2 Tone bands, the later-day ska writers used their music to make political and social statements. Sections with dub-style vocal inserts were often included in their recordings.

Summary

The development of both ska and reggae in Jamaica served as an example of an interesting musical synthesis that resulted from mixing people of different cultures. Blues, jazz, and rock all came out of similar intercultural mixes in the United States. Ska developed out of mento, rhythm and blues, and other music heard in Jamaica. It shared characteristics of those styles but also developed a distinctive sound and rhythm of its own. During the midsixties, ska musicians slowed down their music and added a heavy bass line after hearing American soul music, particularly Memphis soul. That new sound was called rock steady, and when it was played faster it became reggae. Reggae was the music of the Rastafarian religious movement, and it became a vehicle for both religious and political statements.

It was the political rebelliousness as much as the musical style of reggae that made it attractive to British punk bands during the late seventies. Reggae's backbeat and its emphasis on the bass made it attractive to many other rock musicians who left politics out of their performances. Ska was updated when rock musicians combined it with punk. Both ska and reggae became internationally important musical styles, although more so in Britain, Europe, and Africa than in the United States.

discussion questions

Reggae is music of politically and socially oppressed people in Jamaica. Is the international popularity of reggae most likely to be based on its identity with those people, or is it popular more because it is good dance music? Might the reasons for reggae's popularity in England be different from those for its popularity in the United States? What current bands play ska or reggae?

Punk Rock and New Wave

"The reason punk felt so good was: not only was music really powerful and exciting then . . . but it was a great weapon to attack everyone else with!"

—JELLO BIAFRA OF THE DEAD KENNEDYS

The musical style called punk rock developed in the United States out of the raw and ener-getic music played by the garage bands of the midsixties. Most of these bands were formed by teenagers who learned to finger basic guitar chords and flail away at drums and cymbals in their own garages, while playing at as high a decibel level as their neighbors would tolerate. The resulting sounds were rough, raw, and musically undisciplined, but they expressed the interests of teenagers and brought rock music back to their level.

At the same time recordings by teenaged garage bands were hitting the pop charts, a slightly older, artistically trained but jaded group of musicians in New York were writing poetry and singing about urban decay. That sort of idea for artistic expression had been at the root of several literary, artistic, and musical styles in the twentieth century, including the Beat movement. The Beat poets and writers of the fifties—Allen Ginsberg, Jack Kerouac, William Burroughs, and others—directed their feelings of anger at what they considered a fat, self-centered, and self-righteous society that gave lip service to freedom for mankind but still excluded anyone who was not white, male, heterosexual, and economically stable. The manner in which the Beats openly confronted the problems that most people ignored was at the philosophical root of the punk movement, which eventually spawned a style of music.

Early Influences on the Development of Punk

Lou Reed (born in 1943) wrote poetry about street life, prostitution, and drugs in New York. He had been trained as a classical pianist, but no Mozart or Beethoven sonata could express what he had to say about, or to, society. While a student at Syracuse University, Reed played the guitar in rock bands with another guitarist, Sterling Morrison. The pair met avant-garde composer and multi-instrumentalist John Cale in 1964. Cale's principal instruments were the piano, viola, and bass; and Reed, Morrison, and Cale decided to work together, leaving tra-ditional rock and roll styles aside to experiment with new forms of expression. They added a drummer and called their group the Primitives, the Warlocks, and the Falling Spikes before they settled on the Velvet Underground. Reed recited his poems to simple and repetitious melodies, while Cale played a continuous, pulsating drone on his electric viola. Their first drummer quit and was replaced by Maureen Tucker.

The Velvet Underground met pop artist Andy Warhol in 1965. Warhol was already well known for his transfor-mation of soup cans and other mundane images into art. Interested in mixing media, Warhol had the Velvet Under-ground play for his traveling artwork, the Exploding Plastic Inevitable. He painted a banana for the cover of their first album and had them add a singer/actress friend, Nico

(Christa Päffgen), to sing on some cuts. *The Velvet Under-ground & Nico* was recorded in 1966 but was not released until a year later. Reed's songs concentrated on harsh themes such as drug addiction and sadomasochism. He sang as if he were intimately aware of all aspects of urban street life, but coolly above it and alienated from any con-cerns about the people involved. The music was repetitious, unemotional, and only vaguely related to most commercial rock. A listening guide to "Heroin" from that album is on page 233.

> " At the time people thought that we were being very negative and bleak and dark and 'anti' where, as the lyricist, I thought that we were an accurate reflection of segments of New York that you can't ignore. "
>
> –Lou Reed

The Velvet Underground's next album, *White Light/ White Heat* (1968), expressed themes similar to those of its predecessor. Drugs were an important element of street life, and the album's title track was Reed's anthem to amphetamines. Traditional song and musical forms were ignored, and repetitious drones, occasionally interrupted

Listening Guide

"Heroin"
as recorded by the Velvet
Underground (1966)

Tempo: The tempo varies greatly throughout the recording. The introduction opens with a pulse on the half-beats (eighth notes) establishing a tempo of 72 beats per minute, with four beats in each bar. In bar ten, another guitar enters with a lead pattern, at which point all of the instruments speed up gradually to about 96 beats per minute. Each A section speeds up more to about 144 beats per minute and then slows back down to about 96 beats again. The tempo returns to about 72 beats per minute at the very end.

Form: After the introduction, the form is based on three A sections of thirty bars each and then a final A that is extended to over double that length. A new set of lyrics begins each section, but the beginning and ending of each section is established as much by the tempo changes (back to 96 beats per minute) as by the vocals. The longer final section extends the middle, which is played at the fast tempo of about 144 beats per minute and includes many chaotic

sound effects created by electric guitars and electric viola.

Features: Even beat subdivisions are maintained throughout the recording.

No backbeat is present. The bass drum is hit on beat four of each bar of the introduction and then at irregular intervals in the slow parts of the recording. The drum is used to support the intensity of the faster parts by playing on each half-beat.

Once the rhythm guitar enters at the first beat of the second bar of the introduction, it plays on the first beat of every bar through the rest of the recording, alternating between just two chords.

Lyrics: The song portrays the effect heroin has on the addict. Sung from the addict's point of view, the exhilaration as the drug enters his body is expressed in the lyrics and in the increasing tempo of the music. The addict says he knows the drug has caused his alienation from the rest of society, and he knows it will kill him, but he still cannot and will not do without it.

by screeching feedback, were established to accompany his monologues. The work was not commercial, but it functioned to express the coldness and gloom Reed saw in the world. Cale eventually left the group to do his own recording and to produce albums for other nonmainstream musicians. The Velvet Underground continued with Doug Yule replacing Cale, and they maintained the group name with other musicians after Reed's departure in 1970. Reed went on to enjoy a successful, often controversial solo career. In 1989, he and Cale reunited to perform a piece called *Songs for 'Drella*, their tribute to Andy Warhol, who had died in 1987. Original members

of the Velvet Underground regrouped under the name of their drummer, Moe Tucker, for her 1991 album *I Spent a Week There the Other Night*. They toured Europe in 1993. After the tour Reed, Cale, and Tucker continued their solo careers. Sterling Morrison died of non-Hodgkin's lymphoma in 1995.

"There's a certain amount of discipline that I learned while I was studying that comes in handy. I mean the way musical

> "structures work. Even if you are improvising, the fact that beforehand you know certain things will work helps you to make those improvisations successful most of the time."
>
> –John Cale, about his classical background

The Velvet Underground's first efforts influenced the development of punk as a musical style. Their emotionless portrayal of themes centering on alienation from human concerns and their use of repetitious musical ideas became characteristic of both punk and new wave. The highly emotional expression of anger at the heart of most punk music came from the garage band sound. Musically, this anger was expressed through a constantly pounding eighth-note beat (often strummed on the guitar or plucked on the bass) and shouted vocals. Behind the fast throbbing pulse of the guitar or bass, the drums usually played a traditional rock backbeat.

A high school rock band called the **MC5** (the Motor City Five) from Lincoln Park, Michigan (just outside Detroit), developed a loud and angry style. Formed in 1965, they moved to Detroit after graduation and by 1967 had connected themselves with a radical political group called the White Panthers. The MC5 drew attention to themselves by playing for those who rioted at the 1968 Democratic Convention in Chicago. Their first album, *Kick Out the Jams* (1969), was criticized and refused airplay because of its obscene lyrics, which their record company, Elektra, replaced on a reissued version of the album. With two guitars and plenty of distortion, the MC5 combined the power of heavy metal with the raw garage band sound, all infused with their own belligerent, indignant attitude.

> "It was mainly about clang bang, clang, clang, clang, bang, bang, bang, loud, loud, loud and annoying, and the more annoying it was, the better."
>
> –Iggy Pop

> "Musically we never played one track that adheres to the standard punk approach. But we had an attitude. . . . Then the Ramones, the Sex Pistols took it

> more in the direction of the pub, frankly. The first pogoing, stage diving, snarling, use of the word 'destroy' and the word 'punk' in reference to us, that all started with us. . . . I was the first to walk out onstage with the clothes already ripped too."
>
> –Iggy Pop

While a student at the University of Michigan, James Jewel Osterberg sang and played drums with a rock group called the Iguanas (from which he took the name Iggy). In 1967, he formed his own band, Iggy and the Stooges, and played repetitious, angry, and pessimistic music. At first Iggy called himself Iggy Stooge; then he changed that to **Iggy Pop.** On stage, Iggy Pop, who is sometimes referred to as the Godfather of Punk, acted out his disgust with society by hitting himself with his microphone and by cutting his skin with pieces of glass and then smearing the bloody mess with peanut butter. John Cale, who had recently left the Velvet Underground, was hired to produce the group's first protopunk album, *The Stooges* (1969). Iggy Pop developed an addiction to heroin, and his career might have ended after that album had he not been befriended by David Bowie, who produced albums and wrote songs for him. Pop's career continued into the twenty-first century, but his importance to the punk movement lay in his early self-destructive image.

New York Punk

The loud, raw, rebellious sound of the MC5 and the Stooges and the alienated attitude of the Velvet Underground were picked up in the early seventies by the **New York Dolls,** who added some glitter to punk and then passed it on to other New York groups and to the angry youth of London. Formed in 1971, the New York Dolls were five men who donned lipstick, heavy eye makeup, and stacked heels to perform songs about "bad" girls, drugs, and New York street life. The themes were similar to those of the Velvet Underground, but the attitude was less serious. From the MC5 and the Stooges, the Dolls took heavily distorted guitar lines and a powerful pounding beat, which they combined with Rolling Stones–like rhythm and blues. A listening guide to "Personality Crisis," from the group's debut album, *The New York Dolls* (1973), is on page 235.

The New York Dolls established a large following in late-night clubs in New York, but despite their attempts, failed to gain commercial success in other parts of the

The New York Dolls in their dressing room (standing, left to right); Jerry Nolan, Johnny Thunders, Killer Kane, and Sylvain Sylvain (seated): singer David Johansen

Listening Guide

"Personality Crisis"
as recorded by the New York Dolls
(1973)

Tempo: The tempo is about 155 beats per minute, with four beats in each bar.

Form: The recording begins with a sixteen-bar instrumental introduction.

The piano enters, in a honky-tonk style, at bar four.

The basic structure is composed of eight-bar periods organized according to an AABA song form. The B sections repeat lyrics about the frustrations of having a "personality crisis."

A short break (of silence) occurs between the second and third AABA sections.

Features: Each beat is evenly subdivided into two parts, creating a constantly throbbing pulse twice the speed of the basic beat. The fast pulse is created by the guitarist, the chords played by the pianist's right hand, and the drummer on the cymbals.

The drummer maintains the backbeat on the bass drum (in rock, the backbeat is usually kept with the snare drum).

The vocals are shouted almost in a **monotone** (a single, unvaried tone), although there are occasional pitch changes when the chords change or to emphasize a particular word.

The guitarist uses heavy distortion.

Lyrics: The lyrics are about a person who plays a role dictated by society during the day but then goes wild at night in an effort to shake off the day's frustrations.

country. By 1975, most of the group members had left the band, although singer David Johansen and guitarist Sylvain Sylvain continued performing as the New York Dolls for another two years. After the demise of the Dolls, David Johansen recorded several solo albums and then reemerged in the late eighties with a new persona, calling himself Buster Poindexter and singing songs in a variety of older rhythm and blues styles. Several albums by the New York Dolls were released during the eighties, but they were all old recordings that were made back in the seventies. Johnny Thunders and Jerry Nolan both died in the early nineties.

A nightclub in the Bowery district of New York City, called CBGB & OMFUG (Country, Blue Grass, Blues & Other Music For Uplifting Gormandizers, usually shortened to **CBGB's**), was the starting place for many New York punk bands, including Television, the Patti Smith Group, and the Ramones. **Television** was formed in 1973 by poet/singer/guitarist Thomas Miller, who gave himself the stage name Tom Verlaine, after the French symbolist poet Paul Verlaine (1844–1896). The original Verlaine was known for his use of symbolism, metaphor, and lyricism, all of which Miller tried to emulate in the lyrics he wrote for Television. The group's first bass player, **Richard Hell** (Richard Myers), spiked his hair and wore torn clothing, creating an image that later became standard for British punks. Television's music combined a Velvet Underground–influenced punk sensibility with melodic lead guitar lines and psychedelic-style wandering improvisations. Members of Television went their separate ways for just over thirteen years and then reunited in 1991 to record the album *Television* (1992) and to perform at the Glastonbury Summer Festival in England. They took another break and then regrouped in 2001.

Patti Smith (born in 1946) was an artist and writer from Chicago who established herself professionally in New York. She wrote poetry, plays, and articles, many of which were published. Rock journalist and guitarist Lenny Kaye provided simple guitar accompaniments for Smith's reading, and later singing, of her poetry. Ex–Velvet Underground member John Cale produced the Patti Smith Group's debut album, *Horses* (1975), which combined the musical simplicity of the Velvet Underground with Smith's gutsy and energetic vocals and a pounding punk beat. The album included a new version of the song "Gloria" (recorded by Them and the Shadows of Knight, both 1966). Smith's singing of a male text was intended to shock the average listener in much the same way that Beat poetry had years before. The next year she covered the Who's "My Generation" (the Who in 1965, Patti Smith in 1976), in which she shouted obscenities, making it clear that hers was a new and angrier generation. Smith eventually married Fred "Sonic" Smith, ex-guitarist for

the MC5, and moved to his home in Detroit, where she continued to write while also raising their children. A more philosophical, even guardedly optimistic Patti Smith released the album *Dream of Life* in 1988. A book of Smith's poetry entitled *Early Work: 1970–1979* was published in 1994, and later that same year her husband died. She continued on, however, and made occasional concert appearances. She has recorded eight albums since 1996.

Another New York–based band, the **Ramones,** formed in 1974 and named themselves after Paul Ramon, a pseudonym Paul McCartney had used for a time early in his career with the Beatles. Each group member adopted Ramone as a last name. Only their drummer, Tommy Ramone (Tom Erdelyi), had worked as a professional musician; consequently, he became both manager and producer of the group, continuing in these roles even after he stopped playing with the group in 1977. The Ramones' very simple, fast, high-energy music and monotone vocals became the prototype for much punk rock to follow. Most of their songs lasted two minutes or less and were written by the group members as a team. The Ramones did not release their first album, *Ramones*, until 1976, but their performances in England helped influence the beginnings of the punk movement there in 1975.

The Ramones remained a high-energy punk band until the early eighties, when they began branching out from punk to experiment with new styles. Early sixties wall-of-sound producer Phil Spector was brought in for the *End of the Century* album (1980), but the result was a disaster in the minds of the Ramones' punk fans. The album included a hilarious rendition of "Baby I Love You," the 1964 Ronettes hit that Spector had written and produced. After other experiments with nonpunk styles of music, the Ramones returned to their punk energy for *Too Tough to Die* (1984), produced by their original producer and drummer, Tommy Erdelyi. The Ramones played on for another eleven years and then left their fans with their final album, *Adios Amigos* (1994). The Ramones were the first punk band named to the Rock and Roll Hall of Fame.

British Punk

Groups of British lower- and middle-class teenagers in the midseventies had grown to detest the lifestyles and traditional values of their parents and had come to believe they were caught up in an economic and class-ridden social system over which they had no control—one they viewed as relegating them to a life of near poverty with no hope of securing jobs that would pay them enough to better themselves. Entertainment, even movies or dances, was too expensive for them. Rock music played by wealthy stars surrounded by grandiose stage sets and light shows meant nothing to them. Stylish clothes were out of their reach. The attitude of those teens was one of anger, frustration, and violence. They were antigovernment, antisociety, and antifashion. The theme of anarchy heard in British and American West Coast punk begins here. The bands dressed in torn secondhand clothing with large safety pins holding the pieces together. The look reflected their rejection of the standard image of respectability and became a symbol of their feelings of alienation.

The raw, pounding music of the New York Dolls and the Ramones was transported to London by Malcolm McLaren (born in 1946), the owner of an antifashion clothing store in London called Sex. He was sympathetic to the feelings of the angry youth to whom he sold torn clothing, some of which was even made out of plastic trash bags, and wanted to produce a sound that would express their attitudes. He was impressed with the New York Dolls, whom he saw in London and eventually contracted to manage, but their breakup left McLaren to form his own group in London. McLaren knew that one of his employees at Sex, Glen Matlock, played bass with his friends, guitarist Steve Jones and drummer Paul Cook, in a group called Swankers. He had an angry young customer, John Lydon, who did more hanging around than

buying. Lydon had no experience as a singer, but the sound McLaren was after required no more polish than the rebellious youth already had. McLaren put the quartet together, changing Lydon's name to Johnny Rotten, and used his store's name as the basis of their group name, the **Sex Pistols.**

Just as McLaren wanted, the Sex Pistols evoked disgust everywhere they went. Their music had the constant pounding and loud distorted guitar that had been part of the punk sound in Detroit and New York; but unlike the New York Dolls, this group was not just toying with rebellion. They were completely caught up in highly emotional anger. They wanted to repulse the establishment and provoke authorities into retaliating against them, and that attracted more fans than their music by itself did. Performances were stopped in midsong, concerts were canceled, and radio programmers pulled their music off the air. Their first single, "Anarchy in the U.K.," was recorded in 1976 under the EMI label and sold well in Britain in early 1977, but EMI removed it from record stores because of the vulgar language the group used on a British television program, *The Today Show.* Matlock left the Sex Pistols, and Rotten brought in a friend, John Ritchie, to play bass. The group renamed Ritchie Sid Vicious.

The Sex Pistols perform in front of Union Jacks that have the *God Save the Queen* album cover logo on them in 1977 (left to right): Sid Vicious, Johnny Rotten, Paul Cook, and Steve Jones

Listening Guide

"God Save the Queen" as recorded by the Sex Pistols (1977)

Tempo: The tempo is about 145 beats per minute, with four beats in each bar. Each beat is evenly subdivided into two parts, creating a constant, throbbing pulse.

Form: The recording begins with a four-bar instrumental vamp followed by an eight-bar instrumental introduction.

The form is based on eight-bar periods, organized according to an AABA song form with added C sections.

Most A sections begin with the words of the song's title.

Two full AABA sections are followed by another A section with vocals, an instrumental period, another A with vocals, and then three new C periods based on repetitions of words from earlier B periods.

Features: Although the guitar and drums both keep the fast pulse of the beat subdivisions from time to time, it is most clearly maintained by loud, repeated bass notes.

The drums maintain a backbeat.

The guitar is very heavily distorted, creating a background mood of anarchy and disorder.

Most of the vocals are shouted in a monotone by Johnny Rotten alone, with the group joining him in the C section.

Lyrics: The lyrics express a very depressed view of Britain's economy, social system, and government, emphasizing that there is no hope for anything positive in the future and that anyone who is hopeful is only dreaming.

British hit singles: number two

The Sex Pistols had gained such a reputation that other bands began forming, copying their distorted guitar, bass, and drums instrumentation with monotone-shouted vocals even before the Sex Pistols had an album out. The energy level of the music was high, and violence at their performances became common. A punk dance—or a sort of nondance—called the **pogo,** in which people simply jumped straight up and down, was popularized at the Sex Pistols' concerts. The Pistols lost record contracts as fast as they signed them, and they finally ended up on the Virgin label.

One sure way to anger a respectable English citizen is to show disrespect for the Queen. Queen Elizabeth II was celebrating her Silver Jubilee (the twenty-fifth anniversary of her coronation) in 1977, and in her "honor," the Sex Pistols released a single whose title was the same as that of the English national anthem—"God Save the Queen." The Sex Pistols' lyrics were so foul and insulting that the song was banned from British radio and television; the title was not even allowed to be printed on chart listings, so it made its way up the charts as a black line. It reached number two on the British pop charts. A listening guide to the recording is included here.

> " Why should we pay 25 percent of everything we earn to some dreary hippie who dictates how we should sound? It's our music. No one should tell us what we should sound like. I simply loathe producers. "
>
> –John "Rotten" Lydon

The commercial success of "God Save the Queen" and the album that followed, *Never Mind the Bollocks, Here's the Sex Pistols* (1977), made it clear that the punks spoke for many young people in Britain.

The Sex Pistols toured Europe and the United States—they had to tour if they wanted to continue to perform because no promoters in England would hire them. They tried to stir up American youth by changing the "U.K." to "U.S.A." in performances of their British hit "Anarchy of the U.K.," but in most places they were received more as oddities than as a musical group. With nowhere left to go, but having made their statement and begun a movement, the Sex Pistols disbanded in early 1978. Vicious moved to New York with his girlfriend, Nancy Spungen, whom he was later accused of killing (an event brought to movie audiences in *Sid and Nancy* [1986]). Vicious died of a drug overdose before the investigation was completed. Johnny Rotten took back his real name, Lydon, and formed an alternative rock band called Public Image, Ltd., that only toyed with punk.

The MC5 and Iggy Pop and the Stooges were the musical influences on another Malcolm McLaren–managed British punk band, the **Damned.** In addition to playing fast, angry music, the Damned engaged in such punk stage activities as taunting and spitting at the audience while accepting the same in return. The first British punk band to release a single, "New Rose" (1976), and an album, *Damned, Damned, Damned* (1977), the Damned traveled to New York and played at CBGB's. Not a commercial success, the Damned were denied their request to tour with the Sex Pistols. For the most part, the Damned played fast, hard punk music that stressed anger for anger's sake. They toured the United States in 1977 and, along with the Sex Pistols, served as a major influence on the development of the punk movement in California. The Damned remained together until their breakup in 1989, having placed hits on the British pop charts through almost every year of their career. They regrouped in 1993 and continue to record and tour.

One of the most important and longest-lasting groups of the British punk movement was the **Clash.** Except for their bass player, Paul Simonon, who picked up his first bass when he joined the group, the members were experienced musicians. Singer/guitarist Joe Strummer (John Mellor) had been with a rock band called the 101'ers, and both guitarist Mick Jones and drummer Tory Crimes (Terry Chimes) came to the Clash from the London S.S. Crimes was replaced by Nicky "Topper" Headon after the group recorded their first album. Instead of just expressing the multidirectional anger the Sex Pistols had, the Clash's songs zeroed in on some of the central causes of punk rebellion: youth unemployment, racism, and police brutality. In addition to using punk's familiar rhythmic throb, they took Jamaica's music of rebellion and added a reggae beat to some of their music. They signed with CBS records, a move criticized by some fans who believed that all punk belonged underground. British punk fans had

learned to use the music as background for their own expressions of anger, and violence flared at concerts. At one concert auditorium, seats were actually torn up from the floor during a Clash performance. The Clash had two top-forty U.S. hits with "Train in Vain (Stand by Me)" (1980) and "Rock the Casbah" (1982).

Through several membership changes, Simonon and Strummer were still with the Clash to record *Cut the Crap* in 1985, but the band folded within the next year. Old material was rereleased on several collections during the early nineties, and the Clash had its only number-one British hit with the 1991 rerelease of "Should I Stay or Should I Go" (originally released in 1982) after the song was used in a commercial for Levi's jeans.

The Sex Pistols, the Damned, and the Clash were only three of many British punk bands that formed and recorded in 1976 and 1977. Among those other bands, Chelsea expressed the anger of the unemployed in their single "Right to Work" (1977); Billy Idol, singing with Generation X, released "Your Generation" (1977); and X-Ray Spex and their female singer Poly Styrene (Marion Elliot) brought a violent feminist message to punk with the single "Oh Bondage Up Yours!" (1977). London did not have a monopoly on British punk. The Buzzcocks formed in Manchester and expressed rebellious, youthful attitudes in their singles "Breakdown" and "Boredom" (both 1977). Many bands stayed with the short songs, fast pulse, and shouted vocals of the Sex Pistols and the Damned, while the Clash's inclusion of reggae added some variation to the punk style. The energy level and simplicity of punk soon spread beyond its original antigovernment and antisociety causes and themes.

Hard-core Punk on the West Coast

When British punk bands like the Sex Pistols and the Damned toured the United States, their music, although not commercially successful, struck a nerve in both San Francisco and Los Angeles and sparked a punk movement there. Punk groups from California used the same rock instrumentation as the British punks, but their attitude was much different from their British counterparts. Whereas the Sex Pistols and other British punks spoke for angry youth who were experiencing a desperate economic situation, the American punks had jobs, food, and clothing readily available to them. That did not keep anger and violence out of their music, however; the groups had plenty to say about their ex-hippie parents' worn-out (or worse yet, sold-out) values and the U.S. government's involvement in the politics of Asian and South American countries as well as its support of an oppressive regime in South Africa.

Jello Biafra, lead singer of the punk rock group Dead Kennedys, performing on stage in April 1981

The **Dead Kennedys** formed in San Francisco in 1978 and played fast, heavily distorted music with shouted monotone vocals that condemned the U.S. government and other institutions for a multitude of offenses, and yet also displayed a sense of humor. The Dead Kennedys' lyricist/singer, Jello Biafra (Eric Boucher), adopted his stage name when he heard that the government had sent a shipment of Jell-O to the starving people of Biafra in Africa, calling it foreign aid. Their debut album, *Fresh Fruit for Rotting Vegetables* (1980), included "Holiday in Cambodia," inspired by the Sex Pistols' "Holidays in the Sun." Also on the album was "Kill the Poor," which made a strong satirical statement against those who put money into the development of the neutron bomb (a device that killed people, but left structures intact) but resisted governmental aid to America's poor. The satirical position was reminiscent of *A Modest Proposal* by Irish satirist Jonathan Swift (1667–1745), in which Swift proposed the English solve the problem of starvation in Ireland by eating Irish children. A listening guide to "Kill the Poor" is on page 241.

The Dead Kennedys attacked the Moral Majority on the EP *In God We Trust, Inc.* (1981). Their album *Plastic Surgery Disasters* (1982) left the government alone for a while, instead criticizing average American lifestyles in "Winnebago Warrior" and "Terminal Preppie." After a break of several years, during which its members produced and supervised recordings by other punk bands for their Alternative Tentacles label, the Dead Kennedys were back with their usual political and social satire in *Frankenchrist* (1985), which contained a reproduction of a painting that the L.A. City Attorney charged was "harmful." The trial took over a year and ended with a

deadlocked jury and a dismissal. The time and defense legal fees became the subject of some of Biafra's later spoken word performances. True to their agenda of criticizing what they saw as wrong with the world, the Dead Kennedys' next album, *Bedtime for Democracy* (1986), even attacked the punk community itself in "Chickenshit Conformist" and "Macho Insecurity."

A large hard-core punk culture developed in Los Angeles during the late seventies and early eighties and included such bands as Black Flag, the Germs, X, and Catholic Discipline, all of whom were featured in the movie *The Decline of Western Civilization* (1980), directed by Penelope Spheeris. One of the first and longest-lasting of the L.A. bands was **Black Flag,** a name chosen because a black flag is a symbol for anarchy. The group's music shared the fast beat, distorted guitars, and monotone vocal style of British punk bands like the Sex Pistols, and their short songs decried the meaninglessness of their lives and the anger they felt toward the establishment and all authority figures. So much violence erupted at their concerts that most Hollywood clubs banned them. Their personnel changed fairly often, with only guitarist Greg Ginn remaining through their career. The group remained true to violent punk-styled music until 1984, when they broke away from hard-core punk and included some very long songs with heavy-metal characteristics such as elaborate distorted guitar solos and repeating bass riffs. Black Flag broke up in 1986, and Ginn worked with a group called Gone before continuing on with a solo career, under both his own name and under the stage name Poindexter Stewart. Black Flag's singer, Henry Rollins, had considerable success with the Henry Rollins Band and with a band he called Henrietta Collins and the

Listening Guide

"Kill the Poor"
as recorded by the Dead Kennedys
(1980)

Tempo: The recording has a slow introduction sung in a tempo of roughly 96 beats per minute, with four beats in each bar. After the introduction the tempo suddenly jumps to about 208 beats per minute with four beats per bar. The fast pulse that earlier punk superimposed on top of a slower beat becomes the main beat through the placement of the drummer's backbeat at the faster speed.

Form: The recording begins with one eight-bar vocal introduction intoned by Biafra, accompanied by guitar distortion and occasional drum rolls; the drums begin a regular backbeat in the seventh bar.

The vocal introduction continues with another period, this time of seven bars, followed by a fast drum roll that serves to introduce the fast beat pulse of the rest of the recording.

A four-bar instrumental vamp establishes the faster tempo.

A series of repeating A and B periods separated by two four-bar instrumental vamps and two eight-bar instrumental periods follows. The A periods feature Biafra intoning lyrics at such a fast pace that they are barely understandable, and the B periods feature the constant repetition of the title lyrics, "kill the poor."

Features: Even beat subdivisions are maintained throughout the recording.

In the fast section, the bass keeps the pulse by playing repeated notes.

The harmonies are more complex than those of most other punk rock.

Lyrics: The lyrics satirically praise the U.S. government for developing a bomb that can kill people while leaving property undamaged, and suggest that, in order to save money otherwise wasted on welfare, the bomb be used to kill poor people.

Wifebeating Childhaters. Like Jello Biafra, Rollins has performed as a spoken-word artist.

Another L.A.-based punk band, **X,** was welcomed at the clubs that had banned Black Flag. X played both high-energy punk and Velvet Underground–influenced pulsating drones, but they also added occasional touches of country music, rockabilly, and heavy-metal styles. Their producer was Ray Manzarek, the Doors' organist, and their first album, *Los Angeles* (1980), featured him performing on their cover of the Doors' "Soul Kitchen." X was formed in 1977 by singer/bassist John Doe, singer Exene Cervenka, guitarist Billy Zoom, and drummer Don J. Bonebrake. Zoom admired fifties rock styles such as rockabilly and the music and guitar style of Chuck Berry and often played solos showing those influences. Doe and Cervenka, husband and wife, were both modern-day Beat

poets, and their duo vocals, sung in a monotone unison or at the interval of a fifth, became X's trademark. Zoom left the group in the mideighties and was replaced by Tony Gilkyson, with whom X continued their career as the most popular punk band in Los Angeles. X was still doing occasional live concerts and recording during the midnineties, having lasted through Cervenka and Doe's divorce and their continuing solo careers.

American New Wave

During the late seventies, many rock fans felt that rock music had gotten old, fat, and complacent and was in need of an infusion of new energy. Punk certainly had the necessary energy, but it was far too violent and anti-establishment to appeal to the mass audience. Punk's half-beat pulse, monotone vocals, and emotional alien-ation were adopted by groups that played within more mainstream popular rock styles, and the term *new wave* began to be used to categorize the music of some of those bands. In actuality, almost any new sound from the sixties onward was temporarily dubbed new wave until it became mainstream and a newer wave took over, but the label finally stuck for the postpunk music of the mid- to late seventies.

Whereas punk was almost always played only by gui-tar, bass, and drums, new-wave bands often added elec-tronic keyboards, saxophones, or other instruments. Punk guitarists and bass players used distortion to cloud melodies or chord changes; new-wave musicians pro-duced a clean, slick sound. The throbbing pulse that punk bands created by angrily strumming their electric guitars was transformed by new-wave bands into a fast, clear playing of repeated notes on the electric bass.

One of the best examples of a new-wave band that stressed a slick version of the fast pulse of punk along with chantlike monotone vocals was **Devo.** Devo was formed by singer/keyboardist Mark Mothersbaugh and bass player Jerry Casale, who were both art students at Kent State Uni-versity in Ohio. Their main purpose in putting together a band was to produce *The Truth about De-Evolution* (1975), a film that took a humorous and sardonic look at the dehu-manization of modern society. Their group was named as a play on "de-evolution." After completing the film, Devo recorded the single "Jocko Homo" (1976), which was so unemotional it sounded as if it were being performed by robots. Devo used their dehumanized image on stage and in videos, often appearing with a little robot mascot they

Devo (left to right): Bob Mothersbaugh, Bob Casale, Mark Mothersbaugh, Alan Meyers, and Jerry Casale

called Booji. Devo put their early singles on their first album, the title of which, *Q: Are We Not Men? A: We Are Devo!* (1978), came from lyrics in "Jocko Homo." A listen-ing guide to "Jocko Homo" is on page 243.

> " Devo, I think, is great. I love them. They are like dadaists to me. Everything that they express is a complete reaction against everything that we stood for. But they did it so well, theatrically speaking . . . and with a great sense of humor. I love it. "
>
> –Joni Mitchell

Devo's clean electronic sound and their songs about a modern world in which human beings are dehumanized by the increasing dependence on robots and computers were entertaining and accessible to a mass audience. Their second album, *Duty Now for the Future* (1979), rendered emotion-less one of the most common rock song themes, human attraction and love, with the songs "Strange Pursuit" and "Triumph of the Will." Devo's later work continued to use humorous, dehumanized electronic music, but much of it had also evolved (devolved?) into commercialism, and Devo began to stress a dance beat and older rock styles instead of continuing to make statements about modern society. They even commercialized to the point of recording "elevator music" for Muzak during the eighties. Devo did some tour-ing in the early nineties, took a break, and then regrouped and are planning a new album for release in 2010.

Another new-wave band whose early recordings employed punk-influenced musical characteristics in much the same way that Devo had was **Talking Heads,** formed in New York in 1975. Like Devo, Talking Heads was formed by art students. Singer/guitarist David Byrne and drummer Chris Frantz had attended the Rhode Island School of Design and had played in a group called the Artistics. After leaving that group, they formed a trio with a classmate of theirs, Tina Weymouth, who played bass and synthesizer (Frantz and Weymouth later married). The three moved to New York and were hired to play at CBGB's. The name Talking Heads came from their obser-vation that television often avoided full body shots and showed only people's heads, talking. The trio recorded the single "Love Goes to Building on Fire" (1977), but by the time they recorded their first album, *'77* (1977), they had added another member, guitarist/keyboardist Jerry Harrison. Harrison had played with Jonathan Richman

Listening Guide

"Jocko Homo"
as recorded by Devo (1976)

Tempo: The tempo is about 240 beats per minute with seven beats in each bar of the first section ($\frac{7}{4}$ meter), and about 120 beats per minute with four beats ($\frac{4}{4}$ meter) in each bar of the second section.

Form and
Features: An instrumental (electronic) introduction begins with four bars of a seven-beat pattern in which each bar is subdivided into a four-plus-three accentuation. The next four bars of the seven-beat pattern are then subdivided into a three-plus-four configuration. The effect of the unusual and uneven seven-beat patterns, and the effect of the shift in the accenting of the subdivisions, is one of instability, as if one is lost in an electronic web.

Even beat subdivisions are maintained throughout the recording.

No backbeat is used, even in the four-beat section of the recording.

The seven-beat patterns continue through three periods on monotone vocals, including a section involving a call-and-response exchange maintaining that the members of Devo are not human.

Between the second and third vocal periods, an instrumental section repeats parts of the introduction.

After the three vocal periods in a seven-beat pattern, an instrumental section repeats parts of the instrumental introduction sequentially; that is, the same music is repeated at different pitch levels. In this case, the pitch of each repetition is higher than that of the previous one.

The fast pulse of the beats in the seven-beat section is maintained with pulsating repeated notes in the bass as the tempo turns to a slower four-beat pattern.

A new melody is used at the beginning of the four-beat sections, but later in the section, a variation of the earlier melody is sung.

At the very end, the fast seven-beat pattern returns for a short instrumental section.

Lyrics: The lyrics express the belief that the coldness of the modern world has had a dehumanizing effect on mankind.

---

and the Modern Lovers, an early seventies group that concentrated on keeping the style of the Velvet Underground alive. Talking Heads' simple, pounding rhythmic pulse with Byrne's forced, near-monotone vocals on bizarre songs like "Psycho Killer" placed the band well within the new-wave category.

Many of the bands formed during the mid- to late seventies played with enough of the musical characteristics of punk or new wave to gain a reputation within those styles, even though much of their music did not really fit into the new-music genre. **Blondie,** for example, formed in 1975 and debuted at New York's CBGB's. Their first album, *Blondie* (1976), put them on the commercial outskirts of new wave, but their later music was even less characteristic of the style. Deborah Harry, their blond lead singer after whom the band was named, seldom sang in a new-wave monotone and tended more toward pop-style melodies. Blondie toyed with disco in "Heart of Glass" and "Call Me" (both 1980), reggae in "The Tide Is High" (a 1980 cover of a reggae song by the Jamaican John Holt), and a commercial brand of rap in "Rapture" (1981). Blondie broke up in 1982 and individual members pursued solo careers, but none matched the success they had known as Blondie. Back together in 1999, Blondie recorded *No Exit* (1999) and then *The Curse of Blondie* (2003).

Part of the attraction of new wave was its simplicity when compared to the grandiose scale of the performances by many glitter and progressive-rock groups of the seventies. That simplicity, in many ways, was not only a reaction against the excesses of the other styles but also a return to what rock music had been during the fifties. New-wave groups such as the **Cars,** from Boston, combined the unemotional (almost monotone) vocals and the pounding beat of punk music with Chuck Berry–influenced guitar and an angular version of a rhythm and blues beat to form a tradition-rooted new-wave style. Singer/guitarist/writer Ric Ocasek formed the Cars in 1976 and remained their central figure. His songs were not as cold and unemotional as those of the New York groups, but the Velvet Underground–style sense of alienation from emotional attachments was well represented in "My Best Friend's Girl" (1978), in which Ocasek coolly reported that his friend's girl had once been his own girlfriend. Feelings like jealousy were considered old-fashioned to new-wave modernists. *Door to Door* (1987) was the last album the Cars recorded together, but several of the members continued to do solo work under their own names. In addition to recording for himself, Ocasek produced albums for other bands. Two former members of the Cars teamed up with Todd Rundgren in 2005, calling themselves The New Cars.

Just after Talking Heads had stretched their new-wave style to include soul, and Blondie had expanded theirs to include disco, the **B-52**'s from Athens, Georgia, produced a self-titled album that took a lighthearted look at new wave. They played simple music with monotone but chatty and conversational vocals and combined it with early-sixties teen dress and slang expressions. Their name was a slang term for the heavily ratted and smoothed-over bouffant hairstyle that had been popular during the early sixties and was worn by the group's two female members, Cindy Wilson and Kate Pierson. Most members had had little musical training when the group formed, but its music was simple and they learned to play well enough to meet the demands of their style. Many of their songs and stage acts poked fun at the pop dance steps of the early sixties.

British New Wave

Punk and new-waves' emphasis on simplicity put rock music back into intimate settings. In New York, those settings were nightclubs like CBGB's; in most parts of England they were pubs. **Pub rock** was an English back-to-the-roots movement that began during the early seventies but did not become commercially successful until later in the

Elvis Costello

decade when many fans finally grew tired of large-scale rock. Many of the pub-rock bands, such as Brinsley Schwarz, Ducks Deluxe, Rockpile, and the Rumour, were popular alternatives to punk, and musicians in those groups became important as British new-wave artists.

Few performers from the pub-rock scene attracted as much attention or were as influential as **Elvis Costello** (Declan MacManus, born in 1955). MacManus was raised in Liverpool, where the American sound of Buddy Holly and the Crickets was popular and being updated by such groups as the Beatles and the Hollies (from the neighboring city of Manchester). MacManus wrote songs throughout his teenage years and then joined a British bluegrass band called Flip City, moving to London to perform with them and record demos of his songs.

MacManus signed with Stiff Records in 1975, but he, his producer Nick Lowe (a pub-rock musician originally in Brinsley Schwarz and later with Rockpile), and one of Stiff's owners, Jake Riviera, left the company so Riviera could manage MacManus's career at Radar Records. With the new stage name Elvis Costello, MacManus took Buddy Holly's boy-next-door image and changed it from naive to neurotic. As befit that image, many of Costello's songs centered on relationships, and in particular on insecurity about relationships with women. Another favorite subject was politics, as was heard in his first single, "Less than Zero" (1977), which attacked fascism. Costello teamed with a California-based country-rock band called Clover (without their usual singer, Huey Lewis) to record the album *My Aim Is True* (1977). In true pub-rock tradition, most of the music on the album followed a Buddy Holly–influenced pop-rockabilly style, but the angry and critical lyrics of "Less than Zero" hinted at his future direction. Costello's second single, and his first hit in Britain, was the reggae-influenced "Watching the Detectives." (The song was included on the American version of his debut album but not on the British version.)

For the album *This Year's Model* (1978), Costello formed a new backup band, the Attractions, and his music moved from pub rock to new wave. The Attractions provided a clean, strong accompaniment to Costello's vocals. He projected an arrogant yet insecure image, in contrast to the angry confidence most punk singers displayed. The pounding half-beat pulse of punk was present on some cuts, but, as was also true of American new wave, its production made it clean-sounding, not wildly distorted. The beat and vocal style were exactly the modern sound new-wave fans wanted, and Costello's career was launched. A listening guide to "Radio Radio," from *This Year's Model*, is below. The song reached number twenty-nine on the British pop charts.

> " Critics take me to task for being vague or obscure sometimes but that's far outweighed by somebody coming up to me privately and saying 'that song of yours, I pondered it and it meant this to me,' so you see I think there is a virtue in that more impressionistic use of words. "
>
> –Elvis Costello

Costello followed *This Year's Model* with an album that gained him more attention and commercial success in the

Listening Guide

"Radio Radio"
as recorded by Elvis Costello
and the Attractions (1978)

Tempo:	The tempo is about 144 beats per minute, with four beats in each bar.
Form:	The recording begins with an eight-bar instrumental introduction, made up of a two-bar pattern played four times.
	The overall form is made up of two eight-bar A sections, a sixteen-bar B section, an eight-bar C section, two more A sections (with new lyrics), and a repetition of the B section and lyrics.
Features:	The bass uses repeated notes to establish a fast (eighth-note) continuous pulse.
	All of the A sections have a strong backbeat maintained by the drummer, but the B sections have no backbeat.

The C section contrasts with the music that precedes and follows it by modulating to a key a minor third higher than the rest of the song and having a lighter vocal tone quality, with organ in the background.

Lyrics:	The lyrics stress the dependence some teens have on the radio for both entertainment and advice. Costello comments that the people he hears talking on the radio do not understand the young generation, so they try to use the power of radio communication to control young people's minds. Costello makes use of the old cliché "Never bite the hand that feeds you" in the lyrics to the C section, changing it to express his own bitterness toward the people who control radio.

British hit singles: number twenty-nine

United States than had any previous releases by British new-wave artists, *Armed Forces* (1979). Not surprisingly, the song themes dealt with power struggles, but in this case they were on both a personal and an international level. The song "(What's So Funny 'bout) Peace, Love and Understanding" suggested that tolerance be practiced.

Costello continued to record in his pop/new-wave style until 1981, when he traveled to Nashville, Tennessee, to record *Almost Blue,* an album of American country music with covers of songs by Hank Williams Sr., Merle Haggard, and Gram Parsons. Knowing that some of his British fans might not be fans of country music, he put a warning label on the U.K. pressings of the album: "This album contains country & western music and may cause offence to narrow minded listeners." He returned to his former style for later albums, which included political comments criticizing the Falklands War, Margaret Thatcher, and the domestic problems of Prince Charles and his then-wife, Princess Diana. Costello continued to work with the Attractions during the middle eighties, but he also played with another acoustic group called the Confederates and performed some solo acoustic concerts. He broke up the Attractions in 1996.

Elvis Costello began his career by portraying an extreme example of male insecurity in modern culture, whereas singer/writer/guitarist Chrissie Hynde (born in 1952) displayed a strong, tough, and yet somewhat vulnerable female image. Hynde was born and raised in Akron, Ohio, and played guitar with a rock band while an art student at Kent State University. A fan of British bands such as the Kinks and the Who, she moved to London in 1973 and got a job as a music reviewer for the *New Musical Express.* She decided to find a band to play with and worked with several musicians who later formed the Damned, as well as with Mick Jones, who later formed the Clash. In 1978, she recorded a demo tape that secured for her a contract with Real Records (Sire Records in the United States). Contract in hand, she hired British musicians to form the **Pretenders.**

In addition to Hynde as a singer, writer, and rhythm guitarist, the Pretenders included lead guitarist James Honeyman-Scott, bass player Pete Farndon, and a temporary drummer who was replaced by Martin Chambers after the recording of their first single, a cover of the Kinks' "Stop Your Sobbing." A strong backbeat and heavy-metal-influenced guitar lines gave the Pretenders a hard-rock sound that was new wave because Hynde's vocals were generally void of any sort of tender emotion. The energy and often the anger of punk were present, but Hynde made the element of melody, whether it was her singing or Honeyman-Scott's guitar playing, more important than the fast, pounding punk beat.

The original membership of the Pretenders did not last long. Within a year after the release of their second album, *Pretenders II* (1981), Farndon left the band, Honeyman-Scott died of a drug overdose, and Hynde became pregnant. Determined to continue with her music, Hynde put together new musicians for the *Learning to Crawl* album (1983), and then another new group, which included American funk and fusion musicians, for *Get Close* (1987). Through the many personnel and musical changes in her band, however, Hynde maintained her tough new-wave image and stage personality. The 1994 album *Last of the Independents* provided a strong return for the Pretenders and included "I'll Stand by You," which charted in the top twenty. Hynde continued to work with the Pretenders, but in the two-thousands she is the only original member.

Summary

The general label of "new music" may be applied to punk and new wave. Messages of song lyrics differed from one style to the other, with punk generally expressing multidirectional anger and new wave displaying a cool, modern, detached approach to life, unaffected by emotional concerns. Both styles were trimmed down from the grandiose rock styles of the seventies, which had created an unbridgeable distance between the performer and the audience. Punks resented music that was so complex most teens could never achieve the necessary technical proficiency to be able to play it—at least not without years of serious study. They were aware that rock had once been a young people's music, and armed with simple guitar, bass, and drums instrumentation, they performed music meaningful to them and their peers.

Although new wave used modern electronic instruments and made other concessions to commercialism, the style maintained punk's energetic pulse. Historically, nothing was really very new about any of the new-music styles, but to listeners who had grown accustomed to hearing progressive-rock groups use racks of synthesizers and dozens of instruments, or to heavy-metal bands with stacks of screaming amplifiers behind them, the sound of new wave was refreshingly clean, clear, and modern.

discussion questions

Punk is angry music, and it is the most effective when the anger is directed at some particular issue, person, or practice. Could a positive message, a religious one, for example, be delivered in a punk style and be taken seriously? What about new wave, which is generally fairly alienated from emotion? Could it express a positive message effectively?

Funk and Disco

> *"All these parts jump around on each other—maybe that's why it makes you dance; because these parts were bouncing off each other it was just one of those things that all fit together perfectly. The horn line flowed across all of it."*
>
> —FRED WESLEY, FROM JAMES BROWN'S BAND, DESCRIBING THE POLYRHYTHMS IN FUNK MUSIC

> "To me his horns were his backup singers."
>
> –Khalis Bayaan, of Kool and the Gang, about James Brown's use of the horn section

chapter 17

247

Funk music predated disco by almost ten years. Yet the two styles share enough musical characteristics that some musicians played either and some recordings had characteristics of both. Part of the reason was that both styles are rooted in soul music of the sixties, although funk began with James Brown's very gospel-oriented soul style whereas disco was an outgrowth of the more pop-oriented soul sound from Philadelphia. Philadelphia soul sometimes even used orchestral instruments to back singers, not something typical of black gospel music. Other differences between funk and disco include the fact that funk uses polyrhythms. Sometimes only the drums in a funk group keep a steady beat—the bass player and horns go off in other rhythmic directions. Disco, on the other hand, is all about dancing and, therefore, the entire rhythm section stresses each beat of each four-beat bar. In disco, those beats are often subdivided into four faster beats, yet the subdivisions are regular and even to keep the stress on the beat itself. Funk groups commonly have electric guitar, electric bass guitar, sometimes a keyboard, a horn section, and drums. Disco often includes all those same instruments, but then adds strings or synthesized strings, orchestral woodwind and brass instruments, and even orchestral percussion instruments such as timpani.

Funk

Funk was a very distinctive style that used polyrhythms, syncopated bass lines, and short vocal phrases with a considerable amount of repetition of those rhythm patterns and phrases. Funk vocals were often sung in a work-song style with a conversational delivery. The first examples of funk were recorded by the Godfather of Soul himself, James Brown. Brown's soul style was deeply rooted in black gospel music, but his funk style was influenced by polyrhythmic music straight from Africa.

Brown's backup musicians maintained a constant rhythmic accompaniment using polyrhythms among the bass, drums, and horn section while still having a clear accent on the downbeat. Horns were used to punctuate the rhythm but not to play melodic lines. Both the bass and guitar parts involved either repeated riffs or rhythmic pulsations. Chord changes were generally minimal. The recording that introduced this style, "Out of Sight" (1964), was followed by a more successful recording in a similar style, "Papa's Got a Brand New Bag" (1965), for which a listening guide appears on page 249. "Papa's Got a Brand New Bag" was number eight on the U.S. pop charts and number one for eight weeks on the rhythm and blues charts. It was number twenty-five in Britain.

Although Brown used the blues chord progression in "Papa's Got a Brand New Bag," other recordings in Brown's new protofunk style maintained a single chord for long sections of the music, drawing attention to the rhythms instead of the chords or melody. As an example of the types of

polyrhythms in Brown's recordings, the following notation shows how the four-way polyrhythms were used in "Papa's Got a Brand New Bag." Only the rhythms are notated—not the pitches for the horns and bass.

Brown's new style had such an appealing, hypnotic sound that other groups copied it. One of these groups was **Sly and the Family Stone.** Sly Stone (Sylvester Stewart, born in 1944) and his brother, Freddie Stewart, grew up singing gospel music in their San Francisco church. Sylvester took classes in music theory at Vallejo Junior College and learned to play several instruments in addition to working as a singer and songwriter. He produced a number of recordings by San Francisco bands, including the Beau Brummels, the Mojo Men, the Vejtables, and the Great Society (with Grace Slick, who later sang for Jefferson Airplane).

The Stewart brothers started a group called the Stoners in 1966, but it lasted only a year. They added more musicians and formed Sly and the Family Stone. The word *family* referred both to the fact that Sly's siblings were in the group and that the group included black and white members. The interracial, family-of-human-beings image

Listening Guide

"Papa's Got a Brand New Bag"
as recorded by James Brown (1965)

Tempo: The tempo of the beat is about 126 beats per minute, with four beats per bar.

Form: The twelve-bar blues form is followed throughout, with an introduction and six full choruses.

Features: The basic beat subdivision is even, but Brown's vocals sometimes relax into uneven subdivisions.

The backbeat is accented by the guitar.

Even sixteenth-note subdivisions strummed on the guitar add energy at the end of each chorus (except the last).

Polyrhythms are created among the horns, the bass, and the drums. Each maintains its own rhythmic pattern that is simple and repetitious but different from that of the other instruments.

Lyrics: The lyrics tell us that Papa's "bag" is dancing.

Billboard pop charts: number eight; *Billboard* rhythm and blues charts: number one for eight weeks; British hit singles: number twenty-five

made an important statement in support of the civil rights movement that was under way at the time. The group also included female members playing instruments, such as trumpeter Cynthia Robinson and pianist Rose "Stone" Stewart, at a time when women instrumentalists were not common in rock groups. By the time they recorded "Dance to the Music" in 1968, the group had taken James Brown's polyrhythmic vamps using minimal chord changes, added electronic fuzztone, and imitated Motown's stress on all four beats, avoiding the strong backbeat common in most styles of rock music.

Bigotry was a concern to Sly Stone, and the group's song "Everyday People" (1969) made fun of hangups about skin color as well as other forms of bigotry. Other songs, like

Sly and the Family Stone perform on a TV show in 1968 (left to right): Cynthia Robinson, Jerry Martini, Sly Stone, Gregg Errico, Rose Stone, Freddie Stone, and Larry Graham

"Don't Call Me Nigger Whitey" (1969), made an even stronger statement about the same subject. "Everyday People" was more rock-styled than the group's other recordings, with a heavy backbeat, gospel-style call-and-response vocals, and the even beat subdivisions common in early Motown recordings.

The recording by Sly and the Family Stone that had the greatest influence on the development of funk music was "Thank You (Falettinme Be Mice Elf Agin)" (1970). The recording was reminiscent of the Memphis soul sound of Booker T. and the MGs, updated with fuzztone guitar and polyrhythms set over minimal chord changes. A listening guide is below. The song was number two for two weeks on the U.S. pop charts and number one for five weeks on the rhythm and blues charts.

"You add the thumpin' and pluckin' with drums. . . . You know, you get the percussion thing. . . . My foot's on a distortion box."

–Larry Graham, bass player for
Sly and the Family Stone

"He actually start poppin' and playing accents while he was playing melodically the low end in the bass. That's how he developed that. It was the beginning of slap bass."

–Members of Sly and the Family Stone,
about Larry Graham's playing

Listening Guide

"Thank You (Falettinme Be Mice Elf Agin)"
as recorded by Sly and the Family Stone (1970)

Tempo: The tempo is approximately 108 beats per minute, with four beats in each bar.

Form: The form is comprised primarily of eight-bar sections, most of which have new lyrics on each repetition; other sections serve as a refrain by repeating the title of the song.

An eight-bar instrumental introduction is followed by two eight-bar sections, the eight-bar refrain, and then a four-bar instrumental section. The major part of the song has two more eight-bar sections with new lyrics and the refrain, one more new eight-bar section, and then four repetitions of the refrain with a fade-out on the last one.

Features: Each instrument repeats its own rhythmic patterns, but polyrhythms are created between the separate patterns of the electric guitar, bass, and drums as notated below (only the rhythms are notated—not the pitches):

The beats are subdivided evenly throughout the recording.

Lyrics: The lyrics refer to street fights and violence, and efforts on the part of the singer to avoid those problems and "be himself" through family unity and music.

Billboard pop charts: number two for two weeks; *Billboard* rhythm and blues charts: number one for five weeks

The polyrhythmic funk style of Sly Stone influenced other funk musicians who followed him, and his use of bizarre spelling as seen in the song title "Thank You (Falettinme Be Mice Elf Agin)" was also used by other funk musicians as a play on jive talk.

During the sixties soul styles developed in many cities in addition to those discussed in Chapter 6. Chicago and Philadelphia were two of the most important because of their influence on the development of seventies funk and disco styles. Sixties Chicago soul tended to have a smooth rhythmic flow with doo-wop-influenced vocals that reflected a more controlled emotional expressiveness than many of the soul recordings from Memphis, where rough and gritty vocals were the standard.

In many ways, the **Impressions** defined sixties Chicago soul. As was true of many soul styles, the Impressions were formed by gospel singers who decided to branch out and sing secular songs. One of their early hits was "For Your Precious Love" (1958), for which Jerry Butler sang the lead vocal. Butler left the Impressions for a solo career in 1959, and **Curtis Mayfield** (1942–1999) took his place singing lead. Mayfield was with the Impressions for eleven years, during which the group recorded some gospel songs that became pop chart hits such as "Amen" (1963). Other songs were intended to give support and encouragement to African Americans during the civil rights movement, including "I'm So Proud" (1964), "Keep on Pushing" (1964), and "We're a Winner" (1968). Mayfield left the Impressions in 1970 and created the greatest success of his career by writing and producing the soundtrack for the film *Superfly* (1972). By the time Mayfield was recording for the movie, his style had progressed from soul to its offshoot style, funk.

Superfly has been described as a "blaxploitation" (black exploitation) film because of the way it portrayed life in a black urban ghetto and focused on a drug subculture. Some saw the movie as making a critical statement about the civil rights movement for its failure to improve the economic lives of urban blacks. Most of the movie's characters were completely involved in drug dealing and could find no way out of that life. In the movie, "Fat Freddie" was a drug dealer who ended up getting hit by a car and killed. Mayfield's soundtrack reflected the antidrug-culture theme of the movie, and some of the songs from it were released as singles. A listening guide to one of the hit songs from *Superfly*, "Freddie's Dead," is included here.

Listening Guide

"Freddie's Dead"
as recorded by Curtis Mayfield (1972)

Tempo: The tempo is approximately 92 beats per minute, with two beats in each bar.

Form: The lengths of sections vary to follow the vocals. The recording begins with a seven-bar instrumental introduction. The vocals begin with a sixteen-bar refrain. Other sections of text vary from eight, to twelve, to sixteen, and, in one place, twenty bars in length.

Features: The instrumentation is voice, guitar, funky syncopated electric bass guitar, drums, other percussion, and an orchestra.

The introduction is comprised of a two-bar bass and guitar riff played three times, followed by one bar of solo drums.

The refrain is sung five times through the recording, with some variations in the text. The third refrain references Freddie's death, and the fourth refrain warns the listener might die too.

The drums play even beat subdivisions throughout, but the bass plays the riff more freely around the drums, creating a funky sense of rhythmic freedom.

The orchestra enters at the first verse (with the first statement that "Freddie's

(continued)

dead") and continues through much of the recording.

A flute joins the bass and guitar on the riff pattern toward the end of the recording.

Between the fourth and fifth verses, the bass, guitar, and drums play a sixteen-bar vamp that includes repetitions of the riff.

Lyrics: Freddie was a low-level cocaine dealer and addict in the movie *Super fly* who is hit by a car and killed (the suggestion is that it is in retaliation for informing on fellow dealers). The song uses

Freddie as a universal symbol of low-level participants in the illegal drug trade (as in "a Freddie") to underscore their short and unhappy lives. The song purveys a better and sardonic sensibility, contrasting technological progress (this early 1972 song was written at the time of the Apollo moon "rockets") and, as in the movie, the assertion that drug dealing in the ghetto is ultimately controlled by a white power structure (as in pushing dope for "the man").

Billboard pop charts: number four; *Billboard* rhythm and blues charts: number two for four weeks

Mayfield provided music for other films and continued to tour and record. He suffered severe injuries when a light fixture fell on him during a rehearsal in 1990. He was paralyzed from the neck down but managed to continue to sing. A quadriplegic, he recorded a new album, *New World Order,* in 1996. He died in 2000.

During the seventies, a funk style called **street funk** developed. Street funk was generally dominated by strong bass guitar lines, harmonies filled in by guitars or keyboards, complex rhythms played by a variety of drums (including Latin bongo and conga drums), a flat-four beat (all four beats accented evenly), and often included a party atmosphere complete with whistles, tambourines, and conversational vocals. Kool and the Gang, the Ohio Players, and George Clinton and his groups Parliament and Funkadelic were popular street funk groups.

" **Most white people, when you listen to their music they turn up the treble whereas black people turn up the bass. . . . That's where the music is rooted, in the rhythm section. . . . Funk is when that bass line is just pumpin' in conjunction with the drums.** "

–Larkin Arnold, Sr. VP of CBS Records

Singer, songwriter, and producer **George Clinton** (born in 1941) formed **Parliament** (originally the Parliaments) as a vocal group styled after Motown's Temptations. Clinton had moved to Detroit and was hired by Motown as a staff writer, but none of his groups recorded for Motown. It is quite possible that he was not asked to perform at Motown

because Clinton's bizarre stage persona was too much for Berry Gordy's tightly controlled production company. Clinton's group Parliament was signed on the Revilot label and his group Funkadelic on Westbound Records. Both groups recorded using Jimi Hendrix–like distorted guitar lines and the funky polyrhythms of Sly and the Family Stone, along with the conversational vocals the Temptations had used in "Cloud Nine." Clinton created science fiction characters and stage sets for Parliament that sometimes made reference to social conditions.

George Clinton

In 1968, Clinton formed a new group he called **Funkadelic.** Both Parliament and Funkadelic had flexible membership, and some musicians were common to both, but he had them record on separate labels and maintain their separate identities in performances. In contrast with Parliament's science fiction characters and stories, Funkadelic's music was built around images and sounds from horror movies. Clinton later combined both groups' members and images and called them the Mothership Connection, Parliafunkadelicment Thang, or P-Funk All-Stars. Clinton himself had several colorful names including Dr. Funkenstein, Maggot Overload, and Uncle Jam.

Sometimes important political statements came through in the otherwise very entertaining music and shows. Parliament's album *Chocolate City* (1975), for example, concentrated on telling a story that placed African Americans where they had not been seen before, such as in the White House holding important government jobs. Through the story, there are constant repetitions of the words "Gainin' on ya!" as if to suggest a future in which African Americans are no longer controlled by others.

"I think P-Funk was a religious something going on, it was a holy sancti-fool type feeling. . . . We always cut good records . . . , but to me the P-Funk revival thang was really what was happening. . . . We could never perform on record like we perform in concert."

—Bootsy Collins

Clinton worked with such constantly changing groups of musicians that his style varied quite a bit over the years. One change that became an important influence on later funk music was the replacement of electric bass guitar with synthesized bass lines. That sound was introduced on Parliament's hit recording "Flash Light" (1978). A listening guide to that recording appears below. It was

Listening Guide

"Flash Light"
as recorded by Parliament (1978)

Tempo: The tempo is approximately 108 beats per minute, with four beats in each bar.

Form: After a four-bar introduction with pickups, the recording is based on a continuous repetition of four-bar sections, some of which are paired with vocal phrases.

Features: Most of the instruments use even beat subdivisions, but the vocals often follow uneven subdivisions.

Hand claps stress the backbeat.

The initial bass riff imitates the rhythm played by the drums at the very beginning of the recording.

A synthesizer plays the bass lines.

Polyrhythms are created between the separate patterns of the synthesized guitar, bass, and drums.

The recording includes long, extended repetitions of the four-bar sections that include dubbing of prerecorded fragments of music, rhythmically random lines played on a synthesizer, and vocal interpolations all held together with the rhythmic playing of the drum beat, hand claps, and bass line.

Lyrics: This song, released at the height of disco's popularity in the late seventies, evokes images of stereotypical seventies disco clubs (the sparkling ball being the song's core image), but the scene is overlaid by a self-conscious celebration of the "funk style," which was far more polyrhythmic than disco music.

Billboard pop charts: number sixteen; *Billboard* rhythm and blues charts: number one for three weeks

number sixteen on the U.S. pop charts and number one for three weeks on the rhythm and blues charts.

Clinton took a break from performing from 1983 through 1989, but portions of his music became popular with new, young listeners when used as backup samples by rap vocalists. He produced the album *Freaky Styley* (1985) for the Red Hot Chili Peppers. Merging his own style with one he had influenced, his 1989 album *The Cinderella Theory* included vocals by Public Enemy's Chuck D and Flavor Flav. With the tremendous popularity of rap during the nineties, Clinton has been featured as an old master of funk in recordings and videos by many rappers. He performed on the *Lollapalooza* tour of 1994.

One of Clinton's bass players, Bootsy Collins (born in 1951), had worked with James Brown before being recruited for Clinton's groups in the midseventies. While continuing to play with Clinton's various groups, Collins also started a group of his own, Bootsy's Rubber Band. They did not have the pop chart successes that Clinton's P-Funk had, but they placed many hits on the rhythm and blues charts well into the nineties. Bootsy Collins became known for his wonderful sense of humor, displayed by his wearing star-shaped eyeglasses. Some of his song titles such as "Psychoticbumpschool" (1969) and "Bootzilla" (1978) also serve as examples.

> **"Bootsy was a big silly dude that could play a gang of bass who has so much imagination that . . . he had that rhythm and that vibe of James Brown."**
>
> –George Clinton, about Bootsy Collins

Disco

The term *disco* was first used in post–World War II France when clubs began playing recorded dance music rather than using live bands. During the sixties, such clubs were called discothèques. Disco music of the seventies began with the soul styles of Detroit (Motown Records) and Philadelphia (Philadelphia International Records) that became popular in homosexual and African American clubs in New York before the dance craze spread to the rest of the country. The musicians and singers of disco music did concertize, as have most other rock musicians, but the essence of disco lay in the clubs themselves, where the dancers were the performers.

Because the music was intended to be played from records by disc jockeys, many disco records had "bpm" (beats per minute) indications on the labels so that recordings could be chosen to easily **segue** from one to another without changing the speed of the beat. Many disco records began with a rhythmically free introduction to allow the tempo to change from that of the previous record played and to give dancers time to get out on the dance floor. Other recordings, such as Donna Summer's "Love to Love You Baby" (1975), were longer than singles normally were, again, to allow dancers a continuous flow of music.

Musically, disco was somewhat related to seventies street funk in that each beat was strongly accented, although not always at an even dynamic level. Many disco recordings also featured group backup vocals that created a partylike atmosphere or used whistles and other sounds to invite listeners to join into the festivities and dance.

One of the earliest important disco singers, songwriters, arrangers, and producers was Barry White (born in 1944), whose disco records were made with a forty-member orchestra he called the Love Unlimited Orchestra. White was born in Texas, where he sang and played the organ for his church. In Los Angeles as a teenager, White became a singer and pianist with a rhythm and blues group. He spent time working as an A&R (artist and repertory) man at a record company before 20th Century records contracted him as a singer. After the top-ten success of his single "I'm Gonna Love You Just a Little More Baby" (1973), he formed his Love Unlimited Orchestra and made one hit disco record after another through the seventies. As the popularity of disco waned in the eighties, White had fewer records making the pop charts, but he did continue to record. His deep, lush voice made it back onto the pop charts in 1994 with the album *The Icon Is Love* and its hit single "Practice What You Preach."

By the midseventies, disco was beginning to separate into substyles. One of those was called **eurodisco,** and its leading producer was indeed a European, Giorgio Moroder. He was Italian-Swiss and a record producer in Munich, Germany, when he first worked with Donna Summer (Adrian Donna Gaines, born in 1948; "Summer" was from her married name, Sommer) to record "Love to Love You Baby." Moroder later relocated to Los Angeles and continued to work as a disco writer and producer. The essence of his production sound centered on his use of Moog synthesizers to create funky, electronic timbres. Donna Summer's recording of "Hot Stuff" serves as an example of Moroder's eurodisco style. A listening guide to that recording is on page 255. "Hot Stuff" was number one on the U.S. pop charts for three weeks and was number three on the rhythm and blues charts. It was number eleven in Britain. It was one of four number-one hits for Summer, who also had many more top-ten and top-forty hits as well. She won a series of Grammy awards and soon came to be considered the Queen of Disco. As

Donna Summer

Listening Guide

"Hot Stuff"
as recorded by Donna Summer
(1979)

Tempo: The tempo is approximately 120 beats per minute, with four beats in each bar.

Form: The form is based on eight-bar phrases, repeated as follows: AABCCABC CAACBA. The A sections are based on the beat pattern and chord progression with which the recording begins. The B sections are vocal verses. The C sections are refrains with repetitions of the words "hot stuff."

Features: The first A section stresses the steady beat with a chordal background but no melody. It includes strongly accented backbeats whereas the rest of the recording has fairly equal stresses on all four beats of each bar.

A synthesized four-bar melody plays twice during the second A section, and all four beats in each bar are almost pounded out very clearly.

When the A section returns the next and last times, it sounds much like it did the second time in the introduction.

The pair of A sections before the last refrain (of "hot stuff" repetitions) and verse serve as instrumental improvisations in which the synthesizer plays new melodic material.

The recording ends with a fade-out.

Lyrics: The singer is an amorous woman looking for a male sex partner and she wants him that night.

Billboard pop charts: number one for three weeks; *Billboard* rhythm and blues charts: number three; British hit singles: number eleven

disco's popularity began to wane in the eighties, Summer continued to make hit records, although many were in more of a rhythm and blues style than disco. She continued to perform into the twenty-first century.

The lyrics to disco songs were often about love, sex, or dancing, but not always. One of disco's biggest hits, Gloria Gaynor's "I Will Survive" (1978), was about her ability to survive the end of a relationship. That recording won Gaynor the first and only Grammy award for Best Disco Recording in 1980. Despite the real-life-related survival message of that recording, sex was still the favorite theme for disco songs. The image of disco's roots in gay nightclubs was popularized by the Village People. The group members dressed as different macho male stereotypes: a biker, a policeman, a soldier, a cowboy, an Indian, and a hard-hat construction worker. The homosexual orientation of many of their songs such as "Macho Man" (1978), "Y.M.C.A." (1979), and "In the Navy" (1979) appealed to large international audiences of dancers and were big hits in England as well as in the United States.

KC and the Sunshine Band's funky disco style has sometimes been referred to as the Miami sound, and the band is indeed from Florida. The group was formed by singer/keyboard player Harry Wayne "KC" Casey and included bass, guitar, drums, congas, two trumpets, saxophone, and trombone. Additional members joined later to give them as many as eleven musicians for part of their career. They had a whole series of hits, with five that were number one, including "That's the Way (I Like It)" (1975), "(Shake, Shake, Shake) Shake Your Booty" (1976), and "Please Don't Go" (1979). After a break during the eighties, KC reformed the band to continue to record and make television and concert appearances.

The movie *Saturday Night Fever* (1977) presented disco dancing as an escape from an otherwise negative and dull life and helped spread the popularity of disco dancing to a massive mainstream audience. The Bee Gees had already had considerable success on the American pop charts with "I've Gotta Get a Message to You" (1968) and many other hits, but with the popularity of *Saturday Night Fever* and its hit soundtrack album they had three number-one hits, "How Deep Is Your Love," "Stayin' Alive," and "Night Fever," and enjoyed continuing success after that. A listening guide to "Stayin' Alive" is included here. Other top-forty

Listening Guide

"Stayin' Alive"
as recorded by the Bee Gees (1977)

Tempo: The tempo is approximately 104 beats per minute, with four beats in each bar.

Form: After a six-bar instrumental introduction, the recording includes three eight-bar verses, three repetitions of an eleven-bar refrain, one two-bar instrumental interlude between the first refrain and the second verse, and five repetitions of a twelve-bar section that begins as an instrumental but has repetitious vocal additions. Those sections are ordered introduction, verse, refrain, two-bar interlude, verse, refrain, instrumental/vocal, verse, refrain, and four repetitions of the instrumental/vocal section.

Features: The instrumentation consists of three voices (the three Bee Gees), guitar, bass, keyboards, drums, and other percussion.

The drums maintain a very steady, repetitious evenly subdivided beat, as is typical of disco.

A riff repeats through much of the recording, only changing to a more standard accompanying bass line during the refrains.

The verses all begin with the word "Well," the refrains begin with "Whether you're a brother . . ," and the vocals, during the partly instrumental sections, start with "Life goin' nowhere" and asking for help.

Lyrics: Despite the ever-present troubles of his hard life and upbringing, the singer exults in his ability to transcend his existence through dancing with the "wings of heaven" on his shoes.

Billboard pop charts: number one for four weeks; *Billboard* rhythm and blues charts: number four; British hit singles: number four

Chic (1980)

hits from the *Saturday Night Fever* soundtrack were the Trammps' "Disco Inferno" and Tavares' "More than a Woman." Kool and the Gang and KC and the Sunshine Band also contributed to the movie soundtrack.

" Disco was funky when you take one record at a time. It's just that they narrowed it down to one beat to try to corner the market on a particular music and when you do that with rhythm you're talkin' about something that will get on your nerves. "

–George Clinton

One of the most successful and influential of the disco groups of the late seventies and early eighties was **Chic.** Formed by bassist/writer/producer Bernard Edwards and

Listening Guide

"Good Times"
as recorded by Chic (1979)

Tempo: The tempo is approximately 108 beats per minute, with four beats in each bar.

Form: The recording is based on the constant repetition of a four-bar pattern, with the lyrics often pairing with that repeated pattern to make up eight-bar phrases.

Features: Even beat subdivisions are used throughout the recording.

Each beat is solidly accented by the bass.

Drums and hand claps accent the backbeat.

The harmonies avoid any sense of cadence at a tonic chord, creating a feeling that the music could play on forever.

A synthesized string section is used to play fills at the ends of vocal lines.

The bass plays a riff pattern that uses a Cuban-influenced rhythm.

Lyrics: The lyrics celebrate the pre-AIDs "good times" of the late seventies associated with disco dancing and promiscuity.

Billboard pop charts: number one; *Billboard* rhythm and blues charts: number one for six weeks

The Language of the Disco Disc Jockey

Beat-mix—Overlapping the ending and beginning of two recordings, keeping their drum beats constant.

Cueing up—Preparing the next record to be played.

Cutting up records—Playing (beat-mixing) sections of recordings as short as ten seconds each from one record to the other back and forth.

Double up—Having two copies of the same recording on two different turntables and beat-mixing from one to the other to greatly increase the length of time they could continue to play.

Phasing—Playing two copies of the same recording at the same time but slightly out of synch to create a dramatic echo effect.

Reedit—Cutting and splicing a tape recording in order to reorder sections of the recording as well as to extend its length.

Remix—Separating the tracks (vocal, guitar, bass, drum, and so forth) on a recording and mixing the chosen ones back together.

Slip cuing—Holding the disc still while a felt pad (a slipmat) on the turntable turns under it ready to let the disc go at precisely the right moment to release it and seamlessly connect it to a record that just ended.

Twelve-inch single—A recording of a length that could fit on a seven-inch disc but, instead, is put on a twelve-inch one with the grooves spread farther apart. Twelve-inch singles were favored by disc jockeys because they were easier to manipulate and could play louder than seven-inch ones.

guitarist/writer/producer Nile Rodgers in New York, Chic also included two female singers and a drummer. Beginning with "Dance, Dance, Dance (Yowsah, Yowsah, Yowsah)" in 1977, their top-ten hits also included "Le Freak (Freak Out)" (1978), "I Want Your Love" (1979), and "Good Times" (1979). Their style was characterized by the pounding beat found in most disco, interesting and active bass lines, and Cuban-influenced rhythms. A listening guide to their most influential recording, "Good Times," is on page 257. It was number one on the U.S. pop charts for one week and number one on the rhythm and blues charts for six weeks. It was number five in Britain.

Later records that bore the influence of Chic's "Good Times" included the Sugar Hill Gang's "Rapper's Delight" (1980) and Queen's "Another One Bites the Dust" (1980). Chic broke up in 1983, but both Edwards and Rodgers continued to be successful as producers. Bernard Edwards produced Robert Palmer's album *Riptide* (1985), which included the hit single "Addicted to Love." Nile Rodgers produced *Let's Dance* (1983) for David Bowie, *Like a Virgin* (1984) for Madonna, and *She's the Boss* (1984) for Mick Jagger. The pair reformed Chic in 1992, but the group has not been able to recapture their past success.

Disco's steady, pounding beat was an important influence on music during the eighties and nineties, particularly on American new-wave bands such as Blondie. It was also an influence on the synthesized dance music called techno, which was still popular in the early nineties. Much of the music sampled or imitated to provide background for early

rap recordings also came from funk and disco recordings. The widespread use of video screens throughout former disco clubs has made the visual images of performers more important than they were in the disco era. Whether disco dancing returns to the popularity it experienced in the late seventies or not, disco music continues to make its mark on the popular culture of the two-thousands.

Summary

James Brown created an early funk style in 1964 when he put conversational vocals over a repetitious, polyrhythmic accompaniment. Just four years later Sly Stone further developed funk by adding a distorted guitar sound and an even four-beat pattern to Brown's basic formula. Curtis Mayfield added more serious, political statements in his soundtrack for the movie *Superfly*. Other writers and performers, such as George Clinton, created elaborate science fiction characters and bizarre stage shows and made funk into a party music. Street funk featured party sounds, whistles, and conversational vocals.

Disco was party music with an emphasis on dancing. The steady, throbbing beat of disco music was intended for one thing and one thing only: to encourage every listener to get up and dance. Both funk and disco have continued to be important influences on later music styles including techno and rap.

discussion questions

Along with most rock music, funk is a style that is primarily dominated by male performers (at least as group leaders), whereas many disco stars are female. How do those styles each compare with other rock styles that are or are not also male dominated? Are the male-dominated styles ones that women would not care to perform, or is there something inherently macho about them to the point that fans do not want to hear female performers? Are there any characteristics about disco that give it particular appeal for women and homosexuals?

The NINETEEN EIGHTIES

"Government has an important role in helping develop a country's economic foundation. But the critical test is whether government is genuinely working to liberate individuals by creating incentives to work, save, invest, and succeed."

–President Ronald Reagan (1981)

"In order to ensure the safety of nuclear power plants around the world, we need much greater commitment, communication, and active cooperation among those who make these systems safer."

–Dr Najmedin Meshleati, Institute of Safety and Systems Management, University of Southern California (1985, one year before the disaster of Chernobyl)

"I touch the future, I teach."

**–Christa McAuliffe, the teacher
who died in the Challenger disaster (1986)**

"We need a new system of values, a system of the
organic unity between mankind and nature and the
ethic of global responsibility."

–Soviet leader Mikhail Gorbachev
(1990, on acceptance of the Nobel Peace Prize.)

**"Mr. Gorbachev. Open this gate! Mr. Gorbachev, tear down
this wall!"**

–President Ronald Reagan (1987)

The seventies had consolidated many of the trends of the sixties, but the eighties reversed much of what had gone on in the previous decade. During the eighties, the "free love" attitudes of the seventies dissolved with the identification of AIDS; vinyl record albums were replaced by CDs; young adults rejected the hippie looks and concentrated on smart business dress and became yuppies; and the seemingly endless growth of the Soviet Union's power ended with the destruction of the Berlin Wall and the dissolution of the Soviet empire.

The decade began, however, marked by the seventies, with high rates of unemployment, homelessness, inflation, and interest rates. President Reagan, who took office in 1981, increased defense spending while also lowering corporate and personal income taxes. Eventually, inflation and interest rates came down. The stock market was riding high until Black Monday, October 19, 1987, when it crashed, but the crash was shortlived. The market soon recovered.

More young adults than ever took their college degrees in business management. They joined the workforce with much dedication to working long hours with the goal of a high lifestyle, spending much of their hard-earned income on clothing and cars that displayed their success. These young urban professionals came to be called yuppies. But increased interest in shopping was not limited to the yuppies. Not only did shopping malls become more popular than ever during the eighties, but also QVC and the Home Shopping Network allowed and encouraged Americans to use their credit cards and shop right from their own homes.

As far as music was concerned, the decade began with the devastating news of the assassination of former Beatle John Lennon. Lennon was only forty years old and at the beginning of a revival of his successful solo career, and his death drained the optimism of many fans. Less than a year after Lennon's death, MTV (Music Television) was introduced, allowing rock videos fans to view twenty-four hours a day. MTV sparked many new fashion and dance trends, as well as the careers of featured performers. Even rap music and the break dancing that went along with its hip-hop culture were popularized nationally by the show "Yo! MTV Raps."

News reports of widespread famine in Africa as well as the well-publicized problems experienced by American farmers caused many gatherings of rock stars for recordings and concerts to raise money for the needy. Michael Jackson and Lionel Richie's song "We Are the World" (1985) was recorded by an all-star group and raised more than fifty million dollars for relief organizations in Ethiopia. Later that same year, Live Aid, which was a fourteen-hour-long concert broadcast from both London's Wembley Stadium and Philadelphia's JFK Stadium, raised more than seventy million dollars for the same cause. Farm Aid followed and raised more than eight million dollars to aid U.S. farmers.

Punk fans continued to identify themselves by wearing torn clothing, to which the eighties' punks added multiple earrings, other piercing, and brightly colored hair. Another look for young people began with African American rappers and included oversized clothes (sometimes, but not always, sweat suits), brand-name sneakers without laces, and baseball caps turned sideways or backward. Madonna's "Material Girl" (1985) look was playfully decadent compared to the "dress for success" conservatism of the yuppies. All of these styles made the long-haired, bearded hippie look from the sixties and seventies seem very dated indeed.

Sports fans missed some competitions and games in the eighties. President Carter refused to allow the United States to participate in the 1980 Moscow Summer Olympic Games to protest the Soviet Union's invasion of Afghanistan. Along with the United States, the boycott included sixty-six countries, leaving many athletes unable to compete and many disappointed fans. Several communist countries joined the Soviet Union in boycotting the 1984 Los Angeles Olympic Games, creating further negative reactions to the mixing of politics with sports. Major league baseball players went on strike in June 1981, canceling 713 baseball games and creating bad feelings among players, team owners, and fans. In 1989, a World

Series baseball game was postponed at the last minute when a 7.1 magnitude earthquake struck San Francisco where the game was about to begin.

Several environmental disasters caused many to reconsider the safety of chemical plants and sources of power. An American-owned insecticide plant in Bhopal, India, leaked toxic gas, killing or injuring many Indian citizens. Longtime fears of the potential release of radioactive materials from nuclear power plants were realized when an explosion in a nuclear reactor did just that over an area of thirty-two thousand square miles in Chernobyl, Soviet Union in 1986. That event, along with the increased costs of maintaining nuclear power plants, caused a reversal of plans to build several new plants in the United States. Cheaper and cleaner ways of producing electricity were found through new research in the use of oil and coal. Oil was not necessarily all that safe to transport, however, as was seen in 1989 when the Exxon *Valdez* oil tanker hit a reef and spilled close to eleven million gallons of oil into the waters of Alaska's Prince William Sound. Much wildlife and life in local fishing villages was wiped out by the spill.

The eighties saw much war and other turmoil in the Middle East. Egyptian president Anwar Sadat was assassinated by Muslim extremists for having negotiated a peace agreement with Israel. Iraq and Iran were at war during most of the decade. The United States managed to stay out of that battle but did get involved in aiding Afghan guerrillas against the Soviet Union in Afghanistan. The Soviets finally pulled out in 1989.

Both horrible and amazing events occurred in science during the eighties. The Challenger space shuttle blasted off into space, carrying a high school social studies teacher, Christa McAuliffe, on board along with a crew of experienced astronauts. The plan was to give McAuliffe the experience of space travel that she would then share with students, teachers, and laypeople from all over the country in a series of lectures. Schoolrooms nationwide had students gathered around televisions to watch the takeoff, and no one was prepared to see the shuttle explode only seventy-four seconds later.

Acquired immunodeficiency syndrome (AIDS) was first discovered in 1981, and the research to find the virus responsible for the disease, as well as efforts to control it, lasted well beyond the eighties. Hundreds of thousands of Americans were infected and many died. On the other hand, many lives were saved from a variety of tumors and other disorders with the development and use of magnetic resonance imaging (MRI) and nuclear magnetic resonance (NMR), both of which allowed doctors to diagnosis problems that traditional X-rays would not have been able to show. The first artificial heart, Jarvik-7, was implanted into patients in the eighties. The first heart kept the patient, Dr. Barney Clark, alive for 112 days, and the second kept William Schroeder alive for 620 days. The end that the doctors had hoped for was yet to come, but these two successes were an important beginning.

Personal computers were introduced in the late seventies and were first popular in many U.S. homes as a tool for playing games such as Pac-Man. By the end of the eighties, however, computers had become essential tools for writing, research, and other educational projects. *Time* magazine called the computer the Man of the Year in 1982. This was the only time in the magazine's history that an inanimate object had been given that honor.

Of all of the successes and tragedies of the eighties, the end of the cold war might have been the most important. Even before the fall, Soviet leader Mikhail Gorbachev instituted *perestroika,* which was a restructuring of the Soviet economy, and followed that with a new policy of openness and freedom of speech for Soviets called *glasnost.* Presidents Reagan and Gorbachev also negotiated a reduction in the numbers of nuclear missiles each state had aimed at the other, and the Soviets withdrew from Eastern Europe. The terrible symbol of the early sixties cold war, the Berlin Wall that separated East and West Berlin for twenty-eight years, was torn down in 1989. Many Eastern European countries were left with new battles to establish themselves as independent from the Soviet Union, but the American fear of the communist menace was all but gone.

Chronology Chart

Historical Events	Happenings in Rock Music
1980 U.S. boycotts Moscow Olympics. Eight Americans are killed in ill-fated attempt to free hostages in Iran. Mt. St. Helens erupts. Carter reinstates draft registration. CNN first airs news twenty-four hours a day.	Frank Zappa starts his Barking Pumpkin company. *The Decline of Western Civilization* is filmed. John Lennon is murdered in New York. Bon Scott, Ian Curtis, John Bonham, and Steve P. Took die.
1981 Reagan becomes president. Fifty-three American hostages are freed by Iran. AIDS (HIV) virus is discovered. Assassination attempt on life of Reagan. Air traffic controllers strike. Sandra Day O'Connor is appointed to U.S. Supreme Court. Major league baseball strike cancels 713 games.	Rap develops out of dubbing. Heavy metal splits into progressive, glam, and thrash in addition to older blues style. MTV airs. Popularity of Sony Walkman pocket tape players increases demand for cassette tapes. Bill Haley, Bob Marley, Mike Bloomfield, and Harry Chapin die.
1982 U.S. supports U.K. in Falklands. Peace Week demonstrations for disarmament. ERA is defeated in vote for ratification. Space shuttle Columbia completes first operational flight. Dr. Barney B. Clark receives first permanent artificial heart.	The Who on "final" tour. Stray Cats revive rockabilly. CDs introduced in the U.S. John Belushi, Randy Rhoads, Murray "the K," Lester Bangs, Lightnin' Hopkins, Tampa Red, and James Honeyman-Scott die.

1983   U.S. military is sent to Lebanon. U.S. Marine headquarters and French paratrooper barracks are bombed in Lebanon. Korean jet is shot down in Soviet airspace. Cellular phones first available.

Duran Duran introduces British new romantic style. Muddy Waters, Dennis Wilson, and Karen Carpenter die.

1984   Famine in Ethiopia. First female vice presidential candidate. Vietnam vets settle with chemical companies over Agent Orange dispute. L.A. Olympics. Vanessa Williams resigns as Miss America. Bishop D. Tutu is awarded Nobel Peace Prize.

Band Aid and USA for Africa raise money to help feed starving in Ethiopia. Everly Brothers reunite. Madonna releases debut LP. Jackie Wilson and Marvin Gaye die.

1985   Ethiopians starve while food rots on docks. U.S. sends aid to Contras in Nicaragua. U.S./U.S.S.R. disarmament talks begin. Government cuts student loan funds. *Achille Lauro* hijacking. New tax law passes. Baby boomers begin to turn forty. Mikhail Gorbachev becomes premier of the Soviet Union.

Live Aid, Farm Aid, Artists United against Apartheid concerts. Organized efforts to censor rock lyrics with warning labels. Soul stars celebrate fiftieth anniversary of the Apollo Theatre in Harlem. Big Joe Turner and Rick Nelson die.

1986   First Martin Luther King Day is observed. Nuclear accident in Chernobyl, U.S.S.R. AIDS crisis escalates. U.S. astronauts die when Challenger explodes after takeoff. U.S. attacks Libya; Quaddafi threatens retaliation. U.S. imposes economic sanctions on South Africa. Hands Across America fund-raiser. Iran-Contra scandal begins.

First annual Rock and Roll Hall of Fame bash in New York. Violent outbreaks plague Run-DMC concerts; deaths at Ozzy Osbourne and Judas Priest shows. New Age music pacifies the yuppie generation. Amnesty International's Conspiracy of Hope tour. Richard Manuel, Ian Stewart, Sonny Terry, Cliff Burton, and Albert Grossman die.

1987   Marcos leaves the Philippines. Gay rights rally in Washington, D.C., displays AIDS quilt. Stock market crashes. Scandal causes Gary Hart to pull out of presidential race. Scandal causes Jim and Tammy Bakker to resign from P.T.L. leadership.

Paul Simon's *Graceland* features South African musicians. Metal bands dominate the charts. American and Soviet bands unite in Russia for the July Fourth Disarmament Festival. Farm Aid II. Lynyrd Skynyrd survivors reunite. Lee Dorsey, Buddy Ric, John Huston, John Hammond, Jaco Pastorius, Paul Butterfield, Peter Tosh, and Andy Warhol die.

1988   I.M.F. Treaty is signed. Launch of Discovery successful. U.S. Navy warship mistakenly shoots down a commercial Iranian airliner. Jimmy Swaggart scandal. Glasnost becomes a distinct possibility when the Soviet Union withdraws from much of Eastern Europe.

Atlantic Records celebrates fortieth anniversary. Nelson Mandela Freedomfest in London honors imprisoned South African leader. Amnesty International's Human Rights Now! tour. Alternative rock bands combine old styles in search of new ones. Nico, Roy Buchanan, Andy Gibb, Dave Prater, Clifton Chenier, Gil Evans, Brook Benton, Memphis Slim, Chet Baker, Will Shatter, Eddie Vinson, Hillel Slovak, and Roy Orbison die.

1989   George Bush becomes president. Exxon oil spill in Alaska. Gorbachev visits Cuba and China. U.S. recognizes P.L.O. U.S. troops invade Panama. Students in Beijing demonstrate for Chinese political reforms. The Berlin wall is removed. Oliver North fined for role in Iran-Contra scandal. The Ayatollah Khomeini issues a death sentence on author Salman Rushdie.

Cat Stevens voices support of Iranian death threats against author of *The Satanic Verses*. Glam and metal bands are featured at Moscow Music Peace Festival. "Yo! MTV Raps" is added to MTV lineup. James Brown is jailed. Salvador Dali, Abbie Hoffman, Nesuhi Ertegun, Gilda Radner, Graham Chapman, Keith Whitley, and John Cipollina die.

chapter 18

Hip-Hop and Rap

" Manipulating sound with just your hand is like a miracle. The basic root of scratching is that the turntable is a musical instrument. You're figuring out all these time signatures and rhythms and patterns and notes. "

—DJ Q-BERT

The hip-hop culture and rap music originated in New York during the midseventies and grew to nationwide popularity in the eighties. Rap involved spoken lyrics performed in a rhythmic patter over complex, funk-styled rhythms. Spoken poetry has long been important in African and African American culture as a form of communication. Griot singers in Africa kept track of and commented on their history through spoken and sung poetry. During the days of slavery, the poetic lyrics of spirituals included at least two levels of meaning, allowing slaves to tell one another about pathways to freedom while sounding like simple religious songs to white listeners. The term for this is *signifying,* and it relates to much rap music.

A group of writers in Harlem during the twenties wrote honest and insightful works that portrayed ghetto life. At times, they even used common street dialect and speech patterns that were not considered to be "correct" English. Langston Hughes (1902–1967) was one such poet who was criticized by his own people for exposing that underground language. Hughes added to the African American flavor of his poetry by using phrases that imitated the rhythmic flow of jazz melodic lines, and he often mentioned the music in his works. Despite the initial criticism aimed at the writers, the movement, which became known as the Harlem Renaissance, soon came to be credited for the open-minded honesty of the works, and "ghetto language" became more openly recognized as an important expression of life in Harlem and other African American communities.

Singers of country blues and other rural styles of the twenties and thirties such as Blind Willie Johnson, Pine Top Smith, and Memphis Minnie sometimes used patter speech in sections of their songs. American rhythm and blues singer Louis Jordan had used rhythmic speech patterns in songs such as "Saturday Night Fish Fry" during the forties, and James Brown used a similar style in message songs of the sixties such as "King Heroin" and "Say It Loud—I'm Black and I'm Proud." Disc jockeys in Jamaica during the late sixties developed a style of patter-talk called toasting or dubbing that may have been influenced by Louis Jordan's or James Brown's speech patterns. Funk disc jockeys in New York imitated those Jamaican disc jockeys to create their vocal style.

Hip-Hop Culture and East Coast Rap

Hip-hop began with **break dancing** in the tough ghettos of New York's South Bronx and soon spread to Queens and Brooklyn. The dancing was a form of competition that not only required a great amount of practiced skill, but also provided a bit of positive relief from life in neighborhoods where gang violence was common. To provide music for the dancers in the streets, disc jockeys would plug their sound systems into electric power from streetlight poles and play funk or even disco music. One of the first disc jockeys to manipulate the sound of the records played for the dancers was **DJ Kool Herc** (Clive Campbell, born in 1957), who had moved to New York from Jamaica. He called his sound system "Herculoids," after his own stage name. Very familiar with the Jamaican styles of disc jockeying and toasting, he also liked to break dance. Many times he would watch the dancers while he was playing records and see that they enjoyed certain parts of the recordings more than others. He decided to play from two turntables so that he could switch from a particular section of one recording that dancers seemed to like the most to a favorite section of another and not bother with playing any of his records all the way through. He used Jamaican styles of toasting to add interest

to his disc jockey performances. In many ways, DJ Kool Herc is the Father of Hip-Hop because he was the first to introduce Jamaican disc jockeying techniques and toasting into New York's break dancing performances, a combination that led to the development of rap. He continues to perform as a DJ in the mid-two-thousands.

> **"I had the attitude of the dance floor behind the turntables. I'm a dance person. I like to party."**
> –DJ Kool Herc

Herc influenced another early hip-hop disc jockey, **Afrika Bambaataa** (Kevin Donovan, born in 1960), whose stage name was that of an African Zulu chief and translated as "Chief Affection." Bambaataa liked to break dance, and he organized his neighbors into what he called the Zulu Nation. He encouraged people of all races to join, and the organization eventually had chapters outside the United States. The basic values around which they organized were freedom, justice, equality, knowledge, wisdom, and understanding. The groups organized neighborhood cleanup projects, food drives, mentor programs, and talent shows. The music they identified with and danced to was hip-hop, which involved disc jockeys manipulating whatever records they had, including ones by James Brown, Sly Stone, and George Clinton, as well as others by any number of rock bands such as the Rolling Stones, Led Zeppelin, or Queen. Rap was the patter-talk that sometimes went along with the record manipulation.

Break Dancing Techniques

B-boy/B-girl—A breakdancer.
Electric boogie—Controlled movements that begin at one appendage and gradually shift to other parts of the body in a wavelike motion.
Locking—A move in which appendages relax and then jerk back into position.
Moonwalk—A mimelike motion in which the dancer stays in one place while moving as if walking.

Popping—A move in which appendages jerk as if put out of joint.
Robot—A style in which individual body parts move while the rest of the body is stationary.
Spins—The dancer places his or her head, back, or hand on the ground and spins around like a top.
Up-rocking—Martial-arts-like motions.

" Flash was in the south Bronx, we was the south east Bronx, and you have Herc in the west Bronx. . . . But we respect each other. "

–Afrika Bambaataa

The neighborhood orientation of much early hip-hop led to the physical identification of city and subway walls by "tagging," or painting markers that identified whose territory the wall was in. This tagging developed into a very elaborate urban graffiti art form that went beyond mere identification to become elaborate murals in which the graffiti artists took great pride. Afrika Bambaataa's crew of artists named themselves the Black Spades.

" Zulu Nation is no gang. It is an organization of individuals in search of success, peace, knowledge, wisdom, understanding, and the righteous way of life. Zulu members must search for ways to survive positively in this society. Negative activities are actions belonging to the unrighteous. The animal nature is the negative nature. Zulus must be civilized. "

–Principles of Afrika Bambaataa's Universal Zulu Nation

The style of patter-talk that DJ Kool Herc used came from his homeland of Jamaica, but it and the vocal styles of other hip-hop disc jockeys were also influenced by a sixties group from Harlem called the **Last Poets.** The tensions of the civil rights movement and agreement with strong statements by Malcolm X and others were expressed through their graphic lyrics. Their first album, *The Last Poets,* was released in 1970 and included such protest songs as "Niggers Are Scared of Revolution." As had been true of the earlier writers from Harlem, jazz, rhythm and blues, soul music, and African drumming patterns were heard along with their poetry.

Lots of the disc jockeys' shows were tape-recorded and the tapes circulated in their neighborhoods, but there was little thought that such recordings would be of interest outside of New York. The owner of Sugarhill Records, Sylvia Robinson, had heard "Master Gee" Guy O'Brien, "Wonder Mike" Michael Wright, and "Big Bank Hank" Henry Jackson rapping at a party and asked them to record for her. They agreed and improvised their way

The Language of the Hip-Hop Disc Jockey

Backspinning—Turning or spinning the record back to the desired place.
Beat box—A Vox percussion box with keys that play the sounds of bass and snare drums as well as high-hat, castanets, and timbales.
Beat juggling—Rearranging the beat with fast changes from one record to another.
Breakdown—A DJ's slowing down a drum pattern by stopping the record between beats and playing beats from a second record between them.
Cutting—Segueing one recording into another using a varispeed control to maintain a constant beat pattern through the change.
Double backing—Playing two copies of the same record at the same time, but with one slightly ahead of the other.
Dub reggae—Hip-hop to a DJ's music.
Loop—A short drum pattern that is repeated over and over.

Merry-go-round—Cutting from the favorite section of one recording to a favorite section of another.
Mixing—Fading down one recording as another increases in volume level.
Ready-made music—Recordings on the records manipulated by disc jockeys.
Sampling—Taking selected sections from previously recorded records and repeating and mixing those sections to create a background sound to accompany new vocals.
Scratching—Changing the record's rotation from forward to backward repeatedly to create a rhythmic pulse.
Turntablist—A DJ for whom a deck of turntables is played like a musical instrument.
Varispeed control—A phonograph control that allows disc jockeys to vary the speed (and hence the pitch) at which a recording is played.

through a seventeen-minute recording that they called "Rapper's Delight" (1979). Their lyrics were casual and allowed each rapper a chance to boast about himself and his image within the neighborhood. The musical backing was the rhythm track from the disco record "Good Times" by Chic. The trio called themselves the **Sugar Hill Gang,** after the name of their record company, and the record ended up being the first ever hip-hop hit, having made it up to number thirty-six on the pop charts and number four on the rhythm and blues charts. A listening guide is included here.

When the success of "Rapper's Delight" indicated that there was commercial appeal for what many rappers had been doing in their live shows for some time, many of them began to put out their own records. Because rap was primarily a vocal style with roots in disc jockeys' use of prerecorded records as background, rappers chose to sample background music for their records as had the Sugar Hill Gang. **Sampling** involved taking selected sections from other recordings and repeating and mixing those sections to create a background sound. Of course, many

of the artists whose music was "sampled" saw the practice as stealing, and the ensuing lawsuits caused rap vocalists to credit the sources of their samples. This eventually included sharing royalties. Without using samples, the vocalists had to come up with their own newly recorded accompaniments, and synthesizers and drum machines became common replacements for samples.

> "To actually know that you have inspired a genre, a whole movement. . . . I look at these guys and think, 'We started that shit.' It's incredible what these guys took from us, and there's no end to it."
>
> –Grandmaster Flash

Kurtis Blow (Kurt Walker, born in 1959) was the first rapper to sign with a major label (Mercury). He produced

Listening Guide

"Rapper's Delight"
as recorded by the Sugar Hill Gang
(1979)

Tempo: The tempo is approximately 108 beats per minute, with four beats in each bar.

Form: The recording is based on the constant repetition of a four-bar pattern, with lyrics rapped over it.

Features: The instrumental backing for the rapped vocals was taken from Chic's recording of "Good Times" (1979), discussed in Chapter 17. The Chic instrumental was probably not sampled but played by a group called Positive Force, imitating Chic's playing. When the writers of Chic's song (bass player Bernard Edwards, and producer Nile Rogers) complained about stealing their music, they were given partial writers' credit for "Rapper's Delight," along

with Wonder Mike, Big Bank Hank, and Master Gee of the Sugar Hill Gang.

The three members of the Sugar Hill Gang trade off rapping throughout the recording.

A very steady backbeat is hand clapped throughout the recording.

Lyrics: All three rappers take turns assuming larger-than-life, almost Herculean personas, particularly in regard to their sexual abilities and magnetism. (There is a Greek myth that Hercules had sex with fifty women in one night.) Big Bank Hank goes so far as to compare himself favorably both to Casanova (renowned for his sexual conquests in Venice in the 1700s) and to Superman.

Billboard pop charts: number thirty-six; *Billboard* rhythm and blues charts: number four; British hit singles: number three

Listening Guide

"The Message"
as recorded by Grandmaster Flash
and the Furious Five, featuring Melle
Mel and Duke Bootee (1982)

Tempo: The tempo is approximately 102 beats per minute, with four beats in each bar.

Form: After an eighteen-bar instrumental introduction, the first eight bars of vocals repeat a phrase that returns at the end of each of five refrains. The refrains vary in length depending on how many times the opening text about life being a jungle is repeated. The verses vary in length as well.

Features: Even beat subdivisions and a strong backbeat are maintained throughout the recording.

    The vocals are sometimes spoken with the accents of the four-beat meter, and sometimes they are syncopated around it.

    Beginning at bar three, electronic sounds ascend for one bar, break for one bar, and then descend for one bar. Those electronic sounds are played during the vocal verses.

    Duke Bootee and others are added for the final verse that becomes a dialogue. It is quite effective to end with such a dialogue because it puts the recording into a "real-life" setting.

Lyrics: The rapper presents a collage of urban decay and degradation worthy of Dante's *Inferno* (progressively worse horrors of hell). His own brother steals from his mother, his son wants to drop out of school and risk the horrors of prison. Violence and early death are ubiquitous. The refrain reiterates the rapper's struggle to keep his sanity and integrity in the face of such unrelenting and dehumanizing conditions.

Billboard pop charts: number sixty-two; *Billboard* rhythm and blues charts: number four; British hit singles: number eight

a number eighty-seven pop chart hit (number four on the rhythm and blues charts) with his recording "The Breaks" (1980). **Grandmaster Flash** (Joseph Saddler, born in 1957) was one of the most successful of the turntablists to follow DJ Kool Herc; in fact, Flash either invented or at least perfected many of the techniques such as **scratching, backspinning, cutting,** use of a **varispeed control,** and others that continued to be the basis of hip-hop music for a long time. He put together a rap vocal group he called the Furious Five that featured the lead rapper Melle Mel (Melvin Glover) and made such records as "The Message" (1982) that expressed a serious view about ghetto life, describing it as a jungle that could easily pull him "under." This type of lyric message represented a major change because previous rap lyrics had been about partying and dancing. "The Message" reached number sixty-two on the pop charts and number four on the rhythm and blues ones. A listening guide to "The Message" is included here. Afrika Bambaataa responded by putting together a group he called Soul Sonic Force that included synthesized sounds, creating a new type of electro funk rap with his recording of "Planet Rock" (1982). That recording soon became the most sampled record in hip-hop.

The group that did the most to popularize rap among those in the mainstream rock culture was Run-DMC. They were the first rap group to get widespread acceptance with white audiences as they toured nationwide during the early to middle eighties, and they were the first to get airplay on MTV. Run-DMC's first hit on the rhythm and blues charts was "It's Like That." The non-funky clarity of the instrumental production and the vocals that stressed stark realities of urban life created a new hip-hop style called **hard-core rap,** which helped open the door for gangsta rap on the West Coast later in the

Listening Guide

"It's Like That"
as recorded by Run-DMC (1983)

Tempo: The tempo is approximately 126 beats per minute, with four beats in each bar.

Form: After a thirteen-bar instrumental introduction, the recording is structured into eight-bar sections with a twenty-eight bar instrumental in the middle. All of the eight-bar verses end with "It's like that . . ." and are rapped in pairs. The eight-bar instrumental sections occur between each pair of verses and begin with the vocalization "Huh." The last verse is repeated to create another pair of verses. The structure is as follows: introduction, verse, verse, instrumental, verse, verse, instrumental, verse, verse, twenty-eight-bar instrumental, verse, verse, instrumental, verse, verse, instrumental, verse, verse, instrumental, verse, final verse repeated, extended instrumental that fades out at bar thirty.

Features: The two rappers, Joseph "Rev Run" Simmons and Darryl "DMC" McDaniels trade off rapping lines in the verses.

The instrumental background is created by drum machines and occasional synthesized accents and other sounds, including Jason "Jam Master Jay" Mizell's work as a DJ.

The drum machine creates a strong backbeat and the beat subdivisions are even.

The vocals syncopate rhythms around the steady drum sound and often stress the half-beats after main beats, not unlike the hesitation beats in ska music.

Lyrics: The rappers focus on the theme of unbending reality, particularly hard, economic reality: "Money can't buy love, but love can't buy clothes. Without marketable skills, your best friend might end up eating out of a garbage can." The rappers advise traditional, "small c" conservative values to make the best of reality (the way it is): "Go to school, learn a trade, 'get taught,' and even take a bus to school or church and stop playing, start praying."

Billboard rhythm and blues charts: number one

eighties. A listening guide to that recording is included here. When Run-DMC decided to try rapping over Aerosmith's "Walk This Way," and then asked Aerosmith singer Steve Tyler and guitarist Joe Perry to work with them on the recording, they created something that helped rock fans relate to rap in a new way. The Run-DMC/Aerosmith recording of "Walk This Way" (1986) was number four on the pop charts and number eight on the rhythm and blues charts. They continued to record in the nineties but broke up when Jam Master Jay was shot to death in 2002.

Popularity with white audiences was bound to lead to white performers in the field, and such was the case with the New York–based hard-core punk band the Beastie Boys. "Beastie" stands for "Boys Entering Anarchistic States Toward Internal Excellence." When the Beastie

Boys began recording rap, the style was still dominated by African American artists. It was Rick Rubin, a white owner of Def Jam Record Company, who signed and promoted them to help broaden rap's popularity with white listeners. His idea worked, and the Beastie Boys' first album, *Licensed to Ill* (1986), was number one on the pop album charts for seven weeks. The album included the number seven pop chart hit "(You Gotta) Fight for Your Right (to Party)." The Beastie Boys' music got funkier with their later albums, and they toured with Dr. Funkenstein himself, George Clinton, as well as Smashing Pumpkins and others, in Lollapalooza '94. They received a Grammy nomination for Best Rap Performance by a Group for their *Alive* (1999) album. Their 2004 album, *To The 5 Boroughs,* hit number one on the album charts.

The goal of many of the political and social statements in East Coast rap was to encourage more unity among African Americans and urge them to make stronger demands for equality. Some band members and their fans wore "X" on their shirts or caps to represent their support of the teachings of Malcolm X. As mentioned earlier, Grandmaster Flash and the Furious Five described some of the problems related to life in a ghetto in their recording of "The Message" (1982), but that song did nothing to support African American pride or, for that matter, to encourage any changes to aid their situation. However, it may have awakened white listeners to the realities of inner-city life.

Def Jam Records signed a group that was sometimes called the Black Panthers of rap, **Public Enemy.** They spoke out from New York to let the world know what they thought about the low-class status of many African Americans. Their primary rapper, **Chuck D** (Carlton Ridenhour, born in 1960), began his career as a disc jockey on a college radio station. He had grown up seeing police brutality and a growing drug problem in his own community as well as the ways in which African American artists were often ignored by commercial radio and video stations, and he decided it was time to make his own statements to the world—and to make them as strong as possible. He referred to his rap lyrics as the CNN (Cable News Network) for African Americans. His goal was to let people know what the lives of real African Americans were like and to say he and his people were not going to put up with "ghetto life" any longer.

Chuck D's fellow rapper and "minister of information" Professor Griff laid the groundwork for others to attack Public Enemy for racism when he made anti-Semitic remarks to an interviewer for the *Washington Times.* When one's reputation is built on an antiracist stand and one attacks another race (or culture), humanism ceases to be the issue and self-centered supremacy rears its ugly head. Well aware of this, Chuck D made it clear that Griff's remarks did not represent the beliefs of other members of Public Enemy by firing Griff. Chuck D used the recording "911 Is a Joke" (from the album *Fear of a Black Planet*) to point out his thoughts about ineffective public assistance programs in his neighborhood. A listening guide is on page 273. "911 Is a Joke" was number thirty-four on the pop charts and number fifteen on the rhythm and blues charts. The backup track included samples from "Think (about It)" by Lyn Collins in 1972.

Where Chuck D had gained a reputation for his angry remarks between songs at concerts in the past, his performances in the nineties included serious talks about his personal commitments rather than a mere venting of rage. The state of Arizona was often a target of attack because (until the November 1992 election) it did not recognize the national holiday for the late Dr. Martin Luther King Jr.'s birthday. Chuck D released his feelings through his rap in "By the Time I Get to Arizona," and told members of the audience who were from Arizona to think about their state's affront to African Americans. If one can step back and look beyond the emotional charge

Flavor Flav (left) and Chuck D (right) of Public Enemy

Listening Guide

"911 Is a Joke"
as recorded by Public Enemy (1990)

Tempo: The tempo is approximately 104 beats per minute, with four beats in each bar.

Form: The form is based on eight- and sixteen-bar phrases ordered as follows: ABC Extension BC Extension CA.

The eight-bar A sections are basically instrumental, but include verbal comments in the background.

Each B section contains sixteen bars of rap vocals. The rhythmic patterns of the rap vocals are made up of four-bar antecedent and consequent phrases paired into eight-bar periods.

The eight-bar C sections function as a refrain, beginning with the words "get up" and then including the song title, "911 Is a Joke." The first C is followed by a four-bar extension that begins with a laugh and the second is followed by an eight-bar extension similar to the first extension.

Features: Even beat subdivisions are maintained throughout the recording.

The drums play a strong backbeat through most of the recording.

The bass, guitar, and horn (or synthesized horn sound) sections play funk polyrhythms.

The production includes much mixing and overdubbing, creating a very full background. That background includes indistinguishable vocal chatter that sounds as if the recording was done at a party.

Call-and-response vocals are used in the extensions to the refrains.

The recording ends by fading out.

Lyrics: The singer claims he had called the emergency number 911 a long time ago, and no one has responded. He believes the whole idea of the emergency squads' availability to help people is a cruel joke because they will get paid whether they do their job or not, so the squads don't really care about people, particularly those in African American neighborhoods.

Billboard pop charts: number thirty-four; *Billboard* rhythm and blues charts: number fifteen

---

of much of Public Enemy's raps to analyze the basic messages behind their lyrics, similarities can be drawn between their antiracist stance and that of what James Brown, Bob Marley, and even Bob Dylan had to say through their music. The title of Public Enemy's 1994 album, *Muse Sick N Hour Message* (Music and Our Message), played on the differences between the written and the spoken word.

Gangsta rap was born in L.A. where gangs were a constant problem in African American communities. By the nineties, however, New York had its own set of hard-core rappers such as Notorious B.I.G. (Chris Wallace, 1972–1997). B.I.G.'s first album, *Ready to Die* (1994),

was backed by George Clinton–influenced funk music. He had many pop and rhythm and blues chart hits, including "Hypnotize" (1997), which was number one on both charts for three weeks. Recordings by Slick Rick and Herb Alpert were sampled for that single. Early in his career, Notorious B.I.G. got along well with L.A. rapper Tupac Shakur, but the two soon became bitter enemies to the point that B.I.G. was suspected of being behind the shooting death of Shakur in Las Vegas in 1996. Notorious B.I.G. was shot to death himself only six months later. Neither murder was ever solved. Ironically, his second and last album was released just three weeks before he was murdered and was called *Life after Death* (1997).

"Ever since I was a kid, I been dreaming about dying saving somebody. I feel like I'll probably die saving a white kid. . . . I'm serious, I see me dying . . . getting shot up for a white kid. In my death, people will understand what I was talking about. That I just wasn't on some black-people-kill-all-white-people shit."

–Tupac Shakur

West Coast Rap

Sugar Hill Gang's hit "Rapper's Delight" was the primary influence on the beginnings of rap in California. **Ice-T** (Tracy Morrow) first heard the recording while in the army with guys from New York. He memorized the lyrics from that as a start at rapping and then began to make up his own lyrics. When he finished with his army duty, he bought turntables to try his hand at hip-hop disc jockey techniques but gave that up to concentrate on rap vocals. His early jobs as a rapper were at parties, and he copied the New York style of rapping to lyrics that fit the party type of chatter. Since his real concerns were about gang violence in his neighborhood, he decided to rap on that subject. His first gangsta rap, as the genre was soon titled, record was his "Six 'N the Morning" (1986).

Ice-T received a large amount of negative press in 1992 when his heavy-metal band recorded the song "Cop Killer" on their *Body Count* album. The song referred to going out and "dusting off" some cops. Ice-T's vocals on that song were not rap, but because of his reputation as a rapper, the controversy still caused many to see it as another example of gangsta rap having gone too far. After his record company, Sire, received death threats, its parent company, Time Warner, had the song removed from the album. They also began to censor artwork on album covers, and Ice-T canceled his contract with the company over a dispute about the artwork planned for his next album. The independent label Priority issued that album, and Ice-T followed its release by signing with Virgin Records, which released *Born Dead* (1994). Ice-T has also done a lot of acting, including a role as a detective on *Law & Order*.

"If it wasn't for rap there would be no poetry in America. I think we went directly from Walt Whitman to Ice-T."

–Frank Zappa

Modeled after Ice-T's example, many other young African American men in Compton began to rap about the way in which the police handled (or, they would say, contributed to) street violence. They insisted that the kids they spoke for didn't have the slightest idea about political figures or the government because the kids had daily problems dealing with violence on the streets—a violence politicians knew existed but ignored. At times, the rappers were accused of encouraging violent behavior when, from their point of view, they were merely reporting about it from an inside perspective.

"If you grow up in any black neighborhood, they got gangs, I ain't been to one of them have no gangs. So you gotta deal with that. . . . It's bad, I'd say, Compton. I ain't gonna say it's the worst place in the world. Compton's the same as every black ghetto I've been to. That's the bottom line."

–Ice Cube

Among the most outspoken of the West Coast rap groups of the late eighties and early nineties was **N.W.A.** (Niggas with Attitude). "Gangsta Gangsta," from their *Straight Outta Compton* (1988) album, even begins with gunshots. That album's title track makes it clear that N.W.A. planned to continue to "say it like it is" in their Los Angeles neighborhood. A listening guide to "Straight Outta Compton" is on page 275.

N.W.A.'s lead rapper, Ice Cube (O'Shey Jackson, born ca. 1969), left the group for a solo career and was replaced by former solo rapper, Eazy-E (Eric Wright, 1973–1995). Their album *100 Miles and Runnin'* (1990) did well on the pop charts and their *Efil4zaggin* (a backward spelling of "niggaz 4 life," 1991) broke commercial records for rap by entering the pop charts at number one. Of course that may not have happened had *Billboard* not just changed its chart research system to the new SoundScan computer system so that the charts were based on actual sales figures instead of interviews with record store managers. Nevertheless, N.W.A.'s sales did make it appear that they had come to express attitudes shared by many others. N.W.A. broke up after the *Efil4zaggin* album. Eazy-E died of complications from AIDS in 1995, and other members, Ice Cube, Dr. Dre (Andre Young, born in 1965), and M. C. Ren (Lorenzo Patterson), continued to record and perform as soloists.

Dre went on to found Death Row Records, produce recordings by other successful rap artists such as Snoop Doggy Dogg, and continue to record hits of his own. His recording of "No Diggity" (1996) featured the female rap

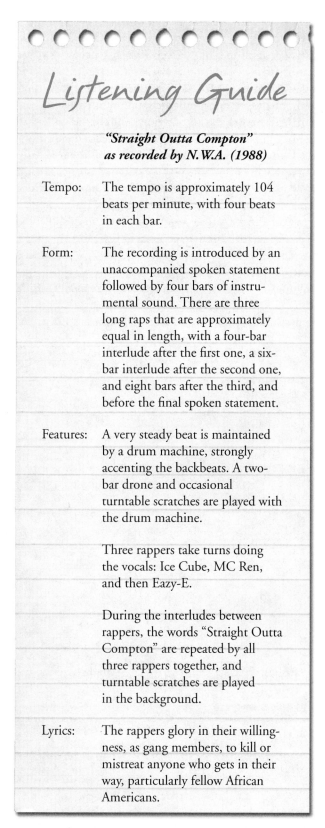

Listening Guide

"Straight Outta Compton" as recorded by N.W.A. (1988)

Tempo: The tempo is approximately 104 beats per minute, with four beats in each bar.

Form: The recording is introduced by an unaccompanied spoken statement followed by four bars of instrumental sound. There are three long raps that are approximately equal in length, with a four-bar interlude after the first one, a six-bar interlude after the second one, and eight bars after the third, and before the final spoken statement.

Features: A very steady beat is maintained by a drum machine, strongly accenting the backbeats. A two-bar drone and occasional turntable scratches are played with the drum machine.

Three rappers take turns doing the vocals: Ice Cube, MC Ren, and then Eazy-E.

During the interludes between rappers, the words "Straight Outta Compton" are repeated by all three rappers together, and turntable scratches are played in the background.

Lyrics: The rappers glory in their willingness, as gang members, to kill or mistreat anyone who gets in their way, particularly fellow African Americans.

Ice Cube

two-thousands was Eminem (Marshall Mathers, born in 1974). There is no hiding Eminem's foul language. His first hit single was "Just Don't Give a F***" (1999). His lyrics are violent at times; for example, his song "Kim" has the sound of him slitting his wife's throat. Rap listeners have long since ceased to be shocked by anything, and despite the content of his lyrics, he did extremely well at the Grammy awards ceremony in 2001: "The Real Slim Shady," a song about Eminem's alter ego, won Best Rap Solo recording; his album *The Marshall Mathers LP*, won Best Rap Album; and his duo with Dr. Dre, "Forgot about Dre," won Best Rap Performance by a Duo or Group.

The violent world from which many of L.A.'s rappers came was clear in 1996 when Death Row Records star Tupac Shakur was shot to death while riding in a car with the owner of his record company, Marion "Suge" Knight. At the time of his murder, Shakur was waiting for an appeal of his conviction for sexually abusing a nineteen-year-old girl. Knight had also been in and out of jail for various charges, including assault and probation violations. Death Row Records' other star rapper, Snoop Doggy Dogg, had recently been acquitted of murder charges at the time of Shakur's death.

> **"I don't think music can make you kill or rape someone any more than a movie is going to make you do something . . . but music can give you strength."**
>
> –Eminem

group Queenpen and sampled "Grandma's Hands" by Bill Withers. It was number one on the pop charts for four weeks.

Another rapper, this time young and white, whom Dr. Dre produced for in the late nineties and into the

The reputation of anger and violence associated with rap from L.A. was somewhat mitigated by the light-hearted, nonviolent work by Coolio (Artis Ivey, born ca. 1972). It is not that Coolio's music was untouched by problems in his community. "County Line," from his first album, *It Takes a Thief* (1994), pointed out problems experienced by people on welfare, but the album cut "Fantastic Voyage" expressed the fun of a dream trip to the beach. The title cut from his *Gangsta's Paradise* (1995) took a thoughtful look at the world of gang rivalry and the people who are more hurt than helped by it. This view was certainly a change from earlier statements that tended to portray street violence as unpreventable.

> "Every time a relative sues me or a critic slams me, I sell more records."
>
> —Eminem

Latino Rap

Many Spanish-speaking Puerto Ricans, Cubans, or other Latinos in New York and Mexicans/Chicanos, Cubans, or other Latins in Los Angeles identified with break dancing and other aspects of hip-hop culture from its very beginnings. The result was the development of a rap style that used a combination of Spanish and English and slang from the Latin American barrio. Latino rap became particularly important in Los Angeles because of the competitive desire to match the ethnic orientation of gang raps by African American rappers. One of the leaders of the Latino rappers was **Kid Frost** (Arturo Molina Jr., born in 1962). Like N.W.A. had for African Americans in L.A., Kid Frost used his raps to point out instances of street violence and police brutality in his own neighborhood with songs such as "Homicide" and the title cut from his *Hispanic Causing Panic* (1990) album. "La Raza (La Raza Mix)," from that same album, became an anthem representing Latin rap.

Listening Guide

"La Raza (La Raza Mix)"
as recorded by Kid Frost (1990)

Tempo: The tempo is approximately 108 beats per minute, with four beats in each bar.

Form: The form is based on the repetition of a one-bar bass riff. After a four-bar instrumental introduction, the vocals and instrumental sections that feature saxophones form eight-bar sections, but the riff and the two chords it uses remain constant, allowing for no real contrasting sections.

Features: The backbeat is stressed by the drums.

Both even and uneven beat subdivisions are used. Even subdivisions are maintained by the drummer using a stick on a closed high-hat, and uneven subdivisions are used in the vocals and by the saxophones.

The most distinctive instrumental part is the riff played on an electric bass guitar.

A guitar plays a two-bar pattern that reaches across the repetitions of the one-bar riff.

Two saxophones play the same melody a single beat apart, creating an interesting reverberation or echo effect.

A xylophone improvises in the background of the last part of the recording.

The instrumental background is based on a sample from "Viva Tirado—Part 1" (1970) by El Chicano.

Lyrics: The lyrics are made up of phrases in Spanish, English (together called "Spanglish"), and Gypsy patois used in parts of Spain and Mexico. The lyrics include phrases that express pride in "La Raza" (the race), and various in-group comments about people known to Kid Frost and his group.

A listening guide to that recording is on page 276. "La Raza" was number forty-two on the pop charts.

As can be heard in "La Raza," background music used by Kid Frost and other Latino rappers varied from much African American rap because it often used Latin rhythms and samples from sixties recordings by Santana and others. Incorporating samples from such artists helped to emphasize their ethnic identity. By the midnineties, Kid Frost had changed his name to "Frost." Other important Latin rappers from L.A. included Cypress Hill and the more politically outspoken Proper Dos.

The Big Punisher (Christopher Rios, 1971–2000) was among the important Latino rappers from New York. He often recorded with the group Cuban Link and had several hits on the pop charts and, as was common for rap, more on the rhythm and blues charts. He was a very big man and died of a heart attack before his last album, *Yeeeah Baby* (2000), was released.

Summary

Rap is a patter-talk vocal style that developed out of a variety of vocal styles, mostly of African or African American origin. Jamaican disc jockeys popularized the rhythmic speech patterns with their toasting and dubbing styles. Funk disc jockeys in New York picked up the Jamaican sound and popularized it through live and radio performances before it was recorded for commercial sales.

Rap lyrics varied greatly, from some East Coast groups that spoke out about racism experienced by African Americans in Harlem or other ghettos to a number of West Coast groups that decried messages about gangs and street violence. Rap vocals did not always carry angry or violent messages, however, as many rap groups represented positive images and themes. Whatever the message behind the lyrics, rap singers wrote of common experiences from a personal level, lending a sense of sincerity to their music.

discussion question

Rap music often tends to have a racial identity. To what degree does that reject the idea of racial integration as an ideal?

MTV

"Wow, Dad, I like that song . . . I wonder what it
looks like."
—A CHILD LISTENING TO THE RADIO

Rock fans have always wanted to see their favorite performers play live if possible. Other than at live concerts, opportunities to do that were limited through most of rock's history. Several teenage dance programs were televised in local areas of the United States during the early fifties. The first to be broadcast nationally was *American Bandstand* in 1956. Those shows played records and sometimes had rock-pop artists on to lip sync to their recordings, but the shows were more about dancing than live music making. Variety programs such as *The Ed Sullivan Show, The Perry Como Show,* the Dorsey Brothers/Jackie Gleason's *Stage Show, The Milton Berle Show, The Steve Allen Show,* and others sometimes had rock-pop artists scheduled to do live performances, but those performers would only play one or two songs and took very little of the hour-long shows. By the midsixties, the Monkees performed on their self-titled television show. In fact, the group was formed for the show, and their records and appearances as a rock band were secondary to that.

Also during the midsixties, several rock variety shows were aired, allowing for many currently popular artists to reach their fans. Many of the performances were still lip synced to recordings. Those shows included *Shindig, Hullabaloo, Where the Action Is,* and *Hollywood a Go Go.* In the early seventies, the popularity of *The Sonny and Cher Comedy Hour* drove other performers to create their own shows, including *Donny and Marie, Tony Orlando and Dawn,* and *Sha-Na-Na.* Some major cities created their own performance programs, including Chicago's *Soundstage,* Austin's *Austin City Limits,* and New York's *Midnight Special,* all of which gained widespread appeal. The dance show *Soul Train* became a modern-day *American Bandstand* for rhythm and blues music and dance styles of the early seventies.

All these TV programs had fairly large followings. Performers on the shows could boost their record sales by their appearances. In general, however, record and tape sales had dropped by 10 percent from 1978 to 1979. Sales of videos, video games, and other home-tech products, however, were growing. During the late seventies and early eighties, a few people in the radio/video business were beginning to see that there were possibilities for music television beyond the individual shows of the past. Cable TV seemed to be the best vehicle for such a project, but it was still very new and in few areas of the country. Because it required cables to be installed under- or aboveground, it took several years to expand the service nationwide.

Robert Pittman had had much success as a program director for radio stations in Chicago and New York. He supervised production of a television music program called *Album Tracks* that showed short rock videos and found the show to be quite popular. It occurred to him that a television channel that showed rock-related shows twenty-four hours a day might be a possibility. Former Monkee Mike Nesmith produced a video show called *Popclips* for the Nickelodeon channel in 1981, but Nesmith refused to sell the rights to it to larger companies and was not able to make it the continuing hit it might have been on his own. The show was canceled after only one season, but Pittman was not discouraged from trying his own station. He gathered videos from a variety of record companies and used them, along with a crew of **veejays**, as the basis for a new cable station, Music Television, or MTV. Its first program was televised on August 1, 1981. The show was immediately popular among the small numbers of people who were able to receive it, and some of the first people to see real benefits from the station were the artists and bands whose videos were shown. Their record sales went up dramatically from having been on MTV.

Within a year, MTV was clearly a success and growing. The British company EMI took a big step in funding the production of three very expensive videos of songs from Duran Duran's *Rio* (1981) album. Album sales increased dramatically after the videos were put on MTV. An article on MTV in *Time* magazine said, "*Rio* was being sold out at half the record stores in Dallas and gathering dust in the other half. A check of the local television listings showed that parts of the city that were wired for cable and carrying MTV were the very same parts where the album was flourishing." Other groups such as the Stray Cats and Men at Work similarly gained much larger followings from being featured on MTV during those first months.

MTV's popularity grew along with that of its stars. It had been on three hundred cable systems in 1981, and that had expanded to almost eighteen hundred in only two years. Part of the reason for the great success of the channel was that it geared its music to the tastes of the large rock-pop audience. On the other hand, that particular market caused them to reject many African American artists' videos, and critics began to question that point. The perfect African American artist to satisfy the musical tastes of MTV's audience had just seen his second solo album reach number one. That was **Michael Jackson** (1958–2009), and the solo album was *Thriller* (1982).

This book cannot possibly include information on every major rock-related star whose career was aided by MTV. The few whose careers and music are discussed in this chapter display the variety of styles that were widely popular during the era.

Michael Jackson

Michael Jackson had been a child star at Motown records in the late sixties when he sang lead in his all-sibling group the Jackson Five. He also recorded solo at Motown, but he primarily worked with his brothers. After the family, except for Jermaine, left the Motown Company, Michael continued to sing in his brothers' group, renamed simply the Jacksons. Michael Jackson emerged as a solo star when his first solo album, *Off the Wall* (1979), had four top-ten hits. His music was funky and fun, and he was a terrific dancer and entertainer. His *Thriller* videos on MTV helped the album continue to sell extremely well and also helped MTV out of the bind of having too few African American artists. Sales of the album, which was already a hit and also boosted by appearances on MTV, went to over forty-five million copies worldwide, the best-selling album to that time. The album was number one in the United States for thirty-seven weeks and number one as well in Britain and many other western European countries. By this time, Michael Jackson was truly the King of Pop, and MTV was there to let the world of cable viewers know.

> **"I don't believe in stylizing or branding any type of music. I think a great artist should be able to just create any style. . . . Just wonderful music where anybody can sing it from the Irish**

Michael Jackson

farmer to a lady who scrubs toilets in Harlem. If you can whistle it and hum it that's the most important thing."

–Michael Jackson

"Billie Jean" was on Jackson's *Thriller* album. The single was number one on the pop charts for seven weeks. Jackson danced to "Billie Jean" on the twenty-fifth anniversary of Motown in 1983, and his inclusion of a "moonwalk" (inspired by break dancers who often employed that same technique) was the hit of the show. It was reported that the famous dancer Fred Astaire actually phoned Michael Jackson after seeing the show on television and said, "You're one hell of a mover." A listening guide to "Billie Jean" is included here.

Jackson had been very generous in donating to charities of various kinds, and he co-wrote "We Are the World" (1985) with Lionel Richie. His *Bad* (1987) album broke his own record of four hit singles on an album by including five number one hit singles. The follow-up albums, *Dangerous* (1991) and *HIStory: Past, Present and Future, Book One* (1995), also sold well but did not outdo his previous successes.

Michael Jackson's career was already well established and only aided by MTV. His youngest sister, Janet Jackson (born in 1966), was just beginning her career in the early eighties. Her talents as a singer would most likely have given her much success without videos on MTV, but

Listening Guide

"Billie Jean"
as recorded by Michael Jackson (1983)

Tempo: The tempo is approximately 118 beats per minute, with four beats in each bar.

Form: The recording begins with a fourteen-bar instrumental introduction that begins with drums. A bass enters at the third bar. The song is based on eight-bar sections, with the first and third verses, and the first and last three choruses extended to twelve bars through repetitions of sections of text. The form can be outlined as the instrumental introduction (fourteen bars), verse 1 (twelve bars), verse 2 (eight bars), bridge (eight bars), chorus (twelve bars), verse 3 (twelve bars), verse 4 (eight bars), bridge (eight bars), chorus (eight bars), chorus (twelve bars), instrumental chorus (twelve bars), chorus (twelve bars), chorus (twelve bars). The recording ends with a fade-out.

(continued)

Features:	The drums play a strong backbeat.		Backup vocals support Jackson's lead vocals through repetitions of text.
	Even beat subdivisions are kept throughout.	Lyrics:	The song is a cautionary tale about promiscuity, where the singer feels trapped by the allegation he has fathered a child, even though he does admit that the baby has his eyes.
	Synthesized orchestral chords sometimes play on beats one and the half-beat after two. Other orchestral background includes synthesized strings and horns.		

Billboard pop charts: number one for seven weeks; *Billboard* rhythm and blues charts: number one for nine weeks; British hit singles: number one

her looks and dancing abilities helped her achieve super-stardom as part of the MTV generation.

Prince

Another African American performer to provide MTV with popular videos and gain much audience appeal as a result was **Prince** Rogers Nelson (born in 1958). Both soul and funk are important

Prince (2007)

elements in his music. Prince wrote and produced his own first album of erotic dance music when he was only eighteen years old. His father, John Nelson, was a jazz musician whose stage name was Prince Rogers, and his mother was a singer. Although the young Prince never had formal music lessons, music and instruments were readily available to him, and he eventually learned to play many instruments, including piano, guitar, and drums. Prince wrote his own music and played his own instrumental parts on almost all the tracks on his first five albums, although he kept some of his old friends such as bass player André Cymone (André Anderson, who later had his own solo career) for occasional support in the studio and to back him on tour.

Prince's style basically combined funk with rock, but it also showed the influences of new wave, disco, and rap. His songs merely toyed with eroticism until his 1980s *Dirty Mind* album, which was too explicit to get any airplay. Its mixture of funk and pop music with fuzztone guitar still attracted a large audience, despite the lack of radio publicity.

A listening guide to Prince's first top-ten hit single, "Little Red Corvette" from his first top-ten hit album, *1999* (1982), is on page 283. It reached number six on the pop charts and number fifteen on the rhythm and blues charts. It was number thirty-four its first time on the British charts and reached number two when it was reissued in 1985.

Prince decided to add a backup band he called the Revolution for his next project, *Purple Rain* (1984), which included an album, film, and concert tour. That project clearly established Prince as a major star. Five top-forty hit singles were released from the album, and it won three Grammys and an Oscar for Best Original Song Score. The movie (directed by Albert Magnoli) was Prince's acting debut and gave fans an insightful look at a very human celebrity who, in the film, lets his stardom ruin him. Prince added Sheila E. to sing backup vocals on the *Purple Rain* soundtrack and gave her career a boost by contributing to her first solo album, *The Glamorous Life* (1984), and having

Listening Guide

"Little Red Corvette"
as recorded by Prince (1982)

Tempo: The tempo is approximately 126 beats per minute, with four beats in each bar.

Form: After about nine bars of introduction, the form is based on eight-bar sections. The sections are ordered as follows: AABAAB Instrumental CBBBDBBBB.

The B sections are made up of a four-bar phrase that is repeated. The repeated phrases function as refrains. They usually repeat the same lyrics, but the lyrics are varied and drop out at times during some of the repeated B sections at the end of the recording.

The instrumental section is based on the B section and features a guitar solo.

The C section is eight bars long; the D section is sixteen bars long.

Features: Even beat subdivisions are used through most of the recording, but the vocals sometimes relax into uneven subdivisions.

The drums play a strong backbeat through much, but not all, of the recording.

The instrumental background is rather full and features an electronic organ.

Prince plays all the instrumental parts and sings the lead vocal except for the addition of a guitar soloist and two backup singers.

The recording begins by slowly building up volume out of silence and ends by fading out very slowly.

Lyrics: The singer analogizes a promiscuous girl to a red Corvette sports car. He advises the girl to find monogamy (a love that will last) before her body fails like a car that is driven too roughly.

Billboard pop charts: number six; *Billboard* rhythm and blues charts: number fifteen; British hit singles: number thirty-four

her open his *Purple Rain* concerts. In 1985, Prince established his own record label, Paisley Park (distributed by his former record company, Warner Brothers), and continued to produce movie soundtracks and other albums with much success. Later soundtracks included music for the films *Under the Cherry Moon* (1986) and *Batman* (1989).

"Very simply, my spirit directed me to do it. And once I did it, a lot of things started changing in my life. . . . One thing is people can say something about Prince, and it used to bother me. Once I changed my name, it had no effect on me."

—Prince, when asked why he changed his name

Prince's career experienced many ups and downs during the nineties. His new band, the New Power Generation, worked well with him on *Diamonds and Pearls* (1991) and *The Symbol Album* (1992), both of which included hit singles. The New Power Generation also included rapper Tony M (Anthony Mosely), adding a hip-hop connection to Prince's widely diverse style. Prince followed these successes by changing his name to an unpronounceable symbol, baffling all but his most dedicated fans. "Since then he has been called "Formerly" or "The Artist," both names being shortened versions of the "the artist formerly known as Prince." His recordings of the midnineties showed that his career was on a downswing. He went back to calling himself Prince and continued to record and tour into the two-thousands.

Madonna

Roles played by female performers changed by the midseventies and continued to evolve in the eighties. In the fifties and early sixties, female singers generally portrayed meek and sweet personalities as had female pop singers before them. By 1964, Mary Weiss of the Shangri-Las had a bit of a "tough" image, but that was more a reflection of her relationship with the "leader of the pack" than it was a reflection of her own personality. In the late sixties, Janis Joplin and Grace Slick displayed some independence, but they both showed vulnerability at times. The feminist revolution and the sense of individual freedom of the punk movement came together to change these perceptions in the stage personality of Patti Smith, who went so far as to invite a woman to visit her room when she sang the male

lyrics to "Gloria." Several punk and new-wave groups had women as instrumentalists, including the Velvet Underground with Maureen Tucker as drummer, Talking Heads with Tina Weymouth as bassist, and the Pretenders with Chrissie Hynde as guitarist, writer, and singer. On the West Coast in the midseventies, Ann and Nancy Wilson assumed the leadership of Heart, and the Runaways formed as a quintet of tough and independent young women who were out for a good time and didn't care how they got it. From the Runaways, guitarist/singer Joan Jett continued this sense of independence with the Blackhearts, lead guitarist Lita Ford went on to a solo career, and bassist/singer Micki Steele joined the female quartet, the Bangles.

> "Ultimately, I want my music to be reviewed, not whether my rib cage is too small or not. . . . Men are allowed to not meet the conventional standards of beauty and still be celebrated. It's much harder for women."
> —Madonna

Other female singers of the late seventies and beyond played less tough but still more realistic roles than had most of their counterparts twenty years earlier. Blondie's Deborah Harry was cold and detached, and Madonna made it clear that she was an individual who did not care what other people thought, as long as she got what she wanted. Singer/songwriter Tracy Chapman, on the other hand, managed to express a great deal of independence while being anything but tough or cold. Her music and image made a new statement for women in general, and, perhaps more important, for African American women.

Of all of those female performers, **Madonna** (Madonna Louise Ciccone, born in 1958) gained the most commercial appeal and success, with the help of MTV. Her debut album, *Madonna* (1983), hit the charts in both Britain and the United States, and many successful albums and singles followed. The dance orientation of her music was influenced by her longtime involvement with dance. Madonna's lead role in *Desperately Seeking Susan* (1985) launched her career as a movie star and led to other movies and a live theater debut in *Speed the Plow* (1988) on Broadway in New York. Many of Madonna's video and movie roles play up her sex symbol image, but in her hit recording "Papa Don't Preach" she portrayed a young woman in need of her father's approval. A listening guide to that recording is on page 285. It reached number one on the pop charts in both the United States and Britain.

Madonna

Listening Guide

"Papa Don't Preach"
as recorded by Madonna (1986)

Tempo: The tempo is approximately 126 beats per minute, with four beats in each bar.

Form: After a sixteen-bar introduction, the form is structured as follows: AABCABC Instrumental BCC₁ Instrumental.

The A and B sections are eight bars each, except for the third B section that is extended with two extra bars of lyrics that add emphasis to the last vocal phrase about the singer's being in love.

The ten-bar C sections are eight-bar phrases followed by two bars of extension stressing the singer's decision to keep her baby. The C section begins with the words of the title, "Papa Don't Preach," and functions as a refrain.

The first instrumental section (within the text of the song) is based on the A section.

The sixteen-bar C_1 section is made up of the first four bars of the C section sung through four times.

The final instrumental is sixteen bars based on the C section. It fades out by the final bar.

Features: Even beat subdivisions are maintained throughout the recording.

A synthesized string orchestra plays the first eight bars of the introduction and then adds to the background in the remainder of the recording.

The drums enter at the ninth bar of the introduction, playing a strong backbeat through the rest of the performance.

In addition to the drums, rock instruments used include electric bass, keyboards, both acoustic and electric guitars, and percussion.

Backup vocalists support the lead vocal in the final C_1 section.

Lyrics: The singer is telling her father that she is pregnant, in love with the baby's father, and planning to marry him and keep her baby. She knows that her father does not like her boyfriend, and begs him to not preach to her, but just give them his blessing. She also asks for advice, but nothing in the song seems to indicate that she is prepared to accept it.

Billboard pop charts: number one for two weeks; British hit singles: number one

Bruce Springsteen

Bruce Springsteen's (born in 1949) recording career began in the seventies, but his worldwide fame developed during the eighties when his videos were shown on MTV. Bruce Springsteen's music developed out of youthful experimentation with almost every rock style imaginable, from the rockabilly and rhythm and blues styles of Elvis Presley and Chuck Berry to Dylanesque folk-rock, from the wall-of-sound pop style of Phil Spector to the raunchy protopunk sound of garage bands. Out of these styles he fashioned an energetic, tradition-based rock and roll style that, especially through its song texts, spoke to the American working class on its own level.

Having worked solo and in groups for years, and having achieved some local popularity in his native New Jersey,

Bruce Springsteen playing "Born in the U.S.A." to a sellout crowd in Washington, D.C., in 1985

Springsteen was signed to Columbia Records in 1972 by John Hammond Sr., who had discovered Bob Dylan a decade earlier. His first album, *Greetings from Asbury Park, N.J.* (1973), included folk-rock-style productions comparable to those of singer/songwriters like James Taylor. The album received favorable reviews from critics but sold poorly. His next effort, *The Wild, the Innocent, and the E Street Shuffle,* released later the same year, was more rock-oriented and featured many of the musicians who would make up Springsteen's E Street Band. It was at this time that Springsteen began to attract attention for his dramatic stage performances and emerged as a headline act. In 1975, the group found the national spotlight with the critically acclaimed album *Born to Run,* recorded using Spector-influenced wall-of-sound production, and followed it up with a national tour. Shortly thereafter, Springsteen appeared on the covers of *Time* and *Newsweek,* and the magazine stories depicted him as the new rock phenomenon.

❝ Basically, all my songs are about how we treat ourselves and how we treat one another. So, the

audience has to be willing to take that trip. ❞

–Bruce Springsteen

Lawsuits between Springsteen and his manager kept Springsteen from recording for two years, but he continued to tour and to write new material. Some of his songs were saved for his gloomy 1978 album *Darkness on the Edge of Town,* and others were given to other artists to record first. His song "Fire" was recorded by Robert Gordon in 1978 and a year later by the Pointer Sisters. Springsteen collaborated with New York–based punk rock singer/poet Patti Smith on "Because the Night."

Springsteen experimented with a more commercial sound for the double album *The River* (1980), which contained the hit single "Hungry Heart." The album's title track served as a particularly good example of Springsteen's compassion for the underprivileged. In the song, Springsteen uses the river to represent a young man's passion for life and love. Early in the song, he and his girlfriend dive into the river, but once family responsibilities and difficulties finding enough work overtake them, the young man goes back to find that the river is dry. Some of that feeling of hopelessness carried over to the lyrics of many of the songs on the album *Born in the U.S.A.* (1984), but the driving beat of the music gave it a more commercial appeal. Through the album's title song, Springsteen attacked the lack of support, both from the government and in the job market, given to veterans of the Vietnam War. Many people did not bother to listen to the song to find out what Springsteen was really saying and made grandiose statements about its being a great patriotic statement. The listening guide to that recording is on page 287. "Born in the U.S.A." reached number nine on the pop charts.

Springsteen separated himself from his hard-rocking E Street Band in 1989 and released two albums, *Human Touch* and *Lucky Town* (1992), both of which contained songs about changes in his personal life—the breakup of one marriage and raising a family with his second wife, singer Patti Scialfa. In 1992 Springsteen performed on MTV's *Unplugged* series, but he played only one song on an acoustic guitar. When the album came out, it was called *In Concert/MTV Plugged.* Springsteen won an Academy Award and four Grammys for the song "Streets of Philadelphia" that was featured on the soundtrack of the movie *Philadelphia* (1994).

Throughout his career, Springsteen's music has ranged from tender, personal statements in a folk style to hard-driving rock and roll. His work supported many of the causes expressed in his songs, including efforts to raise money for Vietnam veterans and to support union workers

Listening Guide

"Born in the U.S.A."
as recorded by Bruce Springsteen (1984)

Tempo: The tempo is approximately 122 beats per minute, with four beats in each bar.

Form: The entire recording is based on almost hypnotic repetition of a two-bar riff. The eight-bar instrumental introduction and the phrases of lyrics are organized around eight-bar sections, each section being comprised of four statements of the riff. The sections that repeat the title lyrics and slight variations of them give them the impression of being refrains, but they are lyric refrains that are not based on contrasting music.

Features: Uneven beat subdivisions are maintained through most of the recording.

The constantly repeating riff and a strong backbeat in the drums are the most outstanding features of the instrumental portion of the recording.

Springsteen's powerful vocals support the sense of anger in the lyrics.

Lyrics: The song is sung from the point of view of a Vietnam veteran who returned to the United States after having lost his brother in the war and was turned down for a job, given no assistance from the Veterans Admission Office, and ended up in prison. Ironically, though, the power of the chorus has tended to obscure the song's otherwise sardonic message; in the years since its release the chorus has been used in various contexts to express pride in the United States even though the story of the lyrics was considerably darker.

Billboard pop charts: number nine

---

on strike. His concerts swept his fans through over three hours of music, through songs that reflected the concerns of much of the American middle class. Springsteen's level of performance energy brings him as close as anyone to a real competition with James Brown for the title of the Hardest Working Man in Show Business.

Springsteen returned to working with his E Street Band in 1999. In 2002, he won three Grammy awards for the album and song *The Rising,* which was composed as a reaction to the September 11th terrorist attacks in New York and Washington, D.C. Springsteen continues to use his music and reputation to support political causes such as Amnesty International and other human rights organizations. He continues to record and tour in the two-thousands.

Expanded Programming

By the mideighties, MTV had received many criticisms for its very pop-oriented programming. The channel's directors responded by adding a number of other programs, plus another channel, MTV2. Among the new programs were *120 Minutes* (1986), which featured alternative or underground rock videos; *Headbangers Ball* (1987), with heavy-metal videos and news; and *Yo! MTV Raps* (1988), with rap videos and news. In the early nineties, MTV added a new request channel, *Dial MTV.*

In later years many other channels took over the broadcasting of rock videos and MTV expanded far beyond videos. Reality shows, awards programs, movies, political programming (including information on how to register to vote), and even animated cartoons became common.

Summary

Televisions became common in American homes during the fifties, and several shows gave rock fans an opportunity to see their favorite artists perform live, or at least appear to do so while lip-syncing to their recordings. Television shows that included performances by rock stars became more numerous through the decades to follow just as rock music itself was growing in popularity. By the eighties, the availability of cable television opened up new opportunities for fans to see performing artists. MTV was the first regular station to air rock videos or other related programs twenty-four hours a day. When studies that compared the availability of MTV with record sales clearly indicated that the videos did much to popularize musicians and sell records, MTV became one of the most influential aspects of the music business. By the late nineties, other stations began to compete with MTV to attract the rock audience, just as satellite providers competed with cable television. Despite such competition, MTV had already changed the rock world, and its influence continued to be important.

discussion questions

Did MTV help provide a vehicle for personal expression, or was it a means of control? Did MTV expand diversity and artistic innovation or narrow them?

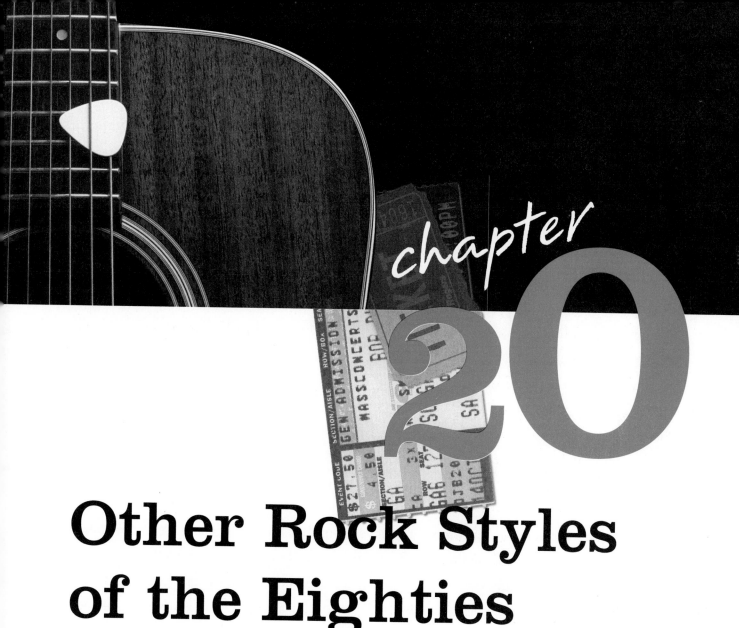

Other Rock Styles of the Eighties

"*A lot of people our age and younger have been brought up with these notions of Reagan-era fueled affluence, then when you suddenly see a lot of those dreams subside because of this particularly brutal recession, and class warfare, race warfare, it makes you very angry, very fearful, very alienated. And those are qualities that lead to an unusually rebellious, passionate rock.*"
—JONATHAN PONEMAN, CO-OWNER OF SUB POP RECORD CO.

After the shock of energy the punk movement gave to late sixties and seventies rock, many bands in the eighties began searching for something new. Some concentrated on combining elements of older rock styles in new ways; others experimented with the possibilities afforded by the use of synthesizers and electronic sound effects. Out of all of this experimentation, a few styles emerged that captured the interest of college-age rock fans who desperately needed a sound they could identify with—music that provided an alternative to the Beatles, Rolling Stones, and Led Zeppelin songs their parents still enjoyed. They also wanted music far removed from the Tiffany and New Kids on the Block songs their younger siblings liked. Many different styles of music fit under the heading of alternative rock, but in general it was geared for this audience of young adults with their own particular interests and attitudes. Some alternative rock songs dealt with traditional themes about love relationships, and some expressed concern about broader social, political, and economic issues. By the late eighties and early nineties, the economy in both Britain and the United States was especially bad for those just finishing school or entering the job market. The resultant social and economic strains were reflected in the negativity of some underground and alternative rock music, particularly industrial and, to a lesser degree, Gothic styles.

Underground and alternative rock fans did not want their groups to "sell out" to large record companies or change their styles to try to appeal to a mass market. Some bands began as alternative, but once they hit pop chart success became mass market. They had sufficient appeal to hold many of their original fans despite their shift from alternative status, but for bands that wanted to maintain their appeal to alternative fans, a hit on the *Billboard* charts was about the worst thing that could happen. Along the same lines, alternative bands generally avoided being dictated to by business executives at record companies or performance venues. The band Fugazi, for example, insisted that their CDs cost no more than eight dollars (when twelve to sixteen dollars was the standard in many CD stores) and their concert tickets be priced no higher than five dollars. They even had a mail-order address for their CDs in case a fan found them to be overpriced at a store. Changes in *Billboard*'s rating system and the addition of "alternative" video television stations forced some alternative music up the pop charts, but in general alternative and underground bands tried everything possible to avoid being "stars." The most important thing was to stay on the same economic level and continue to express the thinking and concerns of their fans.

While punk and new wave were still being played by a number of bands during the mid- to late eighties, their influences had also spread to new bands that used punk's pounding beat in a pulsating bass but did not otherwise show characteristics typical of the style. One such band, **R.E.M.,** came from Athens, Georgia, and redefined southern rock for the eighties. Not only did R.E.M. not stress complicated or highly technical instrumental solos, but they did not even place Michael Stipe's vocals in the position of prime impor-tance. Their drummer, Bill Berry, usually maintained a strong backbeat, and on top of that the sound of Peter Buck's guitar often overlapped the bass lines played by Mike Mills, so that no one part stood out clearly from another. Stipe had some of Bob Dylan's and Lou Reed's ability to maintain a low, dronelike vocal quality, but unlike them he allowed himself to blend in with the instruments. Especially in the early phase of the group's career, Stipe's lyrics were difficult to understand, and the band's overall sound was almost a single layer of texture without the clear divisions between parts found in most rock music.

> " When you're talking about Destiny's Child, where you can sell 10,000,000 more records if you get the right video and promotional push, that is where you need a major label. If you're talking about someone who is playing . . . a smaller artist, there is almost no need for a record company. Essentially, I think a lot of things are going to go through MP3, the Net. "
>
> –Peter Buck of R.E.M.

In R.E.M.'s later music, particularly their *Document* album (1987), Stipe separated his vocals from the texture of the band more than he had in the past. One reason may have been because *Document* contained many songs that made statements he wanted understood, such as the comment on the U.S. government's involvement in Nicaragua in "Welcome to the Occupation," and the anti-right-wing-extremist song "Exhuming McCarthy."

R.E.M.'s *Out of Time* (1991) album included "Losing My Religion." The album, that single, and its video all won 1992 Grammy awards. For *Out of Time*, R.E.M. expanded their instrumentation to include mellotron, harpsichord, pedal-steel guitar, mandolin, bowed strings, horns, and even a female vocal group. Whereas R.E.M.'s previous album, *Green* (1988), had dealt with political issues, *Out of Time*'s songs expressed the more personal themes of time, memories, and love. *Automatic for the People* (1992) made some dark and personal statements about life while also touching on politics with "Ignoreland"—a satire about the Reagan/Bush era. Bill Berry quit the music business to become a farmer in 1997, but R.E.M. is still recording and touring in the two-thousands.

The Dublin-based band **U2** emerged as a symbol of optimism and peace for the eighties, and like R.E.M., they did not stress the solo styles of individual instrumentalists but instead worked together to craft a thick instrumental timbre to which vocals were added. Drummer Larry Mullen Jr. and singer/lyricist Bono Vox (Paul Hewson) were both born and raised in Ireland, but their guitarist/keyboardist, "The Edge" (David Evans), was originally from Wales, and bass player Adam Clayton was from England. The members of U2 grew up listening to such New York punk bands as Television, the Patti Smith Group, and the Ramones, but to

Bono of U2

create their own sound they took the rhythm and blues soulfulness of their countryman Van Morrison, the personal commitment of Bruce Springsteen, and the careful use of electronics to fill out, but not overcomplicate, their basic guitar, bass, and drums instrumentation.

> " I'd like to think that U2 is aggressive, loud, and emotional. I think that's good. I think that the people who I see parallels with are people like John the Baptist or Jeremiah. They were very loud, quite aggressive, yet joyful, and I believe they had an answer and a hope. In that sense, I think we have a love and an emotion without the flowers in our hair, and we have an aggression without the safety pins in our noses. "
>
> –Bono

As has been the case with many other bands whose careers have lasted for any period of time, U2's song themes changed as the group members grew older and their interests and concerns changed. They were all nineteen or twenty years old when their debut album, *Boy* (1980), was released, and the songs on that album, at least in part, were a look into some of the confusion and even trepidation suffered by young people. Sound effects such as breaking bottles added to the sense of tragedy and confusion on the album.

Personal experiences were still the basis for songs on their second album, *October* (1981). Bono's mother died in an accident when he was a teenager, and he had been haunted by his memories of her funeral; he wrote the song "Tomorrow" about his sense of loss. In all their music, U2 made a conscious effort not to be trendy, but instead attempted to make honest, meaningful statements, many of which became passionate cries for both personal and political peace.

In later years, U2 tended more toward the expression of political and international concerns rather than their earlier themes of personal introspection. They confronted the problem of war on their album *War* (1983). The Edge varied his guitar timbre by avoiding the guitar's bass strings to maintain a separation between the tone quality of his instrument and that of the bass. The overall group sound was filled out with echo effects. During concerts, Bono often waved a large white flag as a symbol of surrender and an end to war; the all-white flag had no nationalistic markings, making it a symbol of internationalism.

The Joshua Tree (1987) was a compassionate album that included songs of a personal nature, tributes to specific people and events, and songs that made general statements in support of the work done by Amnesty International.

Listening Guide

"With or Without You"
as recorded by U2 (1987)

Tempo: The tempo is about 108 beats per minute, with four beats in each bar.

Form: The recording begins with a twelve-bar instrumental introduction. The first four bars feature very soft arpeggio patterns on the synthesizer backed by drums. An eighth-note pulse played on the bass enters at the fifth bar.

The form is based on eight-bar periods in which the A periods each have new lyrics, the B's repeat the words in the song title, and the C's repeat lyrics about giving of oneself. The first B period is only four bars long, but the rest are eight bars. The form is organized as follows: AABABCACBBB.

An instrumental section occurs between the second B period and the first C, but it does not include the fast, technical solos typical of other rock styles; instead, it serves as a break or an interlude between the vocal periods.

Features: Even beat subdivisions are maintained throughout the recording.

The bass plays repeated notes at each half-beat, which was typical of much punk and new wave, except that the speed of the beat (and also the half-beat) is much slower than in most punk or new wave.

The drums maintain a backbeat throughout the recording.

An ethereal or otherworldly background sound is played on a synthesizer.

The recording uses crescendos and **decrescendos** for a dramatic effect. It begins very softly, gradually builds in volume, then softens rather suddenly only to rebuild and then fade out.

Lyrics: The song is a statement of pained love, in which the singer expresses both the wish to be with his lover and the realization that the feeling is not reciprocated.

Billboard pop charts: number one for three weeks; British hit singles: number four

(The album insert even included addresses for those who might want to join the organization.) *The Joshua Tree* was also produced by Eno, whose style is obvious in the album's clean electronic background effects and the presence of a new-wave-influenced repeating pulse in the bass. This style is apparent in "With or Without You," as discussed in the listening guide on page 292. The recording was number one on the U.S. pop charts for three weeks; it was number four in Britain. Bono has done much to aid impoverished people the world over and was recognized for that work, along with philanthropists Bill and Melinda Gates, in sharing the 2005 "Person of the Year" award given by *Time* magazine.

Alternative Rock from Britain

Many British groups and solo artists who were considered alternative in the United States enjoyed pop chart success in Britain. One such band was the Smiths. During the four years they were together, from 1983 to 1987, they released seven albums (plus a greatest hits collection and a live album) and seventeen singles, many of which made at least the top twenty in England. In the United States, they maintained an alternative following with more airplay on college radio stations than on commercial ones and had no singles or albums that charted in the top forty. The Smiths' most noticeable member was singer/lyricist **Morrissey,** whose James Dean–like image and pensive, introverted songs often described loneliness and seclusion. Morrissey's choice of a fifties-style image was not surprising because the Smiths were from Manchester, where American fifties artists and images had been popular for decades. Earlier groups or solo artists from the Mersey area of England (which includes Liverpool) had been greatly influenced by Buddy Holly's fifties image, including the Beatles, the Hollies, and Elvis Costello.

The Smiths' musical direction was primarily controlled by guitarist/songwriter Johnny Marr, whose layered guitar tracks provided full but catchy support for Morrissey's vocals. Marr left the Smiths to give himself the freedom to work on various projects with other singers, including Bryan Ferry, Paul McCartney, David Byrne (with Talking Heads), the Pretenders, and Kirsty MacColl.

Morrissey followed the breakup of the Smiths with a successful solo career, releasing one album a year beginning with *Viva Hate* (1988). His choices of backup musicians varied from album to album, at times including former members of the Smiths. As can be heard in "Everyday Is Like Sunday," he also had grown fond of the fullness provided by a synthesized orchestral background sound. During his solo career, Morrissey's song themes expanded to include subjects of worldwide concern, including

Morrissey (1990)

problems in the economy and fear of nuclear war. The listening guide to "Everyday Is Like Sunday" is on page 294. The recording was in the British top ten for six weeks, but it did not enter the top forty in the United States, where Morrissey remained an alternative rock artist.

Just when it seemed that new groups from Britain were never going to make it big in the United States again, the release of *Definitely Maybe* (1994) by the Manchester band **Oasis** brought back memories of British bands from the past and gained favor with American listeners. Some even considered Oasis to have created a new British invasion. The U.S. pop chart success of their second album, *(What's the Story) Morning Glory?* (1996), and its hit single "Wonderwall" made it seem that the group was, indeed, unstoppable. Problems between singer Liam Gallagher and his brother, guitarist Noel Gallagher, however, caused them to cancel several dates on their 1996 American tour and return to England early, leaving many questions about their future ability to work together effectively and further their success. The Gallaghers worked out their problems enough to continue on with Oasis in the early two-thousands, but they broke up again in 2009.

One of the most popular and longest-lasting alternative bands from England was the Cure, formed by Robert Smith, who grew up in the small town of Crawley, in

Listening Guide

"Everyday Is Like Sunday"
as recorded by Morrissey (1988)

Tempo: The tempo is approximately 116 beats per minute, with four beats in each bar.

Form: The form repeats and contrasts as follows: Introduction ABAABACAB Instrumental AA.

Each section is eight bars long except the C section, which has sixteen bars.

The second, fourth, and fifth A sections begin with the title words "everyday is like Sunday" and function as refrains.

The second instrumental A section fades out to end the recording.

Features: The instruments maintain even beat subdivisions, but Morrissey's

vocals sometimes lapse into uneven subdivisions.

The drums maintain a strong backbeat.

The electric bass keeps an eighth-note pulse most of the time. The bass pulse often repeats a single note as was common in much new-wave music of the late seventies.

A guitar is sometimes featured, but a great deal of the instrumental background is played by a full-sounding synthesized orchestra.

Lyrics: The theme is the banality of all events, even apocalyptic ones. The singer imagines a post–nuclear war world that is just another gray Sunday in an English coastal town.

British hit singles: number nine

Sussex, England. Smith was singer and guitarist for Easycure, which he started in 1976. They had shortened their name to the Cure by the time they released their first album, *Three Imaginary Boys* (1979, later reissued as *Boys Don't Cry*). Although influenced by the sense of freedom and nihilism inherent in the punk movement, the Cure's music was not centered around the anger of British punk. Instead, the group played catchy guitar lines and a rhythmically pumping bass as a danceable accompaniment for songs that were often about loneliness and existentialism. The existential aspect of some of Smith's song themes was misunderstood by what he termed "Philistine" critics. The song "Killing an Arab" (1979), for example, was dubbed as racist, although, as Smith later explained, it was really a direct reference to the fatalistic indifference felt by the man who shot an Arab in the existential novel *The Stranger* (*L'Étranger,* 1942) by Albert Camus. As esoteric as the Cure's music and song themes may have

seemed to some, their following continued to grow through the eighties and into the nineties, even having a top-ten hit with "Love Song" from their most successful U.S. release *Disintegration* (1989). As far as image was concerned, Robert Smith's darkly lined eyes staring out from his pale, powdered face, as well as some of the depressing themes of his songs, approached the gloom of what became associated with the movement known as Gothic rock. The Cure continued to chart singles in the U.S. top one hundred through most of the nineties, but none of those matched their earlier chart ratings. They continue to record and tour in the two-thousands.

Gothic Rock

To latter-day followers of the punk movement in Britain, the word *Gothic* evoked images of gloomy medieval castles sitting atop isolated hills, still echoing screams from their torture chambers. Following that mood, some rock musicians abandoned the intensity of punk music to create a rock style known as Gothic rock, or death rock. The style gained many followers in England through the eighties and had become an important underground movement in the United States by the early nineties. Of course, different bands approached their music in different ways, and the instruments they used varied greatly, but some basic characteristics remained fairly constant. Because the underlying theme of the music was portrayed by images of ancient powers that humans could not control, the music tended to stress low voices, bass instruments, and fairly slow tempos. Drones, common in secular music of the Middle Ages, were also common in Gothic rock. Electronic effects were applied to create almost hypnotic repetition of short melodic phrases that often approached, in style, the slower works by minimalist composers such as Philip Glass or Steve Reich. Perhaps because an active drummer would spoil the gloomy mood of the music, many of the bands used drum machines that did not always stress a rock backbeat. When organs, real or electronic, were used, they were made to sound like those in large, stone medieval cathedrals through the use of electronic reverberation. Songs sometimes had very long (as much as five-minute) instrumental introductions to set the mood.

However, the castles portrayed in Gothic novels and the secular music of the Middle Ages were only part of the sources for Gothic rock music. A development out of the negative view of society expressed in the punk movement, Gothic bands went back to the protopunk music of the Velvet Underground, which also used drones and powerful thumps on a bass drum in place of standard rock drumbeats. David Bowie's deep and dramatic vocal timbre was copied by many of the male singers in the Gothic movement, except the Gothic singers deepened the effect by singing at lower pitch levels.

Bauhaus' debut EP, *Bela Lugosi's Dead* (1979), introduced Gothic rock to Britain's underground market. Bela Lugosi was the Hungarian actor who played the title role in the 1931 movie *Dracula*. Appropriate for that character, the nine-and-one-half minute song "Bela Lugosi's Dead" included song sections of haunting electronically produced sound effects that imitated the wind and were full of rattles and buzzes. A throbbing beat and backbeat pounded through most of the recording, and a very low descending bass line repeated through much of it. Bauhaus' singer Peter Murphy maintained a repetitious monotone in his vocals, which were more spoken on pitch than sung. Adding to the gloomy mystery of the repetitions of the words "Bela Lugosi's dead" were the many repetitions of the words "Bela's undead," something

horror stories often claim about vampires, including Dracula. The effect was connected to the sense of mystery many Gothic novels created.

Bauhaus came to an end when Peter Murphy left the group to pursue a solo career. The three remaining members of Bauhaus survived Murphy's departure by first splitting up and experimenting with other musicians and then by regrouping under the name Love and Rockets. As Love and Rockets, they reacted against the darkness of Bauhaus and even managed a top-ten hit with one of their first singles, "So Alive" (1989). As with a number of other groups who began in the alternative market, such success brought into question the band's previously earned underground standing. Murphy returned to Bauhaus in 2005 and sang the group's old classic "Bela Lugosi's Dead" while hanging upside down like a vampire bat.

The city of Leeds gave the Gothic rock movement two important bands, the Sisters of Mercy and Mission (UK). Vocalist and principal song writer Andrew Eldritch was the central figure of the Sisters of Mercy. He stood on stage wearing dark sunglasses, shrouded in black, singing in a hollow voice so deep and velvety that he sounded like David Bowie singing from the bottom of a well. Song themes often portrayed a depressing view of corruption among politicians and the media. Despite the fact that the band was English, they commented on American political figures as well as their own. The title of their album *Vision Thing* (1990) came out of a statement made by President Bush, who was quoted as having asked his speech writers to change their direction because he felt that his speeches lacked the "vision thing." Musically, the Sisters of Mercy avoided the use of acoustic drums and instead relied on a drum machine they named "Doktor Avalanche." Medieval touches included low drones (long-held notes) and an almost minimalistic use of short, repeated melodic fragments.

Several membership changes occurred through the ten-plus years the Sisters of Mercy were together; in fact, **Mission (UK)** was formed by former Sisters of Mercy guitarist Wayne Hussey and bassist Craig Adams. (The "UK" was added to the band's name for publication in the United States because a rhythm and blues band in Philadelphia held the copyright to the name the Mission.) The listening guide on page 296 analyzes the Gothic elements in a track from Mission (UK)'s debut album, *God's Own Medicine* (1986). "Wasteland" was written by members of Mission (UK) and was probably influenced by T. S. Eliot's (1888–1965) poem "The Waste Land" (1922), which depicts the world as a place of spiritual drought. The poem also makes reference to medieval imagery.

Listening Guide

"Wasteland"
as recorded by Mission (UK) (1986)

Tempo: The tempo is approximately 132 beats per minute, with four beats in each bar.

Form: The form is based on eight-bar periods and is structured as follows: Introduction Extension AAAAB Instrumental AAB Instrumental A_1A_1BBB.

The recording begins with a spoken sentence.

The instrumental introduction is made up of two eight-bar periods followed by an extension of three four-beat bars and one three-beat bar.

Each A and B section is eight bars in length. The B section functions as a refrain.

The first instrumental section (after the introduction) is made up of two eight-bar periods.

The second instrumental section has five eight-bar periods.

The vocal line is different in the A_1 sections than it is in earlier A sections, but the chords and instrumental riffs are too similar to the other A sections to call them C sections.

The end of the last B section devolves into electronic sound effects that end the recording.

British hit singles: number eleven

Features: Even beat subdivisions are maintained throughout the recording.

A soft backbeat played in the introduction is replaced by a very strong backbeat played by the drums through the rest of the recording.

A four-bar chord progression is repeated through the entire recording, each eight-bar period playing that progression through two times. A bass riff also repeats during each four-bar pattern, creating what would be called a passacaglia in classical music.

The thick production sound includes layers of riff patterns played by the guitars and bass.

The patterns repeat in a minimalism-influenced way, not unlike some of the backgrounds that Brian Eno added to recordings by U2 and others he produced.

The deep, dronelike sound of the vocals is greatly influenced by some of David Bowie's vocals, except that Wayne Hussey (in this recording) sings in a lower register than Bowie generally used.

Lyrics: The song portrays the world as a wasteland where good and evil have been combined and pain is pleasure. As he laments at the beginning, the vocalist feels ignored and rejected by God. This homage to T. S. Eliot's poem continues his themes of the spiritual isolation and emptiness of the modern world.

Postpunk in the United States

Minneapolis was an important center for postpunk bands of the eighties. The Replacements and Hüsker Dü stand out as Minneapolis bands that achieved a national following without crossing over into mainstream success. After hearing the Sex Pistols, guitarist/songwriter Paul Westerberg envisioned a whole new future for himself. He quit playing guitar in the band Neighborhood Threat because he was tired of playing covers of music by bands like Rush. Because Johnny Rotten's singing affected him as it did, he decided he needed to put together his own band. That band, the Replacements, never actually was a punk band in the sense that the Sex Pistols were, but they played loud and fast music that fit that general style. As Westerberg's songwriting matured, the band moved away from their angry punk roots voiced in such songs as "Shut-up" and "Kick Your Door Down" from their first album, *Sorry Ma, Forgot to Take Out the Trash* (1981), to some rather sensitive expressions of loneliness and insecurity as can be heard in "Answering Machine" (from *Let It Be,* 1984) and "Hold My Life" (from *Tim,* 1985). Hard-rocking songs such as "I.O.U." (from *Pleased to Meet Me,* 1987) and "Bent Out of Shape" (from *All Shook Down,* 1990) indicated that Westerberg was as unlikely as ever to sell out to pop styles.

Hüsker Dü created a Sex Pistols–influenced sound of their own with thick, high-volume buzzsaw guitar timbres that served to blur the distinctions between melody and rhythm. Their driving bass lines, pounding beat, and Bob Mould's sometimes-shouted monotone vocals were also derived from punk influences. A listening guide that serves as an example of their style is included here.

Listening Guide

"Could You Be the One?"
as recorded by Hüsker Dü (1987)

Tempo: The tempo is approximately 160 beats per minute, with four beats in each bar.

Form: After a two-bar introduction, the form is organized as follows: AB with Extension AB with Extension C Instrumental ABCC.

The A sections are eight bars long.

The B sections begin as eight-bar periods followed by extensions. The first extension adds six bars and the second adds two bars.

The C section is fourteen bars in length and uses melodic and lyric sections from the B section. The C section functions as a refrain.

The instrumental section is based on a full A section followed by a B section with a six-bar extension.

The recording ends by fading out.

Features: Even beat subdivisions are generally maintained through the recording.

The drums keep a strong backbeat.

The high intensity level created by the "buzzsaw" guitar timbre and active bass line are very much influenced by the instrumental effects in punk music.

As was also true of most punk rock, guitar, bass, and drums are the only instruments used.

Also in the punk tradition, the vocals are generally in a monotone.

Lyrics: The singer is searching for meaning in a relationship and asking if the person to whom the song is addressed might be the one for him. He must have been hurt before because he says that he is crying inside and wonders whether what he wants even matters at all.

After Hüsker Dü disbanded in 1987, singer/songwriter Bob Mould experimented with a completely new direction for his *Workbook* album. It may have been his move from the noise and constant activity of the city of Minneapolis to the quiet of the Minnesota countryside that caused him to approach his music with a more relaxed acoustic sound. Some of Hüsker Dü's buzzsaw guitar style returned with Mould's midnineties band Sugar.

Washington, D.C. has had a strong and political punk movement called *straight edge* since the early eighties, and the nineties band **Fugazi,** which formed in 1987, was born out of that movement. Fugazi's guitarist, vocalist, and primary songwriter, **Ian MacKaye** (born in 1962), screamed out against drugs, alcohol, and people who were content merely being followers with his band Minor Threat back in 1981. After the breakup of that band, MacKaye moved on to the short-lived band Embrace, and he continued to attack drug usage and widened his social criticisms to condemn the uncontrollable greed for money and power he saw around him in the nation's capital. The late eighties saw a more mature, but still aggressively critical MacKaye co-writing and sharing vocals and guitar solos with Guy Picciotto in Fugazi. The term *fugazi* meant "crisis situation" during the Vietnam War, and Fugazi's songs pointed to the money-grubbing values most Americans hold as being exactly that—a crisis situation. In support of their position that money should not run the world, Fugazi released its recordings on its own label, Dischord Records, at a cost far below the normal prices. As mentioned earlier, Fugazi also kept ticket prices to their concerts at no more than five dollars. The band allowed no merchandise sales at their concerts—"This is not a FUGAZI T-shirt" shirts available at concerts were bootlegs the band had nothing to do with. Fugazi also allowed no age limit at concerts and requested no backstage catering, limousines, or other special treatment. Musically, Fugazi played hard-core punk updated with funk and reggae influences and maintained a large underground following into the nineties. Fugazi's appeal broadened beyond the underground in 1993 when *In on the Kill Taker* made it into the top 200 on the pop charts.

MacKaye also worked with other bands including members of L.A.'s Black Flag, and with one of the most prominent bands of the feminist **Riot Grrrl** movement, **Bikini Kill.** That movement changed its name to **Revolution Girl Style Now** and included many female bands whose songs spoke out about sexual abuse of children, rape, domestic violence, and female empowerment. The movement was essentially dead by the time another band with ties to it, Sleater-Kinney, broke up in 2006, but the ideas they sang about remain important to many young women.

"I feel completely left out of the realm of everything that is so important to me. And I know that this is partly because punk rock is for and by boys mostly and partly because punk rock of this generation is coming of age in a time of mindless career-goal bands."
–Bikini Kill's drummer, Tobi Vail

Industrial Rock

The industrial rock movement began in England in the late seventies. The term *industrial* was used as a statement against what the movement's originators saw as the decay of urban life and its dependency on work in factory and industrial jobs. Thematically an extension of the punk movement, the industrial bands looked beyond the government and monarchy as reasons for rebellion and saw intrusive controls on every aspect of their lives. They felt that even the art world lacked freedom of expression because of too much concern for form and balanced structure. The industrialists' views on control were influenced by the sadistic desires to dominate all aspects of life and expression described by William Burroughs in his novel *Naked Lunch* (1959). Also inspired by that novel, various forms of sadomasochism became part of the stage performances of many industrial groups, and group members and fans would pierce themselves with pins or other ornaments. A very high decibel level is an important characteristic of many industrial recordings and performances.

Two of the most important early industrial bands were Throbbing Gristle and Cabaret Voltaire. Instruments used by these and other such bands were chosen primarily for the amount of noise they could produce and whether the instrument's noise would sound thick and muddy in the background or stand out over the background. Instruments employed to stand out were horns, especially trumpet or cornet, and electric guitars played with a slide, a small electric fan, or even an electric drill. Synthesizers provided much of the background sound. Throbbing Gristle built their own keyboard instrument that had one octave of "notes," on which each note activated one or more cassette machines loaded with prerecorded tape loops containing electronic sounds and noises such as screaming voices. Even such sounds as an electric shoe polisher were pushed through amplifiers and distortion boxes. Throbbing Gristle subtitled their first U.S.-released album, *Throbbing Gristle's Greatest Hits* (1980), *Entertainment through Pain.* They broke up in 1986, but Cabaret Voltaire was still recording in the early nineties. They broke up in 1994.

Listening Guide

"Stigmata"
as recorded by Ministry (1988)

Tempo:
The tempo is approximately 152 beats per minute, with four beats in each bar.

Form:
Most sections of the form are eight bars long, but many of those are extended into other lengths with no apparent pattern to the extensions. Since the vocals are all screams or shouts, it is impossible to analyze a form through melodic repetitions and contrasts. The two formal sections that do contrast with one another are each identified by their riff pattern. The first riff is one bar long, usually played eight times in succession (the A section). The second riff begins like the first riff, but cuts off early and is lengthened to two bars by drum accents. That two-bar riff is usually played through four times, making for another eight-bar section (the B section).

The introduction is made up of six bars of electronic sound effects; eight bars that include drum accentuations; eight bars of screams; sixteen bars of the first riff (A); eight bars of the second riff (B); and then screams that become electronically distorted. From there the vocals enter with barely audible lyrics and the A and B sections alternate (repeated, extended or not) through the rest of the recording.

Features:
Even beat subdivisions are maintained throughout the recording.

A strong backbeat is kept through much of the recording, but the pattern is sometimes broken.

In addition to drums, the recording includes the use of electronic sound effects, distorted guitars, distorted bass (playing the riff patterns), distorted vocals, and other noises.

The vocals have been electronically altered by removing all high overtones and limiting the low pitches to create a robotic effect.

The repetitious riff and drum patterns, along with the background noises, create the feeling of being caught in a factory and doing and hearing the same things hour after hour.

Lyrics:
"Stigmata" generally means that a person's flesh has been pierced or otherwise invaded by a foreign object, and the vocalist constantly screams about trying to get something out of his eyes (along with other references to such things as chewing on and being cut with glass and walking on splinters). The pain and anger are directed at someone who has lied to him.

By the early eighties, the industrial movement had made its way across the Atlantic and bands such as Chicago's **Ministry** formed to vent their anger at the modern world. The layers of noise for which industrial rock is known can be heard in Ministry's "Stigmata." A listening guide to that recording is included here.

Industrial rock of the late eighties had spread to the United States and gained a new voice in Cleveland when vocalist Trent Reznor overdubbed his synthesizer-produced sounds and recorded his debut album, *Pretty Hate Machine* (1989), under the name Nine Inch Nails.

"You might say that my success was to take industrial music and add a melody to it, add an

Trent Reznor of Nine Inch Nails

element of pop to it. It connected with people in a way that we didn't anticipate. "

–Trent Reznor

Reznor hired musicians to form a band that could take his music on the road. They were featured in the first Lollapalooza tour, and that exposure gained Reznor many new fans. Reznor's song themes were already tortured, angry, and alienated, but after having legal problems with his record company, he took those themes even further in his "Happiness in Slavery" video (1992), in which a tortured man is ground up in a machine. Symbolizing his angst, at least in part, Reznor moved from his Cleveland home to L.A. where he bought and lived in the house in which followers of Charles Manson had murdered actress Sharon Tate and others back in 1969. Reznor produced the soundtrack from the movie *Natural Born Killers* (1994) and released a new album of his own, *The Downward Spiral,* the following year. He didn't stay in L.A. very long, however. He ended up moving to New Orleans, where he started the Nothing Record Company. Nine Inch Nails had a number seventeen pop chart hit with "The Day the World Went Away" in 1999. Reznor took a break to recover from alcoholism and drugs and returned to continue with Nine Inch Nails in the two-thousands.

Grindcore, a style that combined the power of thrash/death metal with the pounding beat of hard-core punk and industrial noises, emerged in the late eighties. One of the most important bands to represent this style was a British band from Birmingham, **Napalm Death.** Their breakneck tempos and electronically altered vocals provided powerful support for angry lyrics about hypocrisy and injustice in the world. Before signing with Sony, which released their *Fear Emptiness Despair* (1994) album, Napalm Death's record company was Earache Records. Napalm Death's American grindcore counterpart is the New York speed/thrash band Prong.

Summary

Alternative or underground rock was so named because it served as an alternative to rock music that was commercial or performed to please a broad audience. Most alternative bands avoided signing with major record labels or with promoters for fear that doing so might cause them to lose control of their music or their song lyrics. The bands did not want to be seen as rock stars but rather as living on the same level as their fans. Their songs expressed the concerns of those fans, and in an economy that made it difficult for young adults to foresee dependable financial security for themselves, the attitudes in the songs were often depressed or angry.

The most depressed of the underground movements was Gothic rock (also called death rock), which portrayed the gloom and mystery of a Gothic novel with repetitious sounds influenced by music of the Middle Ages. The most angry movement was industrial rock, which portrayed the world as controlling and lacking any sense of freedom. There were elements of the antiestablishment push of the punk movement in most alternative and underground styles, and many postpunk bands used the intense pounding beat, throbbing bass, and distorted guitars of punk bands like the Sex Pistols. Other alternative rock concentrated less on depression or anger but still had lyrics, images, or music that was too individualistic or even bizarre for broad audience appeal.

discussion questions

Much postpunk alternative music is much more depressed than rock music of the sixties, when many musicians and fans were really experiencing war and death in Vietnam. What might have been attractive about death and depressed themes for young people during the eighties? What rock styles express similar themes today?

The NINETIES AND EARLY TWO-THOUSANDS

"This aggression will not stand."
    –President George H. W. Bush, about Iraq's
        invasion of Kuwait

"When I was in England I experimented
with marijuana a time or two and I didn't
like it. I didn't inhale."
    –Presidential candidate Bill Clinton

"Our worst fear is not that we are
inadequate. Our deepest fear is that we are
powerful beyond measure."
    –Nelson Mandela, the leader of
        the African National Congress

"If it doesn't fit, you must acquit."

–Johnnie Cochran, attorney for O. J. Simpson

"America was targeted for attack because we're the brightest beacon for freedom and opportunity in the world, and no one will keep that light from shining."

–President George W. Bush

The nineties were a decade of unparalleled prosperity for a very large number of Americans. Personal and family incomes were the highest they had been since the end of World War II. Americans shared that prosperity in almost every economic class. Jobs were available, particularly for those who were willing to learn new skills, and unemployment remained low. The Welfare Reform Act of 1996 ended the entitlement to welfare that had previously been in the law and required many former welfare recipients to get jobs. Job training was made available for those who needed it, and the result was a marked decline in the welfare rolls. Some, often quite young, resourceful entrepreneurs established their own Internet businesses that were extremely lucrative, making them, at least for a time, into "dot-com millionaires." Few of those businesses lasted to the end of the decade, but the possibilities created a sense of optimism based on investment capital.

The eighties had ended with the tearing down of the Berlin Wall and the end of the cold war, but soon a new adversary emerged. In the summer of 1990, Iraq invaded and occupied the small, oil-rich country of Kuwait. With Kuwait under its control, Iraq was a great threat to the U.S. ally and oil supplier Saudi Arabia. Thirty nations joined the United States in the liberation of Kuwait by Operation Desert Shield. By early 1991, the United States and its allies began a series of air strikes against Iraq in what became Operation Desert Storm. U.S. and allied ground troops went in, and by the end of February 1991 the war was over. Iraqi troops set fire to many of Kuwait's oil fields as they fled the region, creating an environmental disaster.

By August 1990, Soviet leader Mikhail Gorbachev ended the Communist Party's control of the Soviet government. A group of political leaders in the Communist Party attempted to overthrow Gorbachev in 1991, but then president of Russia, Boris Yeltsen, rode into Moscow on a tank and brought about the end of the coup attempt. Gorbachev then dissolved the Soviet Union, freeing all states of the former Soviet empire, and resigned his office. Boris Yeltsin continued on as the president of Russia and faced tremendous problems in his attempts to move the country to a free market economy. The former communist commissars were often the owners of the new "private" companies, and the system ran into one problem after another. The ruble was devalued, and the lives of Russian citizens, for a time, hit a lower standard than they had had under communism.

Former members of the communist legislature revolted in 1993, and Yeltsin had to send in the military to regain control of the state. The next year, the Russian province of Chechnya began a war with Russia in an attempt to gain its freedom, and that conflict was on and off and then on again throughout the nineties.

In the power vacuum left by the Soviet Union, the different ethnic groups in Yugoslavia fought one another in a series of wars that vied with the "ethnic cleansing" horrors of the holocaust of World War II. The United Nations got involved but did little to protect the average citizens from the hatred and bloodshed. In 1994, Serbian leader Slobadan Milosevic signed a peace agreement to stop the Serbs from fighting the Muslims and Croatians, but it took the constant presence of U.S. peacekeeping troops to enforce it. In 1998, Milosevic sent troops to battle against the ethnic Albanians in the Serbian province of Kosovo, and, again, the United States and its allies were required to intervene with a long series of air strikes. The war ended when Serb troops were finally driven out of Kosovo.

In the seventies and eighties, the United States and other countries had restricted trade with South Africa in order to force the end of the system of apartheid (separation of races) there. In February 1990, South African president F. W. de Klerk freed Nelson Mandela, head of the African National Congress, who had been imprisoned for twenty-seven years for his past attempts to gain equality for Africans. The efforts of both Mandela and de Klerk to end apartheid won the two of them a shared Nobel Peace Prize in 1993. By 1994, South Africa had done away with many of its apartheid laws and held elections in which citizens of all races voted. Mandela was elected president and de Klerk the vice president.

The Middle East continued, as ever, to be a place of unrest and frequent fighting throughout the nineties. President Bill Clinton hosted peace talks between Israeli leader Yitzhak Rabin and Palestinian Liberation Organization (PLO) leader Yasir Arafat in 1993. The talks ended with the signing of a peace agreement that gave many hope that the fighting in the region would end, but there were many difficulties in the process of acting out terms of the agreement. Rabin was assassinated by one of Israel's Jewish extremist citizens in 1995, and the fighting in the region continued on.

Unfortunately, violence in the nineties was not all outside the U.S. borders. African American citizens of Los Angeles rioted after four white police officers were found not guilty in a state court for the beating of African American Rodney King. Fifty-five people were killed, more than four thousand injured, and thousands of buildings were badly damaged.

The United States experienced a number of terrorist attacks during the nineties. The World Trade Center in New York symbolized the success of capitalism and became the target of a car bombing by Osama bin Laden and his Muslim extremists in 1993. Six people were killed, but the terrorists were arrested before they could do any further damage. Theodore Kaczynski, a technophobe known as the "unabomber," sent letter bombs to a number of college professors and scientists whose work he believed was contributing to the destruction of the world by technology. Kaczynski was arrested in 1996 and finally pled guilty in 1998. A bombing at the 1996 Summer Olympic Games in Atlanta, Georgia, killed two people and drew far more attention than the games themselves. The bomber was never found, although a security guard was mistakenly arrested and finally released.

One of the worst of the terrorist attacks of the nineties was the truck bombing of the Alfred P. Murrah Federal Building in Oklahoma City, Oklahoma, in 1995. The building not only housed various federal offices, but also a preschool. One hundred sixty-eight men, women, and children were killed and many more injured. Former Army veteran and militia member Timothy McVeigh turned out to be the person primarily responsible for the bombing. The attack was carried out on April 19, exactly two years after FBI agents had ended a standoff with Branch Davidian cult members in Waco, Texas, that resulted in the deaths of the cult members including many children. The U.S. government's handling of that was extremely unpopular and seemed to be part of what had set McVeigh against the government. McVeigh was executed in 2001.

The so-called trial of the century also happened during the nineties. Former football star and popular African American actor O. J. Simpson was tried for the brutal murders of his former wife, Nicole Brown Simpson, and a waiter who happened to be on his ex-wife's property, Ron Goldman. The murders occurred in 1994, and the televised trial consumed the interest of many Americans through much of the following year. Simpson was found not guilty in the criminal trial but was found liable for the deaths in a civil trial that followed.

The late nineties saw five mass shootings at U.S. public schools in which students turned on one another and their teachers. The most notorious was the 1999 shooting at Columbine High School in Littleton, Colorado, where two students killed twelve students and a teacher before killing themselves. The ease with which students were able to get guns and ammunition as well as the violence in video games and on television and in movies became a great concern in the general effort to keep the schools safe. Some schools installed metal detectors, did away with lockers, and had routine searches to try to avoid weapons at schools.

On the positive side, the nineties was a decade of technological innovation that reached and affected the everyday lives of most Americans. The Internet became available in most schools and many homes, allowing research on the World Wide Web, fast communication by e-mail, online shopping, and any number of other advantages. The entire music industry was affected by the way CD-quality sound could be moved over the Internet. Musicians were able to produce their own music and make it available for others to hear without any of the controls of record companies. Some Web sites such as MP3.com provided access to much music at no charge, causing much discussion about piracy and copyright. Cell phones also became cheaper and more plentiful than ever, becoming common modes of communication among people of most economic classes.

Bill Clinton and Al Gore were elected president and vice president in 1992, promising many new reforms in health care and a commitment to having minorities represented in government. The health care reforms did not get far, but Clinton's cabinet did include more African Americans, Hispanics, and women than ever before. Clinton's tax increase angered Republicans whose "Contract with America" won them control of the Congress for the first time since 1954. Clinton won reelection in 1996. Inflation and unemployment were down and family incomes were at an all-time high. Accusations of a sexual affair with a White House intern and lies under oath tainted Clinton's popularity. He was charged with perjury and became the first elected U.S. president to be impeached. Congress did not get the required two-thirds majority of the Senate to remove him from office, however, and he was able to serve out his term. In a very close election in 2000, Al Gore lost to George W. Bush (son of former President George H. W. Bush) in 2000.

As the end of the decade loomed, the year 2000 "Y2K" potential crisis captured much new attention. Early computers had identified years with the last two digits since the first two were considered a given. As the year 2000 approached, four digit years were needed. The fear was that January 1, 2000, would be read by computers as January 1, 1900, and that would cause great problems with things that depended on keeping track of time. Computer experts all over the country worked at solving the impending problem, and many feared that not enough had been done to keep major government, financial, and safety systems going through the year change. Doomsday scenarios were spun, in which planes fell from the sky, financial systems completely collapsed, and energy systems went down, but, happily, none of that happened. The new millennium, which did not actually begin until January 1, 2001, arrived without significant computer-related problems.

The early two-thousands were relatively free of major problems for most Americans. The recession that had been predicted had not yet hit, and no new wars had begun. On September 11, 2001, however, the world changed. Muslim extremists under the direction of Osama bin Laden, a Saudi Arabian living in Afghanistan, hijacked commercial American planes and flew them into each of the twin towers of the World Trade Center and the Pentagon; they apparently also planned to hit either the White House or Capitol building with another of a series of suicide missions. American Airlines Flight 93 was hijacked with the objective of hitting a Washington target but was overtaken by heroic passengers who died with the terrorists by forcing the plane into a field instead of the intended target. In retaliation for the 9/11 strikes, the war against terrorism was launched and a renewed sense of nationalism spread over the United States.

After 9/11 there was a brief minirecession as air travel and tourism took a dramatic decline. The economy steadily recovered in 2002, and the United States experienced a period of economic growth. In 2003, the United States invaded Iraq with the goal of "regime change" of the government of Saddam Hussein. Hussein was executed in 2006, and the continued presence of American troops in Iraq drew increasing criticism at home as total war casualties first rose above three thousand, then four thousand.

The long period of U.S. economic expansion came to an abrupt end in the spring of 2008. It became increasingly clear that many financial institutions had made numerous bad loans (often called "subprime" because the borrowers did not have a "prime" rating) while simultaneously incurring hard-to-meet obligations to other financial institutions (like "credit default swaps," in which one institution promises to make good on another institution's bad loans). The result was a major banking and financial crisis in the fall of 2008, followed by an almost immediate, dramatic downturn in the economy and an increase in unemployment. Gasoline prices more than doubled their previous highest price, creating great problems for Americans, especially for those who had to drive as part of their job requirements. These financial woes, along with what many saw as the unnecessary dragging on of the Iraq War, no doubt contributed in large part to the election of Barack Obama in November 2008. In 2009, the newly elected president attempted to reform the health care system to deal with the ongoing concerns of large numbers of Americans who were without health insurance.

Chronology Chart

Historical Events	Happenings in Rock Music
1990	East and West Germany reunite. Nelson Mandela is released from prison in South Africa. Iraq invades Kuwait. Operation Desert Shield troops leave for Saudi Arabia. Clean Air Act is signed to update the 1970 Clean Air Act.	"That's What Friends Are For" AIDS benefit concert. Judas Priest is exonerated on subliminal message charges. Allen Collins, Tom Fogerty, Stiv Bators, Brent Mydland, Cornell Gunter, Del Shannon, Stevie Ray Vaughan, Art Blakey, Jim Henson, Dexter Gordon, Johnny Ray, and Sarah Vaughan die.
1991	The Gulf War forces Saddam Hussein's troops out of Kuwait. Rodney King beating video taped in L.A. Justice T. Marshall retires from the Supreme Court. Anita Hill testifies at Clarence Thomas confirmation hearing. Charges against Oliver North are dropped. Strategic Arms Reduction Agreement is signed. Magic Johnson announces his HIV infection. Middle East peace talks begin. Soviet Union is replaced by Commonwealth of Independent States. UN expels Yugoslavia because of civil wars. Rajev Gandhi is assassinated.	James Brown is released from prison. Oliver Stone revives the sixties in the movie *The Doors*. Riot at Guns N' Roses concert in St. Louis. Debut of Paul McCartney's *Liverpool Oratorio*. Tenth anniversary of MTV. Postpunk bands join for Lollapalooza tour. "Record" stores stock only cassettes and CDs. Steve Clark, Steve Marriott, Johnny Thunders, Rob Tyner, Rick Griffin, Leo Fender, Doc Pomus, Freddie Mercury, Miles Davis, Stan Getz, Bill Graham, Gene Clark, David Ruffin, and James Cleveland die.

1992   L.A. riots follow verdicts in Rodney King beating case. Independent candidate Ross Perot shakes up presidential race. U.S. military leads Operation Restore Hope to aid the starving in Somalia. Middle East peace talks deadlock. Earth Summit in Rio. Navy sex-abuse scandal. Hurricanes Andrew and Iniki.

Alternative music becomes mainstream through pop chart hits. AIDS benefit tribute to Freddie Mercury in London. Ice-T pulls "Cop Killer" off *Body Count* LP. *Lollapalooza II* tour. Ozzy Osbourne on farewell tour. Rock the Vote movement attempts to attract younger voters to the polls. Mary Wells, John Cage, Eddie Kendricks, Dee Murray, Roger Miller, Stefanie Ann Sargent, Jerry Nolan, and Willie Dixon die.

1993   Bill Clinton becomes president. Czechoslovakia splits into two countries. Thurgood Marshall dies. Massacres and ethnic cleansing in former Yugoslavia. Blizzard of the Century hits twenty-five southern and eastern states. Air food/medical aid drops to former Yugoslavia. Yeltsin battles with Russian Congress over reform movement. New York World Trade Center bombing. Janet Reno becomes first female U.S. attorney general. Branch Davidian disaster in Waco, Texas. Nelson Mandela and President F. W. de Klerk share Nobel Peace Prize. The Tailhook Convention sexual assault scandal is exposed. "Don't ask, don't tell" policy for homosexuals in the U.S. armed forces instituted. NAFTA passes. Vincent Foster dies.

Rock musicians perform at President Clinton's inaugural balls. Time-Warner cancels Ice-T's contract after attacks over lyrics. Broadway musical version of *Tommy* nominated for eleven Tony awards. Walter Becker and Donald Fagen reunite as Steely Dan. Pearl Jam refuses to release singles or make videos from *Vs.* Thomas A. Dorsey, Dizzy Gillespie, Toy Caldwell, Sun Ra, Conway Twitty, and Frank Zappa die.

1994   Yitzhak Rabin and Yasser Arafat share Nobel Peace Prize. Nelson Mandela elected president of South Africa. Fiftieth anniversary of D-Day celebrated. Republican majority is elected to the Senate and the House for the first time in forty years. Trade embargo against Vietnam ends. O. J. Simpson murder trial is televised. Major league baseball strike. Resignation of Jocelyn Elders and U.S. surgeon general. U.S. troops aid Jean-Baptiste Aristide's return to Haiti. Jacqueline Kennedy Onassis and former president Richard Nixon die.

Pearl Jam cancels summer tour because of Ticketmaster's high prices. Heart attack forces cancellation of John Mellencamp's planned North American tour. Three days of music and mud at Woodstock '94. Robert Plant and Jimmy Page reunite, but without John Paul Jones. Michael Jackson and Lisa Marie Presley marry. Kurt Cobain commits suicide. Major Lance, Harry Nilsson, Fred "Sonic" Smith, and Kristan Pfaff die.

1995   Devastating earthquake in Kobe, Japan. Bombing of federal building in Oklahoma City. Louis Farrakahn's Million Man March in Washington, D.C. U.S. troops sent to Bosnia to enforce peace accord. O. J. Simpson acquitted of murder charges. Assassination of Israeli prime minister Yitzhak Rabin.

Paul McCartney, George Harrison, and Ringo Starr reunite to record new Beatle song. "Free as a Bird," made with a tape by John Lennon. The first Beatles Anthology is released. Opening of the Rock and Roll Hall of Fame and Museum in Cleveland. Michael Jackson and Lisa Marie Presley divorce. Latin pop singer Selena murdered. Eazy-E dies of AIDS. Peter Grant, Junior Walker, Bob Stinson, Jerry Garcia, Sterling Morrison, Shannon Hoon, Wolfman Jack, and Rory Gallagher die.

1996   Commerce Secretary Ron Brown and others killed in plane crash near Dubrovnik, Croatia. Unabomber suspect arrested and charged in two deaths. ValuJet plane crashes in the Florida Everglades. Bombing of U.S. military housing complex in Saudi Arabia. TWA flight 800 explodes and crashes off Long Island, NY. Beginning of O. J. Simpson's wrongful death civil trial. Reelection of President Clinton.

Reuniting of the original Sex Pistols. Snoop Doggy Dogg acquitted of murder charges. Death Row rapper Tupac Shakur shot to death. David Bowie releases "Telling Lies" single on the World Wide Web before its CD or cassette release. Gerry Mulligan, Jonathan Melvoin, Ella Fitzgerald, Johnny "Guitar" Watson, and Bill Monroe die.

1997   Madeleine Albright becomes first female secretary of state. O. J. Simpson found "responsible" for the murders of Nicole Brown Simpson and Ron Goldman. Thirty-nine members of Heaven's Gate cult commit suicide in San Diego county. Birth of cloned sheep, Dolly, made public, sparking much debate. Timothy McVeigh found guilty and sentenced to death for bombing Oklahoma City Federal Building. Princess Diana killed in Paris car crash. Terry Nichols found guilty of conspiracy in planning of bombing Oklahoma City Federal Building. British au pair Louise Woodward found guilty of killing baby in her care.

Lilith Fair tour celebrating female performers begins. Some performers featured at some concerts in the two-year tour include Sarah McLachlan, the Indigo Girls, Queen Latifah, Liz Phair, Suzanne Vega, and the Pretenders. Concerts and CDs by Marilyn Manson, 2 Live Crew, and Prodigy banned in some parts of the southern U.S. Col. Tom Parker, Richard Berry, La Verne Baker, Harold Melvin, Notorious B.I.G. (Christopher Wallace), Allen Ginsberg, Ronnie Lane, William Burroughs, Luther Allison, Michel Hutchence, Nicolette Larson, and John Denver die.

1998   Theodore Kaczynski pleads guilty to being the Unabomber. War begins in Kosovo. President Clinton impeached by the House of Representatives. Muslim death sentence against author Salmon Rushdie lifted. Sonny Bono and Linda McCartney die.

The Rolling Stones, Ringo Starr's All Starr Band, Brian May, Ronnie James Dio, and Deep Purple tour Russia. Junior Wells (Chicago blues harpist) and Carl Perkins die.

1999   The U.S. Senate acquits President Clinton. U.S. leads air war in Kosovo and Serbia. Two students kill twelve students and a teacher at Columbine High School in Littleton, Colorado. Five-year-old Cuban refugee Elian Gonzalez caught up in international debate on immigration and parental custody rights. Boris Yeltsin resigns as President of Russia and is replaced by Vladimir Putin.

U.S. Federal Trade Commission and the Justice Department investigate possible connections between teen violence and popular entertainment. Over 2,500 radio stations available on the Internet allow for global radio contacts. Rage Against the Machine album debuts at number one. Hoyt Axton, Rick Danko, Doug Sahm, Curtis Mayfield, and Mark Sandman die.

2000   The year 2000 (Y2K) enters without the feared problems. Russian nuclear submarine sinks killing all 118 crew members on board. The U.S. Food and Drug Administration approves use of RU-486 abortion pill. Milosevic replaced by Vojislav Kostunica in Yugoslavia. 17 U.S. sailors killed when U.S. warship *Cole* is bombed in Yemen. George W. Bush elected president in a close and highly contested election.

'N Sync breaks all records for best release-day album sales. The Standells, Screaming Trees, Cracker, Camper Van Beethoven, and X reform to perform and/or tour. Screamin' Jay Hawkins, Kirsty MacColl, and Johnnie Taylor die.

2001   Representative Gary Condit suspected in disappearance of intern Chandra Levy. The September 11 bombing of New York's World Trade Center and the Pentagon marks the beginning of a major war on terrorism. Anthrax alert and deaths. U.S. gathers international support to remove the Taliban government from Afghanistan.

BMG and EMI propose merger. John Fahey, Joey Ramone, John Lee Hooker, Ernie K-Doe, Rufus Thomas, John Phillips, and George Harrison die.

2002   War on Terrorism and search for Osama bin Laden. Heightened airport security concerns. Wave of suicide bombings in the Middle East. Scandals regarding pedophile priests rock the Catholic Church. Enron bankruptcy shakes faith in business financial statements.

Paul McCartney, the Who, the Rolling Stones, and Kiss all back on tour. Paul McCartney's art works on display in a Liverpool art gallery. Courtney Love leaves Hole for a solo career. The Ozbournes' TV show becomes popular. U2's Bono visits Africa with U.S. Treasury Secretary O'Neill to help draw attention to the economic needs there. Violence at an Eminem concert injures thirty fans. Record companies work to improve copy protection techniques. Run-DMC's Jam Master Jay murdered. Lisa Lopes, John Entwistle, Joe Strummer, and Dee Dee Ramone die.

| 2003 | Bush begins war in Iraq. Fire at the Station club in Rhode Island kills 99 and injures more than 190 people. Antirave bill passes Congress. Actor Arnold Schwarzenegger wins a recall election to become the governor of California. Producer Phil Spector charged with murder. U.S. forces capture Saddam Hussein. |

Many musicians protest the war, some affected by backlashes from fans who support it. Record industry fights illegal file-swappers as traditional record stores Sam Goody, Tower, and Wherehouse either close or suffer big reductions. The regrouped Sex Pistols perform their last concert. Motown singer Edwin Starr, Nina Simone, Maurice Gibb, Barry White, Sam Phillips, Noel Redding, Johnny Cash, Warren Zevon, Robert Palmer, and Bobby Hatfield die.

| 2004 | Janet Jackson's "wardrobe malfunction" at the Super Bowl. Tsunami deaths in South East Asia. George W. Bush is reelected president. Jazz guitarist Barney Kessel and actor Marlon Brando die. |

Ray Manzarek and Robby Krieger reunite the Doors (of the 21st Century) without John Densmore's approval. Melissa Etheridge treated for breast cancer. Arthur "Killer" Kane, Ray Charles, Coxson Dodd, Jan Berry, Niki Sullivan, Rick James, Bruce Palmer, and Johnny Ramone die.

| 2005 | New York's Hit Factory recording studio closes. Terri Schiavo dies after feeding tube is removed. Last company to manufacture magnetic tape closes due to more common use of digital recording systems. Michael Jackson found not guilty in child molestation case. "Deep Throat" informant from Watergate Scandal reveals own identity. Hurricane Katrina floods New Orleans and surrounding area—thousands die or made homeless. Hunter S. Thompson, Johnnie Cochran, Robert Moog, Rosa Parks, Simon Wiesenthal, Pope John Paul II, Johnny Carson, and Richard Pryor die. |

Pantera guitarist "Dimebag" Darrell Abbott and others shot to death by a "fan" in Ohio club. Cream reunites for first time since 1993 for concerts in London. Bono, Melinda and Bill Gates named *Time* magazine's "Persons of the Year" for their fight against world poverty and disease. Ozzy Osbourne retires from Ozzfest. Memphis bluesman Little Milton, British bluesman Long John Baldry, Luther Vandross, Link Wray, and Barry Cowsill die.

| 2006 | Slobodan Milosevic dies in prison cell while awaiting trial for war crimes. Elton John and longtime boyfriend, David Furnish, marry. The first day gay partnerships are made legal in England. Elvis Presley's former home, Graceland, becomes a national historic landmark. 6.3 earthquake in Indonesia kills six thousand and leaves many more injured and homeless. Apparent terrorist attempt causes the banning of liquids and gels on planes. Vice President Dick Cheney involved in hunting incident. Pope Benedict XVI remarks on Islamic faith spark protests. Iraq declared an Islamic state. Saddam Hussein executed. Coretta Scott King, Don Knotts, and former president Gerald R. Ford die. |

iTunes adds one billionth song to offerings. Eminem's rapper friend, Proof, shot to death. The Berklee College of Music awards honorary doctorate degrees to Aretha Franklin and Melissa Etheridge. New York's punk club CBGB's closes with plans to reopen in Las Vegas. MTV's twenty-fifth and MTV2's tenth anniversaries. Chicago hosts *Lollapalooza*. Paul Rogers performs with Queen. The Who release first studio album since 1982. Sly Stone makes appearance at the Grammys. Lou Rawls, Wilson Pickett, Buck Owens, Proof, Gene Pitney, June Pointer, Desmond Dekker, Billy Preston, Syd Barrett, Arthur Lee, Freddy Fender, Ruth Brown, James Brown, and Ahmet Ertegun die.

| 2007 | iPhone and Windows Vista released. Bird flu diagnosed in England. Global warming becomes major policy topic. Al Gore wins Nobel Peace Prize. Three-thousandth American dies in Iraq War. Greek cruise ship sinks at Santorini. Rappers testify before Congress defending objectionable lyrics. Art Buchwald, Kurt Vonnegut, Jerry Falwell, Liz Claiborne, Beverly Sills, Lady Bird Johnson, Ingmar Bergman, Merv Griffin, Luciano Pavarotti, and Jane Wyman die. |

The Police, Van Halen (with David Lee Roth), Led Zeppelin, Genesis, Rage Against the Machine, and Smashing Pumpkins all reunite to tour. Global concert, Live Earth, draws attention to global warming. Record industry reports constant slump in sales of CDs and need to look for new business models. Brad Delp, Denny Doherty, Joe Hunter, Lee Hazlewood, Joe Zawinul, Pimp C, Ike Turner, and Dan Fogelberg die.

2008   Gasoline prices raise dramatically. Stock market crash and subprime mortgage crisis bring U.S. recession. Fidel Castro resigns as president of Cuba, replaced by his younger brother, Raúl. Summer Olympics in Beijing, China. Global financial crisis. U.S. elects first African American president, Barack Obama. William F. Buckley Jr., Charlton Heston, and Paul Newman die.

Madonna's hit "4 Minutes" gives her more top-ten singles than any other artist. Charity concert in London's Hyde Park celebrates Nelson Mandela's ninetieth birthday and raises money for his Aids Foundation. Guns N' Roses releases first original album in seventeen years. Many rock stars support Obama campaign for presidency. The Eagles releases first album in thirty years. Phish reunite. Bo Diddley, Isaac Hayes, Jerry Wexler, Richard Wright, Norman Whitfield, Mitch Mitchell, Isaac Hayes, Levi Stubbs, Alton Ellis, Delaney Bramlett, and Mike Smith die.

2009   U.S. Airways Flight 1549 brought down in Manhattan's Hudson River by an apparent flock of geese, crew and passengers survive. Barack Obama becomes president. H1N1 flu reported spreading from Mexico. Phil Spector sentenced to nineteen years to life in prison for murdering Lana Clarkson. Michael Jackson's memorial service attended by thousands and televised worldwide. Andrew Wyeth, John Updike, James Whitmore, Dom DeLuise, David Carradine, Farrah Fawcett, Walter Cronkite, Robert McNamara, and Senator Edward Kennedy die.

Jackson Browne receives a settlement and an apology from former presidential candidate John McCain for using "Running on Empty" in an anti-Obama commercial. The Beastie Boys canceled a tour so that Adam Yauch could have cancer treatments. Trent Reznor put NIN on "indefinite hiatus." Jimmy Page, the Edge, and Jack White record "It Might Get Loud" together. Alice in Chains and Sunny Day Real Estate regroup and tour. Billy Powell, Jay Bennett, Michael Jackson, Les Paul, Ellie Greenwich, and Mary Travers die.

chapter 21

Rock in the Nineties and Early Two-Thousands

"Nothing separates the generations more than music. By the time a child is eight or nine, he has developed a passion for his own music that is even stronger than his passions for procrastination and weird clothes."

–COMEDIAN BILL COSBY

Sometime in the nineties, rock turned fifty. Exactly when that birthday occurred depends on what specific recording or performance is identified as starting real rock and roll. As rock progressed through the decades since its beginnings, many different kinds of music have influenced and changed it into a great variety of styles. There is now rock music to please just about every listener. This final chapter surveys the more popular styles of rock music today and discusses ways in which those styles are rooted in music of the past.

Punk was a style that began in the sixties, matured in the seventies, and was then followed by many postpunk styles. One of the most important results of the punk movement was that it took rock out of the big arenas, out of the control of big marketing executives, and put it back in the control of the bands and fans. Punk brought rock music back to its roots in small clubs with lots of communication between the performers and the listeners. Postpunk movements all shared the aggressive, pounding beat of early punk styles, but they differed in their themes, the speed at which they were played, or other basic components of their sounds. The postpunk movements that included the buzzsaw guitar sounds of Hüsker Dü in Minneapolis and the antidrug, antialcohol, and antipromiscuity themes of the *straight edge* movement in Washington, D.C., were discussed in Chapter 20. Those styles developed during the eighties. As rock moved into the nineties, Seattle was the first stop.

Grunge Rock

The roots of grunge rock can be found in the music and image of an important and influential "no wave" band from New York, **Sonic Youth.** They experimented with unusual guitar tunings and sound effects created by **prepared instruments.** No wave was progressive-influenced punk rock, and the idea of preparing musical instruments by placing screwdrivers, drum sticks, and other items between the strings did indeed come from art music. Feedback and dissonance were added with thick layers of sound created by the group's two guitarists, Lee Ranaldo (born in 1956) and Thurston Moore (born in 1958). Sonic Youth formed in 1981 and not only influenced the guitar-based sound of several of Seattle's grunge bands but also helped to promote the Seattle sound by having these bands play opening performances at Sonic Youth concerts. Their female bass player and singer, Kim Gordon (born in 1953), has sometimes been dubbed the Godmother of Alternative Rock. In addition to her work with Sonic Youth, Gordon earned that title through her many efforts to advance the careers of other women in alternative rock music. She co-produced Hole's debut album *Pretty on the Inside* (1991), co-directed videos for the Breeders, and worked with many other female bands. Married to Sonic Youth guitarist Thurston Moore, Gordon dressed their little daughter, Hayley Gordon Moore, in T-shirts with "Question Authority" written on them and has often said in interviews that she hopes her daughter can grow up in a world where she knows she can do anything she wants to with her life. Gordon does not even mind if Hayley decides not to be in a rock band.

One of the first Seattle bands to gain a strong following was **Soundgarden,** which recorded its first EP, *Screaming Life,* in 1987. The term *grunge* represented the loud crunch of their typical guitar sound. Soundgarden's singer, Chris Cornell, imitated the style of British heavy-metal singers of fifteen or twenty years earlier. They also reached back to premetal sources for some of their music by playing covers of Led Zeppelin and even Howlin' Wolf songs. Guitar/bass riffs and distortion added to the heavy-metal connection. Soundgarden released their most powerful album, *Superunknown,* in 1994. That album was not only a hit on the pop charts; it also won two Grammy awards for Best Hard Rock and Best Metal recordings for the album cuts "Black Hole Sun" and "Spoonman." Soundgarden was influential on other Seattle bands including Mudhoney and Nirvana.

Mudhoney put out their first EP, *Superfuzz Bigmuff,* in 1988. Like other grunge bands, they combined late sixties and early seventies metal guitar riffs and distortion effects with punk's intensity and noise level. **Nirvana** did not come from Seattle, but from Aberdeen, Washington; however, they were influenced by the nearby Seattle bands and were very much a part of the grunge movement. Nirvana pulled itself out of the underground when it signed with a major label, Geffen Records, recorded the video "Smells Like Teen Spirit," and hit the pop charts with their *Nevermind* (1991) album. The album's title came from the Sex Pistol's album *Never Mind the Bollocks, Here's the Sex Pistols,* and it might also have been intended as a reference to a song by the Replacements, "Nevermind" (1987). "Teen Spirit" was a deodorant that Kurt Cobain's girlfriend used, but Cobain later claimed that he didn't

Kurt Cobain (1991)

Nirvana broke up and their former drummer, Dave Grohl, started the Foo Fighters. Live performances of music recorded before and after the release of *Nevermind* were included on Nirvana's 1996 album, *From the Muddy Banks of the Wish Kah.*

Of the Seattle-based bands that formed in the nineties, **Pearl Jam** took the grunge guitar-based style and anti-establishment message to the largest audiences yet. Pearl Jam's singer, Eddie Vedder (born in 1966), was in San Diego when a friend invited him to join the band, but other members had been in earlier Seattle bands such as Green River, Mother Love Bone, and Temple of the Dog. Pearl Jam became known for its refusal to allow Ticketmaster to control ticket costs, and they unsuccessfully sued the agency for unfair business practices. They also refused to make videos or singles for songs on their second and later albums. Despite the popularity of those and other issues promoted by the band, the group's music was still the basis of its success. The influences of earlier musicians and bands such as Jimi Hendrix, the Doors, the Grateful Dead, the Beatles, and even the Stooges can be heard in Pearl Jam's guitar riffs and complex textures. Vedder's dramatic and passionate vocals effectively expressed the message behind the lyrics of Pearl Jam's songs, many of which deal with such issues as child abuse ("Jeremy" and "Alive" from *Ten,* 1991), loneliness ("Daughter" from *Vs.,* 1993), and problems the band had with the media ("Blood" from *Vs.*). In 1995, members of Pearl Jam performed and recorded an album with Neil Young. Pearl Jam continued to limit its live concert appearances, but each new album is awaited by thousands of fans. Without selling out their messages or their music, they have become one of the most important and popular bands within the alternative market.

know that when he wrote the song. He said he took the phrase from what a friend had said and didn't know he was naming his song after a commercial product. The song and its video with high school cheerleaders wearing symbols of anarchy on black outfits captured the angst and anxiety teenagers around the world felt. The song and video won many awards, but their greatest importance is that they provided an identity for many young people. A listening guide to the recording is on page 314.

Later albums also sold well, but singer Kurt Cobain was torn between the responsibilities those in the limelight have to their fans and the fear that the band's anti-establishment messages were being overshadowed by popularity or missed completely by most of the band's followers. Both Cobain and his wife, Courtney Love, guitarist and singer with Hole, had a series of overdoses and other problems as a result of taking heroin and even came close to losing custody of their daughter, Frances Bean. Fans and musician friends alike feared that Cobain was losing his battle with drugs and the war within himself. He was found shot to death in April 1994. The police determined it a suicide, but many fans believed he was murdered. Following Cobain's death,

> "When our first record came out, I was shocked how many people related to some of that stuff. Something like 'Alive,' so many people dealt with death through that song. Like people dealt with the death of love through 'Black,' and so many dealt with suicide through 'Jeremy.' The kind of letters that got through to me about these songs, some of them were just frightening."
>
> –Eddie Vedder of Pearl Jam

Listening Guide

"Smells Like Teen Spirit"
as recorded by Nirvana (1991)

Tempo: The tempo is approximately 116 beats per minute, with four beats in each bar.

Form: Major sections of the recording are sixteen bars each with a twelve-bar instrumental introduction to the song and four four-bar instrumental introductions preceding each of four sixteen-bar verses.

The third verse is instrumental.

The recording ends with nine repetitions of the words "A denial!" and then a fade-out.

The sections are organized as follows: twelve-bar instrumental introduction, four-bar verse introduction, sixteen-bar verse, sixteen-bar chorus, four-bar verse introduction, sixteen-bar verse, sixteen-bar chorus, four-bar verse introduction, sixteen-bar instrumental verse, four-bar verse introduction, sixteen-bar verse, sixteen-bar chorus, repetitions and fade-out.

Features: The first three bars of the introduction are played by a strummed acoustic guitar.

The drums enter at bar four, and fuzz-tone electric guitar and electric bass guitar come in at the fourth beat of bar four. The instruments play repetitions of a single-bar riff pattern that changes pitch as the chords change.

The four-bar introduction to the verses is more subdued than the general introduction, with drums playing a strong backbeat and the bass playing repeated notes on the half-beats.

During the instrumental verse, a fuzz-tone electric guitar plays the verse melody.

Cobain's vocals are sometimes sung in a melancholy mood and other times screamed.

Lyrics: The lyrics are difficult to understand, partly because Cobain slurs as he sings and also because the text does not follow any particular line of meaning. The lyrics were not printed on the album inserts. Words that can be deciphered just by listening include statements of insecurity and a desire to be with a group where one is accepted.

Billboard pop charts: number six

Pop Punk

When the term *pop* is used, generally that means that the music is popular. Although punk music has a very large following, it is not generally called *pop*. So what is "pop punk"? Pop punk is an outgrowth of punk music by bands such as the Ramones who played hard, aggressive punk rock music, but who also showed their own love of more melodic pop music in songs like "Sheena Is a Punk Rocker," which was obviously influenced by the Beach Boys. In other words, pop punk is punk music that is more melodic than most other punk.

Green Day formed in 1988 in Oakland, California. After one drummer left and was replaced, they became a trio consisting of singer/guitarist Billie Joe Armstrong, bassist Mike Dirnt (Michael Pritchard), and drummer Tré Cool (Frank Edwin Wright III). Their band name came from a song, "Green Day," by Armstrong about the first time he tried marijuana. They played in local clubs and toured locally. In the early nineties Green Day released a second album, *Kerplunk!* (1992). The album resulted in successful international tours and led to a recording contract with major label Reprise Records. However, while the Reprise deal disappointed fans who deplored the idea

Green Day in 2005 (left to right): Tré Cool, Billie Joe Armstrong, and Mike Dirnt

Listening Guide

"When I Come Around"
as recorded by Green Day (1994)

Tempo: The tempo is approximately 100 beats per minute, with four beats in each bar.

Form: The music is structured by repetitions of a two-bar riff that only breaks during three choruses.

The riff repeats instrumentally at the beginning and then the vocals come in at the fourth repetition.

Each of two verses is sung through eight repetitions of the riff.

At each chorus, chords are held and then the riff returns at "When I come around."

Features: The instrumentation is guitar with heavy fuzztone, electric bass guitar, and drums.

Even beat subdivisions are followed throughout.

The drums keep a strong backbeat.

The vocals are almost monotone and the singer sounds quite bored with the subject.

Lyrics: The singer is a promiscuous male who proudly announces he will only visit his girlfriend at his convenience. Against the image of his freedom and indifference to the relationship, the song juxtaposes the girlfriend's loneliness and devotion.

Billboard pop charts: number six

of seeing their band become commercial, it brought Green Day, and pop punk in general, into mainstream acceptance. Their first Reprise release, *Dookie* (1994), won a Grammy for Best Rock Album, and videos of some of the songs won seven MTV video awards. A listening guide to a song from that album is on page 315.

Green Day continued with their very successful career, but took a two-year break in the late nineties to recover from the pressure of touring. The album released after the break, *Warning* (2000), was more pop than punk and so disappointed hard-core fans. A following album, *American Idiot* (2004), was a concept album that brought back fans and won more with its antiwar songs aimed at American President George W. Bush and the war in Iraq. *American Idiot* also won a Grammy for Best Rock Album. Green Day had spent much of their career on tour and their 2005 album, *Bullet in a Bible*, was released with a live CD and a DVD. Other pop punk bands include Rancid, the Offspring, and Blink 182.

Emo

As discussed in Chapter 20, Ian MacKaye of the straight-edge bands Minor Threat, Embrace, and later, Fugazi established a punk style with songs that concentrated on concerns about the individual and how one should live instead of focusing on externals, which had marked much punk of the sixties and seventies. MacKaye was not interested in imitating England's Sex Pistols, who effectively raged against the British government and monarchy, and who also did drugs and, in the case of Sid Vicious, died as a result. Minor Threat's song, "Straight Edge," sparked an entire movement of young people who rejected the popular "sex, drugs, and rock and roll" lifestyle to adopt a way of living that would have nothing to do with drugs, alcohol, tobacco, or irresponsible sex, and they were often vegetarians. MacKaye also spoke out against what he perceived to be the capitalistic "money-grubbing" attitudes held by many Americans. Influenced by the attitudes of the straight-edge followers, some bands in the nineties looked even more into themselves, and they wrote songs about their lives and the way they lived them. Their songs gradually became more expressive of their daily life experiences and emotions. Some songs were nostalgic and even confessional. The music was still hard-core punk, however, so the movement was first called "emotional hardcore," then "emocore," and eventually, **emo.**

❝This was the period when emo earned many, if not all, of the stereotypes that have lasted to this day: boy-driven, glasses-wearing, very sensitive, overly brainy, chiming-guitar-driven college music.❞

–pop music journalist Andy Greenwald

In addition to MacKaye's short-lived band Embrace, early emo bands included the Rites of Spring, Jawbreaker, and Sunny Day Real Estate. By the early two-thousands, Jimmy Eat World, Dashboard Confessional, and Fall Out Boy, as well as many others, brought the style to mainstream acceptance and popularity. Emo bands often toured with such pop punk bands as Green Day and Blink 182, adding new fans to their music.

Jimmy Eat World formed in Arizona in 1994. The group name was taken from a cartoon drawn by Tom Linton's little brother. The cartoon featured their other brother, Jimmy, cramming the entire world into his mouth. Jimmy Eat World released three albums and then lost their record contract despite extensive touring to support album sales. Renewed by a new contract, Jimmy Eat World's fourth album, *Bleed American* (2001), broke records for the popularity of emo music, and the hit single "The Middle" reached number one on *Billboard*'s modern rock tracks chart and number five on the *Billboard* hot 100 chart. A listening guide to that recording is on page 317.

A more aggressive style called screamo developed out of emo. It was called screamo because the singers tended to scream out their emotions in their songs.

Jam Bands

The musical term *jam* refers to musicians getting together and just playing, trying out new musical ideas, and enjoying the experience whether those new ideas worked out or not. The classic jam band was and is the **Grateful Dead.** Since their regrouping after the 1995 death of founding member Jerry Garcia, their name has been reduced to simply the Dead. Unlike the many rock bands that were best known for their recordings and whose tours were made up of performances of exactly the music on those recordings, the Dead never cared to play anything exactly the same way more than once. As all deadheads (fans of the band) know, those live concerts in which just about anything could happen were the very best thing about the band. Another way the Dead broke from mainstream rock was in a different attitude toward the proprietary and legal aspects of their work. While most rock bands try to keep fans from recording their concerts, the Dead never cared about that. They let fans openly record, swap tapes or CDs, and do whatever else they wanted during concerts. So much selling of tapes, CDs, food, clothing,

Listening Guide

"The Middle"
as recorded by Jimmy Eat World
(2001)

Tempo: The tempo is approximately 160 beats per minute, with four beats in each bar.

Form: The song is structured in eight-bar sections that occur as follows: instrumental introduction, verse 1, verse 2, refrain, verse 3, verse 4, refrain, refrain, sixteen-bar instrumental section, verse 1, verse 5, refrain, refrain.

Features: The instrumentation is voice, guitar, percussion, bass guitar, drums, and "synth emulator."

The instrumental introduction is played by the guitar strumming on every half-beat and the bass supporting the beat, but at a very soft dynamic level.

The drums enter at the beginning of the first verse and maintain very even beat subdivisions and a strong backbeat.

Soft vocal responses that repeat part of the text come in on verses 3, 4, the repeat of 1, and verse 5.

The instrumental section within the song is twice as long as other sections, sixteen bars.

The recording ends very abruptly when the final refrain finishes.

Lyrics: The lyrics encourage listeners to feel all right about themselves and to live as well as they can. The song was written and recorded when the band had lost its record contract and was trying to give themselves the courage to go on, as well as to sing the message to others.

Billboard modern rock tracks chart: number one; *Billboard* hot 100 chart: number five; British hit singles: number twenty-six

jewelry, drugs, and whatever else happened in parking lots where the Dead were playing that some fans made a living from the sales and just kept touring along with the band.

Another jam band, **Phish,** had been around and making records since 1988, but they didn't receive national attention until the Grateful Dead stopped performing when Garcia died. By then, in the midnineties, psychedelic drugs were coming back into the drug culture, a fact that increased the popularity of concerts as big jam sessions. Like the Grateful Dead, Phish played free-form concerts that combined folk, jazz, country, bluegrass, and pop styles of music into long, wandering improvisations that recaptured the psychedelic era of the sixties. Phish broke up in 2004, after twelve albums and many successful concert tours. Back together five years later, Phish was on tour in 2009.

A jam band that was very much alive and well as of early 2006 is the **Dave Matthews Band.** Matthews is from Johannesburg, South Africa, although he has also lived in England and New York, and he formed his band in Charlottesville, Virginia. Since their formation in 1993, the Dave Matthews Band has played many concerts that involve long improvisations similar to the ones by other jam bands. In fact, their first album, *Remember Two Things* (1993), is mostly comprised of long improvised jams. On the other hand, some fans consider them a "jam rock" band instead of a jam band because their songs are not always drawn out with endless new material and fans like their performances on recordings as well as their live concerts. Whatever the genre, the band has had many successes in their years together. Along with folk, country, jazz, and pop influences in his music, Matthews's time in South Africa added some of the characteristics of African music to his band's overall sound. Like the Dead and Phish, the Dave Matthews Band had no problem with fans recording their concerts, but they have resented it when fans sell those recordings instead of just sharing them without money changing hands.

The listening guide on page 318 for "What Would You Say" is from the album *Under the Table and Dreaming,* an

The Dave Matthews Band (left to right): Boyd Tinsley, Butch Taylor, Dave Matthews, and Stefan Lessard

Listening Guide

**"What Would You Say"
as recorded by the Dave Matthews Band (1994)**

Tempo: The tempo is approximately 120 beats per minute, with four beats in each bar for most of the recording, but a few short sections have three beats in each bar.

Form: The recording begins with two eight-bar instrumental sections.

Each verse is made up of eight four-beat bars.

The first, third, and sixth verses are followed by sections with four three-beat bars followed by four four-beat bars.

The fourth verse repeats the text of the second verse, and the sixth verse repeats the text of the third verse.

A twenty-four-bar instrumental section is placed between the fifth and sixth verses.

Features: Matthews's voice follows the rhythms of the text, sometimes breaking with the beat patterns accompanying it.

Even beat subdivisions are followed through most of the recording.

The drums keep a strong backbeat through most of the recording.

Group vocals respond and add to Matthews's lead vocal lines.

Instruments take turns playing solos during the very improvisational twenty-four-bar instrumental section.

The song ends with the question "What would you say?"

Lyrics: The song reflects a self-consciously philosophical orientation toward life and death. On his birthday, Matthews notes his mortality and wonderment at life. He has no particular axe to grind other than to say, in a song reminiscent of the biblical book of Ecclesiastes, that we all die in the end.

Billboard pop charts: number twenty-two

album that Matthews dedicated to his sister Anne who died in a home accident. The Dave Matthews Band continued into the two-thousands with new albums and tours. Other popular jam bands include Yonder Mountain String Band and String Cheese Incident.

Alternative Country

Exactly what defines "alternative country" is not clear because many bands play music that combines country, rock, punk, and other styles in various different ways, and no one sound or theme is common to all of them. Even the magazine *No Depression,* which claims to report on "alternative-country music," adds "(whatever that is)" in parentheses after its claim. The last words in parentheses make it clear that even the writers of that magazine understand the great variety of styles that fall under the title. Regardless of whoever does or does not fit into this style category, few would argue that **Uncle Tupelo**'s music helped draw mainstream attention to the style. Uncle Tupelo formed in Belleville, Illinois, in 1990. Their first album was *No Depression,* a title taken from a song by the Carter Family from the 1930s, when the United States was experiencing a real economic depression. Their music combined country, blues, and postpunk by bands like Hüsker Dü. Some of their songs are about people in the Midwest who are cynical about

their lives going nowhere and drink to kill the pain of their existence. Such themes are common in country music, and the band's punk intensity added to the expression of frustration. Uncle Tupelo went all acoustic for their third album, *March 16–20, 1992,* causing them to lose their punk following. The band was together for only four years.

When Uncle Tupelo broke up, singer/guitarist Jeff Tweedy went on to form **Wilco** with other musicians, of whom only bass player John Stirratt remains. Not surprisingly, Wilco's first album, *A.M.* (1995), continued in the Uncle Tupelo tradition of blending country, blues, and rock styles. The addition of guitarist and electronic keyboardist Jay Bennett for their next album, *Being There* (1996), added rhythm and blues, power pop, and even psychedelic sounds to Wilco's music. Looking for a new challenge, Wilco agreed to use a set of lyrics by Woody Guthrie that had never been recorded before as the basis of their *Mermaid Avenue* (1998) album. Recording in their own alternative rock style instead of attempting any imitation of Guthrie's folk style was a great success, and they received critical acclaim and their first Grammy nomination for their efforts. Later albums have vacillated between stressing country and rock styles. *Yankee Hotel Foxtrot* (2002) was their biggest-selling album to date, reaching number twelve on the *Billboard* album charts. *A Ghost is Born* (2004) won two Grammy awards, and Wilco was still recording and touring in 2009.

Wilco (left to right): Jeff Tweedy and John Stirratt

Progressive Rock

Progressive-rock took many forms when it was first developing in the late sixties and the seventies. Many of the progressive rock bands used electronic instruments for special effects just as many avant-garde classical composers had. A contemporary band that combines very sophisticated electronic musical sounds with traditional rock music and instrumentation is **Radiohead.** Radiohead formed in Oxford, England, in 1989 but did not release their first album, *Pablo Honey,* until 1993. The original five members have stayed together into the twenty-first century. Each member plays many instruments, and they switch from one instrument to another, not just for recording sessions, but also during concerts. One of the more unusual instruments Radiohead uses is the Ondes-Martenot, which is an electronic keyboard instrument that has a bank of expression keys that allow the player to affect the tone quality as well as microtonal pitches. The instrument has also been used in works by highly acclaimed classical composers Edgard Varèse, Krzysztof Penderecki, and Olivier Messiaen. Without listing all the instruments each member plays, Radiohead's membership includes vocalist/guitarist Thom Yorke, lead guitarist/keyboardist Jonny Greenwood, guitarist/backing vocalist Ed O'Brien, bass guitarist/keyboardist Colin Greenwood, and drummer/general percussionist Phil Selway.

> **"Whoever has the most weapons is in charge now. It's INSANE."**
>
> –Thom Yorke, Radiohead vocalist

Radiohead's music continued to bring themes of angst and alienation from Britain to the United States in the nineties. Radiohead layered sounds from three guitars, careful use of feedback from the amplifiers, electric piano, bass, and drums to create a thick timbre influenced by such earlier bands as Pink Floyd, Talking Heads, and U2. Their debut album, *Pablo Honey* (1993), contained the single "Creep" that rose to number thirty-four on the U.S. pop charts. The song's lyrics were intensely personal and alienated. The singer, Thom Yorke, described himself as a "creep" who didn't deserve the attentions of "beautiful" people whose acknowledgment and respect he craved. The moods of anguish and insecurity and a desire for satisfaction and even revenge continued to be central to Radiohead's music on their next two albums, *The Bends* (1995) and *OK Computer* (1997). Constant touring and the popularity of the MTV video for the song "Just" from *The Bends* helped boost the album's sales in the United States. It made the top ten on the British album charts. The U.S. pop hit "Karma Police" was from the *OK Computer* album, and the listening guide is on page 321. Radiohead's following two albums, *Kid A* (1999) and *Amnesiac* (2000), were recorded at the same sessions and, therefore, represent similar themes and styles. One stylistic exception was the addition of a jazz quartet on "Life in a Glasshouse" on *Amnesiac.*

The title of Radiohead's *Hail to the Thief* (2003) album was a parody on the song that is generally used to praise or introduce the U.S. president, "Hail to the Chief." The band was asserting that U.S. President George W. Bush

Radiohead in 2003 (left to right): Thom Yorke, Phil Selway, and Jonny Greenwood

Listening Guide

"Karma Police"
as recorded by Radiohead (1997)

Tempo: The tempo is approximately 72 beats per minute, with four beats in each bar.

Form: The recording has two parts. The first is made up of six eight-bar sections ordered as follows: instrumental introduction, verse, verse, refrain, verse, refrain. The second part has four four-bar sections all with the same text, and with extended repetitions at the ending. The third four-bar section is instrumental.

Features: The drums play a strong backbeat in the verses of the first part and through the second part.

Acoustic guitar and piano play a riff pattern, and other accompaniments with electronic background noises come in and out throughout the recording.

An analog synthesizer imitates a choir during the second and third verses and during the second part of the recording.

The second part of the recording is a step higher than the first half. (It abruptly changes from the key of A minor to B minor.)

The recording ends with electronic sound effects and static that ultimately descends to nothing.

Lyrics: The word *karma* refers to the Hindu belief that individuals experience the sum total of past effects. Here, the use borders on the sarcastic, with a vague allusion to Orwell's *1984* and its "thought police." The song conveys a sense that individuals find themselves in conditions that run afoul of socially conforming authorities (who disapprove of how one talks or of one's hairdo) contrasted against the momentary possibility of losing oneself, that is, one's karma.

Billboard pop charts: number fourteen; British hit singles: number eight

---

stole the U.S. presidential election through a controversial vote in Florida. The album also comments on what the band perceives as the lack of interest U.S. citizens showed in the war in Iraq. It begins with "2 + 2 = 5," taken from George Orwell's book *1984* in which a totalitarian government controls its people. Radiohead continues to record and tour. Other progressive-rock bands include the Mars Volta, Muse, and Coheed and Cambria.

Rap Rock

By the nineties, rap vocals had become so popular that groups outside the hip-hop culture used them as well. From Los Angeles, the **Red Hot Chili Peppers** formed in 1983 as an alternative funk-metal-rock group and were among the first such bands to add the patter-talk vocals of rap. The group changed membership many times with only two band members remaining through their career, singer Anthony Kiedis and bass player Michael Balzary ("Flea"). Despite the release of three early albums, the Red Hot Chili Peppers did not gain national attention until *Mother's Milk* (1989). Their next album, *Blood, Sugar, Sex, Magik* (1991), included a top-ten hit, "Under the Bridge." With the release of *Stadium Arcadium* (2005), they had nine studio albums to their credit, although many fans still consider *Blood, Sugar, Sex, Magik* to be their best effort.

Nineties punk-related music fused with many other eighties styles such as rap and thrash metal in the music of **Rage Against the Machine.** As the band's name indicates, their music expressed much anger against what they perceived as the oppressive. Part of their anger at industrialization has concentrated on speaking out for the rights of Mexican American field workers who have been

Red Hot Chili Peppers (left to right): Flea and Anthony Kiedis

unfairly treated by their employers. The band's first single, "Bullet in the Head" (1992), won them a record contract with Epic and a Lollapalooza tour. It took the band four years to release *Evil Empire* (1996), which hit number one on the U.S. album charts. Perhaps it is needless to say that the album title refers to the U.S. government that Rage Against the Machine saw as fascist. Songs on the album *The Battle of Los Angeles* (1999) angered the antiabortion group Rock for Life, and that group called for a boycott against the band and its recordings. Rage Against the Machine's single "Guerrilla Radio" won a Grammy award for Best Hard Rock Performance in 2001.

Rage Against the Machine performed outside the Democratic National Convention in August 2000 to demonstrate their anger about the amount of control that donations of corporate money had on U.S. politics. The L.A. Police Department was there because they expected a riot, and they ended up using rubber bullets and pepper spray to disperse the crowd, angering many fans. Soon after that, the band's vocalist, Zack de la Rocha, quit to pursue a solo career. His former bandmates replaced him with former Soundgarden's singer Chris Cornell and renamed themselves Audioslave.

Hip-hop music and attitudes continued to develop outside of the culture's origins in New York and Los Angeles. **Arrested Development** formed in Atlanta, Georgia, in 1988. They took the funky lightness and pride in African American culture of New York's Native

Tongues' rappers such as De La Soul and Queen Latifah and backed their vocals with drums and sometimes even folk-related instruments such as banjo and harmonica. A writer for the newspaper *20th Century African,* Arrested Development's leader, Speech (Todd Thomas, born in 1968), was outspoken about the need for young people to recognize that not all rappers tell them the truth. He further pointed out that the "f" word young fans should be hearing in the music with which they identify is "freedom." Arrested Development's positive message reached many rap fans with their two top-ten hits, "People Everyday" and "Mr. Wendal" (both 1992). The title of their 1994 album, *Zingalamaduni,* refers to a beehive of culture in the African language of Swahili. After a break in the late nineties, Arrested Development regrouped in 2000.

Also from Atlanta, **Outkast** continued to update hip-hop by adding soul and funk to their sound. Outkast is a duo consisting of Andre Benjamin ("Dre") and Antwan Patton ("Big Boi"). They began rapping together in 1992 and a single, "Player's Ball" from their first album, *Southernplayalisticadillacmuzik* (1994), rose to number one on the rap charts. Source Awards called them the Best New Rap Group in 1995. A listening guide to their hit single, "B.O.B." from *Stankonia* (2000), is on page 323. The hits continued, and Outkast won a Grammy for Album of the Year in 2004 for *Speakerboxxx/The Love Below*. They were also featured in the movie *Idlewild* in 2006 and continue to record and tour.

Nu Metal

Many of the rock styles that developed in the nineties were combinations of earlier rock styles, but nu metal might be the one with the broadest range of origins. The term metal evokes the thought of the powerful fuzztone riffs of most heavy metal, speed metal, and thrash, but nu metal also includes rhythms from funk and hip-hop; screamed, shouted, or rap vocals; and bands use turntables and synthesizers along with more traditional rock instruments. Most nu metal bands want to add the depth of extra-low sounds, and to get that they play seven-string guitars. The seventh string is extra low, tuned to a B note below the E on the sixth string. Nu metal electric bass guitarists often also play instruments with an added lower string, also for depth, and they sometimes slap the strings

Listening Guide

"B.O.B." ("Bombs over Baghdad") as recorded by Outkast (2000)

Tempo:	The tempo is approximately 156 beats per minute, with four beats in each bar.
Form:	After a four-bar introduction, Dre raps through four eight-bar verses. Two eight-bar choruses follow, and then Big Boi raps through four eight-bar verses. Another two eight-bar choruses follow. A choir repeats the text "Bombs over Baghdad!" during two eight-bar instrumental sections. For another two eight-bar sections, Dre inserts the names of the rappers in Outkast. Dre and Big Boi repeat a two-bar text fifteen times and then the recording ends with a choir

repeating a two-bar set of words twenty-three times.

Features:	The rapped vocals are very fast and rhythmic.
	Electronic sounds and drums accompany the vocals.
	The drums keep a steady backbeat.
	Even beat subdivisions are kept throughout the recording.
Lyrics:	The rappers express an ironic indifference toward the world and contemporary events, part detached, part amused, and part appalled.

Billboard hot rhythm and blues charts: number sixty-nine; British hit singles charts: number sixty-one

Listening Guide

"Freak on a Leash"
as recorded by Korn (1998)

Tempo: The tempo is approximately 100 beats per minute, with four beats in each bar.

Form: Much of the recording is constructed of eight-bar sections, at least while the vocals are understandable. Once the rhythmic singing of nonsense syllables begins, there is a twelve-bar section followed by a thirteen-bar section. The second half of the chorus (eight bars) follows, and then "Part of me" repeats to the ending.

Features: The recording begins with an eight-bar instrumental section that includes melodic electronic sound, drums playing a strong backbeat, and bass playing uneven beat subdivisions.

The first two eight-bar verses have almost spoken text, bass and drums playing stop-time breaks at first, and then continuing with a strong backbeat.

The second verse adds soft electronically affected vocal responses to each line of sung text.

The refrain is in two eight-bar sections, beginning with "Sometimes I cannot take . . ." and the second section beginning "Something takes a part . . ." The refrain vocals are accompanied by distorted death-metal-sounding guitar and distorted electronic sounds with an active bass line and drums.

Like the second verse, the third verse has soft electronically affected vocal responses to each line of text.

The full double refrain follows the third verse along with the distorted death-metal-sounding guitar and distortion.

That refrain is followed by a section of rhythmic vocal nonsense syllables with drums. The use of such syllables creates a sort of nu metal form of scat vocals much like jazz singers use to be able to sing without concerns about specific words. At the fifth bar of that section, clean pop-sounding electronic riffs enter and continue for the rest of the twelve bars.

After the word "Go!" is shouted, distorted death-metal guitars return for four bars, and then vocals enter with some understandable words like "So . . . fight" are repeated among more rhythmic nonsense syllables.

The second eight bars of the refrain returns, and then the recording ends with the words "Part of me . . ." repeated.

Lyrics: An anguished soul cries out from an earthly hell marked by a sense of being controlled by unseen forces (the leash). He can fall no lower, yet something in him resists his condition and inspires him to "fight" his condition.

Billboard mainstream rock charts: top ten; *Billboard* modern rock charts: top ten

as they play to create a funk-influenced rhythmic sound. Some of the nu metal bands to emerge in the midnineties are Korn, Limp Bizkit, Kid Rock, Incubus, and Slipknot.

Radio stations used to be essential to support the popularity of a rock band, but when the nu metal band **Korn** was first performing and recording in 1993–1994, they managed to build themselves a large following without radio play. Their energetic live shows were immediate hits with audiences when they opened for such acts as Danzig, Marilyn Manson, Megadeth, Ozzy Osbourne, and

Jonathon Davis of Korn (2008)

Deftones. Korn even produced an online TV show called KornTV that allowed people to call and talk to band members. Their third album, *Follow the Leader* (1998), debuted at number one on the *Billboard* album charts, and the single from it, "Freak on a Leash," hit the top ten, and its video won a Grammy award for best video and best editing. A listening guide to "Freak on a Leash" is on page 324.

Nu metal is a good style with which to bring this book to a close because the music includes so many rock styles of the recent past, all put together in new ways. As we look back at the rock music of the fifties, we hear many different styles based in the blues, country, gospel, or other prerock music. The same variety of styles existed in the decades that followed. Now, as we hear with the current styles we have discussed and others, the variety of sounds still generally described as "rock music" continues to grow.

Summary

This last chapter has provided an overview of some of the styles of rock music popular as we move into the twenty-first century. In each case, the music is based on styles from earlier decades, but also in each case, there is something new. Music from the grunge, pop punk, and emo movements is clearly related to earlier punk styles, and yet none of these modern bands sound exactly like those styles of the past. Jam bands of today, such as the Dave Matthews Band, relate to the old Grateful Dead sound in some ways, but the two bands would never be confused with one another. Alternative country music and progressive rock by Radiohead are new, but they share many characteristics with the more traditional country and classically influenced styles of the past. Rap vocals remain popular and are being used with many different types of backup instruments and instrumental styles.

That is why rock will ever die. It just keeps changing and adapting to new generations.

discussion questions

Is Bill Cosby right in the quote that opens this chapter? Does music really separate the generations? How do bands like Led Zeppelin, the Beatles, and the Rolling Stones, whose music is often popular with both the youngest and oldest rock fans, transcend the generation gap, or do they? What young, new bands today play music that is likely to be enjoyed by many future generations? Singer/songwriters of the seventies and beyond expressed very personal emotions and experiences in their songs. Are emo songwriters the singer/songwriters of today?

GLOSSARY

A

a cappella
Describes group or choral singing without instrumental accompaniment.

aeolian mode
See modes.

AM radio
An early (pre-FM) form of radio using an amplitude modulation (AM) system of broadcasting; the system can be used over great distances but is subject to static and not capable of true high fidelity.

antecedent and consequent phrases
Melodic phrases that occur in pairs in which the first, the antecedent phrase, sounds incomplete and the second, the consequent phrase, brings the first to a final-sounding resolution.

antiphonal choruses
Groups of singers or instrumentalists that are separated by physical distance in performance and sing or play different material in response to one another.

arpeggio
A chord that is broken or played one or two notes at a time instead of all its notes being sounded together.

arrangement
Preplanned music involving written-out parts for instrumentalists in a band.

avant-garde
Very current, modern, and experimental.

B

backbeat
Beats two and four of a four-beat pattern, the accenting of which creates rock's basic rhythm.

backspinning
A hip-hop disc jockey technique for turning or spinning the record back to the desired place.

barrelhouse
A bar, or honky-tonk, originally with whisky barrels along the walls or used as tables; the boogie-woogie-based piano style often played in such places.

bass riff
A low, short, repeated bit of melody, often played by the bass guitar, or by bass and lead guitar together.

Beats
American writers and poets of the fifties and later whose works included social criticisms questioning the lack of individual freedom in American society, their followers were known as *beatniks*.

beat subdivisions (even and uneven)
The subsections into which a single beat is divided. An even subdivision involves two equal notes; an uneven subdivision involves three equal notes, often with the first two notes tied together, making a long–short subdivision.

bebop
A modern jazz style pioneered in the early forties by alto saxophonist Charlie Parker, pianist Thelonious Monk, trumpeter Dizzy Gillespie, and others. Bebop was more harmonically, melodically, and rhythmically complex than earlier jazz and was usually played by small combos of musicians with a great amount of technical facility; also called *bop*.

blue notes
Notes that are lowered a half-step or less. Early blues musicians lowered the third and seventh scale degrees, and bebop musicians lowered the fifth degree as well.

blues harp
A harmonica used to play blues; a technique called *cross harping* makes use of a harp played in a key one step or a fifth below that of the song, in order to have blue notes automatically available to the player.

boogie-woogie
A rhythmic piano style that uses repeating bass patterns.

bottleneck
A glass or metal tube that fits over a guitarist's ring finger or little finger and stops the strings of the guitar

when it is slid up or down the instrument's fingerboard. Originally, the glass tube was the neck of a bottle that had been broken off and sanded down for use by blues guitarists.

break
A technique in which instruments stop playing for a short period of time, allowing a singer or instrumental soloist to be heard alone.

break dancing
An elaborate and competitive form of dancing that started as part of the hip-hop culture in New York's South Bronx in the early seventies.

bridge (of a guitar)
A piece of wood or metal attached to the body of the guitar to which the strings are attached or over which they pass.

bridge (of a song form)
The contrasting, or B, section in a song form that has repeated A sections before and usually after the B. Also called *release* or *channel.*

C

call-and-response
The practice of singing in which a solo vocalist, the caller, is answered by a group of singers. The practice is also used with instruments, but its origins are vocal.

Chicago blues
A blues style that combined country and urban blues characteristics, recorded in Chicago during the late forties and the fifties.

chord
Three or more notes played together.

chord extensions
Notes that lie beyond the normal three or four notes of a chord. These additional notes are dissonant to the basic chord.

classic blues
A blues style of the twenties and thirties, in which female singers

were featured as soloists with blues bands.

claves beat
The rhythm pattern played by the claves in a rumba.

coda
An ending section to a musical work that functions to bring the work to a satisfying conclusion. Codas can be very short or extended with repetitions of earlier themes and occasionally some new material. The term *coda* comes from an Italian word for "tail."

concerto
A multimovement work for a soloist, or small group of soloists, and a large group of players, generally an orchestra, in which the soloist is accompanied by the orchestra.

cool jazz
A style of modern jazz developed by trumpeter Miles Davis, the Modern Jazz Quartet, baritone saxophonist Gerry Mulligan, and others. As the name implies, it is a style that is subdued, and it generally is played by a small group of instrumentalists.

copyright
The exclusive right to control the use of an artistic work for the amount of time allowed by law.

country blues
The earliest and simplest blues style, usually performed by a solo singer accompanied by simple guitar strumming with occasional melodic fills.

cover recording
A recording made subsequent to the original version; it may or may not follow the style or lyrics of the original.

crescendo
A gradual increase in loudness, or volume level.

crooning
The soft vocal style of Rudy Vallee, Bing Crosby, Perry Como, and others who tended to slide from one

note to another giving the effect of warmth, intimacy, and sentimentality.

cutting
A technique used by disc jockeys to segue one recording into another using a varispeed control on the phonograph to maintain a constant beat pattern through the change.

decrescendo
A gradual decrease in loudness, or volume level.

delta blues
The country blues style of Robert Johnson and others who came from the Mississippi delta region.

doo-wop progression
The chord progression of a tonic (I) chord, a submedian seventh (vi^7) chord, a supertonic seventh (ii^7) chord, and a dominant seventh (V^7) chord, commonly used as the basis of fifties doo-wop songs.

dorian mode
See modes.

double time
A tempo that is twice as fast as the tempo that precedes it.

downbeat
The first beat of each bar.

drone
A sustained tone over or under which other music is played. For example, a bagpiper usually plays a continuous drone over which the melody is played.

dubbing (by disc jockeys)
Rhythmic patter-talk used by Jamaican disc jockeys while a recording was being played; also an engineering technique used to cut instruments or vocal parts out of a recording.

dubbing (in recordings)
Also called *overdubbing;* refers to the technique of adding instrumental, vocal, or other sounds to a recording that has already been put on

tape. Dubbing requires a multiple-track tape machine (or two tape machines) to allow one track to be heard while the new one is being recorded.

E

eight-bar period
A section of melody made up of two four-bar phrases that create a sense of completion.

eighth notes
Notes that receive half the amount of time allotted to a quarter note.

electro-theremin
An electronic instrument that produces a tone that changes in pitch when the player moves a slide. Also called a Tannerin, the electro-theremin was invented by Paul Tanner and Bob Whitsell in the late fifties to imitate the sound of a theremin, which is very difficult for the player to control. (Paul Tanner played the instrument on the Beach Boy's recording of "Good Vibrations.")

eurodisco
A funky electronic type of disco music.

F

falsetto
A high male vocal range above the normal tenor voice.

feedback
A naturally produced, sustained, distorted squeal created when high-volume sound coming out of an amplifier is taken in by the pickup on the guitar (or a microphone) and then fed back into the amplifier.

field hollers
Solo singing by African Americans while working in fields. Country blues most likely developed out of, or was greatly influenced by, this singing, which has been described as being rhythmically quite free.

flutter-tonguing
A technique that involves buzzing with the tongue while blowing into a woodwind or brass instrument.

FM radio
A form of radio invented in the early thirties, using a frequency modulation (FM) system of broadcasting. FM did not have the range of AM, and it was used almost exclusively by college and other noncommercial stations until the late sixties, when demand for its clearer sound quality and stereo capabilities allowed FM stations to take the commercial market away from AM.

four-bar phrase
A four-bar section of music ending with a partial or total feeling of completeness, most often paired with another four-bar phrase to make up a complete period ending with a cadence.

front line
The group of lead melodic instruments such as those used in early New Orleans jazz bands, usually including a cornet (or trumpet), a clarinet, and a trombone.

fusion
A jazz style that is influenced by, or fused with, elements of rock music, including even beat subdivisions, electric instruments, and short riff patterns.

fuzztone
A distorted sound effect achieved by cutting through the speaker cone of an amplifier, playing a tube amplifier at a much higher volume than it was intended for, or using an electronic device that creates a controllable version of the sound.

G

glissando
A sliding effect created by playing a series of musical tones in rapid succession.

griots
Oral poets in Africa who memorized and sang the story of their people's history.

guiro
A Latin American percussion instrument made of a hollow gourd with notches cut across the outside over which a stick is scraped.

H

Hard-core rap
An aggressive type of rap that uses confrontational lyrics that stress real-life problems and experiences.

harmonics (artificial)
The same as natural harmonics, except that the vibrating length of a string is changed by its being pressed against a fingerboard, allowing for a great number of harmonics beyond the few available on open strings. Full melodies can be played in artificial harmonics.

harmonics (natural)
High, clear tones produced by touching a vibrating string at a point exactly one-half, one-third, or one-fourth its full length, then plucking or bowing the string at another point to cause it to ring. When the string has been touched at its halfway point, the harmonic produced is an octave above the pitch of the open string; when it is touched at a point at one-third its length, the harmonic is one octave and a fifth above the open string; and a touch at one-fourth the string length produces a harmonic two octaves above the open string.

honky-tonk
A bar or saloon: the boogie-woogie styled piano often played in such places.

hook
A catchy melodic or rhythmic pattern that "hooks" or attracts the listener to want to listen to the rest of the song.

horn section
(1) The section of a jazz band that includes brass and woodwind instruments. (2) A group of French horns.

improvisation
Spontaneous performance of music that has not been written or planned out in advance, based on a progression of harmonies, which can involve a certain amount of interplay among several musicians.

jazz rock
A rock style that includes a horn section somewhat like that of a jazz band, but smaller.

lip-syncing
Moving the lips to synchronize with a prerecorded song, giving the impression that the song is being performed live.

major chord
A chord based on a triad in which the bottom and next higher notes are a major third apart (four half-steps) and the middle and highest notes are a minor third apart (three half-steps). A C-major chord contains the notes C, E, and G.

melisma
An expressive and elaborate melodic improvisation sung on a single syllable.

mellotron
(From *mel*ody + elec*tron*ic) An electro-mechanical instrument invented in England in the early sixties that uses taped recordings of acoustic (often orchestral) instruments to re-create the sounds of those instruments.

mento
A Jamaican folk music that combines a Cuban rumba with African rhythms. The name comes from the Spanish *mentar*, meaning "to mention," referring to the subtle way the music and dance express personal complaints or social criticisms.

meter
The basic repeating pattern of accented and unaccented beats followed through a composition or a section of a composition, usually indicated by the time signature.

microtones
Intervals smaller than a half-step often used in non-Western music.

minimalism
An avant-garde style of composition based on systematically organized repetition of a minimal amount of musical material; also called *systematic music*.

modes
Scalelike patterns based on church music formulas dating from the Middle Ages. The natural notes (that is, notes produced by pressing only white keys on the piano) from C to C produce a major mode, or major scale (also called the *ionian mode*). The other modes are as follows: D to D, dorian; E to E, phrygian; F to F, lydian; G to G, mixolydian; A to A, aeolian (the natural minor scale); B to B, locrian.

Mods
Short for *modernists;* the Mods were a sixties youth subculture in England who considered themselves the wave of the future; they usually had jobs, wore trendy clothes, rode around on motor scooters (rather than motorcycles) and took amphetamines.

modulation
A change of key or tonal center.

monotone
Nonmelodic, repetitive singing of a single pitch.

motive
A fragment, or short bit, of a melody.

musique concréte
An avant-garde type of musical composition in which natural, acoustic sounds have been prerecorded on a tape that is altered to change the sounds for use in performance.

nonchordal tones
Notes that are not part of the basic chord being played. The nonchordal tones may be dissonant with the chord, they may hint at another chord and create a bitonal effect, or they may merely add color to the basic chord. (*See also* chord extensions.)

octave
The distance between one note and the next note (higher or lower) of the same pitch name.

Oi!
A British term for a combination of hard-core punk and ska that avoided commercialism.

opera
A dramatic theatrical performance with orchestral accompaniment in which all or most of the roles are sung instead of spoken.

orchestra
A large group of instruments (generally from thirty to a hundred or more players) that includes instruments from the string (bowed string), woodwind, brass, and percussion families, as well as piano, harp, and other instruments as required for a particular composition.

overdubbing
The technique of adding more tracks of sound to a recording that has already been taped.

P

passacaglia
A form based on a continuously repeating chord progression and accompanying bass line.

patter-talk
Talking in rhythmic patterns; also called *rap*.

payola
The practice of bribing disc jockeys to induce them to play particular recordings on the air.

pentatonic scale
A scale, or mode, that has five notes corresponding to the natural notes C, D, E, G, and A, any of which may be the first note of the series.

Peps
Vocal sounds made by a Jamaican deejay or toaster to "pop up" a record: "chicka-a-took."

pickups
(1) One or more notes that lead into a downbeat at the beginning of a musical phrase. (2) A contact microphone or other device that converts vibrations into electric impulses that allow the sound to be amplified.

pogo
A punk dance in which people jumped up and down as if they were on pogo sticks.

polyphonic texture
The sound pattern created by two or more independent melodies being played or sung at the same time.

polyrhythm
Music in which more than one rhythm pattern is played at the same time.

pop song form
The structure of repeated and contrasting sections of a song in which each section (represented as letters when the form is diagrammed) is usually similar in length and corresponds to an AABA pattern or some variant on that organization.

power chords
The full and deep sound created by two notes that are a perfect fourth or a perfect fifth apart played together on the bass strings of an electric guitar with added distortion. The depth of the sound is created by the resultant tone, or combination tone, that is lower than the notes that are actually played. Power chords are used in most hard-rock and heavy-metal music.

prepared instruments
Traditional musical instruments, usually ones with strings such as grand pianos or guitars, with items placed on, hung from, or woven between or among the strings to alter the instrument's sound. Items used can include bolts, sticks, cloth, paper, paper clips, folded pieces of foil wrap, or other things.

psychedelic drugs
Drugs such as LSD that generally produce a loss of sense of time and dreamlike distortions of the senses.

pub rock
An English "back to the roots of rock" movement of the seventies that reacted against large-scale, theatrical rock styles.

R

raga
A scale or melody used in Indian music.

ragtime
A type of music that used "ragged time," or syncopated rhythms; particularly popular between 1890 and 1915.

rhythm and blues
Called *race music* until the end of the forties, an originally African American popular music in which the backbeat was accented and beats were usually subdivided unevenly.

rhythm section
The group of musical instruments that maintain the beat pattern and the harmonic flow of a piece of music. Rhythm sections include bass, drums, and guitar or keyboard instruments.

riff (melodic or rhythmic)
A short melodic or rhythmic pattern repeated over and over while changes take place in the music played along with it.

rockabilly
Music that combined honky-tonk country music with blues and rhythm and blues. Rockabilly bands in the fifties generally used electric lead guitar, acoustic rhythm guitar, acoustic (stand-up) bass, and drums. (The name is a combination of *rock* and *hillbilly*.)

rock steady
A Jamaican music that was basically a slowed-down version of ska, but it included a syncopated bass line. When sped up, rock steady became reggae.

S

sampling
The practice of taking selected sections from previously recorded records and repeating and mixing those sections to create a background sound to accompany new vocals.

scratching
A technique used by disc jockeys in which a record's rotation is rapidly changed from forward to backward repeatedly, to create a rhythmic pulse over which the disc jockey talks in a rhythmic patter or rap style.

segue
The joining together, without pause, of two different pieces of music.

selector
The person who plays the records to back up a Jamaican deejay or toaster.

signifying
Texts, or song lyrics, that have more than one meaning or message.

sixteenth notes
Note values of which there are four for every quarter note.

skiffle
A very simple British folk music that involved little more than melody and accompaniment by a strummed acoustic guitar, and rudimentary rhythm instruments such as washboard.

slapping bass
A name given to rockabilly bassists' practice of slapping the strings against the fingerboards of their instruments as they played.

solo breaks
Short sections of music in which the soloist sings or plays alone while the accompanying instruments stop playing, or "break." The breaks are usually no longer than one or two bars (measures) long.

spirituals
American folk hymns and other religious songs that originated in the late eighteenth or early nineteenth centuries and developed into gospel music.

stop time
A technique in which instruments play only on, say, the first beat of each bar while a soloist continues performing. There are a number of stop-time patterns: first and third beats, first and fourth beats, as well as patterns stretching over two or more measures (not to be confused with break).

street funk
A seventies funk style generally dominated by strong bass guitar lines, filled-in harmonies by guitars or keyboards, complex rhythms from a variety of drums, a flat-four beat, and a party-like atmosphere.

string bending
A guitar technique used by many blues and rock guitarists in which the player pushes or pulls the string temporarily out of alignment, causing the string to tighten and the pitch to be raised.

suite
In the eighteenth century, a multi-movement work that was generally a collection of dances preceded by a prelude. In the nineteenth and twentieth centuries, the term was also used for groupings of nondance compositions.

swing
A big-band jazz style of dance music popular during the thirties through the fifties.

sympathetic strings
Strings that vibrate and sound as the notes to which they are tuned are played on another string, causing them to vibrate; sitars have a set of sympathetic strings.

syncopated rhythms
Rhythms that do not fit an expected pattern of accents. Syncopations include the accenting of weak beats and the absence of accents (or even silence) on strong beats.

synthesizers
Electronic sound generators (often keyboards) capable of modifying the sound generated.

systematic music
An avant-garde style of composition based on systematically organized repetition of a minimal amount of musical material; also called *minimalism.*

T

tag
A short section of music added to the end of a composition to emphasize that the piece is ending. The term *coda* is also used for a tag ending.

tape loop
A piece of magnetic tape recorded and then cut and spliced to form a loop that continues to repeat the recording, creating an echo effect.

theremin
An electronic instrument that produces a tone that changes in pitch and dynamic level when the player moves his or her hands near

its antenna and loop. The theremin was invented in the twenties by Leon Theremin.

through-composed form
A compositional structure that does not use the usual formal schemes of regular repetition and contrast but rather employs a more extended spinning out of new musical material, although individual themes may reoccur.

timbre
(pronounced TAM-ber) Tone quality as it relates to the characteristic differences among musical instruments or singing voices.

Tin Pan Alley
Late nineteenth- and early twentieth-century area of New York where music publishers often had cheap, tinny sounding pianos.

toasting
A Jamaican name for the rhythmic patter-talk used by disc jockeys.

trading twos (or fours)
A term for a type of improvisation used especially by jazz musicians in which two or more musicians take turns improvising on two- or four-bar sections of music.

trad jazz (traditional jazz)
Dixieland jazz in the style played in New Orleans and Chicago during the twenties.

tremolo
(1) Fast repetitions of a single note. (2) Loud-soft undulations on a pitch; not to be confused with vibrato.

triad, or triadic harmonies
A chord that contains only three notes, each a major or a minor third apart from the next.

twelve-bar blues
The classic blues form, structured in three four-bar phrases, which follows a particular chord progression based on four bars of a tonic chord, two bars of a subdominant chord, two bars of a tonic chord, one bar of a dominant chord, one bar of a subdominant chord, and two bars

of a tonic chord. There are many variations of this basic progression of harmonies.

two-beat bass
A style of bass playing often used in country music in which the bass plays the root note of the chord on the first beat of each bar and the fifth of the chord on the third beat of each bar.

urban blues
A blues style that developed in the big cities and was generally more sophisticated and played by larger instrumental groups than the older country blues style.

varispeed control
A phonograph control that allows disc jockeys to vary the speed (and hence the pitch) at which a recording is played.

vaudeville shows
A type of live variety stage show that included songs, dances, comedy acts, and other types of general entertainment: popular from the middle nineteenth century into the twentieth century.

veejay
A "disc jockey" for video shows.

walking bass
The line played by a bass player that "walks" melodically between chord tones instead of jumping from one chord tone to another.

western swing
A type of country music that developed out of the string bands. It was influenced by certain characteristics of jazz such as uneven beat subdivisions, syncopations, and the use of wind instruments in addition to the usual country instrumentation.

work songs
Solo or group singing along with the rhythm of the work being done by the singer(s).

PHOTO CREDITS

INDEX

C

G

M

U

V

Z